Joshua Chamberlain

Joshua Chamberlain

THE SOLDIER AND THE MAN

Edward G. Longacre

COMBINED PUBLISHING
Pennsylvania

PUBLISHER'S NOTE

The headquarters of Combined Publishing are located midway between Valley Forge and the Germantown battlefield, on the outskirts of Philadelphia. From its beginnings, our company has been steeped in the oldest traditions of American military history and publishing. Our historic surroundings help maintain our focus on military history and our books strive to uphold the standards of style, quality and durability first established by the earliest bookmakers of Germantown and Philadelphia so many years ago. Our famous monk-and-console logo reflects our commitment to the modern and yet historic enterprise of publishing.

We call ourselves Combined Publishing because we have always felt that our goals could only be achieved through a "combined" effort by authors, publishers and readers. We have always tried to maintain maximum communication between these three key players in the reading experience.

We are always interested in hearing from prospective authors about new books in our field. We also like to hear from our readers and invite you to contact us at our offices in Pennsylvania with any questions, comments or suggestions, or if you have difficulty finding our books at a local bookseller.

For information, address:
Combined Publishing
P.O. Box 307
Conshohocken, PA 19428
E-mail: combined@combinedpublishing.com
Web: www.combinedpublishing.com
Orders: 1-800-418-6065

Library of Congress Cataloging-in-Publication Data
Joshua Chamberlain: the soldier and the man / Edward G. Longacre.
     p.   cm.
Includes bibliographical references (p. 367) and index.
ISBN 1-58097-021-4
    1. Chamberlain, Joshua Lawrence, 1828-1914. 2. Generals—United States Biography. 3. United States. Army—Biography. 4. United States—History—Civil War, 1861-1865 Biography. 5. Brewer (Me.) Biography.   I. Title.
E467.1.C47L66 1999
973.7'441'092—dc21
[B]   99-42720

Printed in the United States of America.

For Katie, Jerry, and LeAnn

Contents

Maps

Acknowledgments

Foremost among those who have helped me understand Joshua Lawrence Chamberlain is Gary Leak of the Department of Psychology, Creighton University, Omaha, Neb. Professor Leak, a nationally known authority on personality psychology and an avid student of 19th-century American history, suggested the need for an alternative to Alice Rains Trulock's 1992 biography, *In the Hands of Providence*, which he considers a superficial examination of Chamberlain's traits and motivations. Professor Leak has also contributed a psychological evaluation of Chamberlain using modern techniques of personality assessment as a counter to the flawed methodology of pyschobiography.

Numerous others assisted me, to one degree or another, in researching this book. At least some will be relieved to know that the interpretations, judgments, and evaluations that populate the text are mine alone. My sincere thanks go to William David Berry, Maine Historical Society, Portland; De Anne Blanton and Michael P. Musick, Military Reference Branch, National Archives, Washington. D.C.; Jeff Brown and Art Dostie, Maine State Archives, Augusta; Nan Card, Rutherford B. Hayes Presidential Center, Fremont, Ohio; Anne Englehart and Ellen Shea, Schlesinger Library, Radcliffe College, Cambridge, Mass.; Amy Hague, Sophia Smith Collection and College Archives, Smith College, Northampton, Mass.; James Helms, Florida State Archives, Tallahassee; Emily Herrick, Maine State Library, Augusta; Erik Jorgenson and Julia Colvin Oehmig of the Pejepscot Historical Society, Brunswick, Me.; Diane E. Kaplan and Christine Weideman, Yale University Libraries, New Haven, Conn.; Jennifer King, American Heritage Center, University of Wyoming, Laramie; Gary Kross, Gettysburg, Pa.; Tony Lemut, Parma, Ohio; John Lenthe, Historical Society of Pennsylvania, Philadelphia; Lieutenant Colonel Al Mackey,

USAF, Hampton, Va.; John H. McMinn, University of Miami Library, Miami, Fla.; Leslie Morris and Jennie Rathbun of the Houghton Library, Harvard University, Cambridge, Mass.; Betsy Paradis and Muriel Sanford, Raymond H. Fogler Library, University of Maine, Orono; Susan Ravdin, Special Collections, Hawthorne-Longfellow Library, Bowdoin College, Brunswick, Me.; Dr. Richard A. Sauers, Soldiers and Sailors Memorial Hall, Pittsburgh, Pa.; Sylvia J. Sherman, Maine State Archives, Augusta; Dr. Richard J. Sommers and Pam Cheney, Archives Branch, U.S. Army Military History Institute, Carlisle Barracks, Pa.; Mrs. Abbott Spear, Warren, Me.; Don Troiani, Southbury, Conn.; Connie Williams and Steve Zerbe of the War Library, National Commandery, Military Order of the Loyal Legion of the United States, Philadelphia, Pa.; and Craig G. Wright, Clarke Historical Library, Central Michigan University, Mount Pleasant.

A few individuals who assisted in the preparation of this work warrant a special note of thanks. Dr. T. Adrian Wheat (Colonel, U.S. Army, Ret.), of Gloucester, Va., heed me understand the medical and surgical aspects of Chamberlain's war service. Joseph G. Bilby of Wall Township, N. J., provided insight into the nature of Chamberlain's wounding on the Quaker Road, March 29, 1865. Lawrence T. Long-acre, Perkasie, Pa., and William C. Davis, Mechanicsburg, Pa., assisted in my attempt to view a large collection of Chamberlain letters owned by the city of Harrisburg, Pa. For ably editing and producing the book, I thank Bob Pigeon, David Farnsworth, and Ken Gallagher of Combined Publishing. And for encouraging me to complete this book despite the criticism it was bound to attract, I thank Mark Perry of Arlington.; Thomas W. Crouch of Newport News, Va.; and my wife, Ann, who served ably as my research assistant.

Preface

*E*very age and every society needs its heroes; 20th-century America is no exception. While there is nothing inherently wrong with this, Americans appear to prefer their heroes pure, unambiguous, and one-dimensional, more symbol than han being. A case in point is General Joshua Lawrence Chamberlain of Maine, a Civil War hero of epic stature. A major character in recent fiction including Michael Shaara's Pulitzer Prize-winning novel *The Killer Angels* and Ronald F. Maxwell's film "Gettysburg," Chamberlain is also the subject of numerous biographies published over the past decade, including Alice Rains Trulock's *In the Hands of Providence*, Michael Golay's *To Gettysburg and Beyond*, and Sis Deanes's *His Proper Post*. These volumes supplement Willard M. Wallace's earlier biography, *Soul of the Lion*. Another recent study with Chamberlain at its center is *Stand Firm Ye Boys from Maine: The 20th Maine and the Gettysburg Campaign*, by former Gettysburg National Military Park historian Thomas A. Desjardin. The most recent contribution to the field of Chamberlain studies is Mark Perry's *Conceived in Liberty*. Over this same period, innumerable articles, pamphlets, and lectures have celebrated the officer whose regiment of volunteer infantry held Little Round Top against repeated attacks on July 2, 1863, thereby saving the left flank of the Army of the Potomac and perhaps the army itself.

The outpouring of scholarship not only attests to the stature Joshua Chamberlain has assumed in our time, it reveals the lengths to which amateur and professional historians will go to mythologize an American warrior. Wallace, Trulock, Golay, Deanes, Desjardin, and their lesser-known colleagues appear to agree on most if not all of the following points: Chamberlain was, by turns, a precious and precocious child, a self-confident young man, a master tutor, a loving and supportive husband, a caring father, a patriot of the first rank, an ardent libertarian, a self-taught military genius, a selfless statesman, a farsighted educator, an enlightened businessman, an eloquent opponent of war's wastage and horror, a disinterested historian, and a pristine example of all that is good about America.

Although the modern chroniclers take slightly different approaches to their subject, the thrust of their scholarship is defined by Trulock's claim that "Joshua L. Chamberlain was a great American hero and a genuinely good man. He was also intelligent, creative, handsome, and well-educated—the embodiment of the nineteenth-century ideal of manhood. . . . His leadership and bravery in our country's great Civil War, along with his dramatic action at the surrender ceremony at Appomattox, made Chamberlain's deeds legendary in his own era." Trulock, Wallace, and Deans appear determined to extend the legend to our era as well. While somewhat more critical in their analysis, Golay and Desjardin make fitful attempts to psychoanalyze Chamberlain. Perry's book is the most balanced and objective portrait of Chamberlain to date, but it suffers from the fact that its author is not a Civil War specialist. Moreover, like Golay's book, Perry's is a dual biography: it devotes nearly equal attention to Chamberlain's principal opponent at Gettysburg, Colonel John Calvin Oates of the 15th Alabama Infantry.

To some degree each of these writers either ignores or attempts to explain away possible flaws in Chamberlain's character. Each likewise fails to utilize primary sources that dispute Chamberlain's wartime recollections. The lack of critical evaluation is especially troubling given that the majority of what we know of Chamberlain's life and career comes to us from his own writing, much of it composed decades after the experiences it relates and compromised by a suspect memory and an overt tendency to romanticize.

The present volume seeks to fashion a more rounded, more inclusive, and more objective portrait of Chamberlain as soldier and human being. It does not claim to be a complete, definitive biography; Trulock's massive tome has co-opted that distinction and subsequent studies have only piled on the details. Nor does this book seek to erode the heroic status to which its subject has been elevated over the past 130 years. The author believes that Joshua Lawrence Chamberlain was, and ought to be regarded as, a hero; certainly he acted at Gettysburg and on other fields, civil and military, in heroic fashion, and his deeds had critical, far-reaching implications. But Chamberlain, being human, was also prone to foibles and failings, and those characteristics deserve attention alongside the stirring thoughts, the noble aspirations, and the heroic actions that have captivated so many writers and readers. To overlook symptoms of imperfection is to produce a monument, a marble man. A statue may achieve the status of a work of art, but it remains cold, immobile, and promotive of a surface understanding—a poor substitute for the flesh-and-blood person it seeks to portray.

Brigadier-General Joshua Lawrence Chamberlain.
(Courtesy of the U. S. Military History Institute)

One

FAVORED SON

As a boy, Lawrence Joshua Chamberlain paid breathless heed to the tales told by the watermen and lumberjacks who inhabited his native southeastern Maine. Epic sagas of man against nature on the high seas and in the forest primeval stirred his imagination. So too did the stories recounted by a band of Native Americans who had camped on the fringes of his family's hundred-acre farm near the village of Brewer, where Lawrence had been born on September 8, 1828. "Getting some hold on their way of speaking," he observed years later, writing in the third person, "he listened to their dark, wild stories of old: fierce forays of the dreaded Mohawks; weird myths of Katahdin [Maine's tallest peak], throne of the storm-god; legends of the mysterious Saguenay springing from under a dome of glittering gold, and the seeking from which no mortal ever returned."[1]

The storytellers taught the youngster lessons that he studied the rest of his life. He learned the value of legend not only as moral example but as historical record. He learned the power of myth as the embodiment of cultural ideals and the expression of community emotions. He learned to infuse the past with a romanticism that quenched his thirst for adventure and fantasy. And he learned the superiority of symbolic truth over literal fact.

Other boyhood lessons had geographical, religious, political, and ancestral roots. Coastal Maine, with its rugged terrain, its heavy forest cover, and its isolation from the lower United States, planted in him a sense of independence, a feeling of reserve, and a basic conservatism. The Congregationalism of his family—the religion of Chamberlain's Puritan forebears—taught him responsibility to community and respect for lawful authority and gave him a sense of local autonomy. In his early twenties, while a student at a theological seminary in Bangor, he resolved that he would never "fawn, cringe or supplicate—scarcely *obey*" any "stiff, overbearing, unreasonable man" even when necessary to earn his daily bread.[2]

The Democratic leanings of the Chamberlain clan told young Lawrence to adhere to fundamental American institutions and resist sweeping social change. And his mingled Pilgrim and Huguenot heritage bequeathed to him a strong work ethic, an aesthetic consciousness, and a degree of self-discipline that he considered "good for the conscience and the constitution." Few mid-19th-century American youths could boast a more formidable combination of influences.[3]

These influences were strengthened by the example of Chamberlain's parents. Born in 1800 in what was then northern Massachusetts, Joshua Chamberlain Jr. was a self-made man in every sense. The great-grandson of mid-17th-century English immigrants, he pioneered the region east of the Penobscot River, where arable soil had to be carved, slowly and sometimes painfully, from the wilderness. Joshua Jr. grew up like the land itself: hard, craggy, and forbidding. Throughout his life he maintained an unswerving devotion to the Puritan ethic as well as to that secular religion whose objects of worship include country, family, and hard work. Although Lawrence always seemed closer to his pious and warm-hearted mother, Sarah Dupee Brastow Chamberlain, the descendant of French Calvinists, he gained from his father several gifts, including a love of things military and a worship of heroes. After all, Joshua Jr. had named him for the stalwart seaman James Lawrence, whose War of 1812 battle-cry, "Don't give up the ship," had already inspired a generation of schoolboys.

Through flinty example Lawrence's father also taught him self-reliance, perseverance, and the transcendent power of physical toil. Once, when leading a team of oxen pulling perhaps 400 pounds of fresh-mown hay, the boy failed to prevent a wheel from wedging between "two good-sized stumps." The wagon would not budge, and Lawrence found himself at a loss to follow his father's demand to "clear that wheel." Throwing up his hands, the boy exclaimed, "How am I going to do it?" "*Do it, that's how!*" came the sharp reply, whereupon the youth stooped, put his weight behind the wheel, and, quite impossibly, lifted wagon and contents clear of the stumps. He would always remember the incident less for his feat of strength than for the command that had produced it. Looking back, he decided that his father's instruction constituted "a maxim whose value far exceeded the occasion. The solution of a thousand problems. An order of action for life, worth infinitely more than worn-out volumes of lifeless learning and years of thumbsucking irresolution." Freeing the wagon against every physical law showed him—as did later experiences of a similar nature—the value of forthright action, the pitfalls of hesitation and self-doubt, the need to overcome one's fear of making mistakes, and the worthlessness of "crybaby repentances" for failure.[4]

Such a mature outlook, coupled with the inherent stature of the firstborn, gave Lawrence great influence over his brothers, Horace Beriah, John Calhoun, and Thomas Davee Chamberlain—respectively, six, ten, and thirteen years younger than he—and his sister, Sarah Brastow Chamberlain, eight years his junior. Despite (perhaps because of) the age difference, Lawrence enjoyed a close, warm relationship with each of his siblings, though in temperament and taste he was probably closest to the sister he called "Sae." His status as his parents' preeminent offspring was never challenged. Strictly speaking, Lawrence might not have been his mother's favorite—her "good boy Johnny" would always remain her baby—but everyone knew that he would carry the family's hopes on his shoulders. Neither parent harbored a doubt that their first child would excel in whatever field of endeavor he chose.

That choice promised to be a difficult one. At an early age Lawrence developed an appreciation for music, which he indulged as much and as often as his family's middle-class financial status and his own ingenuity would permit. Once, seized by the desire to play the bass viol but lacking the funds to buy one, he crafted a version of the instrument, complete with bow, from a cornstalk. He also nurtured a love of literature and composition. Encouraged by his mother, in his early teens he considered entering theological school as a prelude to the ministry. At the same time, he was greatly influenced by his family's military tradition. His father had been a lieutenant colonel of Maine militia, his grandfather a full colonel, and his New Hampshire-born great-grandfather a soldier in the colonial wars and the Revolution. Thanks to Joshua Jr.'s oft-repeated references to this tradition, young Lawrence developed a lifelong interest in soldiering. A personality quirk, however, threatened his vision of a military career: he had an aversion to firearms, at least to the extent of using them to kill squirrels and rabbits.[5]

Lawrence had grown up like boys of all eras, fond of games and sports. Years later he recalled his favorite pastimes and what they instilled in him: "Strong, bold swimming was a school of self-command; old-fashioned round ball, where the game was to knock the ball and not each other, fostered manliness." Living as he did in the heart of shipbuilding country, at an early age he became fond of sailing. He made a practice of hanging his hat atop the masthead of every vessel launched on his side of the Penobscot. As a teenager he constructed a land-bound ship of his own, using trace chains for foot ropes, his mother's carpets for sails, and his brothers as crewmen. But although he learned the use and care of firearms, and reportedly owned a rifle, he continued to be "reluctant to kill the animals that seemed so indispensable to the balance of the serenity he found in the forest."[6]

Although the Chamberlains' religion forbade family quarrels, mother and father appear to have waged a muted but determined struggle for the heart and mind of their eldest son. Initially, Joshua Jr. won out, though the contest seems to have ended in a tie. At 14, escorted by his father, Lawrence traveled south to the town of Ellsworth, where he entered Major Whiting's Military and Classical School. In his single term at the boarding school, the teenager learned the rudiments of drill and studied the lives of the great captains. His mother would have rejoiced to know that while he took to the military life he also appreciated the compulsory acquirement of some "practical acquaintance with the French language." This, his initial exposure to the subject, spurred a lifelong interest and proficiency in languages.[7]

Major Whiting's ability to mold his pupil from Brewer ended abruptly in the summer of 1843 when a financial crisis forced Lawrence's family to call him home. The situation stemmed from his father's habit of lending money to local industry in hopes of reaping the kind of profits a small farm could not return. Acutely aware of his position as the least successful member of his family—two of his brothers had emigrated to the Northwest to become financially secure and politically prominent—Joshua Jr. was willing to gamble the family's savings on quick prosperity, a practice that threatened him with ruin when a recession in Portland sank a shipbuilding enterprise in which he had invested heavily. The downturn forced the elder Chamberlain to sell all of his holdings except the farm. It took years for the family to recover fully from his speculation.

His family's suddenly reduced circumstances clouded Lawrence's future. To make ends meet, the boy toiled in a local brickyard, then traveled to Portland to find work as a lumberjack. Though he had grown tall and was capable of hard work, neither profession appealed to him; while he labored indoors and out, his initial interest in the ministry began to revive. His mother encouraged this train of thought, and in June 1845 the 16-year-old went through the rituals required to gain formal admission to the First Congregational Church of Brewer.[8]

Although Lawrence's desire for "saving grace and a loving divine brotherhood" was sincere—he entered fully into the life of the congregation, singing in the choir and each week trudging two miles to teach Sunday school—entrance into the church was also a stepping-stone to a new calling. Inspired by the example of visiting missionaries, he wished to bring the gospel to benighted lands such as Africa and the Pacific islands, "where the social conditions might give him a chance to … show that Christianity is obedience to the law of right living as well as of right worshipping." But church membership was not enough to secure this end; he realized that his ambitions depended upon a college or seminary education—realized, too, that such an education demanded the sort of money his family no longer possessed. But someday, somehow, he would gain the book learning a missionary required.[9]

He was also aware that a religious career demanded the power to speak clearly and dramatically. This fact troubled him, for since youth he had been afflicted by a pronounced stammer caused by an inability to articulate words beginning with the letters *b*, *p*, and *t*. As his journey through adolescence brought him increasingly into formative social situations, Lawrence's stuttering caused him no end of pain and embarrassment. The affliction, he admitted, affected his "habits and perhaps character," in fact "the whole of life." Like many creative people who find it difficult to communicate orally, at an early age he turned to the written word, tapping a talent for writing that he would refine in early manhood. Although capable of powerful, unadorned prose, he preferred to inject his writing with a lush sentimentalism that recalled the tale-tellers of his youth as well as the rich verse of Lord Byron, the only author exempted from the Chamberlain family's ban on fiction and poetry. At this time literate Americans were fascinated by Byron's romantic verse, exotic adventures, and support of democratic causes; the more scandalous aspects of his life, including his incestuous affair with his half-sister, would not become public until the late 1860's.[10]

By close reading he not only improved his writing skills but helped overcome his speech impediment. Preliminary scanning of a text to be read aloud enabled him to anticipate the difficult word sounds and to skip lightly, rather than stumble, over them. In time he developed a rhythmic, almost melodic, pattern of speech that helped hide his syllabic difficulties. Although the stammer would recur throughout his life and his fear of it would never completely abate, the obstacle had been largely surmounted by the close of his college years. Some historians dwell excessively on Chamberlain's youthful trials with stuttering as well as with the specter of poverty; at least one asserts without basis that the Civil War became for the thirtyish Chamberlain "a personal struggle with his childhood insecurities."[11]

To succeed in his formal studies Lawrence would have to master the full range of reading, writing, and reciting. He was prepared to take whatever steps were necessary to attain such proficiency, and to bear whatever burdens it entailed. In 1846, upon the approach of his 18th birthday, he decided that within a year he would enter Bowdoin College in Brunswick, one of Maine's oldest and most respected institutions of higher learning. Both parents accepted his decision with good grace, his mother especially so. Joshua Jr. may have been disappointed that Lawrence had given up his West Point dreams, but Sarah had extracted from her son a promise that after college he would enter the seminary. Both set about helping him prepare, academically and financially, for his studies.

Because classical languages and literature formed the foundation for the liberal education of Lawrence's day, he strove to conquer two subjects in which he considered himself deficient, Greek and Latin. With characteristic energy and determination, he converted an attic room into a study where he shut himself up for half a year, studying up to 17 hours a day. By sheer force of will he committed to memory an unabridged Greek grammar "from alphabet to appendix." Wisely he interspersed physical with intellectual exercise. In winter he chopped hardwood and carried armloads of logs to his garret stove. In summer he careened across the attic floor as he and his father fenced with broadswords.[12]

Near-constant study and recitation would not suffice to make Lawrence college material. His preparation for Bowdoin was enhanced by William Hyde, an alumnus of the college who had briefly taught Lawrence at Whiting's academy. Hyde knew well the Bowdoin curriculum and entrance requirements, and his assistance was invaluable in advancing his pupil's candidacy.

Hyde's teaching did not come free; Lawrence paid him with funds he himself gained from tutoring. During the late fall of 1846 he traveled to the upriver village of North Milford to lodge at a boardinghouse and teach at a rural school. It was at once an exhilarating and a frightening experience. He took on a class of 30 scholars, at least a third of whom were not children but "young ladies and gentleman." His ability to educate and enlighten his younger pupils brought him a sense of accomplishment, but older, more rowdy students threatened to make his life miserable, as they had for his predecessors, more than one of whom they had tossed through the schoolhouse's open window.[13]

Early attempts to rule with a gentle hand proved unavailing. To maintain order he apparently resorted to fisticuffs. He claimed to have hurt none of his pupils—at least not seriously—but his new, fighting image prompted an "increase of local respect" and enlarged his "area of self-command." An environment more conducive to learning having been established, Lawrence loosened up to the extent of starting (despite initial reluctance) a "singing school" that drew students from 10 miles away. Three nights a week enthusiastic if not necessarily cultured voices, accompanied by Lawrence on the old bass viol he had brought from home, helped while away the winter hours and dispel some of the loneliness caused by his estrangement from home and family.[14]

Though brief, his stint in a backwoods schoolroom proved to Lawrence that, speech difficulties notwithstanding, he had a future as a teacher. Although he remained committed to the missionary's life, the experience allowed him to add to his list of prospective professions. He likewise remained committed to passing the entrance examinations that gave entrance to Bowdoin. When not teaching, leading a chorale group, or writing long, determinedly happy letters to Brewer, he pored over his classical texts and recited aloud in his room at the boarding-house, honing his ability to deal with those treacherous syllables.

Despite his determination to enter college on or about his 19th birthday, the time he devoted to his teaching made that schedule unworkable. Not until February 1848, at the start of Bowdoin's winter term, did he consider himself prepared to embark on his studies. That month he took a seat beside Professor Hyde in a sleigh "with a big wooden trunk lashed on behind and the faithful mare ahead." The conveyance took the pair on a 90-mile jaunt along the west bank of the Penobscot to Brunswick, where the hopeful student, "confused with mingled sensations of awe and awkwardness," strode across the Bow-doin campus and went before a faculty committee to take a special entrance examination. For hours the youth fielded questions designed to gauge his proficiency in various disciplines. Despite a bad case of nerves fueled by his shaky grasp of Latin, he comported himself admirably. That evening, some hours after the ordeal, he was informed that in every area but one he had passed with colors flying; he was accepted in Latin on condition he became more familiar with Sallust's *Jugurtha*. Instead of passing, he later punned, he had "expected juggernaut."[15]

His winning performance represented an early life's hurdle deftly cleared. Now he could concentrate on mastering the collegiate life and acquiring the knowledge, poise, and self-confidence that would carry him into adulthood.

* * *

He discovered that to do well at Bowdoin he need not duplicate the strenuous efforts through which he had gained admittance. Although he had entered half-way through the year, he assimilated his studies and passed his freshman examinations without difficulty. Outside the classroom he was a model of decorum and restraint, refusing to partake of cigars or spirituous beverages or to participate in the sprees that less mature members of the student body regularly enjoyed. Whenever a classmate considered inviting Lawrence to join in their merriment, another would reply, "O! no! Chamberlain won't in to it." For refusing to take part, he paid a price. "I have found myself sometimes alone," he confessed to a former pastor, "but all came out right." More than a few of his fellows came to admire his refusal to succumb to peer pressure.[16]

His standoffish attitude moderated during his sophomore year, and his popularity rose; mates bestowed on him the raffish nickname "Jack." He loosened up to the extent of accompanying several classmates on an off-campus excursion aboard a hay cart. Seeking a class tree to plant on the college grounds, the party wandered 10 miles out of Brunswick before attempting to return. By now many in the group, Chamberlain excluded, had acquired liquid refreshment. On the trip back they drove wildly across private property, collided with fences, trees, and private conveyances, and made a nuisance of themselves among the local population.

A chorus of complaints was soon flowing into the college, and next day the suspected culprits were hauled before Bowdoin's stern-visaged president, Leonard Woods. "Jack" Chamberlain, with characteristic regard for sobriety, had advised his fellow tree-seekers against their giddy course. Still, when questioned by President Woods, he refused to identify the other revelers, vowing to betray no confidences. Considering his reticence a product of false honor, Woods reluctantly ordered him suspended for the remainder of the term.

The punishment did not sway the sophomore from his course; he prepared to leave Brunswick for home, confident his family would support his refusal to turn informant. In the end, he did not have to leave. Moved by his plight, till-then-anonymous joyriders confessed their involvement, and a mollified Woods administered to each as well as to their close-mouthed classmate nothing more than a reprimand. The incident taught Lawrence that honesty, forthrightness, and a sense of fair play—especially when combined with righteous indignation over any suggestion he violate a personal code of ethics—would carry him safely over the most perilous terrain.[17]

If his attitude toward "sprees" relaxed a bit during his second year at Bowdoin, his resolve to live the life of a model Christian did not. At every opportunity he immersed himself in the Bible, chaired scriptural study groups, and enthusiastically supported the evangelical revival that overtook Maine in 1848-49. "At the beginning of the term," he wrote his pastor, "there were only two pious persons in this class—there are six now." His piety was respected by classmates and teachers alike: "I have met with nothing but the most gentlemanly treatment—could not wish for better . . . . I really think I never have been so faithful to myself & my duty as since I have been at Coll[ege]. It seems to me that engaging in God's service is a delightful employment and that my resolution to serve him is strengthening every day." He proved his earnestness by playing the organ in the college chapel and by regular attendance at the First Parish Church, a venerable house of worship just off campus at which were held all Bowdoin functions with a religious connection. Inevitably he became acquainted, though not intimately so, with the church's pastor of 22 years, Dr. George E. Adams.[18]

Lawrence's academic efforts kept pace with his religious zeal, and may have outstripped it. Midway through his second spring semester he appears to have recaptured the relentless intensity with which he had crammed for his entrance exams, daily devouring huge helpings of Greek, Latin, and trigonometry. As if not sufficiently occupied, he took on the additional duties of library assistant and teacher at a local Sunday school. The combination of academic and off-campus activities broke his health; by the time he completed his examinations and returned home for the summer, he teetered on the brink of physical collapse.

For weeks he remained abed as the local physician, assisted by Sarah and Sae Chamberlain, tried to repair Lawrence's shattered health. When the usual nostrums proved unavailing, his mother called in a homeopathic practitioner, whose herbs and broth appear to have accomplished what patent medicines could not. Slowly, gradually, he began to improve, strength seeping back into his body as through a half-open tap.[19]

By the spring of 1850 he was clearly on the mend; by then, however, he had missed a year of instruction. When he returned to Bowdoin in the fall, a 21-year-old junior, he found his closest friends to be upperclassmen. He went back to his textbooks, immersing himself in rhetoric, mathematics, and languages including German and Hebrew. As though he had missed not a day of class, Lawrence continued to excel in his studies. He not only acquitted himself well in his year-end examinations but won the top prize in the college's literary and oratorical competitions. The former prize placed him in the company of Bowdoin alumni Henry Wadsworth Longfellow and Nathaniel Hawthorne. The latter award gave an indication of how well he had overcome what short months ago had appeared a crippling handicap. Despite his continuing success, however, he passed through his junior year at a more leisurely pace than before. With the memory of his recent breakdown fresh in his mind, he no longer wished to test the limits of human endurance.[20]

* * *

Comfortable in his decision to slow down and enjoy college life, Lawrence found the time to make new friends. He forged lasting ties with members of his new class—future physicians, lawyers, editors, ministers, and politicians. He also drew close to some of the faculty including Calvin Stowe, the newly hired Professor of Natural and Revealed Religion. Chamberlain's regard extended to Stowe's family, whose house he visited every Saturday evening along with classmates and family friends.

Lawrence especially admired the warmth and wit—to say nothing of the literary ability—of the professor's wife, Harriet Beecher Stowe, daughter of a well-educated and deeply religious family from Connecticut and a frequent contributor of domestic literature to periodicals including the *Atlantic Monthly*. In that winter of 1851, Mrs. Stowe, like her husband a devout abolitionist, had embarked on what would become her most memorable work of fiction, the tale of a Christ-like slave named Uncle Tom, a fugitive heroine named Little Eva, and a loathsome master, Simon Legree. Spawned by a vision the authoress had experienced the previous March during Communion Sunday at First Parish Church, *Uncle Tom's Cabin* would become one of the most influential and forceful screeds against chattel slavery. A national bestseller, its ability to divide the nation along sectional lines was such that in 1862 Abraham Lincoln would address its author—only partly in jest—as "the little woman who wrote the book that made this great war."[21]

While Lawrence Chamberlain would have admired the narrative power of Ms. Stowe's novel and the poignant rendering of her characters, he was less likely to have appreciated her theme or to have shared her point of view. His views on slavery, which he carried well into adulthood, have become the subject of much confusion, partly the result, one suspects, of Chamberlain's liberalized portrayal in 20th-century media. No less than a Pulitzer Prize-winning historian has characterized the antebellum Chamberlain as "a staunch Republican and antislavery man." This assessment is far from the truth.

Scion of a deeply conservative family, inheritor of its Democratic tradition, and distrustful of the abolitionist agenda, Chamberlain the undergraduate—and, for that matter, Chamberlain the postgraduate—sympathized with black people in slavery, but he would not have campaigned to stop it. Growing up in the isolated northeastern corner of America, he would have had little experience with free blacks and none with their brethren in chains. Like most conservatives, he considered the future of the "peculiar institution," and especially the question of slavery's extension into the American territories, issues to be worked out through the slow but effective political process the Founding Fathers had established. Those who agitated for the liberation of slaves would have appeared to him as fanatics; and as he would later admit, "I haven't a particle of fanaticism in me."[22]

His views toward slavery appear ambiguous in light of his post-war pronouncements on the subject. A careful reading of those comments shows that he championed emancipation principally as a military measure, a weapon in the arsenal of the Union, a tool to uproot secession's hold on the South. During the war the only African-Americans he championed were those who fought beside the white soldiers of the Army of the Potomac. In postbellum years he came to view slavery as "so repugnant to justice and freedom." Yet even late in life, when holding political office as a convert to Republicanism, his views on civil rights for free blacks were not enlightened, and his unwillingness to advance the more liberal social agenda of his party often put him at odds with its leadership.

Chamberlain was not an insensitive, uncaring man with an underactive social conscience. He was motivated by a keen sense of duty to his fellow-man and displayed a great sympathy for humanity in general. He was not, however, socially enlightened by the standards of the late 20th century, and to view him as otherwise does a disservice to his memory as well as distorts the truth.

* * *

Soon after he made the acquaintance of Professor Stowe's wife, Joshua Lawrence Chamberlain (as he now styled himself, presumably in honor of his father) met the woman who would occupy a place in his life and heart shared by no other, Sarah Dupee Brastow Chamberlain not excepted. Through his affiliation with the First Parish Church, the Bowdoin junior was thrown into the company of the congregation's sometime organist, 25-year-old Frances Caroline Adams, adopted daughter of the congregation's pastor. The dark-haired, dark-eyed "Fannie" was not a beauty; a prominent nose and a weak chin detracted from an otherwise pleasant appearance. She was handsome enough, however, that Joshua was smitten almost from their first meeting.[23]

At the outset, the Boston-born Fannie did not reciprocate his interest; in fact, she had a reputation for rejecting any number of potential suitors. As the long-indulged daughter of one of the community's pillars, she appeared a prize catch; presumably, she could have had any number of young men at her call. However, Fannie was a stubborn, willful young woman—the combined result of her nature and the manner in which her adopted parents had spoiled her—and she was reported to entertain a dim view of marriage. In his attempt to win her hand Joshua had his work cut out for him.

From the first, Chamberlain saw qualities in her that attracted his interest as no other woman had. He was taken, too, by her social position and ancestry. Over the years he would brag that Fannie's pedigree included forebears who "for 150 years [were] high officers of Government in Connecticut." Another celebrated ancestor was Mabel Harlakenden, "conspicuous in early Colonial history as 'the Princess of New England,' being of royal lineage in the line to which nearly all the monarchs of Europe are related."[24]

Chamberlain was also impressed by her artistic gifts. Fannie had talent not only in music but in poetry and, especially, art; by her mid-twenties she had produced several canvasses that Chamberlain would consider exquisitely rendered. He likewise came to admire her independent, iconoclastic nature and her unwillingness to subordinate herself to the controlling tendencies of men. It is doubtful, however, that he ever saw Fannie's quest for independence for what it truly was, a desperate search for self-control. By the time they met early in 1851 the young woman had long suffered under the domination of her loving but stern and sometimes severe father, who was wont to criticize his daughter's habits and to direct her life's choices even as he indulged her desire for the finer things in life. The prospect of being dominated by another man may account for her dim view of courtship.

Fannie's struggle to shape her own destiny had a physical side. Since childhood she had been afflicted with diminishing vision. Frequent occurrences of sore, swollen eyes and the racking headaches they caused played hob with her literary and artistic endeavors, while the fear of losing her sight—a fear intensified by contact with an aunt who had gone blind—raised the dreaded prospect of becoming totally dependent on others for her day-to-day needs.[25]

The specter of helplessness appears to have cast a shroud of gloom over Fannie Adams, one she could throw off only intermittently. Spells of melancholy bore her down throughout her life; these episodes prompted observers to regard her as ill-tempered, moody, snobbish, and selfish. In truth, she was a caring, sensitive woman capable of deep feelings—some too deep for her own peace of mind.

Willing to overlook certain flaws of nature in she who had captured his heart, Chamberlain pursued her with single-minded determination. He pressed his suit especially hard that fall, when Fannie's recently widowed father traveled to Chicago and returned with a new bride, the former Helen M. Root. Fannie was shocked and upset by this unexpected outcome. She knew that her father had met Helen that summer at a religious convocation, but she did not expect romance to blossom, especially so quickly. Fannie had adored her adopted mother and thus resented the new stepmother who had the additional liability of being only six months older than she. Soon after the couple settled in at the parsonage, the distraught Fannie sought to avoid Helen's company as much as possible, even to the extent of permanently leaving home.[26]

Her dramatically changed situation cast her relationship with Chamberlain in a new light. Although it had become clear that Dr. Adams did not consider him a fit candidate for his daughter's hand, Chamberlain pressed Fannie for expressions of her feelings for him, insisting that her father "has mistaken his man. I am not so easily managed." What professions she made came haltingly, as though she was unsure of her feelings and unwilling to commit herself amid the unsettled conditions of her life. Eventually, perhaps to place between them enough distance to gain a better perspective on their relationship, Fannie left Maine for New York City, there to study music under the tutorship of her stepmother's brother, the noted professor and composer George F. Root.[27]

While seeking Fannie's hand, Joshua was also seeking academic honors. Despite the distractions in his personal life, he successfully completed his junior year at Bowdoin, assuring Fannie that, "I have finished all my writing in a manner quite satisfactory to the Prof's—though I feel entirely exhausted in consequence of the exertion." After a few months in the family fold at Brewer, where he plied his mother and sister for advice on how to win at the game of love, he returned to Bowdoin for a triumphal final year.[28]

As a senior he deftly assimilated romance languages, chemistry, physics, and moral philosophy. His scholarly achievements brought him a Phi Beta Kappa pin as well as membership in two Bowdoin literary clubs, the Round Table and the Peucinian Society. Though his course load was heavy enough, he regretted his inability to choose from a wider selection of science courses. He continued his regular attendance at chapel and choir while taking on the presidency of the "Praying Circle of Bowdoin College," which usually met in his dorm room. Increasingly, however, he found himself preoccupied by earthly concerns. Fannie's absence in New York, and her inability or unwillingness to commit herself to a relationship, weighed heavily on his mind. At times their estrangement drove him to fits of depression from which not even the comforts of religion could save him.[29]

By early 1852 Fannie Adams decided she was in love with Joshua Chamberlain. Yet she harbored doubts about her ability to return his feelings for her measure for measure. A friend in whom she confided paraphrased her dilemma: "You say you love him—yet cannot feel that sort of love for him of which you have for years dreamed so wildly...." The friend advised Fannie to suppress her fears and commit herself to Chamberlain. Not till that spring, however, did she feel confident enough to make her feelings known, and then it was her aunt, Deborah Folsom, another member of the Adams household, who conveyed those sentiments to Chamberlain by showing him an emotion-laden letter Fannie had sent her from New York. Transported to "the loftiest pinnacle" by Fannie's stated willingness to marry him, the object of her affection was soon addressing himself in letters to her as "your betrothed."[30]

Two

ARDENT SUITOR

*A*ssured of a life with the woman he loved, Chamberlain completed his senior studies, shouldering the hefty courseload without breaking a sweat. His capped his scholastic triumph by being named First Orator at commencement. Coinciding as it did with celebration of the college's 50th anniversary, the end-of-year ceremony was a major social event, one made even more memorable by Fannie's presence. Having completed her music lessons, she had returned to Brunswick in time to witness her fiancé's honorary presentation.

For this reason, the speaker was especially disappointed by his performance upon the altar of the First Parish Church. Having recently reached his full height of five feet, ten and a half inches, he cut an imposing figure at the lectern, the audience admiring his fair complexion and finely chiseled features that included gray-blue eyes, a high forehead, a square jaw, and a nose he would later characterize as of "medium size, (& somewhat Roman)." When he began to speak, however, the carefully built impression fell apart. Made nervous by the overflow crowd of school, church, and municipal dignitaries, the First Orator stumbled unexpectedly over portions of his text. Flustered, he lapsed into the stutter he believed he had forever conquered, then made unsuccessful efforts to regain his composure. At the end of his speech, red-faced with embarrassment, he exited the lectern to a smattering of applause.[1]

He would forever recall his humiliation this day, although the occasion apparently marked the last time his speech impediment affected him in public. His mood improved, however, as soon as he left campus for home. Traveling by boat up the coast and into Penobscot Bay, he sailed in company with the future Mrs. Chamberlain. Fannie, on her way to visit friends in Bangor, tried mightily to convince her fiancé that his speech had not been the disaster he knew it to be. Even if she failed in this, his spirits had revived by the time they reached Brewer. There Fannie stayed over long enough to be presented to family and neighbors. To their mutual gratification, everyone in the Chamberlain household—parents, brothers, and sister—greeted Reverend Adams's adopted daughter as though already a part of the family. As the beloved of the family's first, favored son, Fannie should have expected nothing less.[2]

* * *

In the fall of 1852, soon after Chamberlain presented Fannie with an engagement ring, the couple went their separate ways, to remain apart for several months. Hardly an auspicious prelude to a life of wedded bliss, the new estrangement placed strains on the relationship and revealed hidden strengths and weaknesses in the young couple.

In his final weeks at Bowdoin Chamberlain had thought long and hard about his future. He briefly revisited his youthful intention to enter West Point, an idea his father would surely endorse. He retained a strong interest in military life, an interest that would soon prompt him to join a militia outfit, the Brewer Artillery. Embarking on a military education might appear an idea whose time had passed, but other college graduates had moved on to the U. S. Military Academy; Bowdoin's own Oliver Otis Howard (Class of 1850) had done so. Much like Chamberlain, Howard had initially weighed West Point against theological school.[3]

In the end, Chamberlain chose to keep to the course he had set for himself years before, along which his mother had quietly but firmly pushed him. While his predilection toward missionary work had lessened during his latter years at Bowdoin, he still believed he had "a call to preach." Thus, in the fall of 1852 he entered the Bangor Theological Seminary, a bastion of Congregationalism just across the Penebscot River from his family's home. He resolved to pay his own way, as he had when preparing for Bowdoin, by teaching languages or mathematics to students of any age. He only hoped that this time he would not have to resort to fists to gain his students' attention.[4]

While Chamberlain stayed close to home, Fannie left southern Maine for the warmth and lushness of the Deep South. Like her Aunt Deborah, Fannie had resolved to leave the suddenly unhappy household in Brewer as soon as assured of opportunities elsewhere. Late that year, through the auspices of Professor Root, she secured a position as a voice and piano teacher in Georgia's capital city of Milledgeville, where an old friend of her adopted father would serve as her sponsor. In Milledgeville, far from her home and her loving fiancé, Fannie would spend almost three years, much of that time feeling homesick, lonely, bored by her job and the endless socializing required of her, and distressed by her failing eyesight. Still, the job was a godsend, for she owed her father $300—a princely sum for the time—a debt she was determined to discharge before coming home.[5]

In Bangor, Chamberlain experienced neither the homesickness nor the ennui that troubled his betrothed. He kept busy studying not only sacred rhetoric and ecclesiastical history but exotic languages such as Hebrew, Arabic, Syriac, and Chaldee. To each of these he would devote at least an hour per day for the next six years, while striving almost as hard to firm up his grasp of Latin. When not in class he led the seminary choir, taught at another Sunday school, and tutored young ladies in modern languages. His teaching burdens were onerous but they paid his tuition; moreover, he was no longer in danger of being thrown out a classroom window. Returning home on weekends, he could be found every Sunday at the organ of the Brewer Congregational Church. In time he gained appointment as supervisor of schools in Brewer; the demands this position made on his time cannot be determined.[6]

Despite the hectic routine, he had much time to picture, and miss, Fannie. He had never taken her absences well, especially as she never wrote to him as frequently as he to her. Past leave-taking had placed him in a mood darker than any that beset his melancholy fiancée. These fits of depression, which have been overlooked by his biographers, appear to have afflicted him for days at a time. An undated letter in which he describes the agony Fannie inflicted by leaving him, may have been written soon after she went to New York; whether he mailed the letter is unknown. Though his prose is disjointed and in places difficult to follow, its anguished stream-of-consciousness provides a portrait of the young Chamberlain so at odds with the conventional depiction of him as a mature, self-composed young man that it warrants extensive quotation.

He begins with an expression of longing and regret wholly under-standable under the circumstances: "Oh! I wanted to see you so much tonight! I could have said what I can never say now, nor write even; for it will never come again. Oh speak to me, speak, whenever you see me, for you may perchance touch some chord that does not often speak…." At this point he lapses into despair, declaring that, "I can not bear to live—& I am not fit to die, till I am willing to live…. Nobody can answer the phrenzied [sic] earnestness of my heart—nobody can know the meaning of what I say & do, & I am so weary, I try to say & do nothing." Ashamed of the unmanly behavior he displayed in her presence, he prays that Fannie will see him not as "*the silly clown that I seem*," but will take pity on the "heart so dark & dead within me." He realizes the inaptness of that one word: "*Dead!* no! If it were dead it would be still, but there is no rest for it now…. What am I living for? What am I doing? Where can I look for only one moment's rest—only *one* now & I shall not be driven mad." At their parting "I turned away before you could notice my tears, for I am sick of my weak tears. I felt the full tears coming & I could not stay for it would trouble you & I cannot trouble you—it is enough that I be full of such furious agonies that I can only smile like a driveling idiot, to save myself from being a maniac."

The reference to madness unsettles him, and his words flow in a purple torrent: "I am given over to be tempted & tormented by the old [a]dversary. I feel him clutching at my heart beating & tormenting it, dragging it mangled & faint unto death over every rough & jagged rock, piercing it with every thorn & then triumphantly glorying over the ghastly murder with a hideous devilish grimace...." His lament ends with the realization that the demons torturing him will torment Fannie as well: "I see with grief how much you have to sacrifice to my unreasonable demands. I see how you try not to be too cheerful in company when I am looking at you. —Do not think of satisfying me. I am all unreasonable. I require of you all that I would & can give you myself. How much that is you do not know. Thank H[eaven] that you do not know *what* it is.... I am certain that you do not fully understand me. It is the most charitable belief I can have that I cling in hope that at sometime you will see but one single glimpse of me & will know me...." He closes with an expression of his dependence on Fannie's love, a plea for self-awareness, and a prayer that his suffering will soon end: "I cling to you with the eager grasp of the sinking man, so earnestly hoping that you will only kiss me.... am I mad or what & where am I & what am I saying[?] Must I bear it long? Oh, will it, may it, not be done soon, soon that the last dagger be driven & I be out of the way. How wild & strange it must be to be at peace."[7]

While the letter can be viewed as a sophomoric expression of the agonies of young love, it may help explain some aspects of Joshua Chamberlain's relationship with Fannie Adams. Although certainly open to interpretation, his references to "my unreasonable demands" and the "old [a]dversary" appear to have sexual overtones. This reading seems consistent with the established fact that sexual tensions affected their relationship from an early day. The tensions are apparent in the voluminous correspondence that chronicles their courtship.

Contrary to the belief of most 20th-century readers, mid-Victorian couples were capable of an active sexual life before as well as after marriage, not necessarily but sometimes including premarital relations that then, as now, could impact their lives in many ways. It is not clear whether Joshua and Fannie were sexually active; some evidence suggests that they were, but the question lacks a definitive answer. That has not stopped writers from weighing in on the subject. The author of what is considered the most thorough biography of Chamberlain declares they did not consummate their relationship before marriage. Her reasoning rests, however, on the archaic belief that "Frances Caroline Adams was a woman of virtue and Joshua Lawrence Chamberlain a man of honor." She credits their celibacy to "religion and self-respect" as if these virtues rendered them impervious to temptation. At least two historians have speculated that Chamberlain and his fiancée became intimate at some point before their wedding. This view is defensible based on a close reading of the couple's letters, in one of which Fannie confides to him "even as to my own heart, in all innocence and perfect trustfulness, those things which would ever sink me in the estimation and respect of *any* third person; for no other being can know what we are to each other." In another missive, she alludes to Chamberlain having spent considerable time in her bed-chamber.[8]

The timing of their sexual union is less important than an understanding of how sex affected the couple's life together and apart. Fannie, like most young women of her day, would have been suspicious of any attempt by her fiancé to lure her into physical intimacy. But for Fannie the desire to avoid temptation seems to have rested on her belief that sex and its usual result, childbearing, were traps laid by men seeking to enslave women. Early in 1853 the free-thinking young woman wrote Chamberlain of her belief (as he paraphrased it in a subsequent letter) that "marriage has no proper reference to children, being rather a more convenient or at any rate more congenial state or relation in which two persons by mutual agreement or attraction merge their individual lives & personal rights, & that children are the result of a tyrannical cruel abuse & prostitution of woman.... you rebel at all the Bible says about it & deem a man unreasonable who presumes to think of children as a *natural* offspring of marriage."[9]

Like most marriageable young men, Fannie's fiancé hoped some day to raise a family; he did not regard children as a byproduct of gender warfare. But more troubling to him than Fannie's view of childbearing was her implied desire that, whether or not they had already been intimate, their marriage should be sexless. There was more than one possible reason for this stance. Numerous young women of Fannie's time, when contemplating marriage, professed to be passionless as a means of asserting control in the sexual arena. Then, too, the hazards of mid-19th-century childbirth were severe enough to make any young woman think twice about pregnancy.[10]

Fannie's distrust of motherhood may have been real, but her betrothed chose to regard it as a ploy. He decided to play along with her: thereafter, in his letters he elaborately disguised every reference to children as if to show that he took her concerns seriously. An example is his mention of a "quit claim deed of the b****s [babies]," another his assurance that in the matter of childbearing *your will shall be my law.* Beneath the rhetoric, however, he took offense at Fannie's unwillingness to admit her sexuality as well as at her presumed lack of regard for him as a lover. Despite his moral upbringing, deeply held religious beliefs, and choice of profession, Chamberlain had a healthy libido; he would not live without physical intimacy. Thus while repeatedly professing to accept a childless marriage, he let Fannie know he would not tolerate a sexless one: "We can have *mischief* enough," he once told her, "without any *trouble*," adding that unless he missed his guess "you will be as ready for it as I."[11]

As if rising to a challenge, increasingly he filled his letters with sexual references. Once he declared that by the next time they were together "I should be pretty full of mischief. I'm pretty ready to be stirred up." On another occasion he warned her that, "I have such a terrible passion for you tonight that I hardly dare go to bed. I've been thinking about *things* retrospective & *pro*spective, & it stirs me all up, making my physical existence rather inconvenient." He would single out certain words and phrases she had put into her letters and explore their sexual connotations. Her casual mention of a nightdress was "enough to drive a man mad," while a reference (perhaps inadvertent, perhaps deliberate) to an "insertion" prompted this reply: "I don't know what meaning you apply to it. I'm afraid you are getting to be a naughty girl."[12]

Once he told her of a dream in which she carried a precious object obviously symbolic of a baby; in a second dream the two of them behaved in such a way as to make the two visions come "in rather an *inverted order.*" In another letter he told of sleeping with a young, handsome, unmarried woman—finally identifying his companion as a tintype of his beloved, which he had pressed to his chest until falling asleep.[13]

During their separation, Chamberlain would frequently write loving, romantic, "*caressing letters*" to his "precious little girl," his "nice little wife," his "Fannie bird." In our day such references bear a sexist or demeaning connotation (even Chamberlain's most admiring biographers admit that he frequently treated Fannie like a child). Such appellations, however, were intended as heartfelt expressions of his devotion to her and of his hope that their "blessed, blessed" wedding would soon take place. He sometimes made inventive declarations of his love: in November 1854 he sent Fannie a warrantee deed, obtained from an attorney, by which he assigned to her in perpetuity the heart and soul of J. Lawrence Chamberlain.[14]

On other occasions, he was not so "caressing." In some letters he infused his sexual references with a dark and mordant wit that must have chilled rather than titillated his correspondent. One of Chamberlain's biographers notes that he had little or no sense of humor and that his infrequent attempts to be funny were often crude and heavy-handed. This is perhaps the only charitable way to view one comment, made in response to Fannie's preference for a childless union, by which he intended to give her "a grand *scare.*" Perhaps quoting a bit of local doggerel, he asked: "You remember the jar in the cellar-way[?] He would have been three weeks old to day." In a following letter he made clear he was being playful and called on Fannie to admit that "it *was* witty wasn't it[?]" A latter-day reader, however, would be pardoned for wondering what kind of man would inflict on a loved one beset by fears of pregnancy a joke about an aborted fetus.[15]

* * *

Conflicts between Chamberlain and his beloved over the desirability of procreation would appear to be an obstacle to wedded bliss. Other differences of opinion were similarly threatening. By the midpoint of his seminary career the prospective groom gave up his adolescent dream of a foreign mission and began to concentrate on preaching to a congregation. During his final year he gained experience in composing sermons, which, in response to course requirements, he delivered from several local pulpits. In a memoir he mentions having received, during this period, calls to churches in Belfast, Maine, and Wolfboro, New Hampshire—neither of which he answered. In fact, at the end of his seminary career he left Bangor before ordination. Although later licensed to preach, he never became an ordained minister.[16]

By all indications, Fannie exerted a major influence on his career decision. In several letters she made clear that she had no intention of becoming a minister's wife. "My whole mind, character and temperament," she explained, "are entirely inappropriate for that position, and I never could be useful in it." Doubtless the burdens a preacher's spouse must shoulder daunted her, as did the piety that would be demanded of her. Too much a free-thinker, Fannie did not share the devotion her father and Chamberlain held for organized religion. Perhaps, too, the earthy nature of their courtship militated against such a life as her fiancé appeared to be laying out for her.[17]

She hoped that he would become, instead, a teacher, a profession for which she considered him eminently suited—if not a teacher, then perhaps a doctor. More than once she tried to obtain for him a classroom position in Georgia, but the schools she had in mind were too small and too rural to appeal to him. Believing himself fitted for finer things, he rejected every effort in his behalf, sometimes rather curtly. Even so, he gradually altered his course. By April 1854 he was considering studying medicine during his summer vacation. Three months later—not long after expressing certainty that he had a calling to the pulpit—he was insisting that "I am more of a scholar than preacher." [18]

The turnabout in his thinking, his sudden inability to discern life's direction, placed him in a quandary. Several times he wrote Fannie of his indecision and the frustration it produced. He began to consider outlandish propositions such as working the gold fields of California, where, as his father advised him, he might establish a college of his own. In one letter to Fannie he made the mistake of musing about obtaining a "bachelor office" at some institution of learning where their marriage might prove "embarrassing" to his job prospects. To this point, their unspoken agreement had been to marry as soon as he completed his studies, an event scheduled to occur in midsummer 1855. Suddenly Fannie began to suspect that her betrothed had changed his mind without telling her.[19]

Understandably, this prospect left her confused and angry—reactions aggravated by her present situation. By early 1855 Fannie, who had been working in Georgia for almost two years, was wearying of the grind. Like many young women thrust into an unsatisfying career, she began to see marriage as the only way out. "I am afraid," she wrote him, "that if your poor little girl stays here toiling on ... she will indeed have no youth left for you." Then, too, pressure from relatives and friends who expected her to wed was becoming unbearable. Suddenly her letters to Bangor began to exceed his to Milledgeville.[20]

Soon Chamberlain's letters did not have to travel so far south. In mid-year Fannie quit her position and went to Boston to visit relatives. Shortly before Chamberlain received his divinity degree, she wrote him "beside myself with anxiety and suspense. I have seemed to be spending all my time either in writing to you or in crying. It has been dreadfully mortifying & embarrassing to be asked so continually, by my friends, 'when are you going to be married?'...."[21]

Chamberlain's motives for suggesting they postpone their wedding are difficult to gauge. As he quickly reassured her, his ardor had not diminished. In fact, short months before she came north he had longed for her return so they might plan for the future in each other's presence. But there is some question as to whether he was fully committed to the union. Until recently he had kept in touch with at least one other young woman, a distant cousin, for whom he professed romantic feelings. By the time he broke off the relationship, he had been engaged to Fannie for nearly two years. Furthermore, he parted with this "friend of my soul" in words suggesting that the separation need not be permanent: "There is a place for you in my heart which no other can fill, —*I will sooner be blotted out ... than ever let you go.*"[22]

Whether or not he loved Fannie as deeply as he had once, Chamberlain was a man who met his obligations. Not only Fannie's relatives but his own regarded their wedding as overdue. He came to share their view.

As he prepared for entrance into the married state, his career planning began to take shape at last. In his final weeks at Bangor, while composing the oration he would present in partial fulfillment of his degree, he learned of his appointment to deliver a master's oration at Bowdoin. Since he lacked the time to prepare two addresses, his alma mater accepted a repetition of what he would deliver at the seminary a week earlier. As the oration would serve to qualify him for degrees at two august institutions, Chamberlain worked long and hard on his composition and faithfully practiced diction, determined to erase the memory of his graduation-day disaster of three years before.

He delivered his address with perfect composure and impressive elocution, first for his clerical masters at the seminary, then before the secular audience that filled the pews of the First Parish Church. Chamberlain's proud family was on hand for one or both occasions, as was Fannie, recently returned to Brunswick for a heart-to-heart with the man she loved. Declaiming on "Law and Liberty," the speaker drove home his theme that "the superabounding life lavished in the world" proved that human freedom was the natural order of things. "The whole universe," he argued, "showed that freedom was a part of law." Nowhere in evidence was the halting, stammering performance he had given the last time he spoke in the church of his future father-in-law.[23]

Chamberlain's oration was warmly received. Not only did it bring rapturous applause, it attracted newspaper attention in cities throughout the East. Publicity reached as far as New York, where a notice in the *Independent* hailed its author as a theologian with a fresh voice and a sound outlook. Numerous papers closer to home endorsed Manhattan's opinion.

The reception his speech received was so strong that Chamberlain hoped it might land him professional connections, perhaps even a job offer. Hope became reality one day later, when Bowdoin offered him the position of natural theology recently vacated by Calvin Stowe. Without hesitation, he accepted the offer, along with others. Soon after he entered on his duties the college asked him, and he agreed, to become a special instructor in logic as well as theology, with the added duty of teaching freshman Greek.[24]

The pay that accompanied the instructorship was anything but munificent and the position was bottom-rung, but the idea of teaching at his alma mater appealed to him for more than one reason. It would support his marriage; it might lead to a better-paying professorship; and it would place him in close contact with the two brothers who had followed him to Bowdoin: Horace, now about to enter his junior year, and John, on the verge of matriculating. Coming as it did at such a key moment in his young life, Bowdoin's offer seemed to confirm Chamberlain's belief in a spiritually directed destiny. As he would assure his mother nine years hence, "I have laid plans in my day, good ones I thought. But they never succeeded. *Something else, better, did*, and I could see it as plain as day, that God had done it, & for my good."[25]

The metaphysical convergence of need and means persuaded him that teaching was, and ought to be, his life's work. In late September he asked Fannie, who was back in Boston, to marry him at the end of the fall term. She happily agreed and began to pack for home. Less than a week later she was in Brunswick, selecting her trousseau and attending to a myriad of bridal preparations that would have been foreign to her fiancé.[26]

For obvious reasons, Chamberlain may have been distracted as he labored through his first full semester at Bowdoin. Yet his effectiveness in the classroom appears not to have suffered. Three weeks before his wedding day, several of his students wrote to thank him for the "earnest and faithful manner in which you have sought to point out to us the Paths of Life, [and] also of our love and esteem for the kind and brotherly interest, which you have ever shown in our temporal and eternal welfare."[27]

* * *

All distractions were laid aside on the frosty afternoon of Friday, December 7, 1855, when Joshua Chamberlain and Fannie Adams were joined in wedlock, the first church wedding held in the meetinghouse of the First Parish Church. A happy and hopeful Dr. Adams officiated, and the families and friends of bride and groom filled the parsonage. All were made glad by the simple but sacred ceremony that joined two lovers so long apart.[28]

Three

RESTLESS SCHOLAR

*O*n the day his adopted daughter wed, George Adams lamented: "*I feel sadly about poor Fanny* fearing greatly she will not make herself happy." By now the pastor had come to regard his new son-in-law, whom he once considered a poor choice for Fannie, as a man who could fill her life with love and comfort, if only she would let him.[1]

At the outset of her married life, at least, Fannie appeared happy—in fact, almost ecstatic. She would remember with great fondness her wedding night, which the couple spent in her room in Brunswick. There, she later told Chamberlain, "I first pillowed my head on your bosom, your own beloved wife." Chamberlain himself considered that first evening as man and wife "that sweetest & purest & ever to be honored night." Two months later, with the couple again apart—he back at Bowdoin and she on an extended shopping trip—he told her that married life had made him "*happy every day.*"[2]

The glad times seemed destined to continue indefinitely. Chamberlain's first year on the Bowdoin faculty was intellectually rewarding, and when, at the next commencement, he was offered the vacant chair of rhetoric and oratory, at a higher salary than before, he eagerly accepted. He was tickled by the irony of being called to such a position despite "what he had supposed [to be] disqualifying disabilities" of speech and poise. His home life was happy, though the rooms he and

Fannie leased in Brunswick were small and in need of extensive furnishing. This Fannie attended to through the shopping rounds she made locally and occasionally in Boston and other cities.[3]

His wife's tendency to extravagance, nurtured in girlhood, concerned Chamberlain, who feared that not even his new salary would accommodate her tastes for new furniture, carpets, wall coverings, draperies. A year and a half into their marriage he warned her gently that "at the best I can hardly keep up with our expenses," tempering his tone with an admonition to "forgive me, dearest love, I am ashamed to be obliged to say this…. You ought not to have married a poor boy…." Fannie accepted his advice to the extent of shopping occasionally at auction to obtain the best quality at the lowest price, but at other times she continued to spend what her husband considered more than they could afford. They made do by staying with his family when the college shut down for vacation and by taking in brother John as a boarder, his parents paying his rent. (At about this time, Horace Chamberlain graduated, followed in his brother's footsteps by taking a master of arts degree, and prepared to marry and move to Bangor to start a law career.) The extra income represented by John's addition to the household helped allay Chamberlain's fears of impecuniousness, and for the most part his home life continued to be pleasant.[4]

Wedded bliss increased when children were born into the family. Obviously, Chamberlain was able to talk Fannie out of her professed desire for a childless marriage (as he had confidently assumed he could) or he overrode her objections. True to his expectations, both of them were elated by the birth, in October 1856, of Grace Dupee Chamberlain. The proud parents nicknamed her "Daisy" but her father considered his first-born "an angel of God." His elation turned to grief when a son, born prematurely 13 months later, lived only a few hours. In the fall of 1858 another son came into their life and, after some weeks of fragile health, survived to grow up alongside his sister. His parents named him Harold Wyllys but promptly called him by his middle name.[5]

By the time of Wyllys's arrival, his parents had moved into more commodious lodgings in Brunswick. The following spring they moved again, this time into a house on the edge of the Bowdoin campus. The one-story Federal-style house on the corner of Maine and Potter Streets, complete with barn and garden in rear, had been built in 1830 by a Captain Pierce. Ten years later it became home to one of Bowdoin's most celebrated alumni, Henry Wadsworth Longfellow, who, like Chamberlain after him, accepted a professorship in modern languages at his alma mater. At first the Chamberlains leased the house, which was large enough to cost $2,500, more than twice Chamberlain's salary. The young professor was able to afford the purchase only because he impressed a neighbor, a banker, with the time and care he put into gardening around the house. The banker assured Chamberlain he would qualify for a mortgage no matter how steep.[6]

* * *

From 1857 on, strains began to pull at the edges of the Chamberlains' marriage. The family budget, thanks largely to Fannie's unflagging efforts to secure handsome furnishings for their new house, was a continuing source of unease and concern for her spouse. Fannie was sometimes away from home for weeks at a time, buying table linen in Portland and plush chairs in New York. In her absence Chamberlain cared for the children with the occasional help of his visiting mother and sister. When alone, Chamberlain missed his wife terribly, finding the half-empty house "desolate for me." During one of her absences he found a forgotten daguerreotype of her, the sight of which left him "perfectly & uncontrollably wretched ... all [in] a tumult ... sick, faint." Whenever she would extend her trips, as she frequently did, he slept poorly, had morbid dreams, and felt close to tears. Once he wrote her of a dream in which "you did not seem to care much to be near [me]." He decided, with an almost audible sigh, "perhaps I am too much of a lover for a husband."[7]

When at home, Fannie was often quiet or cross, as though she had begun to feel chained to her existence in Brunswick. Her interests in music and art no longer seemed to sustain her. But she was not alone in her susceptibility to gloom. Her husband was almost as prone as she to black moods, some of which came upon him with the force of an explosion. His intermittent fear that Fannie loved him too little underlay one such episode. In February 1857, with his wife traveling once again, he chanced upon a portfolio of hers and found inside some letters she had sent, unbeknownst to him, to a male friend named Akers. Although the contents are unknown, one can assume they contained intimate information, perhaps a discussion of Fannie's feelings for her husband. Their discovery sent Chamberlain into one of the most violent fits of his life.

Apparently he wrote Fannie at white heat, for in a return letter she beseeched him to calm down: "Lawrence! Lawrence! God help me my own Lawrence. Your letter has killed me. I would die for you if I could. If I did not know you had misconstrued those letters of mine, and that there really was no reason for your feelings as expressed in your letter … God only knows what would become of me." She tried desperately to assure him that for Akers she felt only platonic affection. She had considered showing her husband the letters, deciding against it for fear of inducing what their discovery had triggered, "those fearful, morbid states of feeling into which you so often fall." Eventually she was able to explain the matter to his satisfaction, drawing from him a hopeful promise that "nothing of that kind will ever trouble me again…. It's all over now & better than before." But the intensity of his reaction to suspicions of his wife's infidelity suggests that the mood swings and the overwrought imagination that had afflicted Chamberlain as a suitor continued to oppress him as a married man.[8]

* * *

In addition to a latent distrust of his wife's affections, Chamberlain's life in the years leading up to the Civil War was burdened by his and her poor health, by loss and mourning, by the hint of boredom that crept into his professional life, and by the sectional discord sweeping the country in the late 1850s and early 1860s. Fannie's apparent discontent began to express itself in physical ailments not readily ameliorated, such as the blinding headaches that accompanied her eye strain. It reached the point in early 1860 that she was, as her husband explained to his mother, "perfectly 'killed' with neuralgia—day & night." While household chores forced her to work through the day, evenings found her "driven distracted" and often in bed at an early hour. Chamberlain himself was "never so more plagued by pains &

sleeplessness. Rheumatism or some such sort of thing seems to have got a fast hold of me, & has of late struck into my head in such a way as to make me incapable of doing anything which requires attention or mental effort." He treated his afflictions, as his wife treated hers, with remedies so powerful they sometimes incapacitated him.[9]

Chamberlain's headache-induced inability to think clearly would certainly have affected his classroom performance. In 1857 he was partially relieved from his duties in rhetoric and oratory and appointed instructor in French and German. Almost three years later, after what he called "our usual amount of diplomacy ... plotting & counterplotting," the administration named him Professor in the Modern Languages of Europe. Although he preferred the course to any other he had taught at Bowdoin, as the 1859-60 school year progressed he found himself curiously out of step with the rest of the faculty. Increasingly he admitted to feeling restless, disoriented, distracted. Perhaps the life of a professor in a small college was not the path of destiny after all.[10]

When the nation began its tragic but inexorable slide toward civil conflict, he found it difficult to devote full attention to recitations or to grading the hundreds of themes his students submitted each semester. He continued to sing in the First Parish Church choir and to assist at the local Sunday school. For relaxation, he sailed small boats in Middle Bay, and in the evenings he would play the bass viol for the pleasure of his children and his brother John, with Fannie accompanying him on piano. His life seemed serene, at least upon the surface, but his attention was sometimes turned elsewhere, as though to catch the strains of a far-off bugle.

He tried to bury himself in his academic work. In the autumn of 1859 he began to agitate for reform in his department, hoping to expand and liberalize the class offerings and, in defiance of the views of the administration, to make Bowdoin more of a secular institution, less of a training ground for Congregational clergymen. For him a liberal education constituted "a general outline of a symmetrical development, involving such acquaintance with all the departments of knowledge and culture—proportionate to their several values—as shall give some insight into the principles and powers by which thought passes into life...." Despite the radical tinge of his suggestions, school officials permitted him to implement some reforms. One added courses in which student papers, heretofore graded and forgotten, were discussed, revised, and rewritten under his supervision until they became finished products, capable of carrying "a point once [and] for all."[11]

In 1860 events local and national, social and political, coalesced to interrupt the flow of Chamberlain's personal life and professional career. The beginning of the year found him in a contemplative mood, musing uneasily about morality and mortality. On a snowcovered Sabbath in February he wrote his sister that it was "well for us that we have our moods ... that we should be conscious at once of the joy of hope, the contentment of possession, the fear of loss, the resignation in bereavement." His words took on a prophetic ring when, that spring, Emily Stelle Chamberlain was born in the house on Maine and Potter Streets, only to leave it that fall in a tiny coffin. The season caused her grieving father to remember her as having left behind "a summer smile and aching hearts, as she departed with the flowers."[12]

Another family loss was imminent, for in 1860 a lung ailment that had afflicted Horace Chamberlain suddenly worsened in prelude to his death the following year. When he succumbed on December 7, 1861—his brother's sixth wedding anniversary—Horace left behind a young wife and a promising future in the law. For a time Chamberlain was inconsolable, consumed with grief that Horace "should be stricken down at the very opening of his career, & when he had so much reason to anticipate a prosperous course...." He had been in Horace's company only intermittently since adulthood, but his death evoked an almost overpowering sense of loss, making Chamberlain see that "it is not after all for *him*, as it is for the thought of the thing, for myself, & for us all, that I feel sad."[13]

Another mournful realization came to Chamberlain as 1860 neared its end. The long-simmering enmity between North and South had seeped into the national political process, raising the specter of war. War was something that Chamberlain had never wished to see but for years had sadly expected. In November, after the "black abolitionist" Republican, Abraham Lincoln, won the presidency by less than a majority vote, the South prepared in earnest for conflict. Six weeks after Lincoln's election South Carolina left the Union to a cacophony of minute-guns and fireworks. Hearing the news, Chamberlain suspected that the fireworks had just begun.

* * *

On the last day of March 1861 Chamberlain intoned the prayer that ended the first observance of Easter Sunday in Dr. Adams's church. Barely two weeks after celebrating the death and resurrection of the Prince of Peace, Brunswick, along with cities, towns, and hamlets across the country, learned of portentous events in Charleston Harbor, where local cannon had fired on the U. S. Army garrison inside Fort Sumter. In the wake of the fort's surrender on April 14, thousands of young men North and South, motivated by patriotism, adventurism, or both, rushed to defend their homeland and, if necessary, carry the war to the enemy's. The South already had a nation to whom its warriors pledged their fealty. In early February, six states having declared themselves out of the union (five more would follow through late May), their political representatives established the Confederate States of America, thereby giving an institutional dimension to disunion. On the 18th, the new nation on the North's doorstep inaugurated its first president, former Secretary of War and ex-Mississippi Senator Jefferson Davis, a nationally-known and -admired statesman on whom Bowdoin had conferred an honorary degree two and a half years before.[14]

At first Professor Chamberlain watched in bemused detachment as the war fever gripped his town, state, and region. A week after Sumter's surrender he was in Boston on family business. To his growing interest he found "this city of flags & bayonets" agog with war fever. Two months later he was back at home when his fellow alumnus, now-Colonel Oliver O. Howard, led the Washington-bound 3rd Maine Volunteers through the streets of Brunswick to the cheers and applause of a spirited throng.[15]

Though fairly certain that the contest was not his to join, Chamberlain approved of war fervor in the North because he detested the motivations of the South, which he saw as a hotbed of "fire eaters." He could not abide the thought of a divided nation; the Founding Fathers "did not vote themselves into a people; they recognized and declared that they were a people" whose bonds ought not be severed by political, social, or economic grievances. At Fort Sumter "the integrity and the existence of the people of the United States had been assailed in open and bitter war." Men who loved their country had a clear course of duty: they must force the errant states to return to the fold—at sword-point, if through no other means.[16]

Chamberlain saw his own course as through a glass darkly. One of his principal motives in rejecting a military education was his unwillingness to soldier in peacetime. Now, however, he might serve in a war—not just in any war but a conflict of epic proportions, upon which the survival of his nation depended. Yet he was 33 and already graying, a married man with a family, and an educator, not a warrior, one who sought to fill young men's minds, not blow them away. Besides, the war would surely be brief—the might of the manpower-rich, resource-abundant, technologically advantaged North would make quick work of this experiment in rebellion.

In this latter belief he was very wrong, but he did not admit the truth until the conflict was almost lost. By the early stages of summer, 1862, following a year's worth of defeats and setbacks beginning with the near-disaster at First Bull Run the previous July, the mighty legions of the Union had been brought low. The specter of the Stars and Bars flying atop the Executive Mansion in Washington no longer seemed a ludicrous fantasy. In the eastern theater, military fortunes had bogged down on the Virginia Peninsula, where Major General George B. McClellan's Army of the Potomac had been turned away from the gates of Richmond by a much smaller but more formidable force under Robert E. Lee. President Lincoln, who had called out thousands of volunteers when the crisis broke, was now asking 300,000 more to flock to the colors (approximately 5,000 would be assigned to the quota of the state of Maine) in order to "bring this unnecessary and injurious civil war to a speedy and satisfactory conclusion."[17]

By July 1862 Bowdoin's professor of modern languages had seen numerous underclassmen join the two drill teams that had been formed on campus at war's outset. Dozens of his former students had gone off to war in volunteer outfits, many as officers—at least a few of them inspired by the speeches he made at campus rallies in support of the war. Typical of the letters he wrote in his students' behalf to Governor

Israel Washburn Jr., Adjutant General John L. Hodsdon, and other state authorities, was the following, composed in September, 1861: "It gives me great pleasure to say that Mr. Walter J. Poor during his College course gave ample proof of high moral principle and intellectual capacity. I know him to be a man of integrity, of generous devotion to the cause he enlisted in, of great energy and perseverance in executing his plans; and I cordially recommend him as worthy of high trusts."[18]

Each time one of his young men went off to war, Chamberlain felt a sense of regret and, perhaps, the pang of duty spurned. He tried to follow their military careers as closely as possible, and the letters they sent him from the field made him doubt even more the direction his life was taking. A few weeks after his professor had commended him to state officials, Walter Poor wrote Chamberlain from the Peninsula about the lack of effective leadership in McClellan's command. If Chamberlain could have seen the poorly drilled, poorly disciplined ranks "of beardless boys" and the "lifeless and characterless men" who tried to lead them, "you would not be surprised at the panic at Bull Run or our reverses elsewhere."[19]

The reference to "characterless men" may have struck a chord in Chamberlain, who was aware that few of the professional soldiers placed in authority over the young men of Bowdoin shared their breeding and erudition. It must have occurred to him, now and then, to ask whether men of intellectual and moral caliber might not bring a quick end to this protracted and bloody struggle. At length, he decided in the affirmative.

Many of his Bowdoin colleagues professed to have no personal stake in the war, which they considered a disgusting waste of youth and treasure and thus unworthy of their support. Some must have noticed Chamberlain's tendency to restlessness, which they dated from Fort Sumter. His behavior raised a red flag for certain professors because, despite his earlier efforts to tinker with the established order, he was regarded as an ally against others' attempts to liberalize and secularize the curriculum; to lose him now was to lose the fight to keep Bowdoin true to its Congregational traditions.[20]

To hold onto its professor of modern languages, late in 1861 the administration had named him "professor for life" in his department.

Along with tenure had come the privilege of two years' paid leave of absence in order to study abroad and thus perfect himself in his discipline. Historians invariably state that the leave would have been spent in Europe, which makes sense from the standpoint of Chamberlain's academic specialty, but in August 1862 he himself noted that "it was not a condition that I should visit Europe but go wherever I chose…." The visitation, which had also been granted to Chamberlain's illustrious predecessor, Longfellow, had delighted him enough that he made plans to leave for distant parts at year's end, a decision he deferred following the fatal illness of his brother. An 1861 account by a close acquaintance claims that Chamberlain put off going until the war should end. This may well be true; but whether he was to go in '61 or four years later, he did not intend to use the sabbatical, as many historians have claimed, as a cover for jumping ship and enlisting in the army.[21]

Once Chamberlain determined to follow the path of his student-soldiers, he did not reveal his decision to his colleagues. Nor, for that matter, did he tell Fannie until the deed was effectively done. His penchant for secrecy would land him in hot water on both campus and home front. Not until after his return from his July 18 trip to the state capital at Augusta did the faculty learn of his meeting with Governor Washburn. Many were livid over what they considered his duplicity, and some shunned him during the brief period he remained in Brunswick before reporting to training camp.

As one might expect, Fannie was shocked, hurt, and alarmed by the decision he had made without consulting her. With two young children at home, having experienced difficulty in securing help to care for them, and with neuralgia draining her daily energy, the last thing she wanted in her life was a long-absent husband who might never return to her, at least not in one piece. She remonstrated, she raised her voice, quite possibly she wept over the injustice he had done them both by this unilateral act that threatened to send their world careening in all directions. Her husband sympathized, tried to calm her fears, but remained resolute. Whenever at life's crossroads, Chamberlain consulted with his heart, his better judgment, and God—no one else.

Having made up his mind, not even a distraught wife could convince him he had acted selfishly or for the wrong reasons.[22]

His belief that he had made the right decision had been strengthened by his audience with state officials. The diminutive and bespectacled governor, a mild-mannered but forthright statesmen pushing 50, had received him warmly, as though Chamberlain had years of experience in the art of war. In fact, all the governor had to go on as a gauge of his visitor's abilities was Chamberlain's unsolicited letter of July 14, which he wrote "in pursuance of the offer of reinforcements for the war," and in which he offered his services in any capacity he might be thought suited to. Confidently he had predicted: "I believe you will be satisfied with my antecedents," including his militia officer father.[23]

In his letter Chamberlain made no mention of his brief term at Whiting's Academy or his stint in the Brewer Artillery. Instead he emphasized that "I have always been interested in military matters and what I do not know in that line, *I know how to learn.*" To strengthen his claim to a commission, he boasted that "nearly a hundred of those who have been my pupils, are now officers in our army; but there are many more all over our State, who, I believe, would respond with enthusiasm, if summoned by me, and who would bring forward men enough to fill up a Regiment at once." He added that he was willing to forgo the leave he had been granted by the college. He would make himself available for duty immediately after commencement, the first week of August.[24]

It is not known what sort of position Chamberlain believed himself qualified to fill or how much rank he hoped to secure. His military interests might be strong but his education in that line was meager and his field experience limited to a militia muster or two. When the governor replied to his offer by setting up a meeting at the State House, he expressed what Chamberlain called a "favorable opinion" of his correspondent's qualifications but appeared mainly interested in the professor's ability to recruit students to fill one of the five regiments Maine appeared obliged to raise under Lincoln's call.[25]

Presumably, therefore, the Bowdoin professor was mightily surprised by the upshot of his State House conference. Washburn at once informed him that four of the new regiments—the 16th, 17th, 18th, and 19th Infantry—had already been staffed with a full complement of officers and had gone into training camp. There was some question whether a fifth regiment would be needed to meet the state's quota. If the decision were made to organize it, would Chamberlain consider becoming its colonel?

The offer of such high rank, despite his apparent lack of qualifications, must have staggered him. Later he would wonder if he had been the beneficiary of the Republican governor's desire to curry the support of the state's many War Democrats. He blurted out that he would not feel comfortable beginning his war service on such a plateau; he would settle for a lesser position if available to him. After some further discussion, he shook Washburn's hand and entrained for home, wondering if he could learn the duties of a field officer quickly enough to be of any use to his governor, his state, and his country.[26]

* * *

Back at Bowdoin, for days he maintained a discreet silence about his trip to Augusta. The only person to whom he breathed a word of it was now-General Oliver Howard, who had stopped in Brunswick en route to Virginia following recuperation from the loss of an arm in the Peninsula Campaign. Although it seems unlikely that Howard would have betrayed a confidence, a week after Chamberlain's audience with the governor local newspapers announced his appointment as colonel of the 20th Maine Volunteers. The untrue story embarrassed him, prompting him to assure Washburn that he had not been responsible for its publication.

The article also brought a torrent of criticism from his colleagues, who passed a vote (for whatever good it would do) that Chamberlain should either stay in Brunswick or go to Europe. One of their number, fearing the political fallout of Chamberlain's enlistment, went directly to Augusta to tell the governor that, far from being officer material, his colleague was "a mild-mannered common student." The controversy reached a state official in Portland, who at about the same time wrote Washburn that "his old classmates &c here say that you have been deceived; that C. is *nothing* at all."[27]

It is not known how much influence these criticisms had on

Washburn, who soon learned that he must in fact recruit, organize, and staff the 20th Maine. Most definitely he would have given the man at issue the opportunity to defend himself. This Chamberlain did, writing the governor early in August in some embarrassment about the "unexpected degree of opposition in the Faculty of this College. They are unwilling to give me any sort of countenance in the matter" of his quest for a commission. "But," he added resolutely, "I feel that I must go," and thus he hoped that his colleagues' strictures "will have no more weight with you than with me."[28]

Washburn would have lent an ear not only to Chamberlain's detractors but also to supporters such as Dr. John D. Lincoln of Brunswick, who wrote for the professor the same glowing endorsements of character and ability the latter had composed for his students gone into the army. Chamberlain, Dr. Lincoln, informed the governor, was "as capable of commanding a Reg't as any man out[side] of a West Point graduate." He predicted that many men of military age, students and friends of Chamberlain "would rally around his standard as they would around a hero." The recommendation of the politically active physician doubtless carried some weight, and his reference to Chamberlain's ability to recruit for the regiment would have especially impressed the governor.[29]

As though endorsing one of Dr. Lincoln's points, Washburn came to believe that a West Pointer, preferably a Regular Army officer, would be the proper choice to command the new regiment; the untutored Chamberlain had been right to opt for a lesser position. On August 7 Washburn published a general order announcing the formation of the 20th Maine and directing companies already recruiting to go into camp at Island Park, outside Portland, "on or before the 12th inst[ant]., where quarters and subsistence will be provided. The organization of this regiment will be completed forthwith." The following day the governor scribbled Chamberlain a hasty note: "I formally tender you the office of Lt. Col. 20th Reg Me Vol. Adelbert Ames U. S. A. commander of a battery, a native of Maine is Col—& a superb one he will make."[30]

Chamberlain would have been gratified that his services were rated so highly as to be named second-in-command of a new regiment. It is doubtful he knew anything at all about the man under whom he would serve, but what he learned in subsequent days must have impressed him. Adelbert Ames was a 26-year-old native of Rockland who had graduated near the top of the West Point class of May 1861. Two months later, at First Bull Run, the tall, goateed lieutenant had served with a Regular artillery unit that, when placed in an exposed position by its superior, was overrun and captured. In the melee Ames, who served his guns to the last so faithfully that he would later receive a Congressional Medal of Honor, took a serious wound in the thigh.[31]

One well-known historian offers this observation about the West Pointer: "It had been impressed upon him in two ways—one theoretical and the other practical—that discipline is a mighty good thing to have among your soldiers when the shooting starts." Chamberlain should have suspected, as he would soon learn, that despite his youth and relatively brief experience in the field, Adelbert Ames was an Old Regular in discipline—a textbook soldier, a martinet in the truest (but not necessarily the most pejorative) sense of the term. In fact, while gentlemanly and even affable in his dealings with worthy specimens of the breed, Ames had a dim view of the military potential of volunteers. His experience with them, in the role of drill instructor, predated Bull Run; that experience had taught him that citizen-soldiers required strict handling and a large dosage of discipline. By all indications, he would make life difficult for his new troops, doubtless including his junior officers.[32]

If Chamberlain feared being subject to a taskmaster, he may also have decided that in the long run the situation would work to his advantage. Ivory-tower types such as he, had so much to learn about the very basics of soldiering that it was good he would be learning them from a Regular officer. He only hoped the man would be fair and even-handed as well as spit-and-polish.

* * *

On Monday, August 18, Chamberlain prepared to leave home for Portland, where he would take charge of the training-camp until Ames arrived the following week. That morning he donned the stiffly new, smartly tailored uniform of a lieutenant colonel of infantry, pulled leather gauntlets over his wrists, and set an ornate kepi at a jaunty angle on his head. His martial splendor complemented by a fierce mustache such as Colonel Ames himself favored, he finished dressing and went downstairs, where, after a few minutes spent in quiet farewell, he embraced his sorrowing wife and children. Nothing he could say would have made them understand his compulsion to leave home and risk the fortunes of them all, so he did not try. His emotions in tumult, he left them standing by the open door.

Waiting outside, ready for the ride to the train station, was Thomas Chamberlain, now all of 21, his youth only partially disguised by a new crop of sidewhiskers. Nearly as tall as his brother but gangly in a way Joshua had never been, Tom was attired in a new, homemade uniform; his coat sleeves would soon carry a sergeant's chevrons. Having abided by his parents' wish that he not enlist in 1861, Tom had happily left his job as a store clerk in Bangor to serve alongside his older brother in the 20th Maine. Tom's rank was largely a function of his brother's position, but he would quickly prove worthy of it—and, before long, worthy of an officer's commission.

"Take care of Tom," Joshua Chamberlain Jr. would later instruct his eldest in a letter in which he darkly prophecized that "you are in for it. So distinguish yourself as soon as possible and be out of it.... come home with honor as I know you will if that lucky star of yours will serve you...." The words would not have made for pleasant reflection, but they were typical of Chamberlain's father. For all his pride at seeing his offspring answer their nation's call, the anti-war Democrat, who had named his third son after one of the stalwarts of states' rights, could not help but resent the sacrifice his family was making, especially because the struggle raging in Virginia and elsewhere in the divided country was "not *our war*."

In this, of course, he was wrong: it was now his sons' war, as it would be for the next three years unless sooner discharged.[33]

Four

NOVICE WARRIOR

*C*hamberlain found Camp Mason crammed full of would-be soldiers—energetic, enthusiastic youngsters, most of them with even less of an understanding of what lay ahead than their untutored lieutenant colonel. Until Ames arrived, Chamberlain made fitful and largely unsuccessful efforts to turn chaos into order. In this he was assisted by one of the few officers with field experience, Major Charles D. Gilmore of Bangor, a veteran of the 7th Maine. Although not immediately apparent to anyone, Gilmore was a physical coward who would prove of no use in a battle, assuming he ever got into one. Slightly wounded by a shell fragment on the Peninsula the previous April, the major would cite the lingering effects of his injury as the basis of frequent hospitalizations over the next two and a half years. He would go on sick leave virtually every time combat appeared imminent.

His lack of moral stamina notwithstanding, Gilmore was a proficient drill instructor and something of a disciplinarian. His ability to persuade the rank-and-file to act rather like soldiers was a boon to Chamberlain in his early days in camp. Furthermore, Gilmore was willing to help his superior translate into drill-field maneuvers the lessons covered in the numerous tactics manuals that Chamberlain the military enthusiast had collected over the years.[1]

Chamberlain must have been impressed by Gilmore's efforts at giving

Camp Mason a suggestion of military precision; the material at the major's disposal would have made many a drillmaster weep. Looking about at the men he would command, Chamberlain saw life-long civilians ranging in age from 16 to 60, the latter more than a decade older than the official enlistment age. This fact testified to the regiment's formation in the second year of the conflict, when family men were being recruited to complement the avid youngsters who had left home in the first flush of martial enthusiasm. Walking the extent of the camp, Chamberlain found it populated by nearly 1,000 recruits, almost all of whom lacked uniforms, arms, and any semblance of military deportment. He conversed briefly with farmers, lumberjacks, oystermen, sailors, millers, and day laborers—many of them tall, strapping fellows, their skin browned by outdoor life, their hands gnarled and callused by hard work. Despite their unmilitary appearance, he sensed a potential that boded well for the outfit's future. If these men could be taught discipline and tactics, they just might give a healthy account of themselves in a fight.

One quality he suspected the regiment lacked was cohesiveness. Whereas many regiments benefited from an inherent unity derived from being native to the same town or county, the 20th Maine had been recruited from all corners of the state. Much of its manpower came from excess enlistees in the 16th, 17th, 18th, and 19th Regiments, many of whom hailed from the state's interior rather than its coastal region. While not exactly an orphan outfit—state officials would keep in close touch with the regiment throughout the conflict, supplying its needs and trying to recruit it up to strength—the 20th Maine probably lost something in the way of *esprit de corps* by not having a particular section of the state to call its own.[2]

From his first day in camp, Chamberlain took every opportunity to pore over the instruction manuals that would keep him at least a step or two ahead of the men he was supposed to lead. He perhaps read *Rifle and Light Infantry Tactics*, by William J. Hardee, formerly of the U. S. Army and now a Confederate major general; more likely he studied Brigadier General Silas Casey's *Infantry Tactics*, a glorified rehash of Hardee but newer and more accessible to Union officers. A more obscure text Chamberlain is known to have owned and consulted is Brigadier General George W. Cullum's translation of *Elements of Military Art and History*, by the French engineer officer E. D. L. Duparcq. Marginal notes and underlining in the copy Chamberlain carried indicate how closely he focused on several aspects of the text, including a discussion of the moral effects of switching swiftly from a defensive posture to an offensive one.[3]

And yet, the defensive had its merits. The tactics books should have alerted Chamberlain that the face of warfare had forever changed during the past 20 years with the widespread introduction of the rifled musket and its relatively quick reloading process. Early in the century, troops on every continent had enjoyed the luxury of drawing an enemy's fire at a range of perhaps 300 yards and then reaching his line, via a bayonet charge, before his musketeers could reload. By 1862, however, the rifle, capable of delivering an accurate fire at up to 600 yards, had taken the advantage from the attacker and given it to the well-fortified defender. With rifles in the hands of thousands of Federals and Confederates, the battlefields of America were becoming vast killing fields.

Perhaps Chamberlain foresaw that the war he had joined would degenerate into a protracted, bloody contest of maneuver and indirect offensives—or perhaps he did not. The tactics manuals available to him had not caught up with the times; they did not factor in the destructiveness of the new weaponry. Since every manual available to the army of 1862 was based to some degree on Napoleonic warfare, each continued to stress the desirability of taking and exploiting the offensive through massed firepower and headlong assault. Thus, even as they taught civilians-in-arms how to maintain cohesion and poise in battle, Hardee, Casey, and other theorists fostered an outmoded style of warfare that was becoming ever more dangerous to practice. Since the 20th Maine boasted few veterans in its ranks—men like Adelbert Ames and Charles Gilmore, who had seen the disastrous results of offensives launched at Bull Run and on the Peninsula—Joshua Chamberlain and his men would have to learn the truth through the bitter process of trial-and-error.[4]

* * *

In some ways life for Chamberlain got easier, in other ways more difficult, when Colonel Ames made his appearance in camp. The young Regular took one look at the gaggle of recruits he was supposed to form into a regiment, and his year-old wound began to ache. Called into some semblance of formation on the parade-ground of Camp Mason, the recruits of the 20th Maine stood or slouched at attention, arms dangling, heads wagging, feet shuffling. Some men scratched themselves, others spat. After a few minutes given to inspecting the crooked column, his blood pressure climbing, Ames threw back his head in disgust and shouted for everyone to hear: "This is a hell of a regiment!" Looking on from a respectful distance, Chamberlain had the unhappy feeling that Ames held him responsible for the men's wretched appearance.[5]

At once the new colonel set about to make things right. The first step he took was to call together his officers and look them over, probing for strengths and weaknesses. At once Chamberlain monopolized his attention. Ames acted with no deference toward the older man; well aware of Chamberlain's inexperience, he began at once to instruct him in military thinking, behavior, and custom. He found his lieutenant colonel a willing listener who heeded his advice, took notes when appropriate, and asked intelligent questions. Ames's second-in-command would require at least as much instruction, as much seasoning, as the rank-and-file. But Ames respected Chamberlain's erudition and appreciated the fact that he did not presume upon his civilian accomplishments. Ames also sensed that this man, although currently less valuable to the army than the colonel's own horse, would quickly become an asset. He would assimilate the details, the nuances, not just the basics, of his new trade. He would perform his duties faithfully and well if given the knowledge he needed and the proper encouragement.

For his part, Chamberlain liked what he saw in his energetic, impatient superior. It was obvious that Ames was a man in a hurry, anxious to be done with raw recruits, and perhaps understandably doubtful of the military capacity of citizen-soldiers, especially those who got their shoulder-straps by virtue of who, not what, they knew. He realized that Ames would drill and discipline the regiment to within an inch of its life, probably to the point at which many would come to hate him at least as much as their common enemy. But Chamberlain also sensed that, with precious few days available to train, after which the outfit would be tossed into a cauldron, Ames's way of doing things was probably the best—perhaps the only—way. He knew, too, that if and when the 20th Maine proved itself a capable fighting force, Ames would let up on it, permitting its people to do their duty as he had taught them, no longer making rookies' lives miserable, no longer cursing poor marksmanship or berating those who could not keep up on the march.

Chamberlain was impressed not only by his colonel but by many of the lower-ranking officers and the enlisted staff. A few of these officers—in furtherance of Chamberlain's pledge to Governor Washburn that men would follow him into the ranks—were former students of his at Bowdoin. These included Captain Ellis Spear, commander of Company G, a member of the Class of 1858 who had become a schoolmaster in Wiscasset; Lieutenant John Marshall Brown, an 1860 graduate and a Portland lawyer whose administrative talents would gain him the post of regimental adjutant; and Lieutenant William W. Morrell, Class of '61, one of Brunswick's most active recruiters, destined to die as a captain at Spotsylvania Court House in May 1864.[6]

Chamberlain's personal constituency, of course, included brother Tom, whose clerking experience recommended him, in his lieutenant colonel's view, for a quartermaster's position. Other line officers who in one way or another impressed Chamberlain included Captains Atherton W. Clark of Waldoboro, a sometimes crotchety but dependable sort whom his men called "Pap"; Samuel Keene, a flinty, no-nonsense attorney from Rockland; and Henry Clay Merriam, a born soldier who would remain in the Regular Army and years hence, thanks largely to the support of Chamberlain and other political backers, would attain the rank of major general.[7]

Ames and Chamberlain hoped that the "hell of a regiment" they commanded would be permitted to inhabit Camp Mason long enough to absorb at least the rudiments of soldiering. In this they were disappointed. The men barely had time to assimilate their weapons and accouterments. Corporal Holman S. Melcher of Company B reported to his brother in Topsham that "we have received all our equipments, which make quite a load when all packed. 1 Knapsack with straps to lash the blanket on the top. 1 Haversack, a bag on the left side in which to carry food. 1 Canteen. 1 Cartridge-box. 1 Cap pouch. 1 Bayonet Sheath, a rifle (Enfield), neat they are too, and light[weight]." As far as being armed, Melcher seems to have been among a minority; most of the regiment would not be outfitted with the sturdy, single-shot, British-made Enfield rifle until they moved closer to the war zone.[8]

Less than a week after Ames took command, with the men only recently uniformed and only a few of them armed, a Regular Army officer appeared in camp, assembled the outfit on the parade ground, and mustered 975 officers and enlisted men into three years of federal service. Chamberlain, just returned to camp after a few days in Brunswick tidying up his college affairs, could hardly believe the regiment was prepared to assume that responsibility. Ames and Gilmore had only begun to drill them in the manual of arms and to introduce them to the maneuvers they would be obliged to perform on a battlefield.[9]

Some of the men were such poor specimens of soldiery that they had barely passed the perfunctory medical examination the government required. So anxious were the examining physicians to pass enlistees that, as the dry-witted Ellis Spear put it, most "took the patriotism of the volunteer as conclusive evidence of bodily soundness." Not only had the infirm slipped past; so had the too-young, the ancient, and the vertically challenged. Spear recalled that "one fellow, too short, was passed in high-heel shoes, and grew shorter as time and his shoes wore on.... Another passed muster in a black beard, which soon after disclosed an ever widening zone of grey, and he became a veteran prematurely. More obscure bodily defects developed on the first hard campaign, and speedily furnished ample material for the hospital and pension roll." So green were the men mustered in on August 29 that they had not yet begun to complain about the rations issued to them: salted beef, salt pork, dehydrated ("dessicated") vegetables, and the dietary staple known as hardtack, the hard bread ration that Captain Spear described as "homogeneous and amorphous, excepting when wormy. It did not resemble anything in the vegetable, animal or mineral kingdom, except brick."[10]

The men and their officers, excepting Ames and a handful of short-term veterans, may not have been ready for the war, but the war was ready for them and thousands of other new recruits. On the day the regiment was sworn into service, a new Union commander, Major General John Pope, was meeting, on a battlefield known as Second Bull Run, much the same fate that George McClellan had met on the doorstep of Richmond. Outmaneuvered, out-fought, and out-foxed by Robert E. Lee and his brilliant lieutenant, "Stonewall" Jackson, Pope's much larger command was hammered into defeat throughout August 29 and again the next day. By the first days in September his demoralized survivors would be seeking refuge within the defenses of Washington, D.C., and McClellan would be riding out to reassume overall command in the eastern theater. It appeared problematical whether "Little Mac," who had already shown an inability to cope with his opponent, would prevent Lee from exploiting this latest in a dismayingly long series of Southern victories.[11]

On the 2nd of September came word that the unfinished regiment known as the 20th Maine was to be transported next day to the seat of war. Despite his concerns for the outfit's future, Chamberlain saw at least some cause for optimism. After much adversity the regiment had conquered the hurdle of moving from column into line and vice versa, movements absolutely critical to its ability to fight in, and disengage from, battle. "Of course," Ellis Spear cautioned, "the line was not at first the shortest distance between two fixed points, and the process of going from line into column resembled a convulsion."[12]

Although the city had no special claim to the regiment, a small crowd of local residents gathered around Camp Mason during the regiment's final days at Portland. Swelling their number were out-of-state visitors—wives, parents, and friends of the soldiers. A small party came down from Brunswick, including Fannie Chamberlain and Dr. Adams. The object of their attention was touched by his wife's presence on the eve of his departure, and honored by his father-in-law's.

Chamberlain must have felt proud indeed when on that last afternoon the men of his regiment formed a hollow square as one of his hometown friends, William Field, presented to him, on behalf of the ladies of Brunswick, a handsome gray stallion, outfitted in the finest saddelry. Chamberlain would christen the prize animal "Prince." In response to Field's gesture, the former professor of oratory stepped forth and made a brief speech in which he thanked his benefactors but doubted that he deserved such a fine gift: "No sacrifice or service of mine merits any other reward than that which conscience gives to every man who does his duty...."[13]

Some of the well-wishers left for home after the ceremony; others, Fannie and her father among them, stayed to see the regiment off in the morning. Both spent the night in Chamberlain's tent, huddling against the fury of one of coastal Maine's notorious "southeasters." Before dawn, their clothes still damp from the piercing rain, they watched the regiment strike tents, gather up its equipage, and reassemble on the parade ground. When the outfit moved out at 6 A.M., the pair joined a throng that accompanied the men—Chamberlain riding at their head alongside Ames and Gilmore—to the train station. Fannie made the trip by buggy, her white-bearded but hardy father on foot.

No farewell ceremony took place at the depot. Instead, family members, loved ones, friends, and neighbors hugged, kissed, shook hands with, and clapped the shoulders of, the departing troops. Chamberlain took his wife in his arms for what he realized might be the last time. After a few private moments with Fannie, he pumped his father-in-law's hand, saw to last-minute preparations including the loading of Prince aboard a boxcar, then joined the others in one of the passenger cars. He waved bravely out the window until the train came to life and began to pick up speed, rocking along the southward-running track. In a matter of minutes what was once Camp Mason had been left behind.[14]

* * *

The first stopover was Boston, where the men left the train late in the day and marched through the streets to the wharves; a steam transport awaited them. Private Theodore Gerrish of Company H found the sidewalks "covered with people who were eagerly looking at us" as if they had not seen soldiers before. This was manifestly untrue of the city Chamberlain had found so warlike only days after the firing on Sumter. At some point the citizenry came to life and began to cheer and applaud the passersby, making Chamberlain feel as though he and his men were veteran defenders of the Union. At the docks the men were herded aboard the 3,000-ton transport *Merrimac*, which the 20th shared with the men of the equally new and untried 36th Massachusetts. As the ship cast off, Chamberlain stood at the rail, staring across the water toward the horizon, recalling fragments of the past, musing on the future, and wondering if his faith in a benevolent destiny would see him through the months ahead.

En route down the coast, word was received, probably from newspapers taken aboard ship, that McClellan had withdrawn his army from the Peninsula, writing finis to an "on to Richmond" campaign whose prospects had shined like silver not so long ago. Coupled with the recent news of Second Bull Run and later reports that had Pope's army huddling like so many sheep on the heights of Centreville, Virginia, the intelligence was a sobering blow. It left open the question of what Lee might do now that he was no longer contained through close contact with McClellan or Pope. Some aboard the *Merrimac* believed the understrength Rebels would withdraw to Richmond; others feared an offensive in the North.[15]

While disappointed by the news stories and the speculation they provoked, Theodore Gerrish found every man he talked to resolute, determined, anxious to get into battle as quickly as possible and save the army from its generals. At some point a man called for three cheers for "Old Abe." Within seconds everyone was splitting his throat and doffing his headgear. The men cheered, said Gerrish, "until they were hoarse [and] the air was filled with flying caps." Chamberlain—even Colonel Ames—would have appreciated the display of enthusiasm, though neither would have admitted it. The men might not know how to load under fire or execute a right-wheel, but they had spirit. While not as effective as military proficiency, spirit had its place in winning a war.[16]

On the evening of September 6, after three days' of bobbing on the high seas as well as on the Chesapeake Bay and the Potomac River, the transport bumped into the docks off Alexandria, Virginia, staging point of McClellan's Peninsula campaign. Maine and Massachusetts troops, many of them still seasick from their first ocean voyage, hastily debarked. As an experienced sailor, Chamberlain would have walked down the gangplank more steadily than most. Once on land, the Mainers did not move far. Near the landing they spent the balance of the day as well as that night. Next morning, with dew coating their uniforms, they reembarked on a small steamer that carried them across the eastern branch of the Potomac to Washington City.[17]

Colonel Ames immediately marched his regiment to the arsenal that hugged the southeastern corner of the District of Columbia. There the enlisted men formed a line to receive the rest of the regiment's allotment of Enfields. That arm, which had been adopted by the English Army in 1855 and imported in quantity by Union and Confederacy alike, fired a 57-caliber bullet similar to the more common minie ball and could deliver an accurate fire at up to 1,100 yards from the target. Although the Enfield was a well-crafted weapon of tested merit with the additional advantage (mentioned by Corporal Melcher) of weighing little more than nine pounds, many of those issued to Chamberlain's outfit would prove defective; when they could, the Mainers would exchange them for the American-made Model 1861 Springfield Rifle Musket with its minie ball ammunition. Chamberlain, however, would not need to weigh the Enfield's qualities against any other arm; as a field officer he carried, instead, two pistols and a three-foot-long saber which he proudly called his "battle blade, a real tough one." He was expected to do his fighting at close quarters, such as at the head of a charging column, not at a sharpshooter's distance.[18]

After receiving its full complement of shoulder arms and bayonets, the 20th Maine bivouacked near the arsenal grounds, sleeping on what Ellis Spear called "a downy bed of dead cats, bricks and broken bottles." By sunset on September 8 the men were trudging northwestward toward Georgetown, before turning south and recrossing the Potomac. Via Long Bridge, they moved toward Fort Craig on Arlington Heights, one of dozens of defensive works that ringed the federal capital and which had given recent refuge to Pope's remnants. As they marched the outfit learned some interesting facts from the men of veteran regiments whose camps they passed. The previous day, the newly reinstated McClellan had led most of the army north—the opposite direction from the 20th Maine's heading. "Little Mac" planned to overtake and pummel Lee's army which, following its success at Second Bull Run, had ranged above the western reaches of the Potomac. On the 7th, Stonewall Jackson's corps had occupied Frederick, Maryland, threatening the Union garrisons at Harpers Ferry, Virginia, and elsewhere along the eastern rim of the Shenandoah Valley. Digesting the news, the men of the 20th Maine wondered if they had entered the field too late to take part in the critical struggle. A concomitant thought—surely one Lieutenant Colonel Chamberlain entertained—was that, if it was in time to fight, could the regiment hope to contribute to Union success, given its lack of training?[19]

Another bit of information the regiment gleaned this day fixed its place in the army's organization. The 20th Maine had been designated an element of Brigadier General Daniel Butterfield's 1st Brigade of Major General George W. Morell's 1st Division of Major General Fitz John Porter's Fifth Army Corps. Later, when Chamberlain became familiar with the personality of the army, he decided that the regiment's placement had been fortuitous. The Fifth Corps, although the newest component of McClellan's command, had a reputation for tenacity, fighting power, and—considering that it contained the only Regular outfits in the army—discipline and deportment. Chamberlain was likewise pleased to discover that the corps was a bastion of conservative politics. Many of its commanders, including Porter, Morell, and Butterfield, proudly identified themselves not only as Democrats but as friends and supporters of the most celebrated War Democrat of them all, George B. McClellan.[20]

Recently, however, the corps appeared to have suffered for its fidelity to its leader. It had fought bravely and well throughout the Peninsula campaign. Several of its regiments had distinguished themselves in combat while General Butterfield served so meritoriously that he would be awarded a Medal of Honor. The corps' subsequent service had been much less rewarding. Along with other portions of McClellan's army, Porter's people had been detached and sent to join John Pope shortly before Second Bull Run. Porter and many of his subordinates detested Pope, a Republican partisan whom they considered neither a gentleman nor a soldier. Bad blood had marked the merger of the two forces, and in the aftermath of his defeat the outraged Pope had preferred charges against Porter for disloyalty, disobedience, and misconduct in the face of the enemy. Now, as the 20th Maine joined his ranks, it was widely expected that Porter would be court-martialed. Expectations would be met, and in January 1863 Porter would be found guilty on all charges and cashiered from the service. His corps would forever consider its commander a victim of army politics. Long after his departure, Chamberlain would find the command largely shaped by Porter's legacy as well as fiercely protective of his reputation.[21]

To join its military family, Chamberlain's regiment, after crossing Long Bridge, made a moonlight march of perhaps five miles. This, its first long excursion afoot, took a severe toll. Although sunstroke was not a factor, the long, hard road was. Scores fell out at—some even before—the first halt, and by the time the rest reached Fort Craig the countryside was littered with footsore, panting men. Disgusted with the outfit's lack of conditioning, Colonel Ames was heard to roar: "If you can't do any better than you have tonight, you better all desert and go home!" Chamberlain, comfortably mounted on his gray steed, berated no one.[22]

When the hard-breathing Mainers reached their destination, they bivouacked adjacent to the other regiments in Butterfield's "Light Brigade," the 12th, 17th, and 44th New York, the 83rd Pennsylvania, and the 16th Michigan; to the latter regiment was attached a company of Michigan sharpshooters. While two of the New York outfits and the marksmen would later depart, the other units would serve alongside the 20th Maine for the balance of the conflict. In time, the four regiments would become a fighting fraternity of a type not unique to, but especially prevalent in, the Fifth Army Corps. With the 20th Maine now in place, the only piece missing from Butterfield's brigade was Butterfield himself. Now staffing a court of inquiry in Washington, he had been temporarily succeeded by his senior subordinate, Colonel Thomas B. W. Stockton of the Michigan regiment.[23]

Although the newcomers represented a welcome addition to a casualty-depleted brigade, the other units greeted the men of Maine warily. As was customary, the 20th would be on probation until its conduct under fire could be established. Even so, on the rainy morning of September 10 Chamberlain made the rounds of the other camps, exchanging greetings and picking up the latest news. He found the rest of the brigade buoyed up by McClellan's reinstatement, and he learned that within a day or two everyone would be heading north to overtake the forward echelon of the army, now outside Frederick.

Many enlisted men who obtained passes used them to visit their new comrades in the other regiments under Butterfield. Those who remained in camp did some visiting of their own, many chatting with their officers. The disciplinarian in Adelbert Ames was outraged by this practice; that same day, he issued a special order forbidding enlisted men's "loitering about Commissioned Officers['] tents," which he called "unmilitary in the greatest degree…. it tends to destroy the discipline and morale of the Army…." The order made Chamberlain stop and think. In a few days his brother Tom, who had been left behind at Portland due to illness, was expected to rejoin the regiment. When he did, would Ames's decree keep them from speaking except about official duties?[24]

* * *

Early on September 12 the 20th Maine started to war in company with the rest of Morell's division. Leaving Arlington Heights, the regiment crossed the Potomac for the third time in less than a week. About an hour later, it found itself in the Maryland countryside, 16 miles of which it traversed by nightfall. If the trek to Fort Craig had been arduous, this day's march was brutal. Almost 20 years later the historian of the regimental reunion committee would recall that "scarcely a corporal's guard of the Twentieth stacked arms when the brigade went into camp. The stragglers, however, came up in a few hours and the regiment marched with full ranks the following morning."[25]

On the 13th the men, having become somewhat accustomed to the pace, covered 24 miles in a northwestward heading. This day they began to pass stragglers not from a marching column but from the front, the flotsam of the army that inevitably trickled back to the rear—the far rear—when battle loomed. Chamberlain heard a rumor that fighting had taken place near Frederick as McClellan's advance evicted Lee's rear guard. The report was confirmed when, riding along the flank of the marching column, he heard a distant rumble that even his untrained senses took to be artillery fire. Aware that his baptism of battle, as almost everyone else's, was drawing near, he must have felt nearer to God than usual, and hopeful of His love and care.[26]

A third day of marching, adding 12 miles to the 42 covered since quitting Arlington Heights, brought the 20th Maine to the outskirts of Frederick. Now the distant thunder was coming from the west. Out there, somewhere, elements of both armies were locked in combat along South Mountain. Men who had withstood the first two days' exertion suddenly stumbled from accumulated fatigue. Chamberlain did what he could to ease their burdens, at one point carrying on his saddle excess gear belonging to Corporal Melcher.

The fighting may have moved west, but Frederick bore the scars and debris of battle. "Dead horses lie in every direction," Melcher informed his brother, "causing an unpleasant stench and beef-cattle partly devoured, the secesh [i.e., secessionists] not having a chance to savor their beef-steak!" Judging from the firing, he estimated the battle to be only 15 miles off. He predicted bravely that "we shall probably have a chance at the business before tomorrow night."[27]

The corporal's estimate was off by several days. On September 15 Colonel Ames led the 20th through Frederick, stopping for the night at Middletown. The following morning Morell's division moved out along the National Road—America's first government-funded infrastructure project—toward Turner's Gap in South Mountain. On the far side of the pass, scene of sharp fighting two days before, lay the stiff, blackened bodies of the Confederate dead. Scribbling on the back of a pass granted him by General Porter, Chamberlain wrote Fannie his second letter since leaving Maine (the first has been lost to posterity). He spoke of studying the bloated corpses, "piled up & lying in every conceivable position." He claimed to regard the dead matter-of-factly because he was already "accustomed to" such sights. Here he probably exaggerated for Fannie's benefit, hoping she might be less shocked by war's horrors if they failed to shock her husband. Years later, in a celebrated oration, Chamberlain would admit that he had been moved by the sight of a young Rebel "of scarcely sixteen summers," whom he found with his back to a tree, gripping a testament that he had been reading when death overtook him. The angelic look on the boy's face struck at the officer's heart, making him realize, perhaps for the first time, what this war was about. He may have asked God's forgiveness for having become, of his own will, a part in a great, merciless, remorseless killing machine.[28]

From Turner's Gap Morell's division continued west to Boonsboro and Keedysville, Maryland, where it finally united with the balance of its army. When the 20th Maine bivouacked beyond Keedysville, it knew that a fight larger than any along South Mountain was imminent. McClellan had overtaken his quarry near the village of Sharpsburg, along Antietam Creek; there, surely, he would use all the resources at his disposal to halt Lee's invasion.

But McClellan would not use all his resources. Early on September 17 he launched a day-long series of largely uncoordinated assaults across Antietam Creek. In every sector Lee's veterans contested the ground with exceptional stubbornness. The result was a drawn battle as well as the bloodiest day in American history. The carnage might have been greater had McClellan not left in the rear as reserves thousands of troops including the Fifth Corps in its entirety. On the other hand, had he committed Porter, the day might have ended in decisive victory. As it was, the 20th Maine observed, rather than took part in, the fighting at Antietam. Chamberlain, who appreciated the state of the regiment's unpreparedness, attributed its withholding not to Little Mac but to God.[29]

Though closed up on the battlefield, the 20th Maine spent September 17 just above the Middle Bridge over Antietam Creek under what Chamberlain called "a continuous fire of shot & shell." Held several miles from the center of action, the men could see distant columns moving hither and yon and could hear the muffled sound of cannon-fire. When the wind shifted, they could make out the rattle of musketry and even the shouts of charging troops. According to Chamberlain, at least twice during the afternoon orders came to march to the sound of the fighting but before they could move "the scale had been turned without us" and the directives were countermanded.

Late in the day the regiment was moved a mile or more to the right in the event it was needed to support Major General William B. Franklin's Sixth Corps. Before evening, however, the men were returned to their former position near the bridge. The only danger Chamberlain's soldiers faced in either position was when errant shells came shrieking overhead. Most struck harmlessly in the rear, although a few found human targets among other units within sight of the 20th.[30]

The only loss the regiment experienced this day was from illness. A suspicious pattern began to emerge when Major Gilmore reported himself sick the morning of the 17th. He gained the regimental surgeon's permission to return to Washington for treatment. And after the fight, as Captain Spear reported, a member of his company "came to my tent fatally sick, and soon after died." The soldier, barely 21, was the elder of two brothers Spear attempted to recruit in Wiscasset. Unwilling to leave their widowed mother home alone, the captain had refused to enlist the younger boy. Even so, the role Spear had played, however indirect, in the widow's loss never ceased to trouble him. As the older son's death was the first in Company G, "it made a great impression upon my mind, and I thought often of that poor widow in her sorrow, and her sacrifice for the country...."[31]

When the fighting tapered off after sundown on the 17th, more than 23,000 Federals and Confederates had become casualties. Despite the horrific carnage, both armies held essentially the same positions they had assumed at the outset. Another day of heavy fighting seemed likely, and Chamberlain doubted the 20th Maine would be spared two days in a row. "Tomorrow," he informed Fannie, hoping to prepare himself as well as his wife for the worst, "we expect to be in the thickest of it all day & as for me I do not at all expect to escape injury. I hope I should not fall; but if it should be God's will I believe I can say amen. I think of you all whom I love so much & I know how you would wish me to bear myself in the field. I go, as twice today I went serious and anxious but not afraid. God be with you & with me."[32]

Five

COMBAT VETERAN

*L*ieutenant Colonel Chamberlain's worst fears were not realized. Throughout September 18 the antagonists rested in position as though stunned by the previous day's slaughter. At some point in the afternoon Morell's division was moved to the far left, where it took up a position in rear of Major General Ambrose Everett Burnside's Ninth Corps. Most of Burnside's troops lay on the west side of Antietam Creek, guarding the bridge over which they had belatedly advanced late on the 17th. This chore Morell's command assumed soon after arriving, a favor for which Burnside reported himself "much indebted." Even on the west bank, in close proximity to the enemy's positions, the 20th Maine experienced war only as intermittent skirmishing and took no casualties.[1]

That night the battered but still-potent Army of Northern Virginia swung south and crossed the Potomac River at Shepherdstown (or Boteler's) Ford. On the far shore the army was back in its home base. Despite his excessive caution and poorly timed offensives, McClellan had hurt his enemy severely enough to force an end to the first large-scale invasion of what was regarded as Union territory. Lee's retreat had implications beyond the military realm. Considering Antietam enough of a victory to provide a platform for a far-reaching decree, on the 22nd President Lincoln announced his Preliminary Emancipation Proclamation, declaring all slaves in enemy territory, as of the 1st of January next, "forever free." Despite his moderate views on slavery, Chamberlain would come to approve the president's course not only as an economic and diplomatic weapon but as a vehicle for recruiting black men into the army. As a passionate defender of the Union, he increasingly believed in using any expedient—even one devised by a Republican president—against those who would dismantle the world's great experiment in democracy.[2]

Chamberlain contributed his own effort against the nation's enemies—his first performance in combat—on September 20. The night before, two brigades of his corps, under a general whom Chamberlain would come to know intimately, Ohio-born Charles Griffin of the Regular Army, had crossed near Shepherdstown Ford under cover of darkness. The Ohioan was a Fifth Corps favorite, for good reason. One of his soldiers summed him up this way: "Griffin is a brave man and a good fighter and don't drink more than his share."[3]

On the high ground lining the Virginia shore the hard-driving Griffin had encountered the enemy's rear guard. He shoved it south for half a mile, took prisoners, and captured artillery pieces and caissons. The reconnaissance indicated that Lee had retreated along two roads that converged toward the Shenandoah Valley town of Winchester. To verify the information and determine how far the Rebels had retreated, McClellan, early on the 20th, dispatched to the same ford a larger portion of the Fifth Corps, the divisions of Morell and Brigadier General George Sykes, protected by a large bank of artillery on the Maryland shore.[4]

Shortly after sunrise, Colonel Ames led the 20th Maine into the river, the cold water lapping at the men's flanks as they pushed across. Once atop the bluffs on the far side, Chamberlain helped Ames form a column and guide it toward a deep woods, other elements of Stockton's brigade advancing on either flank. No sooner had the outfit started inland, however, than rifle fire crashed out of the woods, hundreds of Union cavalrymen who had preceded Morell's column came galloping back to the river, and bugles shrilled on the opposite bank, ordering everyone to return at once. After some confusion the foot troops complied, at first in good order and then in some chaos as the firing intensified. Quite obviously, Lee had not retreated as far as the high command had been led to believe.

On the Union-held shore the pre-positioned Union artillery opened with a covering fire. Some of the guns loosed defective shells that imperiled the men they were trying to protect. According to Private William T. Livermore of Chamberlain's regiment, the cannonade "would go so near our heads it seemed as though it would take the hair off from my head, and the air was full of shells and some of our own burst overhead and wounded some of our own men."[5]

With haste bordering on panic, men rushed down the bluffs and splashed into the river, several of them falling wounded in the process. Eventually three members of the 20th Maine would become casualties, though none was seriously injured. To stem the chaos and neutralize the enemy's fire, General Morell decided to throw another of his brigades across the stream. At Colonel Stockton's order, Chamberlain—riding a borrowed horse this day, having left his prize steed in camp—strove to bring up the reinforcements. He rode midway across the stream, where he sat motioning the brigade forward, inattentive to the bullets whipping past him. This, his first time under direct fire, was a defining experience for the executive officer of the 20th Maine Volunteers. He was not unaware of the danger he faced in this exposed position—which included a barrage from what he took to be 20 cannon—but managed to do his duty in spite of it.

He remained in the middle of the river, "keeping the men steady & urging them over, until the whole Brigade was across." As he later informed Fannie, "the balls whistled pretty thick around me & splashed on all sides, but didn't touch." But when he finally wheeled to follow, the last brigade having gotten across, his horse went down wounded, throwing its rider head-first into the Potomac. An unhurt Chamberlain quickly bobbed to the surface and sloshed his way to the Maryland side, where a concerned Colonel Ames was relieved to find him alive and well. Ames kept his second-in-command out of the balance of the fight.[6]

When ordered to retreat, some of the regiments under Morell and Sykes, including more than one veteran outfit, had raced to the rear with unseemly speed and had not re-formed as ordered. In contrast, the 20th Maine had withdrawn in tolerably good order and, without being prodded by its officers, had rallied and maintained cohesion. To be sure, the regiment had shown its green tinge in a number of ways; one of its wounded, for instance, had been struck by the discharge of his own rifle. The great majority of the men had nonetheless acted as Chamberlain had, doing their duty under trying circumstances and carrying out the orders of their officers whenever possible to do so. Even the crusty Adelbert Ames ought to have been pleased.

As soon as they received the necessary permission, Ames and Chamberlain led the men downriver and into a trench formed by the dry bed of the Chesapeake and Ohio Canal. From that natural defensive position, as Private Hezekiah Long reported, they exchanged "some pretty sharp shooting" with the Rebels across the water, a diversion that lasted until after dark. Regimental casualties remained at three, which helped morale as much as the obvious fact that the men had behaved on this day quite a bit like soldiers. Those lucky stars Chamberlain's father had alluded to continued to hover above his son and his regiment. Had the 20th Maine experienced its first fight on the killing ground of Antietam, the consequences would have been infinitely more severe for all involved.[7]

* * *

The outfit remained in place along the river, with frequent but slight shifts of position, for six weeks after the fighting at the ford. The men saw to their daily duties, took instruction in the manual of arms when opportunity arose, and in their free time stared down the enemy across the water. Much of the rest of the army moved into the same area, so that on September 21 Corporal Melcher could report that "we are encamped here near the Potomac with the rest of Porter's Corps. Encamped I say, though we have not been in a tent since we left Portland." The countryside provided splendid surroundings. The aesthetic Chamberlain assured his wife that it was the "most beautiful country you ever saw, [complete with] graceful slopes, green valleys, winding streams, fertile fields, & bold mountains...."[8]

Chamberlain could take the unpleasant with the pleasant. He shared with the men the privations of the bivouac, sleeping on the hard earth, going without bathing for days, eating whenever the commissary wagons could find a way to the front, relieving himself in the woods or in the open-air sinks. He was surprised to find he could tolerate this life quite well. His comforts were few, but so were his needs and they were always attended to, with reasonable efficiency, by the government. His world had narrowed, become less complicated. He need not worry so much about his health, the sometimes unpredictable behavior of his wife, the myriad difficulties of childrearing, or his relations with fellow academics.

He appreciated the simplicity of his new situation, and in some indefinable way it pleased him as well. A month after Shepherdstown he was writing Fannie that "I do not find myself in need of much," and although things sometimes troubled him—his fraying uniform coat, his inability to sift through army rumor and discern what lay ahead—he was feeling something remarkably close to contentment. "I feel that it *is* a sacrifice for me to be here in one sense of the word," he wrote, "but I do not wish myself back by any means." Not even the prospect of stopping a bullet could make him regret his course. Quoting from the farewell of a nay-saying colleague, he added that "the '*glory*' Prof. Smythe so *honestly* pictured for me I do not much dread. If I do return 'shattered' & 'good-for-nothing,' I think there are *those* who will hold me in some degree of favor better than that which he predicted. Most likely I shall be hit somewhere at sometime, but all 'my times are in His hands,' & I cannot die without His appointing. I try to keep ever in view all the possibilities that surround me & to be ready for all that I am called to."[9]

As Chamberlain was coming to realize, his ability to withstand the hardships of army life and disregard its hazards meant that his current existence, so different from his life in Maine, tapped a psychological need. Growing in him was the suspicion that he was a soldier by nature and that bivouacs and battlefields were his homes.

* * *

The daily routine of the 20th Maine in its camp by the Potomac was established by order of Colonel Ames, published on September 24. Each day reveille was blown at sunrise, followed immediately by breakfast call. Sick call and police call—where men who were ill or wanted the surgeon to believe they were ill went to his tent and more able-bodied comrades cleaned up the campsite—took place at 7 A.M. From 8:00 to 9:30 and again from 11:00 until 12:00, company drill was held, various elements of the regiment practicing at any given time, other units remaining on post along the river.

Dinner call was blown promptly at noon, and regimental drill, with virtually the entire outfit assembled on the practice-field, ran from 3:30 to 5:00. Dress parade took place at 5:30, with supper served immediately afterward and tattoo, which called the men to their quarters, at 8:30. The regimental bugler blew taps, the lights' out call, at 9:00. (Previously, this call had been based on a European military tune composed many years before. But, a new, more melodious, more poignant rendition of the older "taps" had been composed by the 20th Maine's original brigade commander, Daniel Butterfield. General Butterfield's version had found immediate favor throughout the Union ranks; it would remain a ceremonial staple in the repertoire of U. S. Army buglers for a century, and more.)[10]

The order that Colonel Ames issued on the 24th and which Lieutenant Colonel Chamberlain tried to enforce proved susceptible of violation by officers of the regiment. In subsequent decrees, Ames announced that officers must be personally present each day for reveille, tattoo, and roll calls. Further, every morning promptly at 10:30 officers were to assemble at regimental headquarters for drill and every evening at 6:45 for recitation in the manual of arms.[11]

Ames's belief that his officers needed additional schooling extended to his second-in-command. Ames admired Chamberlain's erudition and was impressed by his ability to quickly absorb large portions of the tactics books directed to his attention. Still, Ames thought he should attend personally to Chamberlain's education. Soon the lieutenant colonel was asking his wife to send him a copy of Baron Antoine Henri de Jomini's celebrated *Art of War*, explaining that "The Col. & I are going to read it. He to instruct me, as he is kindly doing in every thing now."[12]

His instruction was not limited to one or two manuals: "I *study*, I tell you, every military work I can find," he told Fannie, "and it is no small labor to master the evolutions of a Battalion & Brigade. I am bound to understand *every thing*." Nor was his course of study limited to infantry movements. After the war a friend of Chamberlain's recalled that the texts reviewed and discussed that fall and winter included "not only the tactics and evolutions of the Infantry arm but that of Cavalry and Artillery, together with that of the general service of War." The evening study sessions in Ames's tent would bear early fruit. Chamberlain would prove such a quick study, even in advance of receiving his copy of Jomini, that Ames would entrust him with supervising the regiment at daily drill.[13]

* * *

Chamberlain and the 20th Maine shared at least one memorable experience in their Maryland camp. On October 2 President Lincoln, accompanied by cabinet members and other Washington officials, paid a visit to McClellan's headquarters. Lincoln stayed with the army for three days, inspecting it, speaking informally with officers and men, and conferring in private with the army leader on a number of subjects, the foremost being when McClellan expected to cross the Potomac and pursue Robert E. Lee. Lincoln may not have gotten the answer he was seeking, but he considered his trip a success if only because it permitted him to review the various elements of the army, an act that brought him much satisfaction.

On the morning of the 4th Stockton's brigade of Morell's division turned out for the president's inspection. The 20th Maine lined up on its parade ground, which Chamberlain had ordered policed of stones, cornstalks, and other refuse. In his order of October 2—his first as commander of the regiment, Ames being temporarily absent— Chamberlain also directed officers and men to spruce up their uniforms and scrub their rifles and accouterments with soapstone and emery paper.[14]

When Lincoln arrived at the 20th's camp, he found its occupants standing at attention in what they supposed was Regular Army posture, or something close to it. They wore freshly brushed uniforms and the metal parts of their weapons fairly gleamed. Chamberlain himself had expended extra time tidying up his frock coat and headgear; he looked particularly soldier-like astride his handsome gray charger on the flank of the column. As the president, clad in his customary black suit and stovepipe hat, passed down the line Chamberlain and Prince supposedly stole his attention. According to Chamberlain, for an instant Lincoln's eyes locked with his, as each men took the measure of the other.[15]

Another witness to the review, Ellis Spear, claimed that the president did not halt even briefly as he rode past the regiment, and never glanced at Chamberlain. Spear may have been correct, but Chamberlain firmly believed that the president gazed at him with eyes filled with sadness and sympathy, a moment he would remember the rest of his life. He had not voted for Lincoln, nor had he approved of some of the president's policies. Even so, he considered the war effort in able hands, for he thought of Lincoln as a good man, intelligent and honest, motivated by what he believed to be best for the nation, and stooped by the weight of his responsibilities.[16]

Years later, when Chamberlain came to venerate Lincoln's memory, he would recall the man's "outward or inward searching eyes," his "questioning and answering heart," the homely, rough-hewn features that stood for "rugged truth," and that look he gave off, "as from the innermost of things." On the day of the review "we could see the deep sadness in his face, and feel the burden on his heart, thinking of his great commission to save this people, and knowing that he could do this no otherwise than [through] . . . the valor, the steadfastness, the loyalty, the devotion, the sufferings and thousand deaths, of those into whose eyes his were looking. How he shrank from the costly sacrifice we could see; and we took him into our hearts with answering sympathy, and gave him our pity in return."[17]

Once Lincoln left the army to return to Washington, the less prosaic aspects of army life retook center stage. The regiment remained by the river for another three days before moving on the 7th to a site by an iron works near the mouth of the Antietam. There it spent a little more than three weeks, the routine broken only by a brief reconnaissance toward South Mountain on the 12th and 13th. This excursion, led in person by Chamberlain—his first stint in independent command—was designed to overtake and punish Confederate cavalry under the already legendary J.E.B. Stuart. When Chamberlain reached the mountain passes directed to his attention, however, he found that the gray cavaliers had moved on; thus he returned empty-handed.[18]

In the new camp on the Antietam, Colonel Ames redoubled his efforts to make the men proficient at drill. After the war the historian of the 20th Maine Regimental Association wrote that "at times his [Ames's] orders were severe in the extreme, yet the soldierly bearing of the regiment soon became conspicuous." Ames himself was seeing results on the parade ground. Although he kept his feelings to himself, the colonel admitted in letters to his parents that discipline was slowly seeping into the 20th Maine. He was bold enough to predict that when the regiment entered its first true battle it would be ready for it.[19]

Perhaps because of the demands Ames made upon it, more likely due to the severe changes in climate common to Maryland in October, as well as to the regiment-wide lack of shelter tents, and to what Ellis Spear called "the malarious locality" in which they served, the 20th Maine developed a long sick list. When the outfit finally broke camp on the Antietam and poised to advance into Virginia, fully 300 men had to be left behind as too ill or too disabled to march. The regimental historian added that "many of those who remained on duty were reduced to a condition from which they did not recover for months."[20]

* * *

As early as October 23 Holman Melcher was reporting that "a grand move of the army" was imminent. Not for another three days, however, did McClellan begin to cross the Potomac, an operation not completed until the 1st of November. Late on the 30th Chamberlain's outfit finally got the order to move. That evening everyone trudged south toward Harpers Ferry, where next day they crossed the Potomac into picturesque Loudoun Valley. On the Virginia side, the 20th Maine and the other outfits in Stockton's brigade continued south along the rim of the Blue Ridge Mountains. On the far side of the chain Lee's army was moving in the same direction, "up" the Shenandoah Valley.[21]

The leisurely, unmolested withdrawal of the Army of Northern Virginia troubled Chamberlain; he could only assume that McClellan planned to challenge the foe at an early opportunity. On November 3, by which time the 20th Maine had bivouacked along the Blue Ridge pass known (rather gracelessly, Chamberlain thought) as Snicker's Gap, he wrote to Fannie about a "coming battle," calling the regiment "ready to pitch in when called for." The following day combat still loomed and, as before, he tried to defuse his wife's fears: "You need not worry if you hear of a battle, until you know that I was in it; if I am injured, you will hear at once. I expect to get some sort of a scratch when we *'go in,'* but the chances are it will not be serious if anything." He closed with regards to family and friends and with a significant self-commentary: "Tell them I am beginning to understand my business, & shall probably be enabled to look them in the face again if I get home."[22]

Chamberlain's belief in an early battle was not fulfilled. On the 6th his brigade moved slowly south, passing through villages recently occupied by the enemy, including Middleburg and White Plains. The first snowflakes of the season whipped through the valley as the men marched on the 7th. On the 9th they went into a frosty bivouac at Warrenton, not far from the line of the Orange & Alexandria Railroad. There, as was true of every locale they had inhabited since leaving Harpers Ferry, no Rebels were in sight.

The impression that the army was moving too slowly, stopping over too long, and that Lee was meeting too little resistance on his way south, was sweeping through the ranks. For this reason, many were not greatly surprised to learn on or about November 10 that General McClellan had been relieved from command by a president who considered his field leader fatally hobbled by "the slows." Despite the inevitability of the move, many soldiers moaned or cursed the replacement of "Little Mac" by General Burnside. While the army was developing a warm regard for Lincoln, it had long loved McClellan.[23]

The reaction of the veterans of the Fifth Corps was especially strong because at about the same time they learned that General Porter had been replaced by Major General Joseph Hooker. To add to the corps-wide gloom, a few days before General Morell had been removed from his division and assigned to a command along the Upper Potomac; Dan Butterfield, Colonel Stockton's predecessor, had replaced Morell. Neither McClellan's nor Porter's successor evoked reassuring emotions in the soldiers of the Fifth Corps, and Butterfield, while brave enough in battle and an artist with bugle calls, was not known as an astute field leader.[24]

Though relatively new to the army, Chamberlain was sad to see fellow conservatives such as McClellan, Porter, and Morell go. Their departure marked, as he said, "the sundering of long-familiar ties" throughout the army. Like many in the Fifth Corps, he probably viewed the deposed commanders as sacrifices on the altar of administration politics. Although Butterfield was a McClellan man, Burnside and Hooker were favorites of the Radical Republican faction in Congress that supposedly controlled White House policies. Neither was considered to be the soldier his predecessor had been, and it seemed doubtful that either would enjoy the hold on the affections of his new command that McClellan and Porter had enjoyed.

A minority reaction came from Ellis Spear, who, writing after the war, claimed that countless other members of the corps felt, as he did, that McClellan and his deposed subordinates were expendable. Spear refuted Chamberlain's view that the loss of its original commanders wrought havoc on corps' morale. Indeed, some observers considered the commanders themselves hurtful to morale through the "harsh and unconcealed criticisms on the Administration" they frequently delivered in earshot of junior officers. In 1862, at least one of Spear's colleagues, aghast at such insubordination, loudly opined that General Porter was a traitor. Whatever the case, Spear's contention that Chamberlain himself was too new to the Fifth Corps to feel cut adrift by Porter's and Morell's exodus is probably valid.[25]

* * *

As early as the first week in November the men of the 20th Maine heard that the Army of Northern Virginia was falling back on Richmond. Not for several days would Chamberlain's regiment be able to determine the counter-strategy of Ambrose Burnside, which involved transferring the army (recently reorganized into "Grand Divisions" of two corps each) to Fredericksburg, 50 miles north of the Confederate capital. From there Burnside hoped to beat Lee to Richmond as the latter came in from the Shenandoah Valley via Culpeper Court House. Burnside's plan hinged on many variables, including speed of execution; Lincoln endorsed it reluctantly but also hopefully. In retrospect, the president's hesitation appears portentous, for mistakes, missteps, and miscalculations would doom the campaign and decimate the army.

Burnside's plan was set in motion on November 17, when his troops pulled up stakes at Warrenton and headed rapidly southeastward. A week later, after a grueling march in increasingly cold weather, the 20th Maine found itself at a place called Stoneman's Switch on the railroad that ran from Fredericksburg to the Potomac River supply base at Aquia Creek. There, as Private Samuel Miller of Company E recalled, "the regiment settled down to the monotony of camp and picket duty for three weeks." The 20th was not alone in marking time; the rest of the army did likewise.[26]

The men lay idle for so long because Burnside's hope of bringing Lee to bay above Richmond foundered on the shoals of indecision and delay. Originally "Old Burn" had intended to cross the Rappahannock River, take position on the heights above the city, and wait for Lee to make the mistake of trying to dislodge him. Burnside, however, had changed his mind to the extent of moving his army to Falmouth, opposite Fredericksburg, with the expectation of crossing the river on pontoon bridges (the rail and foot bridges that originally spanned the river had long since been dismantled). The change of plan proved to be a major blunder; by failing to seize the heights beyond the town Burnside permitted Lee to do so instead. But the most serious error occurred when the army's pontoon train failed to come down from Washington in time to beat the Confederates onto the south bank.[27]

The 20th Maine spent its first Thanksgiving, November 27, immobile at Stoneman's Switch. The day seemed anything but festive, for the supply trains from Aquia Creek were running late and empty haversacks abounded on the pine-covered hill the regiment called home. Denied even the ubiquitous hard bread, one hungry Mainer recalled that "the repeated shouts of 'hard-tack!' 'hard-tack!' were heard about the camp and the railroad station...." Next day, at last, the trains ran through to Stoneman's Switch, "and the boys received their full rations."[28]

Like the majority of his men, Lieutenant Colonel Chamberlain spent a cold, hungry, uncomfortable Thanksgiving. Shelter tents had finally been distributed to the regiment, but they provided only so much protection against the raw weather. It was surely the bleakest holiday the former college professor had spent in many a year. His sagging spirits drooped even lower a few days later, when he received a letter Fannie had composed on Thanksgiving Day. "We have wanted you with us *terribly*," she declared, although "it has been very pleasant here, a beautiful dinner, the children all well and perfectly happy, tonight a charming little table of fancy cakes, bright red apples, nuts, candies and so forth...." These reminders of hearth and home should have been enough to sink her husband in the slough of despondency, but Fannie finished off the job by complaining that "you cannot imagine *how* lonely to *me*, this Thanksgiving night, when you ought to be at your own home, with all those who long to see you so."[29]

With some effort he managed to uproot the guilt feelings Fannie had planted in his heart. By December 2 he was writing her from the Switch that "we have been here a week & are waiting nobody knows for what. All sorts of rumors arise of course, but our business is to obey orders & it becomes us to be patient as well as obedient. There is a great army here you may be sure & something will be done with it, I have no doubt." On November 29 he had ridden in company with his former student, Adjutant Brown, along the north bank of the river, "only a few rods from the Rebels opposite in Fredericksburg.... They were busy as bees throwing up fortifications & planting cannon." He admitted that "I did not feel fully comfortable, I own, in full view & reach of every one of those ugly looking cannon they are training to slaughter us by." Yet, he would have charged the forbidding weapons had the order come that day: "I could have gone in with all the vigor & earnestness in the world."[30]

He resumed his letter two days later, covering very different matters: "We had two ladies," he wrote, referring to workers of the relief agency known as the United States Sanitary Commission, "to dine with us on tin platters yesterday.... Very proper & efficient they are too. They think I have been well instructed in the manly art of taking ladies bonnets & cloaks properly." Finally he alluded to Fannie's Thanksgiving epistle. He offered no reaction to it but expressed his pleasure at

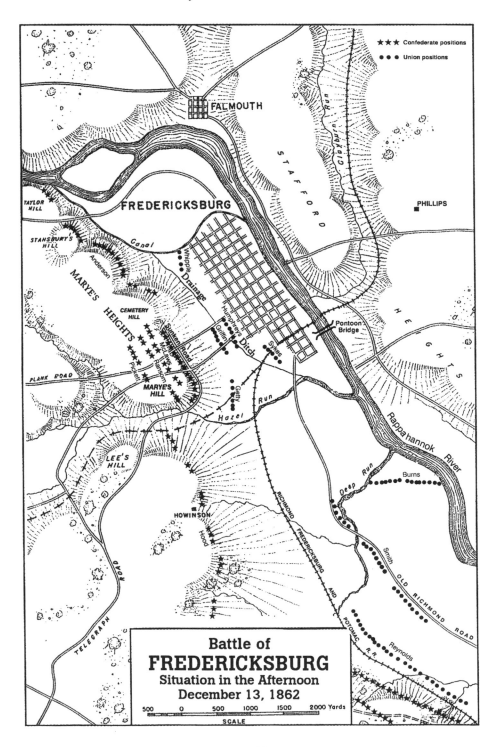

Battle of
FREDERICKSBURG
Situation in the Afternoon
December 13, 1862

receiving gift items she had enclosed: his copy of Jomini, and, even more acceptable under the circumstances, two pairs of shirts and drawers, which were "just what I wanted.... I feel perfectly crazed [at] so much good fortune." He ended with a romantic flourish, "I dreamed of you last night of course," and with a promise to write a longer letter three days hence, on their wedding anniversary.[31]

* * *

On the morning of December 11 the 20th Maine left its hilltop camp for Falmouth, staging area for the crossing to Fredericksburg. Gingerly, Chamberlain led Prince over patches of ice, the remnants of a several-inch snowstorm that had struck a few days before and whose severity had resulted in two members of the regiment freezing to death. When he reached the river at Falmouth, he quickly realized that those would not be the only fatalities the 20th Maine would suffer during the campaign. The guns he had witnessed going into position across the water almost two weeks before had been considerably augmented, and rifle pits and breastworks crowned several of the bluffs below them. It was obvious that General Lee had made good use of the time given him to make his position formidable—perhaps impregnable.[32]

Chamberlain's role in the events of the next several days is a matter of much dispute. Two first-person sources seek to chronicle his Fredericksburg experience: an article in a Maine newspaper supposedly based on a now-lost journal he kept during the campaign, and an article he wrote for a popular magazine 50 years after the battle. Both sources appear to have been composed for an audience that preferred its history dramatically rendered. Moreover, each was edited to an unknown extent. Finally, throughout his 1912 article Chamberlain's memory appears to have worked to his disadvantage.

Despite the time lapse between experience and recollection, the magazine piece has come down as the primary source of information about Chamberlain's thoughts and actions from December 11 to 16, 1862. But when Ellis Spear read the article, Chamberlain's old subordinate became upset by the distortions and fabrications that permeated it. Adelbert Ames, was also alive in 1912 (he would die 21 years later, as the last general officer on either side), and Ames asked Spear to match his own recollections against Chamberlain's. The result was a virtual point-by-point refutation of the article. Spear hoped the critique would correct the record for posterity, but his wish went largely unfulfilled: his rebuttal was not published for another 75 years and then only in a limited edition edited by his grandson. While some of his comments read like carping, others the bitter fruit of jealousy, numerous criticisms appear to hit the mark, making his old commander out to be a myth-maker, a dresser-up of events—at times, a liar.[33]

Late on the morning of the 11th, as the 20th Maine descended the riverbank prior to crossing to Fredericksburg, Chamberlain, again in company with "Mr. Brown," rode to the front in advance of the main body to study the emplacement of Union artillery atop the high ground known as Stafford Heights. The guns protected the engineers who were throwing pontoon bridges across the river—all the while making excellent targets for Confederate riflemen holed up in the streets of the town. Despite the cannon's covering fire, which turned several blocks of riverfront property into rubble, the bridge-builders did not complete their work till late in the day and only after foot troops were ferried across to evict the marksmen.[34]

Observing Burnside's barrage at close range, Chamberlain overheard a conversation between a staff officer from Major General Edwin V. Sumner's Right Grand Division and a battery commander. The artilleryman was cautioned not to fire on a sacred landmark visible on the other shore, the "white shaft" that marked the grave of George Washington's mother. Spear doubts the credibility of this account, believing that the shaft was not standing during the battle. He is correct: while construction of the base of the monument had begun 30 years before, the shaft was not erected until 1883. While this inaccuracy may seem trivial, it helps cast doubt on the body of Chamberlain's Fredericksburg memoir.[35]

After Lieutenant Brown and he had scouted the terrain over which Burnside planned to march, Chamberlain spent the night of the 11th in a wooded bivouac behind the three-story brick home of a family named Phillips. He passed the next day, the eve of the army's crossing, in relative idleness. His journal contains a bare comment: "Not ready yet; moved nearer, however, and waited yet another day."[36]

At dawn on the 13th, the 1st Division, Fifth Corps was marched down to the water, where it was halted at the head of the pontoon bridge across from Princess Elizabeth Street. The men were about to enter their first fight under the gruff, steely-eyed General Griffin, who three weeks ago had replaced Dan Butterfield in command of the "Light Division." As part of the personnel turnover that marked the beginning of the Burnside era, General Butterfield had moved up to fill the vacancy created by Fitz John Porter's departure, while "Fighting Joe" Hooker had been named to lead Burnside's Center Grand Division, consisting of Major General George Stoneman's Third Corps as well as Butterfield's command.[37]

The picture Chamberlain paints of the concentration by the bridge-head in the early morning darkness of December 13 fairly ripples with dramatic tension. Amid the thunder of artillery, the men of the 20th Maine stand on the riverbank and watch breathlessly as troops under General Sumner, who had crossed hours before, make "five immortal charges" against enemy positions beyond and below an eminence known as Marye's Heights. Chamberlain depicts "stern men" in tears and one of their commanders crying in poetic anguish ("Where are the sixty thousand that were so quickly to decide this day?") Commenting on this scene, Spear argues that if the men had wailed and gnashed their teeth for the length of time Chamberlain describes, "we should have soon been exhausted."[38]

In fact they waited throughout the morning and well into the afternoon. By midday the men of the Fifth Corps had heard a credible rumor that elements of General Franklin's Left Grand Division had briefly broken the enemy's right before being tossed back with heavy loss. Franklin's defeat added to the misfortunes suffered by the army farther north, where Sumner's two corps, the Second and Ninth, could not penetrate the Marye's Heights line. In his article Chamberlain describes the travail of Sumner's men as they near the "death-delivering stone wall" at the foot of the heights. The wall is "suddenly illuminated by a sheet of flame, and in an instant the whole line [sinks] as if swallowed up in earth, the bright flags quenched in gloom, and only a writhing mass marking that high-tide halt of uttermost manhood and supreme endeavor." Spear, choking on Chamberlain's overripe prose, calls this passage "such as a man with a lively imagination might write fifty years after of a charge which he saw, in part, at a distance of nearly a mile."[39]

Chamberlain considered it obvious that his army's reserve—Hooker's command—would be committed in an effort to retrieve the fortunes of the day. Yet, through most of the afternoon the men of the Center Grand Division waited for word to cross and move up in Sumner's rear. When the order finally came, at about 4:30 P.M., dusk was descending, but it failed to prevent Chamberlain from observing the "searching wistful look" General Griffin gave his men as they pushed on to the bridge, "not trusting his lips and we not needing more." Spear claims that Griffin betrayed no such emotion and that, had he, no one could have seen it at such a distance, especially under falling darkness and amid cannon smoke.[40]

By Chamberlain's account, the crossing of the pontoon bridge was accompanied by "flying, bursting shells, whooping solid shot. . . fortunately not yet plowing a furrow through the midst of us, but driving the compressed air so close above our heads that there was an unconquerable instinct to shrink beneath it, although knowing it was then too late." According to Spear, Chamberlain may have ducked shells on other occasions, but not this day: "Only one shot fell in our vicinity when we crossed; that was a solid shot which harmlessly dropped from [a] high trajectory just as we turned to the bridge, and nobody was hurt, not even the hot air, when we crossed."[41]

Chamberlain contends that once on the other side of the river, the regiment crossed a water-filled millrace, then encountered a line of fences so constricting that Ames's horse as well as his own had to be sent to the rear. Spear insists that the mounts had been left behind before the river was crossed. He also refutes Chamberlain's gory description of the brigade's advance on the Fredericksburg side, including "crushed bodies" and "severed limbs" lying in the 20th Maine's path. In reality the advance was subjected only to scattered long-range musketry, which produced no casualties.[42]

After passing the fences, Chamberlain has the 20th Maine form in an open field for a push against Marye's Heights. On the naked ground, its right flank exposed by the inability of two New York regiments to keep up with the 20th, the outfit makes excellent targets for a Rebel battery that wheels into position to sweep the Mainers' front and flanks. The resulting barrage draws from Colonel Ames the cry, "God help us now! Colonel take the right wing; I must lead here," whereupon, taking half of the regiment, he leaves Chamberlain and pushes to the front. Spear correctly points out that, had the outfit been subjected to a cannonade, its colonel would not have left half of it under fire while decamping with the remainder. Moreover, Spear heard Ames issue no such order as Chamberlain ascribes to him, which does sound unrealistic. Finally, Spear denies that an enemy battery opened on the regiment as it moved up: "There was a battery which ... before the advance, swung into position, but it was one of our batteries. There was no other...."[43]

If Chamberlain is right about the artillery unit, he never explains what permitted the 20th Maine to reach the starting-point of its charge virtually unmolested. He merely notes that the advance brought the men to a point beyond rifle-range of the enemy, where survivors of the Second and Ninth Corps lay huddled. To get there, however, the regiment had to pick its way "amid bodies thickly strewn, some stark and cold, some silent with slowly ebbing life, some in sharp agony that must have voice, though unavailing...." Reviewing this anecdote, Spear asks, sensibly: "How did all this thickly strewn mass of living, dead and wounded get back to this safe shelter? The living might, and they might bring some of the wounded, but apparently they brought also the dead and placed them on the line, so thickly that Chamberlain had to 'pick' his way."[44]

By Chamberlain's account, the 20th Maine and the rest of its brigade pushed resolutely through the danger zone, charging for a quarter of a mile "up slopes slippery with blood, miry with repeated, unavailing tread. We reached that final crest, before that all-commanding, countermanding stone wall." Then and only then, within sight of the Rebels at the base of the heights, did the 20th Maine realize the futility of a farther advance. After exchanging rifle fire with the enemy "until the muzzle-flame deepened the sunset red," the regiment—presumably at Ames's order—as a man dropped back behind the crest. Protected by a slight ridge, they spent the night there hugging the ground, too close to the foe to advance or withdraw without attracting a fusillade. Chamberlain himself sought sleep "between two dead men among the many left there by earlier assault ... [drawing] another crosswise for a pillow out of the trampled, blood-soaked sod, pulling the flap of his coat over my face to fend off the chilling winds, and, still more chilling, the deep, many-voiced moan that overspread the field...."[45]

Spear challenges virtually every detail of this lurid scene. He seems on firm ground when asserting that the 20th Maine got nowhere near the stone wall: "We advanced no farther than the line to which the repulsed brigades of the Second and Ninth Corps had retired, which was far in rear of the ground on which the severest fighting took place." In fact, it was not expected that the 20th Maine should advance farther than this; by the time the regiment reached the field, the day and the battle were effectively over. The mission of Stockton's brigade at that point was to guard against an enemy advance following the repulse of Sumner's troops. Spear's point helps explain why, rather than being obliterated, the 20th Maine suffered only four killed this day.[46]

As for Chamberlain's famous "bivouac with the dead" passage, Spear finds it artfully written and powerfully descriptive, but wholly untrue. "There were," he writes, "no wounded men on the ground occupied by me, and I saw no dead bodies excepting two [of the] killed in our regiment." Spear's most damning criticism derives from his knowledge of where Chamberlain spent that night: "He was lying with Colonel Ames and Colonel Stockton ... a little to the rear and left of where I lay," not on the "blood-soaked sod," certainly not in the arms of dead comrades.[47]

The accumulation of Chamberlain's exaggerations, fanciful descriptions, and invented scenes caused Spear's indignation to boil. He calmed himself down by wondering if he were "taking all this too seriously. Possibly this story may have been intended for pure fiction."[48]

Nearly 90 years after its publication and 135 years after the events it purports to depict, what can be said of Chamberlain's account? To be sure, it was edited heavily, but what remains still rings with Chamberlain's trademark prose. What seems to have happened is that, wishing to emphasize the horrors of war in general and of Fredericksburg in particular, he subordinated historic truth to the value of his message. In some places a fading memory got the best of him, but elsewhere he took artistic license with the truth. Perhaps he hoped that his readers would regard his account symbolically, not literally. Despite his facetious comment about taking the article too seriously, however, Ellis Spear knew that it would color readers' impressions of the battle for generations to come; that is why he critiqued it so minutely.

As one historian has recently pointed out, Chamberlain and Spear saw things differently. The difference between them, however, was a matter not of point of view but of personality. Ellis Spear was a realist; he saw things plainly and remembered them clearly, in stark, unadorned hues. Joshua Chamberlain was a romanticist; even when describing the horrors of a bloodbath his prose could be colorful, lyrical, even poetic. Spear did not permit himself to see things that way. Even at his most nostalgic, he never confused war with poetry.[49]

Six

UNHAPPY SPECTATOR

Chamberlain claims that at about midnight he rose from his "unearthly bivouac" and went in search of wounded men to succor. Again in company with Adjutant Brown, he ministered to an unknown number of sufferers. "Our best," he writes, "was but to search the canteens of the dead for a draft of water for the dying, or to ease the posture of a broken limb; or to compress a severed artery of fast-ebbing life that might perhaps be saved, with what little skill we had been taught by our surgeons...." The depiction of Chamberlain as a Union "Angel of Marye's Heights" is unconvincing, if only because, given his exposed position (supposedly "before the stone wall" where Rebel riflemen lurked), even in the dark such movements as he describes and the noise they would create would have attracted a harvest of sharpshooters' bullets. Spear is right to rank this scene, too, as fiction or, at the least, dramatic hyperbole.[1]

After running his errand of mercy, Chamberlain supposedly returned to his precarious position of the night before, where he resumed his huddling until dawn. Awakened on December 14 by a resumption of skirmish fire, he states that he and his comrades protected themselves by forming a breastwork of the bodies of dead comrades, yet another assertion that Spear disputes: "We were fairly protected by the ridge behind which we lay, and we were not in such a panicky state of distress

97

as the Story represents." Chamberlain claims he stayed behind this human parapet until well after darkness fell. In the small hours of December 15 came word that the forward ranks should disengage and withdraw in any manner possible. "We got our bodies ready to go," Chamberlain writes, "but not our minds."[2]

Cloaked in darkness, they slipped away to the rear in groups small enough to attract little or no fire. Some members of the brigade did not leave until they could carry off the bodies of the dead "on fragments of boards torn from fences by shot and shell." The dead were removed under the strobing lights of the Aurora Borealis. "Befitting scene!" wrote Chamberlain, as if declaiming. "Who would die a nobler death, or dream of more glorious burial?"[3]

Along with the rest of the regiment, Chamberlain wormed his way over hard, rocky ground, then picked a path through a "field strewn with incongruous ruin; men torn and broken and cut to pieces in every indescribable way." Spear comments: "Absolutely … there was nothing of the horrible scene described. There are ghastly scenes on a[ny] field of battle, and the story teller seems to have collected those of all the war and dumped them upon the field of Fredericksburg."[4]

Some time before dawn, the 20th Maine, along with the other regiments in Stockton's brigade and hundreds of other troops including dozens of stragglers, were withdrawn to Fredericksburg. Chamberlain snatched some little sleep in the town, even though the troop concentration supposedly attracted an artillery barrage—a contention that Spear categorically denies. A short time after midnight on the 16th Chamberlain's regiment and two others were selected for "some special service" which turned out to be manning a rear-guard to cover the army's recrossing of the river. Chamberlain recounts that after Colonel Ames led the outfit back in the direction it had come and formed it into a picket line near the "extreme front," he told his second-in-command, "hold this ground at all hazards." Chamberlain supposedly did so by throwing up earthworks on ground Spear contends was too hard to yield even a thin layer of loose dirt: "My distinct recollection is that we did not dig at all…."[5]

Not surprisingly, Spear rejects some of the more dramatic events Chamberlain mentions while describing the withdrawal, including an overheard conversation in the enemy's camp, a surprise encounter with Confederate pickets which nearly ended in Chamberlain's capture, a confrontation with an overwrought staff officer, an intricate leapfrogging maneuver to the rear, a near-deadly fusillade from Rebels able to discern Chamberlain's movement when the moon peeked through a cloud, and a grisly stroll through windrows of dead Federals whose "open eyes . . . saw not but reflected uttermost things...." Finally the regiment crossed the pontoons that brought it safely to the Union side. But Chamberlain's night was not over. On the north shore he pictures a run-in with General Hooker, whom he takes to task for poor tactics: "That was the trouble, General. You should have put us in. We were handled in piecemeal, on toasting forks." This presumptuous lecture brings neither reply nor punishment from the grand division commander.[6]

Thus ends a nightmarish evening crammed full of spine-tingling experiences. Chamberlain's rendition of those events, according to Ellis Spear, "is like an artist's picture or a cyclorama of a battlefield with everything that ever happened anywhere, collected in one place."[7]

* * *

Burnside's inept tactics had cost his army 12,653 casualties at Fredericksburg. The Fifth Corps was well represented in this ghastly total, contributing nearly 2,200 dead, wounded, and missing. Too late the man who appointed him to command remembered that the general had professed his unworthiness for the position and had refused to accept it until Lincoln insisted. The experience may have taught the president that even a high-ranking officer was capable of an accurate self-evaluation.

After the bloodletting of December 13, the survivors went into winter camp at and near Falmouth. The 20th Maine returned to its hilltop quarters at Stoneman's Switch, thankful that only four of the men who had left camp the week before would not be coming back. Most if not all of the 32 who had been wounded would eventually be discharged from the hospital and allowed to rejoin the outfit.

Once settled, Chamberlain wrote Fannie and his parents to let them know that he did not number among the casualties; nor did Tom, whose steadiness under fire would earn him a lieutenant's shoulder straps to the proud pleasure of his brother. In fact, the regiment as a whole had displayed commendable poise and clearness of mind throughout the fight, proving that its transition from rookies to veterans was well underway. That transition was news throughout Stockton's brigade. On January 10, Colonel Ames confided in a letter to his mother and father that "my regiment has an excellent reputation. I cannot ask for better success than what I have had."[8]

In his post-battle letters home, Chamberlain praised not only the conduct of his men but his own as well. Fannie would have been amazed by his coolness under fire, his clear-headed leadership throughout the fight, the commendation his actions received from Ames and other observers. Such self-praise would not be confined to his first pitched battle; in letters following Gettysburg, Wapping Heights, and other actions he would also describe his participation in glowing terms. After one fight he would inform Fannie that, had Napoleon been present on the field, her husband would have received a marshal's baton.

His lack of humility—so at odds with the conventional portrait of Chamberlain as a selfless, modest soldier—apparently served two purposes. He felt the need to prove to his wife that he was not merely a man of intellect but a man of action—a warrior, a leader, a patriot willing to lose his life in a noble cause. Perhaps this behavior served to solidify, in his own mind, his hold on his wife's affections as well as to gain her respect. The other apparent reason for his writing thus was that Chamberlain had an ego that required steady reinforcement. When he believed he had served ably in battle, he wanted other people to know. Because to praise himself to his comrades would be to exceed the boundaries of manly restraint—a model soldier is a humble soldier—his wife (perhaps his parents as well) constituted the only acceptable audience for his self-portrait as a hero. Chamberlain was not entirely lacking in modesty; after the war, he would sometimes downplay his military achievements, reject praise he considered un-merited, and work to promote others more deserving of recognition than he. But he never eradicated the streak of pride that ran deep within him or fully overcame his tendency to self-promotion.[9]

This tendency had a literal quality to it, a desire for tangible rewards.

In his post-Fredericksburg letter to Fannie, as in later correspondence, Chamberlain revealed a strength of ambition that biographers and historians have shied from discussing. By late December rumors had Adelbert Ames, whose performance at Fredericksburg had been every bit as impressive as Chamberlain's, on the verge of winning a star. If the reports proved true and Ames left the regiment to take a brigade, Chamberlain was the logical choice to inherit his eagles. But because politics could play hob with regimental appointments, he could not be certain of promotion. Thus he instructed Fannie, if the colonelcy came open, to ask local political supporters to agitate in his behalf. In later correspondence, after he had made colonel, he would ask his wife's help in enlisting political support for his promotion to brigadier general.

This effort to win a deserved promotion should not carry a pejorative connotation; officers everywhere have lobbied for advancement since time immemorial. Still, ambition is a trait not often associated with Joshua Chamberlain. Others have portrayed him as somehow too pure, too selfless—perhaps not human enough—to pull strings in his own behalf. Chamberlain may have possessed remarkable gifts as a soldier and a man, but he is not a candidate for hagiography.[10]

* * *

Once back at the old campsite the men stockaded their tents by laying a wooden floor under them. A few erected log cabins, their walls chinked with dried mud, the roofs sporting chimneys made of hollow barrels. Energetic soldiers built fireplaces made of stones or bricks they had foraged off the countryside. Lazier men hauled their portable stoves inside and relied on them not only to cook their rations but to keep their tent or cabin cozy when the wind blew and snow came down. The general result, while not the Astoria Hotel, was a reasonably comfortable edifice that a man could think of as home.

The new camp was soon well enough established to receive visitors. Shortly before Christmas, word came that Dan Butterfield was out as corps commander, replaced by a transferee from the First Army Corps, Major General George Gordon Meade. An irascible old Regular (West Point Class of '35) Meade at an early day made the rounds of the winter camps. He was tolerably well received. While the men of the 20th Maine decided they would give the tall, sad-eyed Pennsylvanian a chance to prove himself a worthy addition to their corps, they wondered if his succession was part of a window-dressing reorganization, something that occasionally followed a major defeat. Then, late in January, General Burnside himself, from his Falmouth headquarters, reviewed Meade's command. This action by the commanding general started a rumor that a movement was imminent. Perhaps Old Burn was out to recoup prestige by another movement against Lee. If so the army hoped he had given up the idea of a head-on offensive.[11]

If another battle loomed, Chamberlain and his soldiers were ready. As soon as he returned to Stoneman's Switch the lieutenant colonel had resumed his study of tactics—a subject in which he had already become proficient—this time under the tutelage of a more experienced volunteer officer, Colonel Strong Vincent of the 83rd Pennsylvania. When not himself learning, Chamberlain helped further his regiment's education. With Colonel Ames frequently absent from camp at division and corps headquarters, Chamberlain took charge of regimental training. To assist him he detailed "Pap" Clark, as acting major (Charles Gilmore was on another of his well-timed sick leaves; it had enabled him to escape the slaughter before Marye's Heights). With Clark's help Chamberlain saw to it that every soldier was tutored not only in the manual of arms but in the Articles of War, which company officers recited to their men every afternoon—20 articles per day—when on parade.[12]

The extra training came in good season. On December 30, following a bleak and glum Christmas Day—the first Chamberlain spent away from home and family—Griffin's 1st Division, the 20th Maine included, left camp for a frosty three-day reconnaissance of the upper fords of the Rappahannock. The mission ended quietly and inconclusively, the only action being a long-distance exchange of rifle fire with Rebel cavalry near Richards's Ford. Stockton's brigade never even got its feet wet; along with another brigade, it waited on the near shore while a third brigade crossed the river and chased off the enemy. After a cold, windy night spent in a wooded bivouac, the 20th Maine retraced its path south, completely in the dark as to the purpose of its movement. Once back at Stoneman's Switch the regiment ensconced itself in its fortified tents and sturdy cabins. There it spent a low-key New Year's. With the carnage of Fredericksburg little more than a fortnight old, there seemed no reason to celebrate, although perhaps some reason for drinking.[13]

The army got in three more weeks of winter camp before another, larger movement served to evict them. This excursion ended on an even louder note of futility than the recent reconnaissance. Unwilling to concede failure in his campaign to outmaneuver and thrash his enemy, Burnside in mid-January put in motion a huge, bold, and poorly-timed plan. His strategy hinged on his ability to hold the Confederates in place at Fredericksburg while the main body of his army hastened upriver, bridged the Potomac above the town, and enveloped Lee's left flank.

What Burnside might have accomplished had he been given an even break will never be known, for nature intervened to prevent anyone from moving with the speed necessary to success. By early on January 19 the operation began with brigades of infantry, battalions of horse-men, artillery caravans, wagons, ambulances, and Burnside's ill-starred pontoon trains streaming past the camp of the 20th Maine, heading in the same direction the 1st Division had taken three weeks ago. As the march progressed, Ames relayed to Chamberlain and the regiment marching orders, but the men went nowhere that day, and on the next, they marched perhaps three miles into a rain-sodden woods, where they spent a most uncomfortable night. The following day, the 21st, as Ellis Spear recorded, the outfit "fell in Early and moved in the mud under showers of rain [for] Several hours, while the artillery went slowly by. Marched through terrible mud 2 or three miles" into another "Cold & drizzly" bivouac.[14]

The inclement weather and the slushy, snow-coated, semi-frozen mud that it created doomed Burnside's opportunity to make amends for December 13. The army literally bogged down on bottomless roads; rumor had an artillery battery, teams and all, sinking out of sight in the monstrous gumbo. Immobilized, miserable, and with too much time to consider how wretched their lives had become, many regiments in the Fifth Corps were in a truculent mood by the third day out.

When an ill-considered whiskey ration was distributed to some outfits, brawls broke out among both officers and men. The demise of the so-called "Mud March" brought a fitting close to a campaign of death, destruction, and disaster. By January 24 the inept and unlucky Burnside had called off the expedition. Late that day the 20th Maine straggled back to its winter camp, feeling about as ill-used as soldiers can get.[15]

* * *

Chamberlain was as unhappy about the aborted campaign as the coldest, muddiest private soldier. But his mood did not spill over into discontent, nor did he despair over the army's fortunes. He expected an early change at the top, and he was confident that under a new leader the army would put the Mud March behind it and go on. Not even the hellish conditions he had endured succeeded in quenching his spirit. He had learned to deal with discomfort as well as with defeat; the hardships of war had not lowered his opinion that soldiering, for the right reasons, was an ennobling experience. Army life was not quite as he had imagined it—the reality was dirtier and more chaotic than the picture-books of his youth had informed him. His saving grace was his ability to filter out the mud, the blood, the squalor, and the sickness and concentrate on what was left—the pageantry, the glory, the nobility of sacrifice, the justness of the cause.

That much said, he leapt at the chance to escape the sights and smells of defeat, if only for a time. On January 28 he applied for a 15-day leave "to attend to business in the state of Maine, involving pecuniary and more important interests." The pecuniary nature of the request may have been his concern that his family was not faring well in his absence. Since October he had tried to send Fannie $100 every month, more than half his pay. But the paymaster could be weeks late in making his rounds, disrupting the flow of funds to Maine. Quite possibly, too, money had been lost in the mail. Leave would enable him to place cash in his wife's hands.[16]

The timing of Chamberlain's request coincided with the change he had foreseen in the army's upper echelon. Three days before, Ambrose Burnside, hobbled by the intriguing of some of his subordinates, and the loss of presidential confidence, told Lincoln that unless disloyal subordinates including Hooker and Franklin were not relieved, he would resign his command. In the end, it was Burnside whom Lincoln relieved, along with Franklin and Edwin Sumner. Instead of canning Joe Hooker, one of Burnside's most vocal critics, the president named him to take over the army. The general with whom Chamberlain supposedly quarreled on December 16 assumed command the day after his former superior was deposed. Hooker began his tenure vowing to revitalize an army he feared had left its morale on a corpse-strewn battlefield bathed in the Northern Lights.[17]

Hoping to find the army in better condition, physically and mentally, upon his return, Chamberlain left for home in the first week of February. Tom had hoped to accompany him but found at the last minute that he could not get away. Traveling alone, the older brother stopped first in Brunswick for a joyous reunion with Fannie, Daisy, Wyllys, and his in-laws. Later he spent a day in Brewer, visiting his parents. He found his sister at home, too, Sae having returned from a stint of teaching at a female academy in New York City. He also had an opportunity to visit with John, who had followed his eldest brother to Bangor Theological Seminary after Bowdoin. In future months John would interrupt his studies to join the relief agency known as the U. S. Christian Commission; later still, he would be offered the chaplaincy of a Maine infantry regiment in the Army of the James.[18]

Chamberlain's trip to Maine had an official side to it. After reuniting with his loved ones, he traveled to the state capital to pay his respects to Governor Abner Coburn, Israel Washburn's recently inaugurated successor. The two men discussed the process for filling the 11 officer vacancies that existed in the 20th Maine—the product of battle attrition and the poor health from which the regiment had suffered both in Maryland and at Stoneman's Switch. Chamberlain stressed to the craggy-faced Coburn that officer losses had left two companies of the regiment commanded by second lieutenants. He named the candidates for promotion on whom Colonel Ames and he had agreed. He may even have advanced his claim to Ames's position should the latter be promoted.

The governor asked Chamberlain to put his recommendations in writing, along with his opinion of the general state of regimental affairs.

This the lieutenant colonel did on February 26, when back in Brunswick. In the letter he supported for promotion four lieutenants, including the hard-bitten Walter Morrill, one of the few pre-1862 veterans in the regiment. He also recommended four sergeants to receive commissions. At the top of the list was his brother's name along with a notation that Ames had named Tom acting second lieutenant of Company D and later first lieutenant in Ellis Spear's Company G. Thanks to the support of his colonel and lieutenant colonel, Tom would gain a full appointment to the higher position, to rank from January 12. As though he considered the vacancies the only item of any consequence, Chamberlain added nothing about the overall condition of the regiment.[19]

Although he managed to extend his leave, his time in Brunswick and Brewer seemed far too brief. Reluctantly breaking free of his family's embrace, he entrained for Virginia in the last days of the month, and by early March he was back on the Rappahannock. He learned that in his absence the regiment had experienced severe weather but had not been forced to campaign in it. He was glad to discover, as Private Alva Small of Company C reported, that "the health of the regt in general is improveing [sic]." One reason was its regular conditioning on the drill field, even when snow was on the ground. Another recent outdoor exercise, a snowball fight, had involved dozens of members of the regiment, "about the same No. on a side," as Company K's Willard Buxton reported. By rapid volleys Buxton's side had forced the other steadily back till it was abutting regimental headquarters, where Colonel Ames looked on in amusement. At that point, "they break & run & their officers could not rally them."[20]

Ames had been getting quite a reputation as a taskmaster, and in some quarters a great deal of criticism. In Chamberlain's absence, his brother, along with Ellis Spear, A. W. Clark, Walter Morrill, and 15 other permanent or acting officers had written a "to whom it may concern" letter of support for the colonel. No doubt seeking newspaper publicity back home, the undersigned refuted the charge that the regiment "has been subjected to harsh and unnecessarily severe discipline ... through the fault of the commanding officer." The truth was that the 20th Maine had "performed no service of any kind that has not been performed by other Regiments of the Brigade." As for Ames, "it is due to him that the Regiment is so well drilled ... that it has been able to face the fire of the enemy with unwavering lines, & fully to sustain the proud reputation of the state of Maine...."[21]

Private Small identified another factor in the regiment's better health. "It is the change in the rations that makes it I think for in place of vegetables once in [every] two weeks," the 20th Maine was now being issued that staple three times weekly. The improved diet was a direct result of Joe Hooker's assumption of command. The new man had decreed that the army would live better and fight better under his regime, and apparently he intended to keep his promise. Tastier and more regular rations, better and more accessible hospital care, and new and improved weaponry had become available within weeks of his replacing Burnside. Chamberlain was impressed by the emphasis on supporting the rank-and-file, and he had the feeling that it was raising morale. Fighting Joe had made a good start; now, if he could prove himself worthy of his nickname, the Army of the Potomac might find the elusive road to victory.[22]

* * *

By the last week in March, as the Virginia winter shuddered to a close (it would produce snow squalls through early April), a new series of reviews consumed the regiment's time, suggesting that a resumption of active operations—the army's first under its new leader—lay not far off. On the 26th the crusty General Meade paid a call on the 20th's brigade, each of whose men now carried on the crown of his kepi the newly designed emblem of the 1st Division, Fifth Army Corps: a red Maltese cross in cloth or brass.

Meade doubtless enjoyed the display of these badges of honor, but he must have been dismayed by some of the afternoon's proceedings. At the outset Colonel Stockton, who seems to have been promoted beyond his abilities, issued incorrect orders, confusing his regimental commanders and delaying the start of the review. When his subordinates mulled about, uncertain of where they were to line up, the red-faced brigade leader pulled his sword and screamed for them to move out. The ludicrous scene inspired Adelbert Ames to laugh aloud, which drove Stockton to the verge of apoplexy. The review proceeded with one minor incident: a staff officer being thrown from his horse virtually in the unsmiling face of General Meade.[23]

Ten days after Meade came calling, the president made a return visit to the army, this time bringing Mrs. Lincoln. On April 7 both were on hand for a grand review of the army, during which General Hooker proudly displayed his rejuvenated ranks. The president was clearly impressed by the healthy, soldierly appearance of the troops, which he took as an indication that, almost two months after Fredericksburg, the army had undergone a revival. On this occasion, unlike his last visit, Lincoln does not appear to have traded glances with the lieutenant colonel of the 20th Maine. Still, Chamberlain was glad to see him. He had been expecting him, too; as the officer wrote years later, "always after a great battle, and especially disaster, we were sure to see him, slowly riding through camp," taking the pulse of the army and giving assurance that it retained the attention and support of its government.[24]

On or about the 10th, the day Lincoln returned to Washington, Chamberlain learned that Fannie was in the capital, seeking a pass through the lines. Evidently she failed to secure the necessary permission, for on the 12th her husband requested of the regiment's acting adjutant—Lieutenant Thomas D. Chamberlain—a five-day pass to meet Fannie in Washington or Baltimore. The request was immediately granted, and a day later he and Fannie were again together. The reason behind her request to visit the camp of the 20th is unknown, as are the circumstances of their meeting and several-day stay in Washington. It can be assumed that their reunion included connubial bliss, for Chamberlain returned to Stoneman's Switch humming a romantic ditty, "Sleeping I Dream Love."[25]

His leave may have put him in a good mood, but only active campaigning would keep his spirits high. By late April his regiment had been hibernating for more than four months, and everyone was anxious to get on with the business of saving the Union. Especially they longed for an opportunity to wipe out in battle the stain Fredericksburg had placed on the corporate escutcheon.

Chamberlain was as eager as anyone to leave winter camp behind. Therefore, he was chagrined to learn that when the army left its quarters for another go at Lee's Confederates, the 20th Maine would remain at Stoneman's Switch. Despite the improved health of the army as a whole, Chamberlain's regiment—much of it, anyway—was sick. Ignoring the mixed results of previous mass inoculations, army doctors had recently vaccinated the regiment against smallpox. Instead of preventing the disease, the poorly prepared serum had promoted an outbreak of it. By April 21, according to Holman Melcher, the recently appointed sergeant major of the regiment, more than 80 of his comrades had developed symptoms of the dreaded disease and four had died.[26]

Alarmed by the results, Surgeon Nahum P. Monroe of the 20th wrote the Adjutant General in Washington warning that continued use of the vaccine might contaminate the entire army. At his urging and that of other medical experts, on the 22nd the entire regiment was relocated a mile from its camp, to the top of an eminence soon known as "Quarantine Hill." Forced to remain there for an indefinite period, it would not participate in the coming advance.[27]

Dismayed by the thought of being denied a role in an important operation, perhaps the most critical of the war, Lieutenant Colonel Chamberlain paid a visit to army headquarters, where he discussed his outfit's predicament with his old corps commander, Dan Butterfield, now chief of staff to General Hooker. Later that day, fearful that he had not conveyed to Butterfield "the precise impression I designed," he wrote the general, pleading to be allowed to serve in the coming movement, even if his command could not. If field service were ruled out, could he at least serve on some general's staff?[28]

It is not known whether Chamberlain himself had been vaccinated; if so, he suffered no ill effects. Whether or not he was physically able to campaign, however, the pleading tone of his letter suggests that its writer had a compulsion to risk his life. Fear of the possible consequences may have motivated him. Although any decision to keep Chamberlain out of action would be someone else's, he may have been concerned about the effect on his reputation if the rest of the army fought and he did not. "If ... there is a battle, & I am left here in a pest-house," he wrote Fannie, "I shall be desperate with mortification."[29]

Another motivation was the lure, the attraction, of battle. Chamberlain had come, by this spring of 1863, to embrace action as much as he rejected the dull routine of camp life. At Fredericksburg the nearness of death had bothered him but not enough to keep him from discharging his responsibilities. Further than this, Fredericksburg had taught him a great truth about himself, one that must have come as a shock: he had never felt so alive, so vital, so in tune with his own nature, as he had on that terrible battlefield.

His letter to Butterfield is also troubling because it represents an effort to gain for himself an opportunity denied to his regiment. This fact makes him appear selfish and self-promotive. Any attempt to serve apart from his troops—especially if it resulted in his being wounded or disabled—could not have been in the best interests of the 20th Maine.

Yet, if Chamberlain was seeking advancement without regard for his regiment, he was not alone. A few days before his audience with Butterfield, Adelbert Ames wrote a similar letter to Hooker's chief of staff. "It seems unnecessary," he argued, "for all the field officers of the Regiment to remain in charge of a hospital camp, when it is earnestly recommended by the surgeon that as few officers as possible should be thus detained." In Ames's behalf (as later in Chamberlain's) O. O. Howard, now commanding the Army's Eleventh Corps, wrote directly to General Hooker. In addition to recommending a field position for Ames during the coming campaign, Howard suggested he be promoted: "If there is a Brigade for him in the Army I know no officer who would command it better."[30]

Ames won his appeal. On April 27, when the rest of the army began to break camp, the colonel was detailed as an aide-de-camp at corps headquarters. Thus he moved upriver, in company with four of Hooker's seven corps, to try to outflank the enemy—strategy unhappily reminiscent of Burnside's Mud March. His departure left the regiment in the hands of a restless, frustrated Chamberlain. For five days, as his regiment's incubation period dragged on, the lieutenant colonel paced atop Quarantine Hill.

By May 1—with more than 100 members of the regiment having shown symptoms of smallpox—the wait had left him frantic with nervous energy. That day the thump of artillery fire drifted down from the place where Hooker's advance had crossed the river toward Lee's left and rear, as well as from the direction of Fredericksburg, where two corps had been left to hold the Confederate main body in place. "We could hear the firing plain," wrote one of Chamberlain's enlisted men, "but there we lay in glorious idleness without being able to lift a finger or fire a gun." No one seemed happy about missing a fight that the rest of the army was involved in, with the possible exception of Charles Gilmore, who had made the mistake of returning from sick leave on the eve of battle—only to be spared from participating by events beyond his control.[31]

Chamberlain made a final effort to gain an active assignment for his outfit. On the afternoon of the first he spurred to Hooker's lightly occupied headquarters, where he found Butterfield in charge. He claims to have told the chief of staff that he would place his regiment anywhere it could do some good, adding that "if we couldn't do anything else, we would give the Rebels the small pox." Later he saw that "the force of my suggestion seemed to be appreciated, for at midnight I received a dispatch ... directing me to be at Banks' & U. S. Fords at daylight to take charge of the Signal and Telegraph lines from Hdqrs. to the several stations on the field of battle, with instructions to put to death any who attempted to disturb our communications."[32]

The assignment was of a rear-guard nature—much work and little glory. Still, he embraced the opportunity. In the wee hours of May 3, he got the healthy members of the 20th Maine on the road to the upriver fords. Through the balance of the night and throughout the 4th as well, they marched along the line of the military telegraph, repairing breaks in the line caused by high winds, fragile cable, vandals, and saboteurs. No members of the latter class, however, were captured and executed. As Chamberlain informed Governor Coburn in a less-than-humble moment, "I was in the saddle *all* the nights [sic] inspecting every inch of the line."[33]

As he had foreseen, the job was thankless and, as it sometimes seemed, trivial in comparison to the work in progress both at Fredericksburg and in the tangled woodland to the north known as the Wilderness. Chamberlain and his regiment moved on to what appeared a slightly more important assignment when they teamed with other units in guarding the crossing at Banks's Ford. Yet the work was not enough; he desired a still larger role in the proceedings.

Early on May 4 Chamberlain saw his chance. Leaving the regiment in the hands of Major Gilmore, he splashed across the river at Banks's. After a long ride he located and fell in with Griffin's division as it sparred with a part of the Second Corps, Army of Northern Virginia. That corps had been Stonewall Jackson's; in the wake of Jackson's mortal wounding two nights ago, it was now led by his colleague and friend, J.E.B. Stuart. As far as the Army of the Potomac was concerned, Jackson's fall had come too late. On the 2nd, Stonewall had almost single-handedly undone General Hooker's strategy by attacking his right flank amid the Wilderness, blunting its drive and rolling it up with textbook precision. First to go under, as Chamberlain had been sad to learn, was General Howard's corps.[34]

By the time Chamberlain entered the battle, it had been effectively decided in the enemy's favor. Lee had dealt Hooker's main body a blow, both physical and psychological, from which it would not recover. The army would remain in the Wilderness for a few more days but by May 6 would be streaming across the river in full retreat, its rear guarded by selected regiments including the 20th Maine. By then the Confederates would also have turned on the Federals occupying Fredericksburg, bloodying them and sending them reeling back to their camps.

Even had he known the fight to be lost, Chamberlain would still have gone in. As it was, on the 4th he attacked on horseback as one of Griffin's brigades moved against a Confederate battle line in a woods. Carried away by the momentum of the advance, the lieutenant colonel rode toward a masked battery, pistol and saber in hand. When the battery opened up, he was quickly unhorsed for the second time in eight months. Prince went down with a shell wound in the head and did not rise. His rider did, rather unsteadily, massaging his forehead, feeling for broken ribs. Realizing that his long-awaited, long-denied battle was already over, Chamberlain—coat torn, pants and cap covered with dirt, and facing the prospect of much walking—went to the rear in abject disgust.[35]

BELOVED COLONEL

*I*n the lurid afterglow of Chancellorsville, the morale of Lincoln's Army began to plummet. Twice in less than five months it had been marched to the slaughter under a commander whose grandiose plans had proved wanting in the execution. Blue-coated forces elsewhere in the country—especially those in the West under Major General Ulysses S. Grant—might be enjoying a run of success, but the Army of the Potomac could boast only a single strategic victory, Antietam, and that battle had ended as a tactical draw. Men who were good soldiers, who had learned well their deadly trade and who rendered faithful service no matter how obtuse their commander, began to wonder if God, fate, or fortune would ever reward them with the battlefield triumph for which the Union hungered.

Joshua Chamberlain underwent no such crisis of confidence. Certain of ultimate victory, he regarded Chancellorsville as another test by the Almighty of men's fortitude and resolve. Shortly after his return from the south bank of the Rappahannock, he wrote his six-year-old daughter a letter that characterized his army's plight in the most matter-of-fact way: "There has been a big battle," he told Daisy, "and we had a great many men killed and wounded. We shall try it again soon, and see if we cannot make those Rebels behave better, and stop their wicked works in trying to spoil our Country, and making us all so unhappy." And he went on to inquire how she and her brother were getting along.[1]

He had reasons to keep in good spirits; for one thing, professional advancement was coming to him. More and more he was being given responsible assignments in recognition of his proven ability, such as replacing a full colonel in command of the brigade's outposts. Increasingly, too, the 20th Maine was becoming his regiment alone. By the 11th, with the outfit no longer isolated from the rest of the army, its smallpox scare over, he resumed publishing orders, filling out requisitions, and drilling the men without Ames's supervision.

The latter was frequently absent from camp on staff duty, and on May 17 he was appointed commander of the guard at the supply depot at Aquia Creek. That assignment effectively severed Ames's connection with the regiment he had organized and trained. A week later word came to Stoneman's Switch that Ames had been appointed a brigadier general of volunteers in order to accept a brigade in the 1st Division, Eleventh Corps. No one who knew Ames would have been surprised that within two months he would be commanding the division itself.[2]

Despite the hell he had sometimes put them through, his Mainers were sorry to see him go, recognizing that he had made them the effective fighters they had come to be. To an extent, Chamberlain was also sorry, but it was a move he had helped along—months ago, he and Major Gilmore had begun writing Governor Washburn, strongly recommending Ames's promotion. Both men may have had an ulterior motive, for they would move up in rank and authority as soon as Ames did.[3]

Like many another native-born unit, the 20th Maine had a dim view of the "Dutch Corps" Ames was joining. Heavily composed of German immigrants, many of whom could not speak English, Howard's command had borne the brunt of Jackson's attack in the Wilderness and had seen its reputation besmirched thereby. Holman Melcher spoke for many in the regiment when he condemned "the disgraceful, cowardly break of the 11th Corps" on May 2. Others expected that Ames's transfer would bring about a change in his new command. "It is not best for them Dutchmen," wrote Willard Buxton, "to break & run under him."[4]

On the day that Ames moved up and out, Colonel Stockton, whom Private Buxton called "our old coward of a Brigadier," retired from the field, to be replaced by a soldier who inspired as much enthusiasm and confidence as his predecessor had elicited concern and condemnation. Colonel Strong Vincent of the 83rd Pennsylvania had distinguished himself on the Peninsula and at Fredericksburg, winning notice throughout the division for coolness in difficult situations. Not a professional soldier but a Harvard graduate and Pennsylvania lawyer, the bewhiskered, 25-year-old had become one of the best drillmasters in the army, a close rival to Ames in his ability to transform awkward recruits into polished veterans. Chamberlain and he had been close since Vincent tutored the older officer in tactics. The Bowdoin man admired the Harvard man's confident air, his solid military sense, his keen eye for terrain.[5]

Although he would not start wearing eagles on his shoulders until late the following month, on May 20 Chamberlain was officially mustered out of the service as lieutenant colonel; his colonel's commission would bear the same date. To fill the vacancy thus created, on May 30 Charles Gilmore would be commissioned lieutenant colonel, and on June 18 Ellis Spear would formally secure promotion to major. Gilmore's appointment came about by seniority, but if Adelbert Ames had had his way, Spear would have received it instead. Before leaving the regiment Ames had hatched a plot to force Gilmore to resign from the service, a plot foiled by Gilmore's demand that he be promoted. Unlike his unpopular associate, Spear had been supported for promotion by the officers of the regiment, several of whom had petitioned Governor Coburn in his behalf.[6]

Chamberlain was of course pleased and gratified by his promotion, a prize he had long coveted and which he doubtless considered his due—as did, it would seem, a majority of his officers and men. One of the advantages of the job was immediately apparent. Lieutenant Brown having accompanied General Ames to his new command, Ames's successor appointed as acting regimental adjutant First Lieutenant Tom Chamberlain.[7]

The colonelcy came with problems as well as benefits. Coincident with Chamberlain's promotion, many two-year regiments were reaching the end of their enlistment periods and departing for home. Two of the three New York regiments in Vincent's 3rd Brigade, the 12th and 17th, did so early in May. As a courtesy to state comrades, on the day Chamberlain made colonel, he led his regiment to the Richmond, Fredericksburg & Potomac Railroad depot to give a sendoff to the recently discharged 2nd Maine Volunteers, veterans of Brigadier General James Barnes's brigade of Griffin's division.[8]

Troubles began when 120 members left behind by the 2nd Maine followed the 20th Maine back to camp. These men, all recruits, had been persuaded by enlisting officers to sign up for three years but with the understanding that they would go home when the term of the regiment expired. When the government refused to sanction the arrangement, the unlucky 120 had been forced to remain in the army, attached to the only other Maine unit in the Fifth Corps.

Considering themselves deceived and swindled, the 2nd Mainers provided Chamberlain with his first challenge in regimental command. The "two year Men ... that cum in to oure Regt last night," wrote the semi-literate John Lenfest of the 20th, "say the[y] wunt due no duty because they cold not go home." The commander of the provost guard that conveyed the would-be mutineers to the 20th's camp at bayonet-point passed on to Chamberlain authority from General Meade "to draw up my Reg't with loaded arms & fire on them if they refused to do duty." The new colonel realized he had a crisis on his hands.[9]

As befitted a man with a gift for controlling others almost as effectively as he controlled himself, Chamberlain defused the situation by resorting not to force but to tact and firmness. At once he rode to Meade's headquarters and gained the general's permission "to manage the men in my own way." His way was to sit down with them, listen to their grievances, sympathize with their situation, and explain the realities of life—although not by way of a dramatic, God-and-country speech such as has been put into Chamberlain's mouth by novelists and filmmakers. He removed their guards, fed them their first full rations in three days, and quietly assigned them to various companies of the 20th Maine, "without giving them any specific orders whatever—expecting them to be treated, & to behave, like other soldiers."[10]

After days of privation and punishment at the hands of their own army, the two-year men responded well to such treatment. As one of their number recalled years later, "though not liking the [20th] Regt at first we got around all right owing to the Disposition of Col Chamberlain and the officers of the Regt to treat us well." Such treatment continued because Chamberlain was happy to add 120 "well-seasoned soldiers, and what is more, well-rounded men, body and brain" to an outfit depleted by battle and illness to fewer than 400 officers and men present for duty. Initially, only seven of the 120 refused to do duty with the 20th; later the number dwindled still further.[11]

After assimilating the newcomers, Chamberlain "found no trouble, except in the case of one or two who were tried by court martial, & whose sentences I afterward succeeded in having remitted. These men of the 2nd were afterward among my very best men, worthy of the proud fame of the 2nd, and the hard earned laurels of the 20th." His first critical performance in regimental command behind him, Chamberlain must have wished his dealings with the Army of Northern Virginia could be resolved so easily.[12]

* * *

On May 28 the 20th Maine accompanied the rest of its division (currently under the command of General Barnes, Charles Griffin being on sick leave) in marching out to the Rappahannock crossings. As other elements of the division took up picket duty lower down the river, Chamberlain, riding his third horse of the war, led his men to a familiar site, United States Ford, where they spent the night in bivouac. Next morning they moved a short distance back from the river and into a fixed camp. When wagons arrived bringing the regiment's tents, everyone expected a long stay.[13]

As the canvas dwellings went up, Chamberlain detailed 100 men to dig rifle-pits along the river, another sign that the regiment would be here for more than a day or two. By May 30, the men had scooped out trenches for a length of 15 rods along the river and had felled trees to provide frontal cover. Five artillery pieces had come up and been masked to guard the approaches to the ford. By May 30 Chamberlain had also formed the men into four parties, each patrolling a several-mile stretch of the North Fork of the Rappahannock. Captain Charles W. Billings of Company C wrote his father that "we are in a more responsible position than ever before except during battle.... Hooker & Lee are watching each other with eager eyes, each eager for an opportunity to injure the other."[14]

Billings noted that Rebel pickets across the river "are anxious to hold communication with our boys and invite them to come over." On the 30th seven Mainers accepted the invitation, remaining on the far side to chat with the Confederates and swap coffee for tobacco. The next day, Chamberlain learned what was going on and in a flash of anger ordered the practice halted at once. Aware that secrecy could be compromised by fraternization, he had his adjutant brother "instruct the officer in charge of the picket to shoot any man" who disobeyed. The uncharacteristically harsh order had the desired effect: no more men swam the river to visit a friendly enemy.[15]

On June 4, no Rebels having crossed near United States Ford, Chamberlain's regiment, in tandem with another from its brigade, was sent 14 miles upriver. Chamberlain led the men up the Warrenton Road, past Richards's Ford, to Ellis Ford, another potential path of Confederate advance. There, wrote Holman Melcher, the regiment "encamped in a beautiful oak woods on dry ground and [with] good water near, about a quarter of a mile from the river." The sergeant-major described his surroundings as "a pretty tract of country ... although quite scarcely inhabited. There has never been any body of soldiers here any length of time before, so that it does not have that look of desolation that about all the rest of Virginia does...."[16]

The men of Maine left the region as unspoiled as they found it, for although enemy units were occasionally sighted across the river, none tried to cross and the only fighting they precipitated was of the spasmodic, long-range variety. On June 7 Colonel Vincent, with characteristic brashness, crossed the stream at the head of a reconnaissance party but returned without locating the enemy. The only other incident to break the monotony of guard duty occurred on the 10th, when Lieutenant James Nichols of Company K, whom Chamberlain had detailed as officer of the day, was found drunk on duty; his colonel ordered him held in arrest for a week.[17]

As of June 12 Chamberlain and the men were under orders to march at a moment's notice, but two days passed before word came to withdraw from the river. Ending two weeks of ford-guarding, early on the 14th the 20th Maine packed its tents and headed northeastward through the hamlet of Morrisville (which Sergeant Albert E. Fernald of Company K described as consisting of "one chimney minus the house") until it struck the Orange & Alexandria Railroad at Catlett's Station. Although occasionally doused with a shower, the men suffered through a long, hard, hot march.[18]

The marching pace and the proximity of the main army—regiments, wagons, batteries, and ambulances, with cavalry units well out in front—told the 20th that a major movement was underway. It would take a few days before conflicting rumors sorted themselves out to produce the reason why: Lee's troops had left the Rappahannock for points north—just which points, no one, not even the high command, seemed able to say. The 1st Division, Fifth Corps, had done its job guarding the river, but someone else had slipped up. The cold, uncomfortable fact was that the army had permitted its adversary to steal a march on it.[19]

* * *

By midday on June 15, following what Sergeant Fernald called the "hardest march I ever had," Vincent's brigade reached Manassas Junction on the railroad, a landmark of two Union defeats. Shrugging off the portents, Chamberlain took a few minutes to write his wife's maiden aunt, Deborah Folsom, explaining that he had "been on the double quick for two days." Although "we are expecting an attack every moment," thanks to the additions from the 2nd Maine "I have 500 men & we are in good spirits, though hard-marched."[20]

Turning to family matters, he mentioned his home in Brunswick and noted with some unease that "Fanny is not there." He had heard from other relatives that his wife was off on another shopping excursion, "but I have no idea where...." This revelation undercuts the view of some historians, that when Chamberlain wrote Fannie from Gettysburg, he had no inkling his wife was not at home.[21]

Chamberlain, in fact, had heard nothing from Fannie for weeks, not an unusual occurrence given her poor writing habits. Tom, however, had recently heard from sister Sae that Fannie was in New York, having left the children in the care of relatives ("did you ever *hear* of such a thing?" Sae asked her youngest brother). Tom did not relay the information to his colonel—perhaps believing that bad news should not be delivered on the eve of his brother's first battle in regimental command.[22]

Fannie had traveled from home—often, far from home— continually since her marriage; her peripatetic ways had not ceased with the outbreak of war. Her family viewed her behavior, especially her virtual abandonment of Daisy and Wyllys, as selfish, irresponsible, and cruel. In mid-19th-century America it was considered acceptable for married women of upper- and upper-middle-class backgrounds, with or without children, to take long, unaccompanied trips, either to visit relatives and friends or to purchase items the family needed that could not be obtained closer to home. It is evident, however, that by traveling so frequently, often without letting loved ones know her whereabouts or destination, Frances Adams Chamberlain exceeded the social norms.

It is possible that she was fleeing from certain undesirable aspects of her relationship with her husband. In today's psychoanalytical terminology, her behavior would be considered a manifestation of an "avoidant attachment style." An avoidant attachment personality fears being too close to others, including his or her spouse, out of fear of rejection. Fannie had experienced rejection, or at least the perception of rejection, at least three times in her relatively young life: by her biological parents, who put her up for adoption; by her adoptive father, who invited into his life a rival for his affections, compelling Fannie to flee the only home she had known; and by her husband, who in 1862 decided his life lay in the army instead of in the home they shared.

Fannie's frequent trips to Boston and New York did not necessarily represent rejection of her emotional dependency on, or intimacy with, her husband. They were, instead, attempts to showcase her own independence. Travel can be a means of manifesting autonomy and self-confidence, and in the world of 1863 America it was one of the few socially accepted ways in which married women could assert a life apart from their husbands.[23]

* * *

The 20th Maine's journey to Manassas Junction and beyond took a toll. Typical was the comment of Corporal Nathan S. Clark of Company H, who "found myself nearly done out by hard marching and the heat." The unrelenting gait was necessary because word had come that a portion of Lee's army was poised to invade Maryland for the second time in nine months—with the apparent intention of ranging much farther north.[24]

On June 17 the march turned killer, four men of Barnes's division succumbing to sunstroke. On the road between Manassas Junction and Gum Springs, several members of the 20th also collapsed from the heat, including Colonel Chamberlain. Soldiers carried him to a nearby house, where he received medical attention for the next three days.[25]

His incapacitation prevented him from leading the outfit into battle on the 21st. That day army headquarters tabbed Vincent's brigade to support the cavalry division of Brigadier General David McMurtrie Gregg in attacking Stuart's troopers outside the Loudoun Valley town of Upperville. In Chamberlain's place, Lieutenant Colonel Freeman Conner of the 44th New York took charge of the 20th Maine. Considering the warm attachment the regiment is supposed ever to have felt for Chamberlain, it is curious to note the reaction of Nathan Clark that "the boys have grate [sic] confidence in" Conner "and feel joyous over" his assumption of command.[26]

Chamberlain would have been pleased to learn that under its temporary leader the 20th sustained its growing reputation as a fighting regiment. Early in the action it advanced as skirmishers, braved artillery fire, and evicted dismounted horsemen from a series of breastworks. The infantry's job done, Gregg's troopers charged the dislodged enemy, driving them through Upperville and toward Ashby's Gap in the Blue Ridge Mountains. Because the 20th ended up in a deep woods, Holman Melcher "could not see the cavalry charge.... Those that witnessed it represented it as grand."[27]

When, carried in a wagon, Chamberlain rejoined the regiment near the village of Aldie, Ellis Spear found him "no better, rather worse." The patient was still doing poorly when Chamberlain's brother John, now an agent of the Christian Commission, reached Aldie on the evening of June 22, exactly three weeks after leaving Maine. Over the next four days, as the regiment rested in its Loudoun Valley camp, drilling twice daily under the supervision of future Lieutenant Colonel Gilmore and Major-to-be Spear, John Chamberlain attempted to minister to the brother who the previous month had invited him to visit the army.[28]

His efforts achieved mixed success. When the regiment broke camp on the rainy morning of June 26 and, in common with other elements of the army, shoved off for Leesburg, Colonel Chamberlain was able to ride. When standing, however, he gave the appearance of a sailor just off a ship. When John suggested that his brother make that day's march in an ambulance, the latter insisted that "he would ride like a man." He did so, keeping to the saddle throughout the day despite intermittent wooziness.[29]

Eventually, he had to turn the regiment over to Charles Gilmore in order to recuperate further. The men disliked the change, temporary as it was, for the great majority trusted and respected Chamberlain. One of these men, Holman Melcher, rejoiced that "our beloved Col.... is on the recovery and we all hail the day he is able to resume his command of the regiment." If this view implied a distrust of the capacity of Chamberlain's second-in-command, Melcher was not alone. While Chamberlain was out of action, Colonel James Clay Rice of the 44th New York kept a close watch over the 20th Maine and especially over Gilmore.[30]

In midafternoon on the 26th—four days after Lee's advance echelon had entered Pennsylvania, and one day after the Army of the Potomac began to cross the river for which it was named—the 20th Maine passed through boarded-up, deserted-looking Leesburg. By sunset, it was waiting its turn to cross one of the crowded pontoon bridges the army's engineers had laid across the water at Edwards Ferry. Once on Maryland soil, the men moved a few miles inland before bivouacking outside Poolesville. The principal topic around the evening cook-fire was the audacity with which Lee had again brought the war north—farther north than ever before.[31]

A good night's sleep aided Chamberlain's recovery, although he was not physically able to resume active command of the regiment until June 29. As he recovered, other officers fell ill, including Spear and Gilmore. Though occasionally prostrated by malaria and weakened by that ever-present soldier's ailment, diarrhea, Spear remained with the regiment. Gilmore, sensing that marching was about to end and fighting to begin, dropped out of the ranks as the regiment neared Frederick City; next day he was admitted to the military hospital there. The major's claim that his Peninsula wound had flared up would result in his transfer to a general hospital at Baltimore, where he would sit out the coming campaign.[32]

The army lay over for a day about three miles below Frederick. There the 20th Maine received its first mail in more than two weeks; among other items, it contained the paperwork to support Chamberlain's and Gilmore's promotions, but not Spear's. Since at the time neither of his superiors was on duty, Spear, who took command of the regiment in his capacity as senior captain, had a right to be frustrated and upset.[33]

Rumor was almost as well-received as mail, especially when it involved stories about the high command. One of the fruits of the grapevine on June 27 was that Joe Hooker had bowed out, the victim of Chancellorsville and post-battle squabbles with the War Department. The new army commander was the Fifth Corps' own George Meade. The following day both rumors were confirmed, to the concern of much of the army. Although swapping horses in the middle of the stream—in this case, perhaps, the middle of the Potomac—could be regarded as a risky move, the men of Chamberlain's regiment probably reckoned that any change was for the better, as long as Hooker was out, even when the next day could bring a confrontation with Lee on Union soil.[34]

On June 29, with a fully recovered Colonel Chamberlain riding at the head of his regiment—silver eagles nesting at last on his shoulders—the 20th passed through Frederick, where the city's many unionist residents greeted it with cheers and gifts of food and drink. The pleasure the 20th felt in moving among people loyal to the Old Flag increased when, later in the day, it trooped through a succession of towns with "Union" as part of its name. That night, the last in June, the outfit camped at Union Mills, only four miles from the Pennsylvania line. To get this far the men—including John Chamberlain, on horseback—had come 25 miles since morning. Over the past six days, they had logged a total of 125 miles. Speed remained of the essence; all day on the 30th, the regiment had beheld signs of Confederate progress northward: burned houses, ransacked barns, captured stragglers, and the intermittent thump of cannon-fire beyond the horizon. The men only hoped they could overtake Lee before he could wreak further havoc on the Commonwealth of Pennsylvania.[35]

In tandem with the rest of Vincent's brigade, the 20th returned to the road at 7 A.M. on the 1st of July. A couple of hours later it crossed into Pennsylvania to the accompaniment of the brigade drum corps playing "Yankee Doodle" and the cheering of thousands of soldiers. By 3:00 Chamberlain was leading his troops through the town of Hanover, beyond which he called a halt. Breaking ranks, the men inspected the dead horses, scattered carbines and tack, and other debris left by the cavalry battle that had swirled through the village the previous day. As they settled down to consume their rations, the visitors paid heed to new rumors filtering back from the front, where the sound of cannon was growing louder by the minute. The advance element of the army—a division of cavalry, supported by two or three infantry corps under Major General John F. Reynolds, Meade's most trusted subordinate, had met the Confederates near a crossroads village named Gettystown or Gettysburg, perhaps a dozen miles west of Hanover.

By sunset every Mainer was back in column, heading west with the balance of the corps. "My men moved out with a promptitude and spirit extraordinary," Chamberlain reported, as if Armageddon were waiting just up the road.[36]

* * *

Chamberlain and his spirited men—still accompanied by brother John—reached the fringes of the battlefield well past dark. After what its colonel recalled as "an hour or two of sleep by the roadside just before daybreak," the regiment left the Hanover road and trudged south under an already blistering sun, halting southeast of Gettysburg some time before noon. By then the action that had flared throughout the previous day, before breaking off in evening, had resumed in full fury.

Thus, the fight was far from over; the Fifth Corps had arrived in time to help decide the outcome.[37]

The previous day the battle had gone against the Army of the Potomac—that portion of the army on the field—largely because Lee's troops were there in greater force and in position to batter both the front and right flank of their enemy. While trying to steady his wavering ranks, General Reynolds had been shot dead. But despite being forced to withdraw from positions northwest of Gettysburg, Reynolds's troops (later placed under O.O. Howard) had formed a defensive line along high ground known as Cemetery Ridge, below Gettysburg. Most of Lee's people took up a parallel line along Seminary Ridge about a mile to the west; other Confederates occupied the town itself as well as high ground immediately below it. Now, at last, the two armies faced each other at close to full strength and the fight could be carried to its conclusion.

At first there was some indecision as to where the 20th Maine and its comrades could be used to best advantage. In the early morning hours of the second, aides from Meade's headquarters guided Barnes's division into position south of Wolf Hill, just off the Baltimore Pike not quite two miles behind Cemetery Ridge. Early in the afternoon, however, the division was escorted south and west, across Rock Creek, past Powers's Hill, and into a reserve position in a peach orchard. There, just off the Granite Schoolhouse Road, the command lay to the rear of the army's left flank.[38]

For some hours, as cannon thundered and rifles rattled not far away, the 20th Maine waited restively, in close proximity to the rest of its corps as well as to elements of three other army corps including units that had been savaged on the 1st. Several times Barnes's division was readied for an advance, only to go nowhere. For Chamberlain it was the rear area at Antietam all over again. "Although expecting every moment to be put into action and held strictly in line of battle," he reported, "yet the men were able to take some rest and make the most of their rations." The majority, it would appear, would rather fight than eat. They longed to do their part to defend their region and to prove Robert E. Lee and his soldiers mortal. Some of the men were also fighting to honor their commanders—if not George Meade, then their old patron George B. McClellan, who, according to carefully orchestrated and wholly spurious rumors, had been returned to command.[39]

As his inactivity stretched on into midafternoon, Chamberlain tried to make sense of the tactical situation. To his dismay he could not determine whether his army was on the offensive or the defensive, or where along the line the Confederates might be concentrating. They were defending ground north of the 20th Maine's position including Culp's Hill, but action was also in progress to the west and southwest, where the roar of combat was climbing steadily. To which area might the 20th be sent?

The issue was decided when the fighting to the west suddenly exploded. Some time before 4:00 P.M., as Chamberlain recorded, "a sharp cannonade, at some distance to our left and front, was the signal for a sudden and rapid movement of our whole division in the direction of this firing, which grew warmer as we approached." In response, the 20th and other outfits were directed down, then across, the Taneytown Road toward the base of Cemetery Ridge.[40]

The commotion in that sector accompanied an attempt by Robert E. Lee to exploit an opportunity along the Union left flank. About an hour before, Meade's Third Corps had advanced without orders from the south end of Cemetery Ridge to what its commander, Major General Daniel Sickles, considered more defensible ground between the lines. By rushing nearly a mile westward, Sickles had blundered at the very hour that Lee's senior subordinate, Lieutenant General James Longstreet, was commencing a belated assault against Meade's left and center with two divisions including that of Major General John Bell Hood. Caught out of position and with fewer troops than his opponents, Sickles was vulnerable to being overwhelmed. And overwhelmed he was, his troops being forced to retreat after offering stubborn resistance in an orchard and a wheat field and suffering hundreds of casualties (Sickles himself losing a leg to a rebounding cannonball).

Forced to concentrate on defending himself, Sickles could no longer protect the heights at the southern end of his army's line: heavily wooded Round Top, and, a few hundred yards to the north, Little Round Top (also known as Sugar Loaf, or Granite Spur), whose eastern crest alone was covered with timber. The vulnerability of this ground invited a Confederate breakthrough. Tactics books of the time favored maneuvers aimed at assaulting an open flank. If exploited through a heavy enfilading fire, such a maneuver might gain the enemy's rear and roll up his line from end to end, regiment after regiment of defenders toppling like dominoes.[41]

The officer who first realized the vulnerability of Little Round Top started the chain of events that drew the 20th Maine into action. Earlier that afternoon Major General Gouverneur K. Warren, chief engineer of the Army of the Potomac (later to become Chamberlain's corps commander and postwar friend), had visited the crest of the smaller elevation and was shocked to find it unoccupied. After determining that a mighty force was poised to strike not only Sickles's men but the hills they had uncovered, Warren sent staff officers galloping in many directions, seeking help.[42]

One who received his message was George Meade's successor as Fifth Corps commander, now-Major General George Sykes. In response, Sykes sent a courier of his own to detach troops from Barnes's division. Barnes, however, was not to be found; according to later rumor, self-protective instincts had sent him to the rear. Fortunately, the more combative Strong Vincent flagged down the messenger and inquired of his errand. When the man insisted he was searching for Barnes, Vincent snapped: "Give me your orders!" Told that Barnes was ordered to send a brigade to Little Round Top, Vincent replied: "I will take the responsibility myself of taking my brigade there."[43]

Already other Fifth Corps troops, along with some Second Corps units, were rushing to plug the gap farther north that Sickles had created. Instead of following them, Vincent temporarily placed the 3rd Brigade under Colonel Rice, with orders that it follow him to the summit of Little Round Top. Along with his orderly, Vincent rode on ahead to scout the position for possible footholds.

In advance of the rest of the brigade, Chamberlain and the 20th Maine advanced to Little Round Top via the road running west from the Wheatfield. By the time the regiment and its trailing comrades began to clamber up the north slope of the hill, Hood's artillery was sending shells screaming their way. Looking to his rear, the colonel was horrified to see not only brother Tom close behind but brother

John—serving today as a surgeon's assistant—riding beside Tom. When a solid shot whizzed just above the heads of all three, the oldest waved his siblings away. The next round might take them all out and "make it hard for Mother."[44]

As Vincent whipped his units into a line astride a secondary ridge of Little Round Top, he chose Chamberlain's regiment to guard his left and rear. A man of few but telling words, the brigade leader instructed his subordinate to hold that vital position "at every hazard." Because of the curvature of the ridge, Chamberlain faced his men south and west and waited for whatever was coming his way.[45]

As the professor-turned-soldier later noted, "these dispositions were scarcely made when the attack commenced, and the right of the Regt. found itself at once hotly engaged. Almost at the same moment ... I perceived a heavy force in rear of their principal line, moving rapidly but stealthily toward our left, with the intention, as I judged, of gaining our rear unperceived."[46]

The 20th Maine—if it had not done so by now—was about to earn its pay.

Eight

DOGGED DEFENDER

Strong Vincent was responsible not only for occupying a strategic position but for the dispositions that would ensure its safeguarding. It was he who led the way up the forested slope via a woodcutter's trail. And it was he who, once at the summit, sized up the defensive possibilities of a lateral elevation—known thereafter, fittingly, as "Vincent's Spur"—that ran for about 100 yards southeast from the main mass of the hill. Bare of trees and some 20 feet lower than the southern crest of Little Round Top, the elevation would prevent the occupiers from being outlined against the sky for the benefit of enemy sharpshooters. From "his" spur Vincent enjoyed a wide and deep view of the valley to the west, watered by Plum Run and studded by a mass of piled rock, a natural sniper's nest known as Devil's Den. In that area Hood's troops were overrunning Dan Sickles's ill-formed salient and were pressing on for Little Round Top.

To hold the right ledge of the spur, Vincent hoped to extend his troops in such a way as to connect with Sickles's corps and its reinforcements. On the left, where the spur sloped south toward the more elevated Round Top and the thick, brushy saddle between, Vincent needed a regiment strong enough and vigilant enough to turn back any attempt to gain his rear. Many students of history assume that he posted the 20th Maine in this position because of the

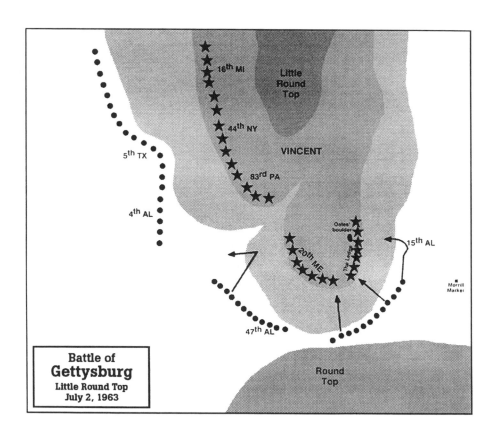

Battle of
Gettysburg
Little Round Top
July 2, 1963

confidence he reposed in its commander and his men. At the time Vincent's brigade reached the summit, however, it was the right flank, already under pressure from enemy forces, that was the post of greatest danger. Rather, the 20th's position as the first regiment in Vincent's column placed it in position to hold the other side of the hill. Next to come on line was the 83rd Pennsylvania, led this day by Captain Orpheus Woodward, which formed on Chamberlain's right, farther down the slope. The next arrival was the 16th Michigan under Lieutenant Colonel Norval Welch, which Vincent had moved from its original position atop the saddle between the hills. At the urging of Colonel Rice, however, the Michiganders were held out of line until Rice's own outfit could take post beside the 83rd Pennsylvania, a favorite fighting partner of the 44th New York. Welch's people then went in on the far right.[1]

In the few minutes that remained before the enemy which had battered Sickles's command reached Little Round Top, Chamberlain sought a way to make his position, if not impregnable, at least formidable. Moving the men by files across the shelf of the spur, he faced most of his line southwestward across the Plum Run Valley, where it would surely make first contact with the enemy. His right flank covered by Captain Woodward's outfit, Chamberlain gave his attention to his left—the far left flank of the Union army at Gettysburg. Calling on his textbook knowledge and calling up the 40 riflemen of Company B, he directed its commander, Captain Morrill, an old veteran who had become one of Chamberlain's most dependable subordinates, to assume a detached position on the left and front of the regimental line, guarding against any attempt to gain the rear. Unable to impart detailed instructions, he enjoined Morrill to "keep within supporting distance of us, and to act as exigencies if the battle should require."[2]

Without hesitation, the stoic Morrill led his marksmen down the south slope of the spur toward Round Top. Later in the day, when cut off from the rest of the 20th by massed attackers, Company B would head eastward toward a wooded lane leading to a farm owned by a Pennsylvania Dutchman named Weikert. In that position, Morrill's men would appear to be too distant from Little Round Top to do their regiment any good in a fight. But at an opportune time they would surprise themselves, the enemy, and their comrades on the high ground.[3]

At about 4 P.M., before the 20th Maine's arrival on Vincent's Spur, Confederate infantry—members of Brigadier General Jerome B. Robertson's Texas Brigade and the Alabama brigade of Brigadier General Evander M. Law—led Hood's assault column toward Little Round Top and points north. When they began their advance, the two brigades consisted of some 3,600 officers and men. Half of Robertson's command was lost to the attack, however, when its 1st Texas and 3rd Arkansas regiments encountered still-feisty units of Sickles's corps in and around Devil's Den. Law supported Robertson in this action by ordering the two regiments on his right flank, the 44th and 48th Alabama, to wheel left and pass across the rear of the column. A third regiment of Law's brigade, the 4th Alabama, kept close to the right flank of the 5th Texas.[4]

All told, these five outfits would either fail to reach Little Round Top or would strike the far right flank of Vincent's Brigade. The 20th Maine would have to contend only with the two regiments that now constituted Law's right flank, the 15th and 47th Alabama, under the command, respectively, of Colonel William Calvin Oates and Lieutenant Colonel Michael Bulger.

Oates would become the Maine regiment's primary antagonist. Like Joshua Chamberlain a former schoolteacher, more recently a lawyer, the 29-year-old native of the Alabama hill country was also a long-time resident of the Texas frontier. Since childhood he had led a rougher, poorer, less genteel life than his Union counterpart, but like Chamberlain, Oates had taken to soldiering like a fish takes to swimming, gaining a reputation as an officer who pushed his men to excel but knew just how far they could be pushed. A hard-bitten veteran of two years of war, Oates was destined to be forever linked with the college professor whose regiment he was committed to destroying.[5]

Oates's and Bulger's outfits totaled nearly 700 men present for duty, 200 more than the number available to Chamberlain. But the attackers could bring only a portion of this total to bear on the 20th Maine. One reason was the path they took toward Little Round Top. Soon after starting out, the regiments diverged southward from the body of

Law's brigade. According to contingency orders from General Law, if the outfits were isolated from support Oates was to have effective command of both.

Law had further directed Oates to strike the Union left only after passing through the narrow valley between the Round Tops. But this plan had gone awry not long after the Alabamians crossed a tributary of Plum Run. Before they came within rifle range of Chamberlain's position, the attackers wheeled still farther south in response to a deadly oblique fire. The rifle blasts came from three companies of a Third Corps unit, the 2nd United States Sharpshooters, which had taken up a position at the base of Round Top. Repeated salvos from the sharpshooters' rifles drove a portion of the 47th Alabama through the flank of its sister regiment. Sorting themselves out and resuming the advance, the Alabamians steadily pushed the marksmen up the wooded southwestern slope of Round Top, and followed them.[6]

Soon after Oates started up the hillside, a courier from General Law arrived to instruct him to make a left wheel and head directly for Little Round Top. But the colonel refused to diverge from his route up the higher eminence in pursuit of the sharpshooters. Only when on the summit of Round Top did Oates assent to another staff officer's order, this directing him "to press on, turn the Union left, and capture Little Round Top if possible, and to lose no time."[7]

By now, Oates no longer had the manpower he and Bulger had started with. Several members of both regiments had fallen prey to the sharpshooters. Another 22 had been detached from Oates's regiment even before the advance began, when early on that sweltering afternoon a detail was sent to the rear to fill dozens of canteens. Oates always regretted that he was compelled to start out before the water carriers returned.

After reaching Round Top, Oates detached another company of his regiment, almost 50 strong, and sent it down the northeastern slope to capture a Union wagon train, thought to be laden with ordnance, which the colonel had spied in park east of Little Round Top. Unfortunately, this unit neither captured the prize vehicles nor made its way back to assist Oates against Chamberlain's men. Finally, three companies of skirmishers in the 47th Alabama had gotten lost during the movement east and had wandered into a position in which they were of no use to Oates. Their loss left perhaps 150 of their regiment to assist the 15th Alabama in its offensive. Thus, the combined force that descended Round Top and climbed the smaller hill to the north had been reduced to a number that made the coming contest against the 20th Maine close to an even match.[8]

* * *

Soon after he was directed into position on Little Round Top, Chamberlain designated "Pap" Clark as commander of the regiment's right wing and named Ellis Spear to command the left. Under the supervision of the three officers, the regiment formed along the rugged spur, the upper part of its line facing the valley of Plum Run as well as southward, the lower line staring toward Round Top. For several minutes Chamberlain paced behind the men as they crouched behind the rocks and scrub oak that afforded the only natural protection. To make himself heard above the din of Confederate batteries to the west, he shouted orders and advice, adding words of encouragement when he considered them appropriate. Otherwise, there was little he could do but stand and wait—wait for the enemy to reach his line and provide the 20th Maine with its first close-quarters fight of the war.

Accompanied by a sharp cessation of artillery fire, the Confederates reached the west slope of Little Round Top some time after 4:30. The initial weight of the attack, wielded by the Texas regiments and the 4th Alabama, fell on the right flank and center of Vincent's position. Suddenly, Michigan, New York, and Pennsylvania skirmishers raced back to the spur, followed by men in gray and brown keening the Rebel yell as they started up the forward slope.[9]

As soon as the enemy came within range, Captain Clark's troops let loose with a volley that materially aided their comrades to the right. Then the left flank of the abbreviated 47th Alabama came into view opposite the 83rd Pennsylvania and Clark's wing. Again the latter joined its Pennsylvania comrades in unleashing volley after volley. The effect was especially devastating on the 20th Maine's front, for Chamberlain had formed his right companies in double ranks. The fire unhinged the open left flank of the 47th, rendered its commander *hors de combat,* and sent most of the regiment careening northwestward to seek refuge with Law's main body.[10]

Chamberlain had barely lent his attention to the fighting on the right when Lieutenant Nichols, recently released from arrest along with the few recalcitrant transferees of the 2nd Maine, came rushing up with dire news. Another Rebel force—Oates's 15th Alabama, supported by the few dozen remaining members of Bulger's outfit—was coming down the mountain, apparently in echelon, toward the left and rear of the 20th Maine. Chamberlain vaulted to the top of "a high rock in the centre of my line where I could see over the heads of the parties then engaged. I perceived a body of Rebels moving by their right flank towards the smooth valley between us and Great Round Top."[11]

Oates's advancing column so widely overlapped the flank of the 20th Maine that disaster seemed minutes away. Reacting swiftly, Chamberlain had the color guard move to the far left, and ordered "my right wing into one rank, by side steps, keeping up a strong fire all the while so as to give the enemy no opportunity to break through...." The sidling maneuver thinned the flank as it extended south and east around the curve of the spur. From the new position of the color guard, Chamberlain directed Ellis Spear to re-form the left wing along the eastern ledge of the spur, so as to protect the rear. When the shift was complete—having been performed with a smoothness and a precision that belied the regiment's relative inexperience—the new line resembled, as Chamberlain said, "a horse shoe, nearly," with the regimental flags where the prongs of the shoe connected.[12]

In their new position, both of Chamberlain's wings let loose as soon as Oates's column came into range. The enemy commander called it "the most destructive fire I have ever seen." It came as a particular shock in that Oates had expected to encounter only the sharpshooters he believed he had driven to the summit of Little Round Top.[13]

Although staggered by the fire coming down from the spur, the gray line kept moving up the slope, breaking after getting to within a few yards of the summit. Almost immediately the 15th Alabama regrouped and came on again, again to be beaten back seconds before it could top the ridge. But Oates's men had taken, as well as received, a toll. Dozens of men in Spear's wing had toppled dead or wounded.

Meanwhile, the companies in Clark's wing continued to fire into what remained of the 47th Alabama, hugging Oates's left.

The men of the 20th Maine were not the only hard-pressed defenders on Little Round Top. While Oates's troops hammered away at Chamberlain's left, Robertson's brigade, supported by Law's 4th Alabama, laid a heavy fire upon the rest of Vincent's line. At one point the Confederates broke through on the far right, sending Colonel Welch and many of his Michiganders to the rear. Trying to rally the broken ranks, Strong Vincent went down with a thigh wound that would prove mortal. To support his vain but courageous effort, General Warren, who had continued to occupy the crest of Little Round Top, commandeered a newly arrived regiment of the Fifth Corps and rushed it to the threatened sector. With only moments to spare, Colonel Patrick H. O'Rorke's 140th New York reached the crest, hurled its weight at the attackers, and by desperate fighting sealed the point of breakthrough. For his valor O'Rorke, too, paid the ultimate penalty, crumpling under a Rebel fusillade.[14]

On Chamberlain's part of the line any break could not be repaired so quickly, for supporting troops were nowhere in sight. The Confederates kept pressing the 20th Maine's left and rear, letting up so infrequently that Oates's multi-effort offensive seemed a continuous operation. "The edge of the fight rolled backward and forward like a wave," Chamberlain would later recall. No sooner did the gray tide break and recede at one point than it began to lap elsewhere at Chamberlain's line.[15]

The colonel met every threat by shifting troops to suddenly vulnerable sectors. Seeing that the repulse of the 47th Alabama had left the two companies on his far right less than heavily occupied, he decided to switch them to the opposite flank. When the companies fell back to make the switch, however, they disarranged the line, causing such confusion that Chamberlain feared the entire regiment might disengage. Rushing to the right, he countermanded the order, restored the flank, and let his men fight on.

By the time the struggle was an hour old, some Mainers were already low on ammunition, and the color guard had been thinned out. The regimental and national banners remained, however, in the sturdy hands of Sergeant Andrew J. Tozier, William Livermore, and 18-year-old Private Elisha S. Coan (Bowdoin '60). Chamberlain feared the guard had been annihilated when a brutal crossfire suddenly ripped into the center of the regiment. But when the smoke cleared Chamberlain could see the three color-bearers, especially the conspicuous Tozier, his left arm wrapped around the flag as he loaded, fired, and reloaded a borrowed rifle.[16]

To close a gap hewn by the crossfire, the colonel sent runners to rally troops at the center, one of them being Adjutant Chamberlain. The errand was so risky that the commander of the 20th Maine wondered if he would ever see his brother alive again. "Take care of Tom," their father had instructed; instead, he had sent Tom into the jaws of death. But he could not dwell on the deed. He had business elsewhere, including trying to secure support for his hard-pressed, ammunition-poor troops. A courier-borne request of Captain Woodward brought word that the 83rd Pennsylvania could spare no men to spell the Mainers. The regiment could, however, extend its left, enabling Chamberlain to move farther south—an offer he gratefully accepted. He was further relieved soon afterward, when his brother returned to him unhurt, having closed the gap as directed.[17]

By 6:00 P.M., the fighting had been raging along Chamberlain's line for nearly 90 minutes. The toll showed everywhere the colonel looked. So many defenders had gone down, including a dozen or more of the old 2nd Maine, that each wing resembled a board fence with slats missing.

One of the wounded is supposed to have claimed Chamberlain's attention at about this time: Private (formerly Sergeant) George W. Buck, a 21-year-old farmer from Linneus. According to a well-worn account, Buck had lost his stripes back in winter camp when the regiment's bully of a quartermaster, Lieutenant Alden Litchfield, in a fit of anger struck and cursed the sergeant, then trumped up charges of insubordination against him. The story has it that on Little Round Top Chamberlain reinstated the dying man to his former rank for "faithful service and noble courage on the field of Gettysburg." Thereupon the vindicated youngster breathed his last. This episode may be factual, but the stilted, sentimental language in which the account is always phrased and its sure-fire themes of a cruel wrong manfully borne and the redemptive quality of bravery appear to weaken its credibility. So does Chamberlain's failure to have righted the wrong done to Buck, with whose plight the colonel claims to have been familiar.[18]

After launching nearly a half-dozen thrusts toward the crest of Vincent's spur, Oates's men, their strength and spirit ebbing, tried yet again, this time aiming well to the rear of Chamberlain's original position. By almost superhuman effort the tired, grimy, thirsty Alabamians once again ascended the rocky slope, near the crest confronting the four companies that constituted the "refused" flank of the 20th Maine. Gaining a fragile foothold along a rock ledge, the attackers slowly pushed back Spear's wing until it nearly touched Clark's companies. From this position Oates claimed to have fired not only into the front of one wing of the 20th Maine and the rear of the other but into the rear of the 83rd Pennsylvania and 44th New York. The colonel also maintained that his troops advanced as far as a large boulder well inside Spear's original position.[19]

Present-day historians generally uphold Oates's contention, but Chamberlain never did. In later years he would admit that on July 2 his regiment had been flanked, very briefly. But he would never concede that his enemy had penetrated so deeply as Oates asserted. The dispute would make enemies of the former officers 40 years after the war ended.[20]

This latest and most successful assault told Chamberlain that a crisis was at hand, as did a sudden crash of musketry farther to the rear, giving him the mistaken impression that his regiment had been surrounded. With sunset coming on, assailed in front as well as from the opposite direction, his line bent and battered and one section of it teetering on collapse, perhaps half his men down with wounds, and the able-bodied left with a round or two in their cartridge boxes, he realized, as he wrote in his battle report, "it was too evident that we could maintain the *defensive* no longer." If they could not hold on, and if they could not retreat without violating their orders, there was but one recourse—to shift over to the offensive.[21]

Chamberlain is generally given credit for accepting the risks inherent in assuming an offensive posture in his regiment's weakened condition. It is true that the shift invited danger; Napoleon himself called the transition from the defensive to the offensive one of the most delicate maneuvers in all of warfare. Yet it was a natural response—in fact, the only response—Chamberlain could have made under the circumstances. The specific source of his inspiration is impossible to determine although the operation was a staple of military tactics. The maneuver had been resorted to innumerable times since the dawn of warfare, and its value had been trumpeted by such diverse tacticians as the eighth-century Chinese warrior Tu Yu and Germany's Frederick the Great. In the present war, the tactic had been exploited successfully on several occasions. Robert E. Lee is said to have remarked of one of his battles, "I was too wreak to defend, so I attacked."[22]

On the present occasion, Chamberlain's instincts alone may have suggested the desirability of this course. More likely, he recalled examples from his early-war textbooks, including Captain Duparcq's volume. Chamberlain's copy of this work contains a heavily underlined reference to the 1805 battle of Caldiero. In that struggle the commander of a French force, finding himself cut off and surrounded by Austrian legions, launched a bayonet charge whose unexpectedness and ability to inspire terror carried the day.[23]

Whatever its antecedents, Chamberlain loudly announced his decision to resort to cold steel. He envisioned a simultaneous charge by both his wings that would so surprise and overwhelm Oates's troops that they would turn and flee—as the Austrians had—before first contact was made. He never got further, however, than the order to fix bayonets, which, as he wrote four days after the fight, "flew from man to man. The click of the steel seemed to give new zeal to all. The men dashed forward with a shout...."[24]

Few men reported hearing Chamberlain order the charge. Ellis Spear, for one, did not get the word to attack until well after Clark's wing had started out, and thus the left flank joined in the assault belatedly. Spear, now-Lieutenant Holman Melcher, and other members of the regiment agreed that the charge was a spontaneous expression of pent-up emotion by many men acting at the same time. In fact, the movement had originated as an effort by Melcher and other soldiers

Engraving depicting the 20th Maine at Little Round Top.

holding the center of the line to rescue wounded comrades who lay a short distance to the front. These casualties had fallen within the 20th Maine's line, but that line had fallen back some distance under Oates's pounding. When the rescuers in the center went forward, so did the color guard; and when the color guard went forward, so did every member of the regiment who could see the flags.[25]

Novels and films, as well as some history books, have painted a picture of Chamberlain not only ordering but leading the charge. No participant ever testified to that effect, except for some postwar reunion speakers who gave the colonel credit for everything the 20th Maine accomplished that day. Although he did take part in the movement, it is doubtful that Chamberlain, who had been twice slightly wounded including in the right instep, could have gotten in front of everyone else to lead the way.

While Chamberlain never sought credit for leading the downhill assault, he did profess to have ordered it, all evidence to the contrary notwithstanding. His battle report, contained in the 128-volume *War of the Rebellion: A Compilation of the Official Records of the Union and Confederate Armies*, contains no such claim; in fact, the report appears to argue that the regiment charged of its own initiative as soon as it received the order to fix bayonets. The *Official Records* fails to indicate, however, that Chamberlain's report was not composed until 1884, 21 years after the date it carries. Having been informed by government editors that his original report had been lost; Chamberlain recreated it from memory—but did an incomplete job.[26]

Unknown to some historians, a copy of the original report, written on July 6, 1863, is extant. It includes Chamberlain's contention that "as a last, desperate resort, I ordered a *charge*." He repeated the same claim, but in different language, in a postwar speech as well as in an 1896 memoir that he contributed to a volume of reminiscences by Medal of Honor winners. Civil War students familiar with this claim wonder why Chamberlain made it. The obvious answer is that he believed it to be true. He might not have had time to give the order aloud, but it was there in his mind and he had told at least one man, Lieutenant Melcher, that he was about to utter it. The result of the charge confirmed Chamberlain's faith in its effectiveness and validated the risks he took in conceiving it. Why should he not receive credit for acting on his own idea, an idea that saved Little Round Top, the army's left flank, and perhaps the army itself? Then, too, given his literary proclivities, the symbolism inherent in his leading a charge he himself had set in motion would have been an irresistible influence.

As to why he backed away from his contention in postwar years, by 1884 the idea of a "soldier's battle," a spontaneous movement lacking a guiding hand, had become an accepted piece of Gettysburg lore. Chamberlain did not wish to add to the controversies over, and the conflicting claims stemming from, the fighting of July 2, 1863, especially when that fight had produced plenty of glory for all involved.[27]

A major reason for the attention given to the charge, and especially to the issue of its paternity, was its outstanding success, success destined to resonate through the decades. Just as Chamberlain had foreseen, just as his French predecessor had discovered, a downhill charge with the bayonet generated unstoppable momentum and scared the wits out of the foe. Even before the charge was launched, Oates's men were in critical condition, having exhausted themselves in their succession of almost-successful advances. When the 20th Maine slammed into them from above, the gray line cracked and broke apart, human splinters flying in all directions.

Although Chamberlain in later years tried to give a different impression, the formation assumed by the charging troops was neither preordained nor precisely executed. In at least three of his postwar writings, including his 1884 report, the 20th Maine's commander claimed to have implemented an extended right wheel. In response, his regiment swept by its left flank across the eastern, southern, and southwestern slopes of Little Round Top, clearing Rebels from the ever-widening arc of its advance. Over the years some students of military history have transformed the maneuver into a double right wheel. Historians familiar with the battle and the battlefield, however, reject both notions.[28]

Chamberlain did not order a right wheel, and his men did not perform one. Whereas Captain Clark's wing charged straight ahead, in a southwestward direction, Spear's wing rushed down the eastern slope, running "over scattered men of the enemy in advance of their own line concealed by the boulders." One of Spear's men recalled of the Confederates in his path, "they had but little time to choose between surrender or cold steel." Once at the base Spear's companies, in hot pursuit of the retreating enemy, took a southward heading toward Big Round Top, where many of Oates's survivors had fled. For all intents, Spear's charge ended at that point and did not constitute a right wheel in coordination with the rest of the 20th Maine.[29]

An event that may have created in Chamberlain's mind the impression of a right wheel was the role played by Captain Morrill's company in harassing Oates's retreat. Since being detached from its regiment, Company B had assumed what modern historians call a "mobile defense." The tiny, isolated band wandered here and there—for the most part between Round Top and the Weikert Farm lane—in search of an enemy force small enough to attack without fear of being annihilated. In this effort it was aided by an unknown number of 2nd U. S. Sharpshooters whom Colonel Oates had driven off Round Top. Company B may also have received support from two companies of skirmishers that had been detached from the 16th Michigan before that regiment was moved from the saddle between the Round Tops to the right of Vincent's line. Even with these additions, Morrill did not consider himself capable of effective action except against a small unit or an incoherent, demoralized force.[30]

He came upon the latter target in the fading light of late afternoon when, in position near the farm lane, his men saw the backs of the 15th Alabama as its men raced down the east and southeast slopes of Little Round Top looking (as their commander himself put it) like "a herd of wild cattle." As if contestants in a turkey shoot, the Mainers and their comrades poured round after round into the runaways, causing them to redouble the pace of their flight. The fire intensified as Morrill pursued his quarry along a line from northeast to southwest, until finally stopped by the company of the 15th Alabama that Oates had sent to capture ordnance wagons. Noting the effect of Company B's pursuit but uncertain of the unit's identity, Chamberlain may have been strengthened in his impression that a right wheel had indeed occurred, in accordance with his order.[31]

As the counterattack continued, Chamberlain, either running or limping, accompanied Clark's people down Little Round Top as they swept up the left flank companies of the 15th Alabama and the remnants of the scattered 47th. En route, the colonel claims, he was challenged by a gray officer whose pistol misfired at point-blank range, sending a ball scorching past Chamberlain's head. After sending his assailant to the rear as a prisoner, Chamberlain reached the base of the hill, where he helped his men round up Rebels prevented from escaping by the speed of the assault.[32]

His hasty count included upwards of 400 captives—not only members of Oates's two regiments but, as Chamberlain claimed, also men of the 4th and 5th Texas of Robertson's brigade. Modern-day calculations suggest that the two Alabama regiments Chamberlain opposed lost only 123 men captured or missing, out of 231 casualties of all types. Whatever the toll, Oates had suffered grievously, as had Chamberlain, 125 of whose men had been killed or wounded. For its heroics the 20th Maine had paid a steep price, but that cost had bought the safety of the Union left flank at a critical time in the battle. That realization salved the pain of injury and loss as much as humanly possible.[33]

Now panting at the base of the hill, Chamberlain's soldiers could hardly believe the success their charge had gained, especially given the difficulties under which it had been launched. As Elisha Coan observed after the battle, people do not always "know what we are capable of untill [sic] we are actually brought into circumstances that will try us." Yet he and his comrades knew how to handle the accolades sure to come their way. "There was glory enough earned on Little Round Top," wrote William Livermore, "for every participant from our distinguished and honored Col. to the humblest private who did his duty."[34]

* * *

To place the 20th Maine's achievement in proper perspective, some facts must be taken into account that may tend to diminish the odds the regiment overcame as well as the strategic significance of its counterattack. By the time they charged, the Mainers had been fighting an enemy weakened by hours of uphill climbing and heavy fighting under a torrid sun and without water. Legend has Chamberlain's regiment battling two-to-one odds, but due to Oates's many detachments, for at least a portion of the fight on Little Round Top almost 500 defenders engaged fewer than 400 attackers. Furthermore, just before the 20th Maine resorted to the bayonet, Oates, aware of his outfit's capabilities and appreciating the futility of further resistance, had begun to withdraw from the struggle. Out of position when attacked, his troops had no recourse but to flee as fast as they could.

As for the value of the Mainers' climactic charge, for decades historians have termed it critical to the Army of the Potomac's ability to remain on Cemetery Ridge. If one regards Gettysburg as the war's most important battle, it is possible to view the successful defense of Little Round Top as the pivotal action of the entire conflict, the single occurrence most responsible for the triumph of Union arms. This theory rests on the supposition that had the left flank gone under, Confederate victory at Gettysburg would have been assured.

While a case can be made to support this view, there appear to be good reasons for rejecting it. Had the 20th Maine been forced off its spur, Oates's attackers would have had to contend with the other regiments in Vincent's brigade, some of which were fresher and less battle-scarred than Chamberlain's. Assuming that the Alabamians could have uprooted these troops as well, they would have had to contend with the 140th New York as well as with other potential reinforcements including much of the 3rd Division, Fifth Corps, under Brigadier General Samuel W. Crawford.[35]

Even had Oates's thirsty, bone-weary men overcome all this opposition, they could not have held the ground they took without artillery support. As one chronicler of the 20th Maine has pointed out, the Confederates would have been hard-pressed to find enough room on the captured crest to train more than eight guns on the Federal line farther north. "No eight cannons on Little Round Top," he writes, "under fire from dozens of Federal batteries in response, could have destroyed any significant portion of the Union army that day." Thus, while well-conducted, highly effective, and gloriously successful, the bayonet charge down Little Round Top does not appear to have played a critical role in forestalling a disaster from which the Army of the Potomac could not have recovered.[36]

* * *

The 20th Maine had relatively little time to bask in the glow of its triumph. Not long after Oates's men had fled, Law's and Robertson's troops farther north either withdrew or clung to positions along the west slope of Little Round Top, hoping to renew their advance on July 3. In gathering darkness Chamberlain was still counting heads and tending to his wounded and prisoners when Colonel Rice of the 44th New York came looking for him. After congratulating Chamberlain on his imaginative defense, Rice announced that he was now in command of the brigade, Colonel Vincent having been carried to a hospital in the rear.

Rice also gave a situation report. The balance of the brigade that included the 140th New York had arrived to help hold the right flank. The infantry was now supported by a battery of light artillery whose guns had been manhandled up the rocky slope. Additionally, portions of Crawford's division, including the Pennsylvania brigade of Colonel Joseph W. Fisher, had assumed a reserve position behind Little Round Top. Rice, therefore, was no longer concerned about the safety of the hill he occupied; when he left Chamberlain he appeared to be in an optimistic mood.[37]

Other commanders were less sanguine about the 3rd Brigade's ability to hold its position. A little after 9:00 P.M. Rice returned to Chamberlain's field headquarters, carrying an order from General Sykes to secure the high ground to the south so as to neutralize the strategic position Oates's survivors had gained following their repulse. Rice told Chamberlain he had directed Fisher's brigade to chase the Rebels off Round Top but that Fisher had demurred, citing his unfamiliarity with the situation and the terrain. Frustrated, Rice asked his subordinate to take on the job. A weary Chamberlain hesitated. As he wrote a few days later, "the men were worn out, and heated and thirsty almost beyond endurance. Many had sunk down and fallen asleep the instant the halt was ordered." Still, he would not refuse an order, even one couched in the form of a request.[38]

Fearing that not everyone was up to the task, Chamberlain asked for volunteers to accompany him and the color guard up Round Top. To a man, it is said, the 20th Maine stepped forward and followed him up the heavily timbered north slope. While most of these men had exhausted their ammunition in the fight against Oates and Bulger, their leader noted in his post-battle report that they had been resupplied with 3,000 rounds brought up late in the day by Colonel Rice. Curiously, in a postwar account that has received much attention Chamberlain asserted that "without waiting to get further ammunition, but trusting in part to the very circumstances of not exposing our movement or our small front by firing, and with bayonets fixed, the little handful of two hundred men pressed up the mountainside in very extended order, as the steep and jagged surface of the ground compelled." By spreading his force so widely he ensured that it would cover as much ground as possible while minimizing casualties should bullets come out of the darkness in response to its approach.[39]

The movement did attract a scattering of rifle fire but fire delivered hastily and inaccurately, as if the shooters were in the act of fleeing. Without returning fire, the Mainers managed to capture 10 members of the skirmish line Colonel Oates had established on Round Top. The other Rebels retreated to prepared positions on the hill's southern and western slopes.

Having broken their opponents' line with little effort, Chamberlain's men suddenly whirled to the right in response to a crash of rifle fire. Belatedly they learned that Colonel Fisher had been persuaded to send two regiments to cover their flank. The Pennsylvanians had provided precious little support, however, before drawing the fire of Alabama troops part way down the west slope. With that, Fisher's troops took off for home, leaving Chamberlain and his 200 men alone on the crest.[40]

Although some historians downplay or suppress the fact, Chamberlain, concerned about his ability to hold his position in the dark against an unknown force, also decided to clear out. Supposedly he withdrew because he lacked enough ammunition to guarantee staying-power, but it would appear that he wanted closer, longer-lasting support than Colonel Fisher could provide. After establishing a heavy picket line on the summit, he withdrew the rest of his troops and formed them at the foot of the heights they had climbed perhaps an hour before. Once in contact with the 3rd Brigade, Chamberlain lined up support from portions of the 83rd Pennsylvania and 44th New York. Backed by soldiers presumably blessed with more fortitude than Fisher's brigade, Chamberlain returned his men to the summit, where he augmented the pickets he had left behind and established an occupation zone.

The 20th Maine remained atop the wooded hill for several hours without incident. Despite the nearness of the enemy's skirmishers, the invaders took no casualties. During the night they were joined by four of Fisher's regiments, including the two that had fled, as well as by other regiments from Barnes's division. Thus secure, the position could do without the 20th Maine, which descended in midmorning of July 3 and retraced its steps up Little Round Top. On the summit, as many of its exhausted men fell dead asleep, the outfit rejoined the rest of its brigade; the two regiments that had accompanied the 20th on its second visit to Round Top had been relieved hours before. Thus ended the seminal phase of the 20th Maine's service at Gettysburg, fated to gleam as the jewel of the regiment's war service.[41]

Disqualifying himself for candidacy as a seer, Chamberlain would always consider the taking of Round Top—despite the minimal opposition he encountered and the few casualties he suffered—as his principal accomplishment at Gettysburg. Somehow he considered the strategic significance of taking the taller hill as outweighing the value of having held the smaller one against tremendous pressure. He could not foresee that the latter exploit would bestow upon his regiment and its leader enduring fame.

Nine

WALKING WOUNDED

*N*ear noon on July 3 the 3rd Brigade, 1st Division, Fifth Army Corps was relieved on Little Round Top by fresh troops and the 20th Maine was permitted to retire from the position it had refused to relinquish to the enemy. The regiment—which thanks to its dogged opponents had been whittled down to fewer than 200 able-bodied officers and men—returned to the site of its recent triumph, now free of blue corpses, discarded weapons, and the other debris of battle. "Nothing but the blood was to be seen," reported William T. Livermore.[1]

After replenishing their cartridge boxes, Chamberlain's troops moved about a mile up the battle line, taking position, along with their comrades from Pennsylvania, New York, and Michigan, behind a stone wall not far from Fifth Corps headquarters. Protected in front by another Fifth Corps brigade, the men of Maine must have felt reasonably safe from enemy missiles for the first time in 48 hours.

In their rear position, the regiment had the time to receive visitors, including members of nearby units who had heard stories of a bayonet charge and craved details. A legend was well on its way to being born. One of the first to seek out and congratulate the regiment was Brigadier General Adelbert Ames, who warmly praised many of the officers and men he had once despaired of turning into soldiers. Earlier that day Ames had sent a hasty note to his old second-in-command that

Chamberlain would long treasure: "I am very proud of the 20th and its present Colonel. I did want to be with you and see your splendid conduct in the field. God bless you and the dear old regiment...." Another visitor, of sorts, was General Meade, who passed the 20th's position late in the morning. Corporal Livermore noted that the regiment gave its old corps leader, who had engineered a great victory only days after taking command of the army, "a tremendous cheer."[2]

Behind its stone wall the regiment passed some easy hours. Private John O'Connell of Company C reported the morning "quiet Except [for] the occasional Picket and skirmish Firing." Suddenly, at about 1:00 P.M., the air for miles around filled with artillery ammunition "the like of which," observed O'Connell, a veteran of the 2nd Maine, "we thought we never heard before although the most of us Passed through the Fiery ordeal of Malvern Hill, Antietam, and Fredericksburg." For hours, according to Private William P. Lamson Jr., of Company B, "there was a shot or shell whizzing through the air all the time. Before one [gun] would stop, another would start." This barrage, the combined might of 120 cannon, constituted the prelude to a climactic assault that Lee had decided to hurl against the Union center.[3]

Fortunately for the tired men of the 20th Maine, combat duty was not required of them this day. Their brigade held a position far enough south of the point of attack that they were not called upon to help repulse Pickett's Charge. When not huddling behind the wall, officers and men slipped away to visit the field hospitals in the rear of the lines, checking on the condition of comrades wounded on Little Round Top. Chamberlain was grieved by the death this day of three enlisted men; several other wounded would succumb over the next few weeks, including Captain Billings and Lieutenants Warren Kendall and Arad Linscott.[4]

It could not be determined how many of the injured died from a lack of medical attention at the regimental level. One of the most vexing problems facing the leader of the 20th Maine was filling the position of surgeon that had been vacant since May 18, when Doctor Monroe resigned his commission over a dispute with a board of medical examiners. Two months earlier, Monroe's assistant surgeon had been dismissed for alleged incompetence. Not until mid-month would the arrival of Surgeon John Benson and Assistant Surgeon Abner O. Shaw solve Chamberlain's dilemma. Especially welcome was the bewhiskered Doctor Shaw, a talented, dedicated physician who would remain with the 20th through the rest of the conflict, in the process saving Chamberlain's life at least once.[5]

On July 4, the 76th Independence Day since the founding of the Republic, Chamberlain wrote his wife his first letter since escaping the maelstrom of death on the second. "We are fighting gloriously," he told Fannie, whom he hoped had returned to Brunswick by this time. He informed her of his safety, his regiment's heavy loss and hard-won glory, the enemy's signal defeat, and the mortal wounding of Colonel Vincent ("the greatest loss that could have befallen this Brigade"). He could not refrain from giving his ego the massage it continually needed: "I am receiving all sorts of praise, but bear it meekly."[6]

The glory he spoke of was not in evidence through the remainder of the day, which the 20th Maine spent quietly behind its wall. Nor was it visible the day after, when, along with the rest of what was now Rice's brigade, the regiment advanced well to the front, crossing Willoughby Run and nearing the Emmitsburg Road. The brigade had been ordered to scout out the enemy, but the enemy had fallen back to points unknown. As the high command would eventually discover, Lee, having exhausted his army in three days' worth of flank and frontal assaults—having exhausted as well his patience waiting for Meade to counterattack—had begun to withdraw. By noon of the 5th, the Army of Northern Virginia was well on its way to its native state, ending another promising but unfulfilling invasion. With few exceptions, Lee's troops would never again act so aggressively, so committed to the offensive, as they had on Pennsylvania soil.

Unimpeded, Chamberlain and his men crossed fields that had seen hard fighting on each of the past three days. They picked their way cautiously among scattered corpses in both blue and butternut, the carcasses of battery horses, and discarded weaponry. Many in the regiment took the opportunity to trade their sometimes-contrary Enfield rifles for the Springfields littering their path.[7]

The 20th advanced as far as a barn that had stood between the lines and in which numerous wounded on both sides had taken refuge. The previous day one of the batteries firing in prelude to Pickett's Charge had set the structure afire, killing all within. Corporal William Livermore recoiled when he peered inside to find "skelitons [sic] of men some all burned up others half burned some with only their clothes burned off."[8]

Gruesome sights proliferated. Crossing a field next to the death-filled barn, Livermore's party literally stumbled upon the bodies of three dozen members of a Pennsylvania Zouave regiment that had suffered heavily on the first day of battle. To behold so many corpses in one compact area was bad enough, but, as Livermore wrote, "they had laid there 3 days in hot July weather." In a letter to his brother in Milo, Maine, the distraught corporal stated that, "I wish I never could see another such a sight. It is nothing to see men that have just been killed. But every man was swolen [sic] as large as two men and purple & Black...." In his diary, Livermore added that the bloated corpses "cannot be moved but are buried as well as possible where they fell. The stench is sickening. Men cannot be recognized. I never saw anything like this." He was grateful when, at dusk, the brigade went back to its starting-point; though it recrossed the same littered fields, darkness hid the most hideous scenes.[9]

Similar sights had the same effect on John Chamberlain, who early that day had left his duties at the Fifth Corps field hospital to check on the health of his brothers. Though overjoyed to find the colonel and the adjutant spared from serious wounds, when he accompanied them on the march John shuddered at the harvest of death all around him. There were too many dead men to count and too few living men who could use the medical attention he could give. For the sensitive youngster the day was a terrible kaleidoscope of scenes "I never, never shall forget."[10]

* * *

For the men of Rice's brigade the last 10 days of the Gettysburg campaign were bound to seem anticlimactic, both because of the epic nature of the struggle on Little Round Top and because of the sparse fighting that resulted from the pursuit of Lee across Maryland. At 6:00 A.M. on July 6 the 20th Maine's division, once again under Charles

Griffin, returned to the march, happy to discover that burial teams had been at work since their last advance. Reaching the Emmitsburg Road, the column swung south and followed the flag with the red Maltese Cross toward the city that had given the byway its name. By noon the men were only three miles short of Emmitsburg; at that point, to everyone's surprise and pleasure, Rice's brigade went into bivouac for the balance of the day.[11]

The stopover afforded Chamberlain the time to compose his first after-action report as regimental commander. In eight pages he covered the events extending from his arrival at Little Round Top at 4:00 on the afternoon of the 2nd to noon on the 3rd, when his men were relieved on the higher hill. Curbing his natural tendency to fat and purple prose, he gave a straightforward account of the action on both elevations as he had come to view it. He made no grandiose claims for his regiment, nor for himself—with the exception of maintaining that he had ordered a right-wheel down Little Round Top. He mourned his dead, officers and men, Strong Vincent as well. He quietly congratulated the survivors for their fortitude and determination, and he thanked other elements of the brigade for their "steady and gallant support," singling out the 83rd Pennsylvania for extending its left at a critical point in the fighting on July 2. "Our role of honor," he concluded simply, was that everyone under his command truly "*fought at Gettysburg.*"[12]

Early on the 7th the march continued through Emmitsburg toward Frederick, the not-long-ago campsite of the 20th Maine. Also reminiscent of that pre-Gettysburg period was the marching pace, which so increased this day—as though Meade had Lee trapped on Maryland soil—that despite the sodden weather the regiment made at least 18 miles and as many as 23. The increased rate of travel proved harmful to Chamberlain, who had not felt well for the past week; he may have been running a low-grade fever. When the hard march and the mercurial weather sapped his strength, he was forced to seek rest, as he had when sunstruck on the road to Gettysburg, in roadside homes. Occasionally he also suffered neuralgia attacks reminiscent of his professorial days.

He tried to fight off the body blows. On the rainy afternoon of July

8 he rode at the head of the regiment as it pushed through Middletown and crossed the Catoctin Mountains. The following day he led the way to historic Boonsboro. At Boonsboro, John Chamberlain, himself afflicted with nausea and chills, bade farewell to Joshua and Tom and left the army to recuperate in the rear. After recovering, he would return to Maine, ending a most eventful visit to the army.[13]

John's leave-taking was a sad occasion, but his brothers were buoyed up by news, received later in the day, of a victory in another theater that had implications for the entire war effort. With cheers and catcalls Meade's army greeted word that Ulysses S. Grant had forced the surrender of the Confederate stronghold at Vicksburg, Mississippi. The victory meant not only the capture of a formidable Rebel army but absolute control of the Mississippi River, the most strategic body of water in the war zone.

The news seems to have had a therapeutic effect on Colonel Chamberlain. The next day, July 10, he was well enough to lead the skirmishers of the 3rd Brigade, including Company E of the 20th Maine, into a sharp fight near Jones's Cross Roads, on the pike between Sharpsburg and Hagerstown. In that fracas the 20th Maine supported Colonel Pennock Huey's brigade of Gregg's cavalry division in driving the Rebel rear guard for more than a mile to the south. Under Chamberlain's supervision, the skirmishers resisted enemy attempts to rally and shove them off the pike. For its part in this success, Company E lost two killed and six wounded—the regiment's only combat casualties during the pursuit of Lee.[14]

On July 12, word reached the 3rd Brigade, then in bivouac near Williamsport, Maryland, within sight of the Potomac, that Strong Vincent had died of his July 2 wound. "I grieve for him much," Chamberlain told Fannie, knowing that the brigade, although in James Rice's capable hands, would miss the man whose eye for defensive terrain had made possible the holding of Little Round Top. Later Chamberlain would contribute to a gift memento, a diamond-studded breast pin presented to Vincent's widow on behalf of the brigade staff. Sadly, the news of Vincent's passing came two days after Rice had drawn up the command to announce that, in recognition of the colonel's conspicuous service on July 2, President Lincoln had appointed him a brigadier general of volunteers.[15]

Minus its old commander, the brigade, and the pursuit, went on. Waiting for the rain-swollen Potomac to recede so they might ford and bridge it, Lee's still-ferocious troops lay behind a quickly built but quite formidable series of works that ran from the Potomac at Williamsport southeastward through Downsville and back to the river, enclosing several potential crossing sites including Falling Waters, where pontoons would be laid.

With Lee stranded on the north bank and some of Meade's subordinates clamoring for a strike before he could return to Virginia—others arguing vocally against any offensive—the Union commander made halting efforts to mount an attack. From July 12 through the 14th, Rice's brigade picketed the roads to Williamsport and awaited the call to strike. It never came. Before the army could be put in position to deliver a successful blow, the river lowered and Lee led his army across it on the evening of July 13. By dawn, all but rear-guard forces had gotten over, and Meade's perhaps-golden opportunity was history.[16]

Uncertain of how it should feel—disappointed that a cornered enemy had not been smitten, or thankful that frightening-looking earthworks had not been assaulted—the 20th Maine withdrew from the river on July 15. That morning and afternoon it made a 20-mile march through Keedysville, the passes of South Mountain, and other familiar territory, to a point near Burkittsville, Maryland, where it encamped. On the morning of July 16 it returned to the Potomac at Berlin. Near that village the following afternoon, the men crossed the wide stream on pontoons. Once on the Virginia side Chamberlain led his soldiers five miles inland, hugging the eastern rim of the Blue Ridge. As the Federals marched, Lee's army was moving in the same direction on the opposite side of the mountain.[17]

It was disheartening to think that after its great success at Gettysburg, after all the sacrifices it had made and the sufferings it had endured, the Army of the Potomac was back in Virginia chasing a still-potent, still-mobile foe. More and more, members of Rice's brigade began to feel that a stronger effort should have been made to keep Lee above the Potomac. "I suppose you are all confounded that we did not 'pitch into' him [Lee] at Williamsport," Lieutenant Melcher, the recent successor to Tom Chamberlain as regimental adjutant, remarked in a letter to his brother. "Well I don't wonder. I am afraid that some of the officers of the regular army wish the war to continue, [General George] Sykes for example. Yet I hope they used the best of their judgement [sic] when they objected to the advance on the rebels Monday." A member of the 83rd Pennsylvania, writing at about the same time, damned the faint-hearted subordinates with whom Meade consulted, adding that "no one seems to find fault with Gen Meade except for holding a council of war" when he should have been attacking.[18]

If Chamberlain had regrets of his own, fast-moving events left him no time to brood. On July 17, in camp at Berlin, he received a letter from Fannie dated New York, evidently the last place he expected her to be. In his reply he scolded her, insisting she should never have left home. Because he feared she would not get the letter he had written on July 4, he penned for her another description of the defense of Little Round Top. As usual, he put his own deeds on prominent display: following the heroics of July 2, when "I rode off from the field at the head of my little scarred & battle-stained band the Brigade Commander took me by the hand, & said, 'Col. C. your gallantry was magnificent, & your coolness & skill saved us'."[19]

As if the praise of another colonel were insufficient to stir the response he desired from Fannie, he added the words of General Sykes, that the holding of Chamberlain's position was "one of the most important [achievements] of the day." Even the enemy had heaped praise upon him: "I took several officers in the fight prisoners—& one of them insisted on presenting me with a fine pistol as a reward of merit I suppose...."[20]

In a letter he sent Governor Coburn from Virginia four days later, Chamberlain offered a further description of his own and his regiment's deeds at Gettysburg. In this account he muted, but did not eliminate, the self-congratulatory tone that pervaded his letter to Fannie. For the most part he praised his regiment rather than himself, and he refrained from trying to claim credit for the charge that broke the enemy line.

He did exaggerate the casualties he inflicted (claiming prisoners from five regiments, the killing or wounding of 150 Rebels, and the capture of more than 300 others). He claimed, further, that an entire brigade had attacked his position, only to be whipped for the first time in its history.

Alluding to the lack of back-home newspaper publicity given the 20th Maine's role at Gettysburg, Chamberlain indirectly asked the governor to spread the word. Then, perhaps concerned that he had overstepped his bounds, he confided that "I fear I have written too freely but this is not an 'official' letter, & I know you desire to be informed reliably of the service rendered by your Regiments." He did mention his pre-Gettysburg sunstroke, from which he "came near dying" but was "providentially able to lead my gallant fellows into the fight."[21]

Other responsibilities besides private and state correspondence occupied Chamberlain upon his return to Virginia. For two days in mid-July he was placed in command of the 3rd Brigade while Colonel Rice was held in arrest for a minor infraction. The experience was too brief and the level of activity too low to leave any lasting impression. Still, he must have sensed that, given the high casualty rate among the army's ranking officers, he would probably return to brigade command before long. He believed himself fully capable of filling the position on a continuing basis. His leadership abilities extended beyond the command of a few hundred men. Furthermore, he had forged suffi-ciently close ties with the other regimental commanders to feel confident of enjoying a good working relationship with them.[22]

Had Rice not been released from arrest so soon, Chamberlain might have led the 3rd Brigade into a fight. By July 20, still in search of Lee's army, the command had come 35 miles since crossing the Potomac. On July 22, Rice guided it southwestward to Rectortown, and the following day directly west toward Manassas Gap in the Blue Ridge. Cavalry under Brigadier General John Buford had seized that mountain pass with the intent of holding it till the army's infantry advance guard, the Third Corps, arrived. Meade's hope—one he communicated to his ranking subordinates—was that the main army push through the gap quickly enough to slice through Lee's thin, elongated marching column on the other side. That done, Meade stood a fine chance of cutting off portions of his enemy's army, defeating each in turn, and completing the destruction begun at Gettysburg.

Late on July 22, Major General William H. French, commanding the Third Corps while Dan Sickles recovered from his Gettysburg wound, reported having taken possession of the east side of the gap, relieving Buford. The next morning French advanced to clear the gap, only to find the way blocked by a small but combative force of infantry. As the unequal confrontation began, the Fifth Corps moved up the road from Rectortown in French's rear. Chamberlain and his regiment spent the day waiting and listening, trying to determine from the sound of the fighting whether a breakthrough had come. It had not. Although French eventually pried the defenders loose, later in the day he was confronted by another line of battle, this one atop lofty, rugged ground known as Wapping Heights. French sent skirmishers down the rocky heights, but although some Confederates were driven out, day's end found the Third Corps on the wrong side of the gap.[23]

Next morning, Griffin's division went forward to spell French's skirmishers. According to Samuel L. Miller of the 20th Maine, General Griffin drew up the command and instructed it to take Wapping Heights at all costs. The position—which consisted of three jagged, foliage-rich hills just north of Manassas Gap—proved to be, as the historian of the 83rd Pennsylvania put it, "the most difficult place over which troops ever advanced in line of battle." In addition to climbing steep slopes, Private Miller and his comrades advanced "through woods and tangled underbrush ... expecting the enemy to open fire at every step." That thought danced in the heads of many men; Holman Melcher remarked that "I was impressed with the solemnity of being shot and buried in such a place...."[24]

Chamberlain agreed with the consensus that Wapping Heights, even more so than Little Round Top, was dangerous ground on which to mount an offensive. In a letter to Fannie he called the movement up the high ground "one of the very hardest we ever had [to make] in the way of natural obstacles, craggy ascents, deep ravines—mountain torrents, treacherous morasses—wild vines & woody thickets—all these in the burning sun & at the 'double quick'...."[25]

At least he did not have to add being shot at to this list of hazards. When his men, their clothing torn, their knees and elbows scraped raw, reached the enemy-held knolls, they found them empty except for a few corpses. In a wire to the War Department, General Meade confirmed that his army's exertions had been in vain: "The enemy had again disappeared, declining battle.... nothing was seen of him but a rear guard of cavalry with a battery of artillery...."[26]

Chamberlain's people spent the balance of July 24 burying the dead, afterwards withdrawing to a mountainside camp, "tired to death," as the colonel noted, "completely wet through as a result of toil & heat." In the relative comfort of his shelter tent, he dashed off a letter to Fannie, praising his latest effort to overtake Robert E. Lee. Then Chamberlain the lover took over, describing his campsite as "a sweet smiling valley between ... the breasts of the Mountain." The sexual connotation stirred him, prompting him to tell his wife of his plans to fall asleep "looking at the moonlight ... in that 'vale' & dream myself there. A kiss & [a] thousand thoughts of you till the early bugle call."[27]

* * *

Chamberlain had been ill throughout the advance up the heights. In his love-struck letter, he told Fannie that "I am not well yet," a fact he hoped would "account for my slight unsoundness of mind." He suspected his sickness dated from his mid-June sunstroke, but the symptoms—fever and debility—seemed more severe this time.[28]

In the days following Wapping Heights, those symptoms worsened. By July 27, with his regiment in camp near Warrenton, several miles southeast of Manassas Gap, he requested of corps headquarters 20 days' leave. "I am convinced," he explained, "that I cannot longer continue these duties without the most serious consequences." His condition continued to deteriorate, but several days passed before his request was approved. Not until July 30 did he leave the 20th Maine with Ellis Spear and go on sick leave. The following day he was admitted to a military hospital in Washington, D. C.[29]

Historians and biographers tend to gloss over this period of illness. Medical personnel who had examined Chamberlain at Warrenton found him to be suffering from a disease without readily identifiable symptoms—"exhaustion of the nervous system produced by the severity of the campaign," in the words of Surgeon Benson. Although an attending physician in Washington claimed to have diagnosed endocarditis, an inflammation of the membrane surrounding the heart, he probably based his finding on the presence of a mild, congenital heart murmur. Significantly, four days later, another hospital surgeon confirmed Doctor Benson's diagnosis, concluding that Chamberlain suffered from "nervous prostration." This generic malady, also known in the medical parlance of the time as "debilitas" or "nostalgia," was a 19th-century version of combat fatigue. While it was a real, not a feigned, illness, the lack of a pathological origin sometimes made the patient look like a malingerer. Perhaps modern-day historians view Chamberlain's illness in this way and are too embarrassed to discuss it.[30]

Chamberlain spent only a few days in the hospital; by August 7 he was at home in Maine on leave. The family reunion was such a tonic that he felt better immediately. He tried to extend his stay that he might bask longer in the glow of familial warmth, but in mid-August he received a request from Colonel Rice, who desired a furlough of his own, that Chamberlain return and take over the brigade "if your health will permit." Over the protests of his family physician, Doctor Lincoln, who believed Chamberlain's "bad condition of the nervous system" precluded an early return to duty—no doubt over the protests of Fannie Chamberlain as well—the patient boarded a southbound train and by August 24 was reporting at the new camp of the 3rd Brigade near Beverly Ford on the Rappahannock River.[31]

Although still somewhat under the weather, Chamberlain at once relieved Colonel Rice. The 20th Maine would continue under the leadership of Ellis Spear, whose long-overdue promotion to major had just come through, until Lieutenant Colonel Gilmore returned from his latest, extended sick leave on August 28. Gilmore would not stay, however; phantom ills would soon return him to the hospital. Thanks to Spear's majority, the 20th would at least remain under the command of a field-grade officer.[32]

Chamberlain would not command his Mainers again for nine months, a situation that would sadden him. As he wrote to Governor

Coburn one day after returning to the army, "I regret being thus obliged to leave even temporarily, the noble Regiment with which I have shared so many hardships & perils, & not a few honors too, but I shall have it still under my eye, & in any case, I shall spare no effort to maintain its high & deserved reputation." He could not take credit for organizing the 20th Maine or whipping it into shape—that honor would always accrue to Adelbert Ames. But he could boast that he had played a major role in bringing the regiment to its present level of effectiveness. He had led it through its most trying times and in such a way as to win imperishable fame for its every member. Accomplishments such as these and the happy memories they would always evoke would go far toward assuaging the pain of separation and loss.[33]

* * *

On August 26, two days after Chamberlain entered upon his new duties, Colonel Rice received word of his appointment as brigadier general of volunteers and his transfer to the First Army Corps. Upon his departure, Chamberlain was officially named to command the 3rd Brigade, 1st Division, Fifth Army Corps. For this honor he could principally thank General Griffin, who at Fredericksburg and Chancellorsville had been impressed by his subordinate's leadership, coolness under fire, and combative spirit. Later Chamberlain would recall with gratitude that more than once during the fall of 1863, Griffin resisted efforts to replace his newest brigade leader with more senior officers sent to him for assignment.[34]

Some of Chamberlain's new troops wondered what Griffin knew that they did not. A few appear to have resented Chamberlain's accession to a position once held by a favorite commander. The historian of the 44th New York, General Rice's old regiment, recalling that Chamberlain had briefly led the brigade the previous month, claimed that "there was some opposition manifested to his being returned to command...." The orderly to the late, lamented Strong Vincent, Private Oliver Willcox Norton of the 83rd Pennsylvania, described Chamberlain in letters to his family as "a very fine man, though but little posted in military matters" and "not much of a military man."[35]

It does not take much of a military man to witness an execution, one of Chamberlain's first duties in brigade command. On August 29 five bounty-jumpers from a Pennsylvania outfit were shot in front of the entire Fifth Corps as an example of what deserters could expect. The macabre, drawn-out spectacle concluded with the firing squad knocking four of the condemned men atop the coffins on which thay had been placed but leaving the fifth sitting upright, quite dead but looking too much alive for the comfort of some spectators.[36]

After the corps was dismissed, a disgusted member of the 20th Maine observed that, "it is a very solemn thing to see human beings led forth to be shot like dogs." The memory of the day made him shiver: "Those who witness such scenes receive an impression that can never be shaken off." A comrade had his doubts; after the war John O'Connell recalled that among the spectators to the execution were numerous substitutes and conscripts, the first of this ilk most of the regiments in the corps had ever seen: "Still this had no Effect for scores of them deserted shortly after arriving in Camp." Whatever the effect of the spectacle on Acting Brigadier General Chamberlain, he revealed nothing of it in the letters he wrote home in after days; these he filled with sweet nothings for his wife, adoring references to his children, and virtually nothing about military matters.[37]

He found that he had taken up brigade command at a propitious time. Because battle was not imminent, he was granted quiet weeks in which to assimilate his new duties. He spent much of his time solidifying his relationships with ranking subordinates, overseeing their drill programs with special emphasis on tutoring the new arrivals, inspecting their camps along the river, and making recommendations to General Meade for promotions.

In turn, others sought for him the rank his new position called for. On September 8 the newly minted General Rice wrote Senator William Fessenden of Maine, asking his help in rewarding with a brigadier's star "this gallant officer's skill and bravery upon the battle field, his ability in drill and discipline, and his fidelity to duty in camp," not to mention his "Christian character." A few days later General Barnes, now commanding the 1st Brigade, 1st Division, Fifth Corps, also supported Chamberlain's candidacy, citing his defense of Little Round

Top against "a much superior force" and lauding his "gallant charge upon the enemy."[38]

A week after Barnes wrote, General Adelbert Ames sent a letter of recommendation directly to Secretary of War Edwin M. Stanton, in which he praised his former subordinate as "a most zealous, faithful and efficient officer." On September 27 Governor Coburn likewise wrote the Secretary of War in Chamberlain's behalf, citing his "gallant & splendid soldiership." Charles Griffin weighed in 10 days later, recommending Chamberlain to the notice of army headquarters as an "officer of education and ability.... He has always exhibited excellent judgement [sic] on the battle field." National as well as state political leaders sang Chamberlain's praises. On October 16, Vice President Hannibal Hamlin, an ex-Democrat and a favorite son of Maine, wrote his boss, Abraham Lincoln, seeking promotion for the former commander of the 20th Volunteers.[39]

Although there is no specific evidence to suggest that Chamberlain had a hand in the filing of these recommendations, it is possible—given the instructions he occasionally sent Fannie to work local and state politicians in his behalf—that he was involved in at least a peripheral way. No doubt the sentiments expressed by those supporting him were genuine, but the fact that their letters were sent over the same six-week period suggests some effort at orchestration.

* * *

In mid-September, activity along the Rappahannock heated up briefly, providing Chamberlain his first field campaigning on the brigade level. On the 13th the army began to cross the river in response to reports that its enemy had scurried southward. The reports proved true: Lee was withdrawing below the line of the Rapidan River in the direction of Orange Court House. Later his opponent learned the reason: a recent conference with President Jefferson Davis in Richmond had persuaded the general to detach James Longstreet's corps and send it covertly to Tennessee, where Federal troops had seized the vital communications center of Chattanooga.

·On September 16, as the main body of the Army of the Potomac followed its advance echelon south, Chamberlain supervised a fording of the Rappahannock. Next day he placed his regiments in camp two miles below the county seat of Culpeper Court House. There they would remain, except for temporary excursions toward the Rapidan River, until the second week of October.[40]

From his new camp he continued to keep Governor Coburn posted on the condition of the 20th Maine as if he had never left it. Charles Gilmore, he told the governor, was again on leave—this time not to play sick but to answer dozens of lawsuits pending against him back home, relating to his tenure as sheriff of Penobscot County (less than two weeks hence, Gilmore, having returned to the army, would depart it again, this time with what appears to have been an actual illness). With or without its lieutenant colonel, Chamberlain assured the governor, the 20th Maine was well taken care of, its officers "performing their duty with great faithfulness & credit." An uncommon restraint kept him from naming names; to any list of dedicated performers he would have added the recently promoted Captain Thomas D. Chamberlain.[41]

While maintaining a lively interest in his old regiment, Chamberlain perforce gave most of his attention to the 3rd Brigade. At Culpeper he ensured that each morning at 9:00 sharp every regiment was drilled by battalions in accordance with Volume II of Casey's *Infantry Tactics*. He even decreed that certain lessons be given greater attention, one day stressing dispositions for opposing a cavalry charge.[42]

At the end of the month, when General Meade reviewed the 3rd Brigade, Chamberlain proudly put his regiments through their paces on his windblown parade ground. Private Norton of the 83rd Pennsylvania wrote his sister that, "we had not had a review for some time and it was quite a novelty. It passed off very well. Casualties none, prisoners none and not much of anything else but dust."[43]

* * *

On October 9 the serenity of camp life between the Rappahannock and Rapidan ended abruptly when Lee crossed the lower river and headed for Meade's right flank. "Marse Robert" had learned that in response to his detachment of Longstreet—an operation that had enabled their western comrades to win at Chickamauga on September

19—Meade had made a similar move. Less than a week after the disaster in northern Georgia, the Eleventh and Twelfth Corps, O. O. Howard at the head of the former, had entrained for Chattanooga, to which their defeated comrades had withdrawn to weather a siege. Now Lee wished to exploit his opponent's weakness by seeking to turn his right flank via a march in the direction of Washington—a move sure to spread panic throughout the government and perhaps through its field forces as well.[44]

Enjoined by the War Department to remain on the defensive until the safety of the capital was assured, Meade reluctantly ordered a withdrawal above the Rappahannock—only to return three of his corps, including the Fifth, to the south bank on October 12 to reconnoiter the area just vacated. Having broken camp early on the 10th to head north, Chamberlain now took his brigade in the opposite direction. He led the way southward aboard Charlemagne, a newly acquired chestnut-colored mount with a Morgan bloodline, formerly the property of a Rebel officer. Some skirmishing occurred below the river but not on the Fifth Corps' front, denying Charlemagne's new owner his first chance to maneuver a brigade under fire.[45]

By October 13 everyone was again turning north, Meade having ascertained that Lee was moving toward his enemy's right under a full head of steam. The line of march carried the entire army—lock, stock, and baggage wagons—up the Orange & Alexandria in the direction of Centreville and the Bull Run battlefields. Early on the 14th, Chamberlain was again cheated of an opportunity to perform in battle. Marching on the west side of the railroad, the 3rd Brigade crossed Kettle Run, not far from Bristoe Station, then halted to boil coffee and devour hardtack. In that position its rear suddenly came under artillery fire. Anxious to retaliate, Chamberlain got his men into line, only to be told by General Griffin to move north without further delay. The order was obeyed without comment.[46]

When shooting continued to the south, everyone in Chamberlain's command realized that the army's rear guard—the Second Army Corps, led by former Chief Engineer G. K. Warren, "the savior of Little Round Top"—was under attack near the Orange & Alexandria depot called Bristoe Station. In addition to the sounds of continued firing, grumbling and grousing accompanied the movement north. Late in the afternoon Chamberlain's soldiers rested in the fields around Manassas Junction, where they expected to remain despite the fracas to the south.

An hour before sundown, the brigade was suddenly ordered to Warren's support. A captain in the 83rd Pennsylvania complained that, "we double-quicked about two miles, during which a great many fell out from fatigue and most of the substitutes took good care never to fall in again." The killing pace went for naught; in the darkness of evening the reinforcements reached Bristoe only to discover that the Rebels had drawn off after a drubbing by the Second Corps. While happy over the result, the brigade was more than a little tired of being yanked, puppet-fashion, in one direction after another. A private in the 44th New York complained about marching "night & day, first forward & then back *double quick* to protect the rear" and without any apparent effect.[47]

After spending a day near the battle-scarred depot, the men of Chamberlain's command retraced their steps under what Private O'Connell called a "fearful Thunder storm." They followed the railroad to Fairfax Court House and across Bull Run to Centreville. Given the hard marching so recently demanded of them, and the miserable weather they marched through, it is not surprising that some of Chamberlain's men straggled on the Centreville road. After sending back a bugler to guide the "play-outs" to their new bivouac via the brigade call, Chamberlain was sitting his new horse in the rain when General Sykes and his corps headquarters entourage rode up. Dimly visible in the darkness, Sykes gruffly called on Chamberlain to identify himself, then berated him for losing so many troops to fatigue, offering the opinion that Chamberlain "could not assemble them for any purpose."[48]

Stung by the unmerited rebuke although uncertain of its source, Chamberlain shot back a heated reply: "I can conceive of no 'purpose' governing this move, but this bugle-call would bring my men through Hell!" Sykes, clearly displeased by the retort, asked Chamberlain if he realized he was talking to his corps commander. Chamberlain had not, but he quickly recovered his composure, replying that General Sykes "would thank me for showing him through this muddle." His mollified superior rode on, calling back that "you are a little sharp on compliments, but I think you will get your men up."[49]

* * *

Above Bull Run, in common with the rest of the army, Chamberlain's troops threw up breastworks and waited for Lee to attack. Skirmishing broke out at points along the stream but no large-scale Confederate offensive materialized. Unwilling to repeat a mistake he had made on July 3, Lee drew off, and by October 17 the fighting along Bull Run began to wind down. Soon the Army of Northern Virginia, having discarded its plan to outflank Meade on the road to Washington, was trudging back to the Rappahannock line.

After determining that Lee had vacated the area, Meade ordered a cautious pursuit. By the 24th, after what Ellis Spear called "a slow and tedious march," the 3rd Brigade was back on the Orange & Alexandria, this time outside the village of Auburn. There it camped for a fortnight as an early hint of winter blew through the Rappahannock basin. Before October was out, a veteran of the 44th New York was complaining that "the days and nights are intensely cold and ... very uncomfortable all the while."[50]

The weather began to affect Chamberlain, leaving him feverish and achy as he returned to a life of stationary warfare. As always, his response to illness was to fight through it. In peak condition or not, he kept to his duties, making the rounds of his camps, inspecting the picket lines, overseeing the drill program, interrogating deserters and prisoners from the front. In off-duty moments he kept up his voluminous correspondence with the home front, read Emerson and Byron, and devoured the newspapers, staying up-to-date on the progress of the war in all theaters. He rejoiced when he read that Ulysses Grant, with the army that had captured Vicksburg plus the reinforcements from Virginia, had not only relieved Chattanooga but in a series of brilliantly executed battles had obliterated the besiegers. The victories in Tennessee had made Grant the man of the hour, the brightest star in the Union firmament. Chamberlain must have wondered what it would be like to serve under such a commander.

As November came in, the weather in middle Virginia gyrated

between warm days and cold nights, and cold days and cold nights. The fluctuations in temperature took their toll on Chamberlain, as did an unexpected spate of hard campaigning. By November 6, as an officer in another Maine regiment, an acquaintance of Chamberlain's, noted in his diary, elements of several corps were poised for action near the point at which the railroad crossed the Rappahannock, "every Regiment being doubled on the centre so as to deploy at a moment's warning. How soon we shall move is only a matter of conjecture, but we all expect to be off very soon."[51]

The young officer was prescient: on the frosty morning of November 7 large portions of the Fifth and Sixth Corps, the whole under the latter's commander, Major General John Sedgwick, readied a surprise assault on the well-fortified bridgehead at Rappahannock Station. Supported by much of the rest of the army, which crossed the river a few miles below the railroad, the Sixth Corps made for the riverline defenses, only to be tossed back with loss. An inconclusive artillery duel consumed the rest of the afternoon.

Skirmishers culled from each regiment in Chamberlain's brigade had supported the ill-fated advance; the force included 80 men of the 20th Maine under Walter Morrill. Defeated in daylight, a party of the Sixth Corps finally took the position by storm under cover of darkness. Although not designated a part of the attack force, Captain Morrill's men advanced alongside their leader's old regiment, the 6th Maine of Sedgwick's command, and had a major part in the fighting. Prisoners were numerous; they included five officers and 65 enlisted men snatched up by Morrill, who for his service this day would win a Congressional Medal of Honor.[52]

Chamberlain's role in the victory was brief, unsatisfying, and no doubt painful. Carrying his rider on a reconnaissance preceding the evening attack, Charlemagne stopped a minie ball, stumbled, fell, and tossed Chamberlain to the ground. Rising mostly unhurt from the accident—the third time a horse had been shot from under him—the colonel led his injured but still serviceable steed to the rear, where the bulk of his brigade had gone into a wooded bivouac.[53]

The after-effects of Chamberlain's fall appear to have been few but the rigorous service demanded of him in winter-like weather aggravated his existing illness. Within a few days of the fight at Rappahannock Station, with the brigade now stationed on the south side of the river, he made the mistake of sleeping outdoors while snow fell. By morning his temperature began to climb and his strength to ebb. He managed to keep going for a few days, attending to his ordained duties, but on November 13 he collapsed, and a surgeon was sent for. His condition was reported to be serious enough that Brigadier General John J. Bartlett, temporarily commanding Griffin's division, ordered Chamberlain to Washington for hospitalization.[54]

On the 17th Chamberlain, accompanied by staff officers and a doctor, took an empty cattle car—the first available transportation—to the Seminary Hospital in Georgetown. While he traveled, his adjutant, Lieutenant William E. Dowell, informed Fannie of her husband's condition, calling his affliction "malarial fever," adding that "he is not in serious danger, but the fever is slow in spending its force and leaves one very low."[55]

In trying to allay the fears of a loved one, Lieutenant Dowell underestimated the gravity of his superior's condition. By the time he reached the District of Columbia, Chamberlain was unconscious.[56]

Bvt.-Major Joshua L. Chamberlain.
(Courtesy of the Library of Congress)

Ten

PERFECT TARGET

Some of Chamberlain's chroniclers, taking their cue from the findings of the attending physician, misdiagnose him as suffering from malaria. There are no prior references in Chamberlain's medical history to malaria, and it seems unlikely that his first exposure to a tropical malady would have occurred in a snowstorm. By using the term "malarial," the surgeon meant that his patient was suffering from a recurrent fever, as he had during the post-Gettysburg campaigning. As indicated by his having lost consciousness, Chamberlain's present condition was graver than his earlier illness, but, as before, its pathological origin would remain undetermined.

He reached Seminary Hospital in Georgetown on November 19, the same day that Abraham Lincoln delivered a brief speech on the battlefield at Gettysburg. Under the ministrations of the physicians who staffed that officers-only hospital, the patient quickly regained his senses but took time to recover from the other effects of his illness. More than a week after his admittance, the hospital's chief surgeon found him suffering from "extreme debility…. He is still confined to his bed and is unable to travel." By then, at least, he was in good hands. In response to the hurried note of Chamberlain's adjutant, Fannie had arrived to supplement the care being given her husband. Also attending the patient was a volunteer nurse, Miss Mary Keene, whose devotion so warmed Chamberlain's heart that years later he helped her—by then a widow—obtain a much-needed and gratefully received pension.[1]

By early December, thanks largely to the support of his wife, Chamberlain was well enough to help cheer the other sufferers around him. One was a Doctor Robinson, the assistant surgeon of a New York cavalry regiment, whose mortal wound would take his life three months hence. Robinson's wife, who despite being several months pregnant attended him at the hospital, was grateful for the kindness the Chamberlains showed her and her husband. Twenty-four years later, following a Memorial Day address by Chamberlain back home in Maine, Mrs. Robinson would greet her husband's benefactor, thanking him anew and introducing him to the daughter the doctor had not lived to see.[2]

By mid-month Chamberlain had progressed sufficiently to apply, with some hope of success, for a holiday furlough in Maine. His optimism proved warranted: on December 17 he left the hospital, a bit unsteadily, Fannie at his side. The couple boarded a train for Brunswick, arriving a few days before Christmas. Chamberlain continued to recover at home, where the nearness of children, parents, and friends, as well as the uplifting theme of the season, soothed him and helped him regain his strength.

While convalescing, Chamberlain kept informed, as best he could, of the war news. Information gleaned from the newspapers, supplemented by first-hand accounts from fellow officers on furlough, told him that his worst fear would not be realized: the war would not end during his absence. In the last days of November the Army of the Potomac had made an effort to bring the Confederates to bay before winter cancelled active operations. Although launched in hopes of maneuvering Lee out of his works along the Rapidan, the campaign ended in failure when the enemy, reacting to the slow, error-marred offensive, secured its once-vulnerable line along Mine Run. By December 4 the invaders had returned to their dreary camps, Chamberlain's brigade going into winter quarters near Rappahannock Station.[3]

More rested now and in better trim than he had been for months, three weeks after Christmas Chamberlain left home and returned to the Washington suburbs. He reported at the Seminary Hospital on

January 18, where his doctors pronounced him recovered from his fever. On the 27th, Special Order Number 41 from the Adjutant General's Office assigned him to court-martial duty in the capital. He took temporary lodgings in the city, where Fannie soon joined him to nurse him through recurrent, though milder, attacks of the disease that had removed him from the field. The extended nearness of husband and wife after so many months of estrangement and tension suggest that the rutted path their marriage had taken since August 1862 was being paved over.[4]

Service on a military tribunal failed to captivate Chamberlain's interest. As the proceedings droned on and his fitness to resume active duty became apparent, he longed to return to the front. He remained on that listless service for more than three months, a period that suggests he served on a succession of courts. When the proceedings went into recess he spent his free time squiring Fannie about the city, writing letters of recommendation for officers applying to him for promotion or better assignments, and keeping up his brigade and regimental accounts. On one occasion he reported the whereabouts of 119 screwdrivers and cone wrenches issued to the men of the 20th Maine.[5]

Early in February he made a report to the assistant chief of the Ordnance Department. In this missive (which Chamberlain's biographers have overlooked or ignored) he stated his intention to resign his commission. His motives cannot be determined. Perhaps his physical recovery was not proceeding as smoothly as he had hoped; if so, he may have doubted his ability to return to the army. If privy to such doubt, Fannie would have worked hard to convince her spouse to return to his home and resume his role as family head.[6]

By April Chamberlain's court-martial service had shifted to Trenton, New Jersey, where he and Fannie again took temporary quarters. Early that month, apparently before the new session began, they traveled to Gettysburg, where they toured the scenes of the 20th Maine's heroics. The visit may have caused the colonel's wounds to throb; it must have increased his impatience to return to Rappahannock Station.[7]

His every thought pointed south. In this first full month of spring, the Virginia roads were drying and the Army of the Potomac was poised to cross the Rapidan yet again, this time under the newly appointed general-in-chief of the Union forces, Ulysses S. Grant. George Meade retained direct command of the army, but the hero from the West would travel with him, making the strategic decisions that would determine the outcome of the Virginia campaign. At the newly revived rank of lieutenant general, Grant—far and away the North's most successful warrior, whose continued success Abraham Lincoln was banking on—was prepared to lead 120,000 troops against the smaller but more compact and more resilient army of Robert E. Lee. Months ago, reading of Grant's exploits in the West, Chamberlain had wondered what it would be like to serve under such a man. Whatever his February doubts, by April he expected soon to live out his imagination.

Before the month was out Chamberlain was petitioning the War Department for his release from inactive service. His desire to retake the field only intensified when he learned on May 5 that Grant and Meade had broken camp and had crossed the river, seeking a confrontation with Lee. He and Fannie were still in Trenton on the 9th when he discovered that for unexplained reasons his earlier request had never reached its destination. That very day he rushed another petition to Washington, claiming a full recovery from his bout with fever and begging to be permitted to rejoin his brigade.[8]

This second effort produced swift results; on May 10 the War Department detached him from court-martial duty and ordered him to report to Washington preparatory to rejoining his command. Giving the lie to his protestations of good health, the telegram found him wracked by another spasm of fever. Fannie, already upset by her husband's determination to trade the safety of inactive service for the perils of the field, must have been especially disturbed by this relapse.

On the other hand, she was not so anxious about his health as to remain with him to the last. On the 10th she left him, shivering with fever in the Trenton passenger depot, and boarded a northbound train. In a letter to Deborah Folsom, Fannie admitted that her husband "was very anxious for me to go back to Washington again with him, but I thought it was not best, unless he became very sick." Instead, she planned to stay over in New York until she learned that he was well enough to start for Virginia; then she would head home.[9]

Her willingness to part with her feverish husband may have reflected her resentment over his decision to leave her for the army. Once again, the war had lured him away from his responsibilities to wife and family, prompting him to risk his life in pursuit of a cause Fannie Chamberlain considered unworthy of such devotion.

*   *   *

Chamberlain reached the front, near Spotsylvania Court House, Virginia, on or about Saturday, May 14. His health having revived, he reported at the headquarters of the 1st Division, Fifth Corps, where he found that much had changed during his six months' absence. The regiments he observed appeared smaller, their men more worn and weary, than he remembered. That, he understood, was the result of the trial by fire through which everyone but he had recently passed. After crossing the Rapidan, the troops under Grant and Meade had collided with Lee's army, hurrying up from the west. Both sides had suffered heavily in two days of violent, confused, and indecisive fighting among the scrub pines and thickets of the Virginia Wilderness. From there Grant had sent Meade's units southeastward toward Spotsylvania, where some of the fiercest close-quarters fighting of the war had consumed the next week as well as thousands of lives. Landmarks of the fighting, with names like Laurel Hill, the Bloody Angle, and the Mule Shoe, would forever define a particularly diabolical brand of slaughter.[10]

In addition to heavy casualties—which included Chamberlain's superior and friend, James Clay Rice, who had died heroically on May 10 from a wound received at Laurel Hill—organizational changes had reduced and redefined the army. Two of its corps, the First and Third, had gone out of existence. Savaged on many fields, shattered at Gettysburg, the regiments remaining to both commands had been assimilated into the rest of the army, divvied up by the Second, Fifth, and Sixth Corps. Another infantry corps, the Ninth, had been brought up from southeastern Virginia under Ambrose Burnside. The new arrivals helped compensate for the decimation of the First and Third as well as for the autumn transfer of the Eleventh and Twelfth Corps to the western theater. As Burnside was senior to General Meade, he currently answered only to Grant. Within 10 days of Chamberlain's return, however, rank would be waived and the Ninth would join the other corps under Meade's authority.[11]

One immediate effect of the reorganization was that the Fifth Corps had a glut of general officers, most of whom had been assigned to brigades. Reporting to General Griffin, Chamberlain found that he had been permanently replaced at the head of the 3rd Brigade, 1st Division—which in his absence had been enlarged to seven regiments—by the officer who had placed him on medical leave, General Bartlett. For months Griffin had fended off attempts by other colonels to take Chamberlain's place, but he could not deny the position to one who outranked the commandeer of the 20th Maine, especially one of such high competence as Bartlett.

Chamberlain accepted his demotion with good grace. For one thing, he admired his successor. Bartlett was not only a gifted tactician but a courageous leader who accompanied his troops into the thick of action. Chamberlain was also buoyed by the hope—one that Griffin probably nurtured—that he would return to brigade command at the earliest opportunity. That opportunity seemed imminent, given the poor state of Bartlett's health. In the meantime, Chamberlain could return to the regiment whose officers and men he had long and dearly missed.[12]

Soon after reporting, Chamberlain was introduced to his new corps leader, the suave, dark-complected Major General Gouverneur Warren. Warren's replacement of the lackluster General Sykes, who had been sent west, owed to his accomplishments on Little Round Top as well as to his successful stint in command of the Second Corps at Bristoe Station the previous October. Chamberlain rapidly developed a close relationship with the former engineer from upstate New York, whom he found to be a rare breed of animal—a professional soldier and a refined gentleman to boot. It would take time, however, for the colonel to become familiar with his superior's mercurial temperament. Warren gave the impression of a slow, quiet, contemplative sort who could not be rushed into decision-making. Whether on the march or in battle, he moved at a deliberate pace, refusing to commit himself or his troops until he had time to analyze his situation. Underneath his placid demeanor, however, smoldered a fierce temper that Warren was not hesitant to unleash on colleagues and even superiors whom he considered inept or derelict in their duty. His anger sometimes took the form of torrents of blasphemy and obscenity that never failed to shock listeners. Warren's chief of artillery, for one, considered such behavior a symptom of madness.[13]

Chamberlain had no opportunity to meet the new man at the top, although he was impressed by what he heard about Grant at Fifth Corps headquarters. Officers who had advanced and retreated under a succession of army leaders were vocal in their belief that the new commander was different from his predecessors. At the end of its two-day hammering in the Wilderness, having gained not a single mile in the direction of its presumed objective, Richmond, the army had expected Grant to emulate McClellan, Pope, Burnside, and Hooker by recrossing the river, returning to camp, and revamping his strategy. Everyone had been pleasantly surprised when Grant led them onward as though shrugging off a minor setback. The army's route, though extended toward the east as Grant tried to curve around Lee's right flank, was generally southward in the direction of the seat of government of the Southern nation and the nerve-center of its armies. As long as that course was stayed, the Army of the Potomac could believe it had yet to suffer a defeat under Ulysses S. Grant.[14]

* * *

After paying his calls at division and corps headquarters, Chamberlain reported to the camp of the 20th Maine for a reunion both joyous and sobering. Major Spear, commanding the regiment during the most recent absence of Lieutenant Colonel Gilmore, welcomed him warmly, as did the other officers who remained with the outfit. The few still on duty told Chamberlain how grievously the regiment had suffered in his absence. It had taken 111 casualties in the Wilderness, several more at Laurel Hill and Spotsylvania. The list included Captain William W. Morrell and two lieutenants, killed, plus many wounded including Captain Walter Morrill and Lieutenant Holman Melcher. Through some special providence, Tom Chamberlain, who could always be found in the front rank, had emerged from the tempest unscathed.[15]

No sooner had Chamberlain resumed regimental command than he moved up to replace an ill General Bartlett at the head of the 3rd Brigade. In temporarily regaining the post he had relinquished in November, the colonel recognized old faces and acquainted himself with new ones. He found himself in charge not only of the 20th Maine, 44th New York, 16th Michigan, and 83rd Pennsylvania, but also of the 18th Massachusetts, the 1st Michigan, and the 118th Pennsylvania, Philadelphia's famous "Corn Exchange Regiment." Although unfamiliar with the new additions, Chamberlain would have been heartened to know that they, in common with the original members of the brigade, were seasoned veterans whose experience on the march and in battle would count for much in the days ahead.[16]

He must have expected to lead the command into battle at an early time. In point of fact, he did see early action but not at the head of the 3rd Brigade. Only hours before he reported at Griffin's headquarters, the entire Fifth Corps had made a night-long march from Meade's right flank, across the rear of the army, to a position hard by the Union left. The corps now lay nestled between the Ninth Corps, on its right, and, on its left, the Sixth Corps of Major General Horatio G. Wright, successor to John Sedgwick, who a few days ago had fallen victim to sniper-fire. There it prepared to attack Lee's right flank, following days of unsuccessful strikes at other sectors of the Rebel line.[17]

Chamberlain's first field assignment after his return is veiled in mystery. In a postwar summary of his military service, he claimed that less than half an hour after reporting for duty he was ordered to "take seven Regts and charge the enemy's works at the C[ourt]. H[ouse].; but the attempt seeming to the Corps Commander too desperate, the movement was deferred till night when the advance was successfully made." No historian has questioned the accuracy of this brief and vague account, although it seems strange that General Warren would assign such a "desperate" offensive to a subordinate so soon returned from an extended sick leave and with whom he was not intimately familiar. Of course Warren would have been aware of Chamberlain's Gettysburg reputation, and General Griffin and other officers may have persuaded their superior of the colonel's ability to handle such an important mission. Although no official report of operations on the Fifth Corps' front on May 14 mentions Chamberlain's participation, two of his biographers surmise that the colonel was involved, minus his brigade, in an effort to retake a disputed position spearheaded by the 2nd Brigade of Griffin's Division, commanded by Brigadier General Romeyn B. Ayres. They provide few details to supplement Chamberlain's memoir.[18]

By the 15th, Chamberlain was back with the 3rd Brigade, which he continued to command in the absence of General Bartlett. The following day, however, before Chamberlain could become involved in a major operation, Bartlett returned and sent his subordinate back to the 20th Maine.

By May 16 Grant and Meade were looking for a means of exiting what had become a stalemate around Spotsylvania Court House. The commanding general was especially anxious to resume his march on Richmond. That day a second army operating in Virginia under Grant's remote control—Major General Benjamin F. Butler's Army of the James, comprising some 30,000 men including a division leader named Adelbert Ames—had attacked the southern approaches to the capital near Drewry's Bluff. Through the blundering of some of Ames's associates, Butler's army was thwarted and sent into retreat by a smaller but more energetic force of defenders under Pierre G. T. Beauregard. Butler would cap his debacle of the 16th by occupying a fortified perimeter between the James and Appomattox Rivers about 12 miles below his original objective. There Beauregard would confront and entrap him, neutralizing half of the Yankee pincers aimed at Richmond.[19]

Unfazed by Butler's blunder, Grant planned to head south yet again, hoping to steal a march on Lee. In the interim, he continued to probe his enemy's positions near the courthouse. Still at the helm of the 20th Maine, on the evening of the 17th Chamberlain advanced his picket line "half a mile … with little loss." By the next morning, he and his men lay 600 yards from the nearest works, where they absorbed an hours-long shelling. The precarious position did not discomfit the provisional brigade commander, who had regained the sensation of being at home in combat. As he wrote Governor Cony on May 18, his service in Washington and Trenton, especially once Grant's Overland campaign began, "was one of the most unhappy of my life. I am making up for it now however."[20]

Ironically, on May 20 Chamberlain was detailed to court-martial duty at corps headquarters. Legal proceedings in the field probably proved just as trying, as frustrating, as they had in the rear; therefore, he would have been relieved to rejoin the 20th on the sultry morning of May 21 as the regiment followed the Maltese Cross southward toward the Ny River. Grant had broken contact with Lee, ending the bloody but inconclusive fighting near Spotsylvania. A race was on, via parallel roads, to clear the next major barrier to Richmond, the network of watercourses that included the Ny, Po, and North Anna Rivers.[21]

On the first day out, Warren's corps—moving at the deliberate but steady pace its commander preferred—crossed both the Ny and the Po, camping on the south bank of the latter. The next morning, May 22, Chamberlain again replaced the recurrently ill Bartlett, leading the brigade down the historic Telegraph Road toward the North Anna. En route, near the village of Bowling Green, his skirmishers made spasmodic contact with what proved to be the rear guard of Lee's army. "Marse Robert" had again beaten his opponent onto roads south.

Characteristically, Chamberlain was up front this day, taking personal command of the skirmish line, when late in the afternoon horse artillery began to shell his position. Making a hasty reconnaissance, he found a considerable force of gray cavalry—Major General Wade Hampton's now, following the recent death in battle of J.E.B. Stuart—drawn up in fields and woods on the south side of Pole Cat Creek. Word came back from Griffin that Chamberlain should clear the way, covering the advance of the rest of the division. Without hesitation, the colonel and his skirmishers pressed forward, seeking to seize the artillery and disperse its mounted supports.[22]

He started out in good fashion; by dusk riflemen north of the creek were blowing holes in the ranks of dismounted troopers. But when Chamberlain ordered the newly acquired 118th Pennsylvania to cross the stream, the regiment came up to a board fence along the water, hesitated, then halted. As a member of the 20th Maine later recalled, "this obstacle checked the Reg't—some hesitated [over] what to do—others scrambled over the fence as best they could and daintely [sic] picked their way through the water...."[23]

Annoyed by their slow pace, Chamberlain rushed to water's edge and collared the Pennsylvanians' leader, whom he ordered across the stream "without delay." When the harried officer replied that he could not compel his troops to follow him, Chamberlain shouted at the nearest soldiers: "Take the fence with you my men—forward!" Within seconds the fence had disappeared under the weight of men clambering into the stream and splashing toward the other side.[24]

The Confederates did not wait to receive Chamberlain's water-logged attack. Before their position could be reached, cavalrymen and horse artillerists took off at high speed, joining the rest of Lee's rear guard in a clean getaway. Chamberlain's biographers agree that the colonel was greatly upset by his inability to take the position, for which he ever held the Corn Exchange men responsible. He must have been especially upset that he had failed under the close observation of his superior and patron, Griffin. Although Chamberlain habitually sought to portray himself as a conscientious but disinterested soldier, one who served without an eye on his career, ambition and desire for advancement were among his salient characteristics. For this reason, May 22, 1864 was not the finest day of his life in uniform.

* * *

Moving on from Pole Cat Creek, Bartlett's brigade reached the North Anna near Jericho Mills early on the 23rd. Shortly after 3:00 P.M. the brigade, as part of the advance element of the Fifth Corps, forded the chest-deep stream and stomped up the steep slope beyond. In the rear, engineers laid a pontoon bridge to accommodate the rest of the corps, while the bulk of the army poised to ford farther downstream. Once on the far shore, Warren's people moved southwestward, Griffin's division in the center, Crawford's division on its left, and the division of Brigadier General Lysander Cutler to its right rear.[25]

For a time the Federals encountered opposition, but only from skirmishers. Making full use of his interior lines, Lee had already placed his army in position below the river, with one of his premier divisions, Major General Cadmus Wilcox's, holding that section of the Virginia

Central Railroad toward which the Fifth Corps was moving. Another meeting-engagement was imminent on the long and tortuous road to Richmond.

Still leading the 3rd Brigade, Chamberlain went into action late in the afternoon, when Wilcox's infantry and artillery came up to challenge the advance. The Rebels landed solid blows at one of the other brigades in Griffin's division as well as part of Cutler's command, sent up as reinforcements. Some of Griffin's and Cutler's troops gave way under the pounding of rifle and artillery fire, threatening to dislodge the rest of the corps. At a critical point, Griffin sent for Chamberlain, who double-quicked his regiments to the most vulnerable sector, filled a growing gap in the line, and stanched the gray tide rolling toward it. Many of Chamberlain's officers and men went down with wounds, including Major Spear, who took a shrapnel wound in the groin as he led in the 20th Maine.[26]

Himself exposed to a withering fire from several directions, Chamberlain acted with great coolness, rejecting the pleas of some of his subordinates to take cover. His firmness paid dividends. Inspired by his courage and aided by a barrage from Colonel Charles S. Wainwright's artillery brigade, Bartlett's brigade held its new position for the balance of the afternoon. Finally, as darkness descended, a battered and thwarted Wilcox disengaged.[27]

That night, despite a fearsome downpour, Chamberlain helped entrench his position, while patching the holes in his ranks. Some time after daybreak on the 24th, as other segments of the army finally crossed the river, the Fifth Corps moved out to locate its departed foe. As part of the general movement Chamberlain led his brigade southward and eastward down the narrow corridor between the North Anna and the Virginia Central. Its heading carried it toward the left center of Lee's mile-and-a-half-long defensive line, manned by the corps of Major General Richard H. Anderson.

On this part of the field there would be no resumption of the sharp fighting of May 23. Perhaps 200 yards short of the enemy, which formed part of an inverted "V," its apex resting at Ox Ford on the North Anna, General Warren called a halt and his men began to entrench yet again. In their hastily dug rifle-pits the dusty, grimy, nearly exhausted Federals spent the next two days, exchanging shots with their equally worn and weary foe. Meanwhile, other portions of Meade's army made fitful efforts that failed to dislodge, flank, or even threaten the Rebel line. As in the Wilderness and again at Spotsylvania, the armies had deadlocked well above the city one was resolved to capture and the other determined to protect with its life.[28]

* * *

Grant the strategist and Meade the tactician realized full well that they had been out-positioned, if not out-generaled. Late on the 26th, after three days of confronting Lee at close quarters, their troops broke contact with the enemy, recrossed the pontoons, swung slightly eastward and well to the south, and left the North Anna country behind. Chamberlain must have been glad to be back on the road after spending the past 48 hours in a trench awash in rainwater and mud. Fresh air and restored mobility would have compensated somewhat for a loss of position; a healthy Bartlett had reduced him yet again to regimental command. He could not know that even as he led the 20th Maine toward the Chickahominy River, events were in motion that would separate him permanently from his old outfit.[29]

Early on May 28 Griffin's division crossed the Pamunkey River via pontoons at Hanovertown. Chamberlain realized that the Pamunkey was one of the last natural barriers to Richmond—only the sluggish Chickahominy remained. The 20th Maine bivouacked a mile from the south bank until retaking the road at 6:30 the following morning. Credible rumors had Lee's army moving on parallel roads that converged on the north side of the Chickahominy. At first Chamberlain suspected that a meeting-engagement was imminent, but at some point on the 29th he heard that the Rebels had fallen back to the south side, as though resigned to taking position inside the Richmond defenses.[30]

Late that day Griffin's people, the advance echelon of the Fifth Corps, halted near Bethesda Church, about 12 miles northeast of Richmond, not far from Gaines's Mill and other landmarks of McClellan's Peninsula campaign. By early on the 30th the division was making contact with opposing skirmishers; one of its brigades drove the Rebels two miles before halting, forming line of battle, and throwing up breastworks. The rest of the corps quickly did the same, Chamberlain joining his men in wielding ax and spade despite a torrid sun.

The army envisioned a major confrontation with its enemy, but this day two of Meade's generals feuded with one another. A nettled Warren bitterly complained to army headquarters about Major General Philip H. Sheridan, the bandy-legged Irishman whom Grant had hauled out of Tennessee the previous month to command the cavalry of the Army of the Potomac. An able combat leader, Sheridan was also an intense, driven man with a temper that rivaled Warren's. When the latter repeatedly told Meade that horsemen assigned to cover his left flank were instead idling in the rear, Sheridan, who believed the criticism unwarranted, took instant and violent offense. May 30 saw a great enmity begin to grow between the two.[31]

On the last day of the month the 20th Maine deeded their freshly constructed works to members of Burnside's corps and moved a short distance to the south. Long-range skirmishing consumed the balance of the day, although at times sharpshooters and cannoneers got the Mainers' range. On one occasion, while striding along the parapet of his regiment's defenses, Chamberlain drew artillery fire. When not even a 10-pounder Parrott shell exploding near his head caused him to take cover, noncommissioned officers reached up and yanked him into their rifle-pit.[32]

Although the enemy's position appeared to be held in heavy force, the Union high command opted for an offensive. On June 1 and again two days later Grant, having lost his patience with side-stepping, hurled the Army of the Potomac and a recently attached force from the Army of the James at Lee's well-entrenched, artillery-braced lines east of a dusty crossroads known as Cold Harbor. On the first, the 20th Maine and the rest of Griffin's division repulsed a feeble attack. Elsewhere along the line, the army gained a foothold in Rebel territory. Two days later, when some of Griffin's units captured a line of rifle-pits near Bethesda Church, Chamberlain's men, attacking through a woodlot, absorbed an enfilade from the northwest that forced their colonel to form his right flank at a 90-degree angle to the rest of the line. In that position the regiment suffered heavily, its colonel several times coming close to joining its casualties. Apparently he had learned nothing from his sergeants. One watched him stride along the front line, trying to get a close-up view of the enemy's position, "while the shell and canister played about him fearfully."[33]

Despite the fortitude and courage of those involved, the army's effort this day proved no more successful than its predecessor. Its near-total lack of coordination, however, and the casualty list it spit out—nearly 13,000 killed or wounded throughout the ranks, two dozen of them among the 20th Maine—made June 3 as dark a day as the Army of the Potomac ever saw. Viewing the carnage his strategy had wrought, a shaken, chastened Grant vowed never again to lose his composure and strike his foe head-on.[34]

* * *

The Fifth Army Corps contained a number of regiments formerly part of the First, among them five veteran regiments from Pennsylvania, the 121st, 142nd, 143rd, 149th, and 150th Infantry. Originally assigned to Cutler's division, during the first bloody month of Grant's Overland campaign, these outfits had been whittled down to an aggregate strength of just over a thousand. They suffered especially heavily—and, perhaps as a result, had been perceived to fight poorly—during the combat in the Wilderness. Originally commanded by an early-war hero, Colonel Roy Stone, the Pennsylvanians had most recently been led by one of Cutler's favorite subordinates, Edward S. Bragg. Convinced that Cutler had failed to employ these regiments properly, on June 6 General Warren, as part of a reorganization that also created a division under General Ayres, transferred the quintet to Griffin's division, whose 1st Brigade they thereafter became. To bolster their staying-power, Warren added a large, untried outfit, the 187th Pennsylvania, to create a command 2,000 strong.[35]

Warren appears to have had no quarrel with Colonel Bragg, who had made a distinguished record and was on the verge of promotion to brigadier general. But on June 6, while the armies traded shots at long range near Cold Harbor, he assigned Chamberlain to command the "Keystone Brigade." That same day—backed by similar endorsements from Generals Griffin and Bartlett—Warren recommended that Chamberlain be promoted to brigadier general. This was not the first time Griffin had done so, but on this occasion he explained his action by observing that Chamberlain's "services and sufferings entitle him to the promotion and I am sure his appointment would add to my strength even more than the reinforcement of a thousand men." This extraordinary tribute may have fallen by the wayside. On June 9, without prioritizing the list, General Meade forwarded Chamberlain's name to the War Department along with those of seven other colonels deemed worthy of promotion.[36]

Despite the lofty recommendation, neither General Cutler nor the men of Chamberlain's new command originally welcomed the change. Cutler released the Pennsylvanians grudgingly, which is the way some of the men received their new leader. At least a few cried favoritism, deploring the failure of the division's senior colonel, William S. Tilton, to gain the position. Others saw Chamberlain, who lacked Pennsylvania ties, as an interloper. Still others praised General Warren's action. Their original commander had worn down the brigade through hard marches and harsh discipline. One of them punned that he and his comrades "had been so long ground under a Stone leader," any change would have been an improvement. Most of the Pennsylvanians, however, met Chamberlain with that wait-and-see attitude soldiers usually adopt toward leaders with whom they are unfamiliar.[37]

For his part, Chamberlain was well pleased with his new command. The Keystone Brigade was large enough and sufficiently seasoned to be regarded as promising material. He embraced the challenge of succeeding with it where someone else had failed. Moreover, the assignment bespoke career progression and the high regard of his superiors. His sole regret was the farewell he was forced to deliver to "my beloved & gallant Regiment, the men who never failed me in any extremity." At least he had the consolation of commending the 20th Maine, one last time, into the able hands of Ellis Spear.[38]

After calling together his new subordinates, making his introductions, and giving them a peptalk that at least one officer believed "did us good," Chamberlain inspected the men, their weapons, their equipage, and especially the position they held northwest of Cold Harbor. For the next five days he scrutinized their earthworks, picket posts, and field hospitals. At the latter site he appears to have forfeited some of the good impression he had made on his officers. A few days after assuming command he issued a preemptory order that two surgeons report to his headquarters for special service. Both doctors, being very busy just then, obeyed the order with something less than good humor. Years later the incident still rankled the assistant surgeon of the 143rd Pennsylvania, who recalled in his memoirs that "I scrupled Colonel Chamberlain's authority or right to command the Medical Corps."[39]

* * *

Early on June 7 Chamberlain's men—in company with the rest of their division—quit the scene of slaughter and stasis. Cloaked in morning darkness, the Federals disengaged from around Bethesda Church, fell back beyond range of enemy guns, then headed south toward the Chickahominy River. They were halted along the north bank and allowed to fall out. There, for the first time in weeks, they were able to rest without fear of drawing bullet or barrage.

Dozens of hot, dusty soldiers threw themselves into the stream, many without doffing their clothing. Most regretted the sport, for while the roiled waters of the Chickahominy were cool and cleansing, they also abounded with leeches. When the bathers left the water, one onlooker observed that they "had to have the bloodsuckers scraped from them." These unfortunates felt somewhat compensated for their distress when, in the next few days, Chamberlain's command was issued a ration of whiskey along with a quantity of that medicinal staple, quinine.[40]

The men of the 1st Brigade, 1st Division passed the next five days on picket duty, a chore they soon discovered they were sharing with Rebel troops farther west. Late one afternoon Chamberlain rode forward alone to try to locate the nearest enemy outpost, only to have its two dozen occupants locate him. According to his postwar account, only the lengthening shadows, the dust he had accumulated—which hid the blue of his uniform—and the orders he gave the startled troops in his best Southern accent enabled him to elude capture, just as he had on the field of Fredericksburg.[41]

On the sodden evening of June 12, Chamberlain received orders to cease picketing and stand ready to march. The next morning the 1st

Brigade crossed the Chickahominy on pontoons adjacent to the charred ruins of Long Bridge, heading in the direction of White Oak Swamp. Everyone supposed he was on the final leg of the road to Richmond, but three days of marching south instead of turning west fueled rumors about a change in strategy. In fact, Grant had adopted a new objective, and was marching toward it. Having run out of ground by which to sidestep Lee and still home in on the enemy capital, the commanding general had determined to cross the James River well east of Richmond and head for Petersburg, 22 miles farther south. To capture the "Cockade City" was to sever Richmond's supply links to the Deep South. With Petersburg taken, Richmond would die outright or wither on the vine.[42]

* * *

At 7:00 A.M. on June 16, the rest of the army having already crossed, Chamberlain's people were ferried across the James at Willcox Landing. By that hour, the advance of Meade's army—more than 50,000 men—were at the gates of Petersburg, seeking access to the northeastern portal of that lightly defended city. Having been duped by regiments left at Cold Harbor into thinking that his enemy remained before him in force, Robert E. Lee had not yet reinforced the threatened sector. In his absence the local commander, General Beauregard, was frantically shifting his limited resources—he held the city's works with approximately 10,000 troops—from one point to another along the outer ring of defenses. All the while he scrambled to erect new works closer to the city; throughout, he begged Lee to come to his aid.

Closing up on Petersburg early on the 17th, Chamberlain and his dusty, footsore troops learned that for the past two days wave after wave of attackers had cannoned into the northeastern works, gaining ground in some places but failing to break through to the city. On this third day of attack, as the Fifth Corps took up a reserve position in Meade's left rear, elements of the Second and Ninth Corps tried to batter their way past Beauregard's latest line. Due to a combination of poor coordination and inspired defense, the attackers again fell short.[43]

Dawn on June 18 offered Grant and Meade one last day of opportunity. Lee, deceived no longer, was rushing his army south. Some time before 5:00 A.M. the Fifth Corps at last moved toward the scene of action, going in on Burnside's left. Astride Charlemagne, Chamberlain led his brigade past sights half-visible in the murky dawn: mangled corpses, bloated carcasses, the splinters of artillery wagons victimized by the previous day's fighting. Moving up, a member of the 143rd Pennsylvania recalled that "I actually slipped in blood, near which lay a man ... literally torn to shreds."[44]

At the point at which they should have made contact with the enemy, Chamberlain's skirmishers found lines of vacated works, their inhabitants having fled behind one last row of defenses, perhaps a half-mile closer to Petersburg. Built atop high ground beyond Harrison's Creek, the semicircular line ran from the Appomattox River on the north to the Jerusalem Plank Road on the southeast. At its terminus, the line jutted westward to link with the original network of forts that curled back to the Appomattox River northwest of the city. The junction of the lines, whose approach was blocked by a deep ravine, was known as Rives's (rhymes with "wives") Salient.

Chamberlain's brigade approached the new line from a point northeast of Rives's Salient, moving along the axis of the Norfolk & Petersburg Railroad. By General Griffin's order, some time after 9:00 A.M. everyone was halted along the tracks and allowed to make breakfast. As the men boiled coffee, Charlemagne carried his rider into plain view of the Rebel works. Peering south, Chamberlain observed an enemy battery just off the main line as it hurled shell and case-shot toward other elements of the Fifth Corps. When General Warren materialized at his side and politely inquired if his subordinate thought he could silence the "very annoying" guns, Chamberlain at once "understood the purport of the mild inquiry. 'Thought,' indeed, was required; but the meaning was action." At once he prepared his men—and himself—for their first assault as a team.[45]

It proved to be a successful, although a difficult and dangerous, undertaking. Some time after 10:00 Chamberlain led the brigade by its left flank along an unfinished cut of the railroad to Norfolk. In a nearby woods he formed an attack column, four regiments in front and two, including the green 187th, in rear. At his order, the lines emerged from the trees and rushed across a clearing toward the

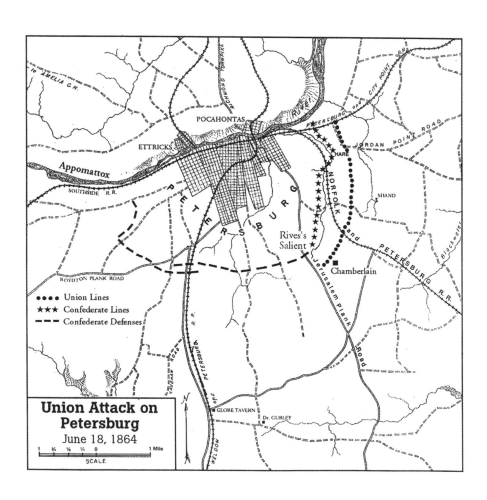

Union Attack on Petersburg
June 18, 1864

• • • • Union Lines
★ ★ ★ Confederate Lines
– – – Confederate Defenses

offending battery and a cordon of infantrymen supporting it. Cannon and rifles opened on the attackers, knocking over several but failing to curb the advance.

Suddenly Charlemagne took a shell fragment in the haunch and threw his rider. Artillery-fire also dismounted Chamberlain's staff and color-bearer. Wobbling to his feet, Chamberlain snatched up the fallen banner and, waving it above his head, rushed forward to overtake his brigade. His presence, although it may have bolstered morale, proved unnecessary. With all of its veteran regiments now in the front line, the command pried the gray infantry from its works. Under incessant prodding, most of the Rebels turned and ran toward Rives's Salient, forcing the guns they had been safeguarding to fall mute.[46]

When he caught up with his command, Chamberlain re-formed its scattered ranks and, finding the captured ground subject to enfilading fire, pulled them back to the shelter of a crest overlooking the scene of triumph. As he dug in, three batteries of Colonel Wainwright's brigade came up in his right rear to confront Rives's Salient and adjacent defenses, which now contained not only Beauregard's troops but the first contingent of reinforcements from the Army of Northern Virginia. Under Chamberlain's supervision, battery personnel sank platforms in the reverse slope of the hill, "so that the guns could be worked out of sight of the Enemy, & when in position the muzzles would lie in the grass on the crest."[47]

*   *   *

After such strenuous exercise, Chamberlain expected a respite. But early in the afternoon a staff officer, a stranger to him, reached his side with orders, purportedly from General Meade, that his brigade attack the main line along the Jerusalem Plank Road, perhaps 300 yards from its present position. Told that he must move out alone—the nearest supporting troops were thought to be a mile or more off—Chamberlain viewed the order as a death-warrant.

At once he sat down and composed a long and rather rambling letter to General Warren, one that no professional soldier would have written. He might have reduced his query to one or two sentences: "Army headquarters orders me to attack. Will I be supported?" He was much relieved when Warren replied that while Chamberlain's brigade should lead the way, the entire army would make the attack. Later Chamberlain believed—for what reason, no one knows—that "my refusal to obey the orders had really been the means of winning the victory."[48]

Early in the afternoon supports moved up in Chamberlain's rear and on his right. Feeling more comfortable about his assignment, he called up his regimental commanders and advised them, when the assault began, to double-quick their men across the intervening ground—down the slope, across a meager stream, Poor Creek, then up the high ground beyond, toward the guns defending Rives's Salient.

He even took the time to confer with General Cutler, whose division had been assigned to support Chamberlain's uncovered left. An acrimonious exchange followed Chamberlain's suggestion that Cutler's men move up in echelon to provide the exposed flank maximum protection. The grizzled commander of the 4th Division, who took offense at Chamberlain's prediction that unless precisely supported his brigade would be "mown down like grass," invariably comes off as the villain of this piece. Yet if the old Regular believed he was being lectured to by a junior officer of volunteers—and it would not be surprising if Colonel Chamberlain occasionally reverted to Professor Chamberlain—Cutler's resentment, and the manner in which he made it known, are understandable.[49]

Chamberlain claims to have had a foreboding about his part in the coming attack. He had grounds for dark thoughts, for in his immediate front were tall, well-constructed works sporting at least a dozen guns that would sweep his lane of approach. He tried to keep his mind on business as the minutes ticked down to 3:00, the appointed hour of attack. He strode along his front line, which lay beyond a sheltering crest, addressing officers and men in a calm voice, calling on them to do their duty regardless of the odds they faced. To break what one sergeant called the "terrible suspense" of awaiting the order to attack, Chamberlain invited everyone to peer over the crest and study the works in front. "This was novel to us," recalled a member of the 142nd Pennsylvania, "for we had been fighting from the Wilderness to this place, with little or no knowledge as to the exact object to be attained, and this new order of things rather captivated the officers and men."

He added that although those who took the colonel's suggestion "could see before them a desperate undertaking, when the order came at three o'clock our line ... went forward with an enthusiasm hardly ever witnessed in battle."[50]

At the appointed time, Chamberlain relayed the order to advance. Along a quarter-mile front his brigade surged forward, shouting a facsimile of the Rebel Yell and pouring down the slope "like a pack of infuriated devils." Before and behind them cannon unleashed a torrent of projectiles, those in front trying to kill them and those in rear trying to cover their advance. At the foot of the bluff, those not cut down by the murderous barrage pushed onward as fast as the marshy, briar-clogged ground would permit.[51]

"Come now, my boys, follow me," Chamberlain shouted as he raced afoot down the hill and through the stream bed. On the other bank he sought to direct the front line toward the left of the salient, where it might evade the hottest fire. Isolated from the bulk of his brigade, waving his officer's saber above his head, he made a perfect target. He was in the act of turning about to speed up his rear echelon when a minie ball crashed into his thigh below the right hip and tore its way through to the other side. The bullet fractured bones, severed arteries, and damaged internal organs. The shock of the blow momentarily paralyzed its victim, but his mind remained clear enough to predict that the wound was mortal.[52]

RETURNING HERO

Significantly, perhaps, it was not of his wife or children, or even of his troops, that Chamberlain thought in the moment of his wounding. As he later related, his first impression was of being struck in the back, a fate worse than death. In that first dazed instant he wondered "what will my mother say, her boy, shot in the back?" His next thought was of the impression his wounding would have on his brigade. Fearing that if he fell to the ground soldiers all around him would be demoralized, he used his sword as a crutch to keep himself upright. As he teetered on that slender fulcrum, blood pouring from his sides, he shouted instructions and encouragement to those rushing past. When he could stand no longer he permitted two of his staff officers to carry him to a somewhat less exposed position in the rear. En route he sent word to his ranking subordinate, Lieutenant Colonel John Irvin of the 143rd Pennsylvania, to assume command. Gingerly, the aides set him down on the ground, where he lay, "half-buried by clods of up-torn earth," expecting to die at any minute.[1]

Many soldiers saw him there as they rushed to the rear, demoralized not by the sight of a fallen commander but by some of the most concentrated artillery and rifle fire troops in this or any other war had ever faced. Despite bursts of almost superhuman effort, the attackers would not come close to carrying their objective. By mid-afternoon the high command would give up the effort as a lost cause, and be content with the few hundred yards Chamberlain's men and their comrades on either side had gained. Even in places where the attackers advanced two miles or more, the enemy's main line held. Toward sundown the Confederates staged a limited counterattack but it was tossed back with small effort and the Federals held their advanced position.

By nightfall the attackers had suffered nearly 1,000 men killed or wounded. The casualty list would help persuade Grant, who now faced Lee's army in force, that Petersburg was impervious to direct assault. Within hours of the failure at Rives's Salient, the Army of the Potomac, along with detachments from Butler's army, would commence siege operations. Grant envisioned an active investment: he planned to strike isolated portions of the Rebel line, stretching its flanks until they reached the breaking-point. Even so, no breakthrough appeared imminent; Petersburg's fall—and, by extension, Richmond's—appeared months away.[2]

* * *

As the highest-ranking casualty of June 18 lay crumpled and bleeding, one of the artillerymen who had supported Chamberlain's assault, Captain John Bigelow of the 9th Massachusetts Battery, sent his cannoneers, with a stretcher, to remove him from harm's way. Chamberlain weakly protested that he was done for and suggested the party look for wounded more likely to recover. Rejecting his advice, the artillerymen rolled him onto the litter and bore him rearward. In the midst of their errand, the rescuers came under a barrage that showered them all, especially the recumbent Chamberlain, with dirt and stones. By good fortune they reached their battery's position without further damage. They placed their burden in as secure a place as they could find. Shielded by guns, limbers, and caissons, Chamberlain lay unmoving, waiting for darkness to descend so that he might be taken to the field hospital, three miles behind the lines. As the day wore on the shock of his injury wore off and searing pain began to course through his body.[3]

It is likely that he lost consciousness; he seems not to have remembered the journey to the divisional hospital. At some point he became aware that he was in the hands of Surgeon Robert A. Everett, who put him under ether prior to probing his wounds. Some time after 7:00 P.M. the anesthetized patient had visitors: Captain Tom Chamberlain, whose regiment had been spared direct involvement in the day's attack, and two other members of his brother's old brigade, Surgeons Abner O. Shaw of the 20th Maine and Morris W. Townsend of the 44th New York. A grim prognosis greeted them: Doctor Everett had concluded that the patient was beyond help. The bullet that struck him after ricocheting from the ground had not only damaged bones and vessels but had severed the urethra and nicked the bladder, before lodging in the left hip. Medical science of the day was powerless to repair such extensive damage to vital organs. The ball could be removed, but that seemed the extent of treatment.

Everett's view of the situation failed to impress his colleagues; Shaw and Townsend made a bold decision to operate. For several hours they worked over their old commander, ranging into the realm of experimental surgery. At one point, supposedly, they stopped, afraid they were merely prolonging the patient's suffering. It is said that Chamberlain roused himself from the anesthetic and urged them to continue.[4]

The nature and the extent of the surgery performed that night remain unknown. In her biography Alice Rains Trulock states that Chamberlain's doctors "managed to patch up and connect things," but she provides no details—indeed, few details are available at this late date. Even so, some of the doctors' decisions and procedures can be intuited. They would have wasted little time on orthopedic repair, for the pelvic fracture Chamberlain had suffered would not have required setting. They could have done nothing to repair the nerve damage he had sustained. And although one of Chamberlain's chroniclers claims that the doctors reconnected the divided urethra, that procedure would have been beyond their abilities, especially given the conditions under which they labored. Even today, such an operation is difficult when performed in a well-lit operating room. Under the flaring oil lamps common to Civil War field hospitals, it is unlikely the surgeons could have visualized the urethra, much less made it whole.[5]

Shaw and Townsend would have been able to do three things, all of them critical to saving Chamberlain's life. They would have extracted the flattened bullet, forestalling further infection. They would have ligated the severed arteries to prevent the patient from bleeding to death on the operating table. And they would have treated the organic wound, although their handiwork would prove as much a curse as a boon to their patient. The bullet had disrupted the flow of urine through the urethra near the bladder. To carry off as much of the urine as possible and allow the wound to heal, the surgeons would have inserted a rigid (in this case, a metal) catheter into the bladder. In the poor light, they must have failed to seat the device properly, for it appears that subsequent operations were necessary to reposition it.

A more serious problem was caused by leaving the catheter in the wound too long. Then, as now, whether a catheter should be used for long periods or briefly and intermittently was a matter of warm debate. In this case the device eventually did its job: after four or five weeks urine stopped being voided through the bullet wound. But the tube was kept in place for so many days that it created a half-inch-wide fistula, an artificial opening in the urethral wall. The fistula helped contaminate the urine (which in its natural state is sterile), inflicting on the patient years of pain caused by periodic, severe infections. The wound had long-range effects other than infection. It made riding—even walking, for quite some time—extremely difficult, and sexual intercourse all but impossible. Then, too, it probably left Chamberlain incontinent for life, forced to wear diaper-like absorbent cloths around his thighs.[6]

* * *

But long-term repercussions from the surgery would not have monopolized Chamberlain's attention on the evening of June 18. His primary concern was to survive the night; the future he would deal with day by day. Another item of interest was the succession of visitors he received that night. One was Ellis Spear, who years later would recall, ungraciously and inaccurately, that he found a post-operative Chamberlain "sitting up, but making some fuss. He was wounded in the penis." More sympathetic guests included Generals Warren and

Griffin, whom Chamberlain greeted with an enthusiasm not even liberal doses of morphine could dull. Particularly welcome was the news they conveyed: they were wiring army headquarters their strong recommendation that Chamberlain be granted a battlefield promotion to brigadier general of volunteers. The patient gasped out his thanks, adding that the honor would be especially gratifying to his family.[7]

Their recommendation made it through the official channels in record time. At his field quarters, Meade endorsed Warren's request of June 19 (which related that Chamberlain had been "mortally wounded, it is thought") and wired his approval to General Grant's headquarters at City Point, Virginia. At Meade's urging, on June 20 the commanding general informed Secretary of War Stanton that he was nominating Chamberlain for brigadier, to rank from the date of his wounding, and asked that his name be sent immediately to the U.S. Senate for confirmation. Grant's Special Order 39 cited Chamberlain for "meritorious and efficient services on the field of battle, and especially for gallant conduct in leading his Brigade against the enemy at Petersburg Va., on the 18th inst[ant]...."[8]

In his memoirs, Grant recalled the appointment and emphasized that Chamberlain had been recommended for promotion several times without result. Thus he acted to ensure that "a gallant and meritorious officer received partial justice at the hands of his government, which he had served so faithfully and so well." Some accounts claim, without basis in fact, that this marked the only time Grant awarded an on-the-spot promotion for gallantry in battle.[9]

Chamberlain received his appointment as brigadier general long after he was conveyed by transport from Petersburg to Annapolis, Maryland, where he arrived the day after his wounding. He was still occupying a bed in the local Naval Hospital during the first days of July when visited by his old executive officer, Charles Gilmore, then on leave from court-martial duty in Washington. Gilmore brought welcome gifts: not only the appointment itself but a copy of the Senate resolution confirming his nomination. Chamberlain was in a certain amount of pain that day, but one can assume that his gratification at reaching this career milestone surpassed, at least temporarily, his physical distress.[10]

All who knew and cared for Chamberlain rejoiced over his promotion. Jubilation was especially prevalent in the camp of the 20th Maine outside Petersburg. Ellis Spear, who informed the outfit of their colonel's survival, initially joined in the merriment. Later, however, his enthusiasm cooled because of what he perceived to be Chamberlain's mendacity. Years after the war Spear corresponded with Oliver W. Norton, Strong Vincent's orderly and the author of a well-regarded book about the struggle for Little Round Top. As Norton informed Spear, Chamberlain had claimed that Grant had witnessed his heroics on June 18 and had promoted him "as a reward for his skillful handling of his brigade, which he had the right to do, subject of course to the President's acquiescence." Norton felt deceived and hurt when he later learned that Grant had not been present for the attack on Rives's Salient and had awarded Chamberlain his star at the urging of other commanders. Moreover, said Norton, despite published claims to the contrary, Grant had been motivated as much by a desire to gratify Chamberlain's family and friends as to honor his skill and valor. Spear came to share Norton's view of the matter, ascribing Chamberlain's version of events to his "inability to tell the truth always."[11]

* * *

In all likelihood, Chamberlain's thoughts were with his wife from the time of his wounding. Assuredly, they were the next day. Although he had come through the operation in tolerable shape, it had left him in great pain as well as weak from blood loss. Despite his suffering, he took up a pencil and scrawled what he feared would be his last letter home: "My darling wife I am lying mortally wounded the doctors think, but my mind & heart are at peace.... God bless & keep & comfort you, precious one, you have been a precious wife to me. To know & love you makes life & death beautiful. Cherish the darlings & give my love to all the dear ones. Do not grieve too much for me. We shall all soon meet...." As his strength ebbed, he closed with words of affection for Daisy, Wyllys, his parents, brothers, and sister, signing off "Ever yours Lawrence."[12]

Word of his wounding preceded Fannie's receipt of the letter. On June 20 the overburdened army telegraph carried the news to Brewer and Brunswick, throwing family members into shock. As Sae Chamberlain reported, everyone was "entirely overcome and could hardly endure the suspense" until further details arrived. The family's fears grew geometrically when it learned that New York and Boston newspapers were reporting their loved one mortally wounded.[13]

Not till the 22nd did wife, children, parents, siblings, and in-laws learn that Chamberlain had been received at the hospital in Annapolis, where it had come to be thought, as Sae Chamberlain wrote him hopefully, "your wound seemed more favorable." By then even the *New York Herald* was expecting him to recover, although no one could say in what condition he would be left. Family members felt the urge to hurry to his side; all wished godspeed to Fannie when, accompanied by a few friends, she entrained for Maryland to sit beside her husband's hospital bed for the second time in seven months.[14]

He seemed to improve from the moment of her arrival, although his life continued to be in danger. He perked up further after Charles Gilmore brought his appointment as brigadier; the following day, the 4th of July, he formally accepted the promotion. Despite the perceptible improvement, Gilmore had cause for worry, writing Adjutant General Hodsdon that Chamberlain's doctors were "by no means certain of *saving* his life…. It is feared that ulcers will form in the Abdomen & terminate his life." Despite his suffering, said Gilmore, Chamberlain had roused himself to discharge some official duties: "He cheerfully recommended the following promotions to be made in the 20th Maine…." The accompanying list must have delighted Chamberlain's visitor, for the name at the top was Gilmore's. Upon the patient's promotion, Gilmore, as senior officer of the 20th Maine, had become eligible for a colonel's eagles. Thus, the officer who had contrived to spend most of his time on sick leave or detached duty was to be rewarded with the promotion of his career. On a more just note, Ellis Spear, so long the *de facto* leader of the regiment, could now move up to lieutenant colonel—although, as it turned out, only by brevet.[15]

A little more than a fortnight after Gilmore wrote him, General Hodsdon received a much more favorable report on Chamberlain's condition, this from the general's brother. Leaving Bangor on or about July 13, John Chamberlain had rushed to Annapolis upon learning that the patient had taken a turn for the worst, probably due to a major infection. Since systemic antibiotics were not then available, the doctors at Annapolis probably treated the condition by irrigating the urethral fistula or by applying topical antiseptics such as carbolic acid. Even this limited treatment seems to have produced results, for by July 16, when John reached the Naval Hospital, the crisis had passed.

Writing two weeks after his arrival, Chamberlain's brother informed Hodsdon that "since then he has gained perceptibly every day, and every thing has worked as favorably as possible. The most excruciating of his pains have ceased, and his wounds have healed greatly; on the left side entirely. His internal difficulties, which are the most serious, have so far adjusted themselves, under his skillful treatments, that we feel quite assured of his recovery." As he wrote, he received a visit from one of his brother's doctors, who confirmed John's optimistic view of things: "His danger is considered passed, and his recovery certain."[16]

If Chamberlain's recuperation was going well, it owed much to his wife's nursing. Fannie rarely left his side, seeing to his wants, bathing him, changing his dressings, calling for opiates when pain flared up, at quiet times reading to him from books and newspaper to while away the bedridden hours. At some point she helped him to his feet and let him lean on her as he took his first, halting steps around the ward.

The nature of her husband's wounds troubled Fannie. The prospect that their sexual life would never be the same meant that their relationship faced a major adjustment. The power she had wielded over the marriage bed—one of the few sources of authority available to a mid-19th-century wife—would now almost certainly be denied to her. Furthermore, the absence of sexual relations would close off an important dimension of their life together. As one historian notes, "for a couple who had been so forthright about their sexuality, this presumably was a great loss." Then, too, they would produce no more children—although their fifth was on the way.[17]

By the time she traveled to Annapolis Fannie was two months pregnant; only the fact that her husband's life hung in the balance would have induced her to make the trip at all. The child Fannie would name Gertrude Loraine Chamberlain had been conceived during the couple's extended, happy stay in Washington. Fannie would have been unusually anxious about her condition, consulting frequently with the doctors at the Naval Hospital and perhaps elsewhere in Annapolis. She would have wanted no harm to come to the last child she would bear—the daughter who, for a time, she feared her husband would not live to see. The child's identity as the last Chamberlain would only deepen the tragedy of her brief life. Born on January 16, 1865, within seven months Gertrude Loraine would join her sister Emile and her unnamed brother in a child's grave. Her death would exert further strain on a marriage badly stressed by the cruelties of war.[18]

* * *

As summer wore on, the mugginess of Annapolis left Chamberlain's bed covers drenched with sweat. Fighting off the enervating heat, he struggled to get well. By late July Colonel Norval Welch, then in temporary command of Bartlett's brigade, wrote Chamberlain that he had heard the patient was making excellent progress and might retake the field. Other correspondents heard that his recuperation was progressing more slowly. In mid-August Lieutenant Holman Melcher of the 20th Maine, himself on convalescent leave following his wounding in the Wilderness, picked up a rumor that his old colonel had died in the hospital. Melcher described the erroneous news as "*very painful*—for as a commander I had learned to love him—and not only that but the Country will miss a brave and gallant defender."[19]

By late August Chamberlain considered himself so far from dead that, despite continuing problems posed by his wounds, he was seriously considering the possibility Colonel Welch had raised. By now able to sit up in bed, he wrote Governor Cony that "I long to be in the field again doing my part to keep the old flag up, with all its stars." Later, in a sickbed letter to his mother, he reaffirmed his belief in a "divinely appointed" destiny "to which we are carried forward by a perfect trust in God." The clear implication was that his destiny lay in a return to uniform.[20]

His hope that the war effort still had a place for him was heightened when, in early September, news reached the Naval Hospital that the armies of General William T. Sherman, following a four-month campaign in Tennessee and Georgia, had captured Atlanta, the industrial and supply center of the Deep South. Until that point the 1864 campaign, in all theaters, had produced discouraging news. Especially in the East, where Grant's effort to maneuver his way into Petersburg had bogged down, stalemate raised the specters of defeat and defeatism. Sherman's success reenergized supporters of the Union and resuscitated Abraham Lincoln's moribund reelection campaign. Added to small but dramatic victories soon afterward in the Shenandoah Valley, where Grant had sent Phil Sheridan to run to earth a small army of Rebels, Atlanta's fall ensured Lincoln's ability to defeat the peace platform on which the Democratic candidate, former General McClellan, had been compelled to run. One vote to keep the president in the White House would come from War Democrat Joshua Chamberlain. Lincoln reelected, the war would continue—as Chamberlain wished—to its ordained conclusion.[21]

On September 21, two days after Sheridan's triumph at Third Winchester and two weeks after his own 36th birthday, Joshua Chamberlain was granted a long-awaited 30-days' leave, the term to be extended as needed. Nine days later (not on September 20, as one of his more recent biographers asserts) he saw the outside of the hospital for the first time in three and a half months. Accompanied by Fannie and family friends, he boarded a train for home, probably making the trip on a stretcher laid across the seats of a passenger car. A few days later, all were relieved to be back in Brunswick, where they were reunited with Daisy, Wyllys and Deborah Folsom, who had cared for the children in Fannie's absence.[22]

Less than a week after reaching Maine, Chamberlain was writing his old superior, Adelbert Ames, that his return to active campaigning was a foregone conclusion. It seemed not to matter that he could take no more than a few steps before discomfort drove him back to bed. Yet pain, weakness, and periodic complications would keep him bedridden for six weeks instead of the six months or more called for by the severity of his wounds.

His great incentive to recovery was the knowledge that the hourglass of war was running out. The coming winter, he was certain, would be the last. When spring came, Grant and Meade would gouge Lee's desertion-depleted, ill-fed, poorly equipped army out of its works to be set upon and destroyed—perhaps in days, not weeks. Chamberlain wanted nothing so much as to be in on the kill.[23]

Fannie's opinion of her husband's resolve can be surmised. For months, even as her strength was depleted by her condition—pregnancy had always been hard on her—she had given unstintingly of herself to return his strength to him. It had been a difficult time for them both, more so for her. Because she had young children to care for, his near-invalid condition while in Brunswick would have taxed both her energy and her patience. One historian suggests that "Chamberlain's frustration at not being with his regiment [sic] in a position of command must have caused tensions, not only because of his agitation about being removed from the scene of action, but also because the 'habit of command' might indeed have become a habit that was unwelcome at home." Now that he was back on his feet, however unsteadily, what had Fannie gained from his recovery? Perhaps only the opportunity finally to become a war widow.[24]

The second week in November brought snow and frigid winds to southern Maine; it also brought Joshua Chamberlain's return to uniform, one that now sported a star on each shoulder. On the 12th—prompted, no doubt, by Chamberlain's repeated assurances that he was fit to resume active duty—he received orders to report to Meade's headquarters for assignment. His old brigade was no longer in existence, having been broken up and most of its regiments transferred to other commands. But he had no doubt that General Warren would tender him a position commensurate with his new rank. He could not yet mount a horse; he had difficulty walking for more than a few minutes at a time; and he had ventured out into public only a few times since reaching Maine. Even so, recommitting himself to that divine providence that had so long guided his steps, he made his farewells to wife and children and took a carriage to the same depot from which Tom and he had gone off to war in the palmy days of '62. Now seven months along, Fannie may not have seen him onto the train, which he boarded stiffly, with lingering pain. Then he was on his way, back to the war.[25]

Virtually every historian lauds Chamberlain for leaving his sickbed for the army, thus placing the needs of his nation above those of his health. His decision to return to Virginia despite his disabilities appears to reflect commendable qualities: devotion to duty, refusal to accept physical limitations as a handicap, and a large helping of courage. It may be, however, that his leave-taking also bespoke ambition, selfishness, even a certain arrogance in its suggestion that he considered his presence in the field somehow essential to the success of the cause. And while his decision may have been in keeping with his nature, it cannot be said that he was acting in the best interests of his family. He was acting, as he had on many another occasion, in the best interests of Joshua Chamberlain.

* * *

On November 19, the new brigadier having reported at army headquarters outside Petersburg, General Meade reassigned him to the Fifth Corps. The order relieved Chamberlain's mind: there had always been the possibility he would be moved into a vacancy in another corps. That prospect had troubled him, for he could not seriously consider campaigning anywhere but under the Maltese Cross. That same day General Warren, who had vocally sought Chamberlain's services ever since it had become known he would retake the field, assigned him, once again, to Griffin's division. In turn, Griffin assigned him to his newly reconstituted 1st Brigade.[26]

Although careful never to express his feelings, there is the distinct possibility that the new arrival was disappointed in the command tendered him—evidence, perhaps, that his superiors doubted his physical ability to handle the larger force to which his new rank appeared to entitle him. In place of the six veteran regiments he had most recently led, he found himself in command of two recently formed outfits, both of them unusually large but composed mainly of raw recruits: the 185th New York, commanded by Colonel Edwin S. Jenney, and the 198th Pennsylvania (14 companies strong instead of the regulation 10) under Brevet Brigadier General Horatio Gates Sickel.[27]

In addition to being dismayed at commanding so many rookies, Chamberlain may have been discomfited to find himself placed over two regimental commanders long senior to him. As it happened, the seniority issue would solve itself. Colonel Jenney—perhaps affronted by the command arrangement—would soon resign his commission, leaving his regiment in the hands of his German-born lieutenant colonel, Gustavus Sniper. And General Sickel, who not only had commanded his own brigade in the Shenandoah Valley but had presided over Chamberlain's new command for the past six weeks, would prove, like Sniper, an obedient and trustworthy subordinate. They would give unflinchingly of their talent and energy to help Chamberlain tackle his most pressing problem, whipping more than 1,800 recruits into shape through a strict training regimen.[28]

That problem, too, was set aright in quick time. Upon reporting at his brigade's headquarters near Poplar Springs Church, four and a half miles southwest of Petersburg, Chamberlain was pleasantly surprised by the proficiency both regiments displayed in camp and on the drillfield. By the last days of November, a private in the New York regiment reported the general as saying "that to see us drill he would not think that we was a new regiment. He said if we will tend to our knitting that we will soon be the best in the division."[29]

Aware of Chamberlain's gleaming record and observant of the respect and support that Sickel and Sniper gave the returning hero, the men warmed to their new brigade leader more quickly than they might have in the normal course of events. In turn, Chamberlain came to forget the size of his command and began to consider himself fortunate in his present position. Especially after General Griffin confided that during future operations he would entrust a second brigade to Chamberlain's control, the latter began to believe that his new command "was really equal to my old one in importance." He also sensed that an uncomplaining acceptance of his lot would pay dividends. Years later he proudly recalled that "my cheerful acquiescence in an assignment of *reduced* importance took the attention of my superiors." Acceptance brought peace of mind, and, in the end, vindication. Later he would describe the 185th as a "splendid" regiment, its commander, Sniper, as "fearless" and "clear-brained," and the 198th as a "stalwart" outfit under "brave veteran Sickel." Beyond the fighting qualities of his officers and men, Chamberlain enjoyed the talents of what his oft-visiting brother, Tom, called "one of the best bands in the Corps."[30]

Picket duty, drill, and target practice consumed the attention of

Chamberlain's brigade during his first three weeks at Poplar Springs Church. He himself spent the time becoming acquainted with his officers, forming a staff, and engaging in such physical exercise as would increase his strength without compromising his health. Band concerts and dress parades broke the monotony of winter quarters, and on November 24 the brigade chaplains read to the assembled troops Lincoln's Thanksgiving Day message.[31]

On the morning of December 7 the brigade left the vicinity of its camp for the first time under its new leader. In concert with the balance of its corps, a division of the Second Corps, and the army's 2nd Cavalry Division, the command headed south along roads that paralleled the Petersburg & Weldon Railroad, Robert E. Lee's supply conduit to the Carolinas. Since late June, Grant had been attempting to sever his enemy's links to areas that provided it with rations, forage, clothing, and other martial necessities. He had captured the upper reaches of the Weldon line, close to Petersburg; now he wanted to deny its still-working lower extremities to the cold and hungry troops opposing him. As he rode south, Chamberlain determined to play well his role in Grant's strategy. Glad to be back in action after so long a hiatus, he would ignore every pain that physical exertion inflicted on him.[32]

His first operation at star rank went relatively smoothly, affirming his faith in his recuperation and his confidence in the military potential of his demi-brigade. On December 8 Griffin's division began destroying tracks and ties near the Nottoway River, 15 miles below Petersburg. The following day, steeling themselves against wintry gusts, Chamberlain's men labored until near midnight, levering up miles of track, roasting sections of rail over bonfires (producing what Chamberlain considered "a grand sight"), and bending them into a semblance of the corps insignia. In this fashion the brigade helped destroy two dozen miles of trackage, a feat that brought them as far as the Meherrin River.[33]

Though the threat of attack was present throughout the expedition, no Confederates disturbed the men's work. The day after they reached the Meherrin, the rail-wreckers discovered its south side fortified by artillery-studded entrenchments. General Warren ended the operation at that point; on the 10th his men followed him north under pelting sleet and icy rain, their mission accomplished.

The return trip produced sights that Chamberlain could never erase from memory. On the raid scores of soldiers—but none in his command—had broken ranks to loot the homes of civilians. Many got drunk on stolen whiskey and brandy; in their inebriated state, some assaulted their unwilling hosts. "This was a hard night," Chamberlain informed his sister days later. "When I brought up the rear, I saw sad work in protecting helpless women & children from outrage.... I am willing to fight men in arms, but not *babes in arms*."[34]

His efforts failed to cool tempers ignited by the criminals in the ranks. Bushwhackers mobilized to even the score; the bodies of captured Federals, many stripped of their uniforms, lined the return route of the Fifth Corps. "In fact," Chamberlain told Sae, "they were murdered—their throats cut from ear to ear." In retaliation, soldiers left the column to burn miles of houses, barns, and outbuildings along both sides of the road. With winter fast approaching, these were truly the darkest days of the war. Chamberlain hoped never to live through another such time. "I had rather," he wrote brother John, "charge lines of battle."[35]

* * *

Despite its unsettling finale, the maiden outing of the 1st Brigade, 1st Division under its new commander had been a rousing success. Chamberlain appears to have come through the operation, however, less well than his soldiers. Although Tom Chamberlain, now provost marshal of Griffin's division, wrote home that Lawrence had returned to camp in good shape, his health deteriorated as the year rushed to a close. Chamberlain pushed himself through days of duty that would have seemed routine to a healthy man but which took a toll he could not ignore. On December 19, as his men began to stockade their tents against the weather, he admitted in a letter to John that although he had managed "to do full duty without much injury, & not a great deal of suffering" during the recent operation, "still I 'was not fit' to return to field duty, & it is very hard to take such chances as we had on the 'Weldon raid'." Evidently, his Petersburg wound was acting up again, probably the result of another infection, one that produced debilitating pain. More surgery appeared inevitable; as he told John, he was "making up my mind where to have it done, that is, the 'knifing'."[36]

Apparently John feared that his brother's devotion to duty might cause him to put off the operation. He may have said as much to their parents, for the first week of the New Year brought a letter from his mother imploring Lawrence to "do dear child take care of your self. Surely you have done & suffered & won laurels enough in this war to satisfy the most ambitious...." His mother's implied criticism—her fear that her son's ambition had begun to outstrip his physical ability to realize it—probably failed to register with him, but he did agree to avoid further damage to his health. On January 9, after consulting with the medical director of his brigade, he petitioned General Crawford, in temporary command of the Fifth Corps, for 30 days' leave of absence "to have surgical treatment for my wound, which cannot be had in the field." Largely due to the doctor's prediction that only surgery could "prevent permanent disability," the petition was granted swiftly. However, probably because no one could predict when campaigning would resume, the leave was reduced to 20 days. The change would seem to necessitate an early operation and a brief recuperation, but Chamberlain knew that an extension would be granted if needed.[37]

On January 13 he handed the brigade to General Sickel, himself recently returned from leave, and headed north. Contrary to latter-day accounts, it appears that he intended to go not to Philadelphia but all the way to Maine, perhaps to be treated by a surgeon in Brunswick. For the early leg of the journey, he traveled in company with Ellis Spear, who was bound for Augusta on army business. For the majority of the trip, however, Spear had to travel alone, for when he arrived in Philadelphia prior to changing cars for the New England run, Chamberlain was "detained" in the city, as he reported, "by the state of my wounds." His reference to the stopover as a "misfortune" indicates that he had not planned to seek medical treatment so soon.[38]

The situation redounded to Chamberlain's benefit for, as he later told Sae, "besides the warm courtesies & compliments I received from every body there I found [that] the services of Dr. Pancoast—the most skilful [sic] surgeon in the United States—not only relieved my existing disabilities, but put me in the mood of a more rapid recovery." Although the identity of the doctor who treated him remains unknown, he may have been Joseph Pancoast, one of Philadelphia's most distinguished surgeons and uncle of Doctor George L. Pancoast, formerly medical director of the Cavalry Corps, Army of the Potomac.[39]

The good doctor's ability to relieve his patient's suffering, while effective in the short term, probably lacked long-lasting results. He might have reseated the catheter in Chamberlain's bladder, but the chief source of the patient's pain and debility was the fistula in the urethra. While Dr. Pancoast may have relieved the symptoms of infection, he probably would have failed in any attempt to close the wound itself. Not for another 10 years or more would surgeons enjoy widespread success in treating wounds of the sort that troubled Chamberlain.

After a few days spent waiting for the palliative effects of the operation to take hold, Chamberlain traveled back to Brunswick, for the second time in four months, to begin his long-term recuperation. At home he would again submit to Fannie's nursing. There he would also make the acquaintance of his newborn daughter and reacquaint himself with Daisy and Wyllys. Throughout the homecoming he would indulge freely in the joys of hearth and home, but he would think of nothing so much as another return to the army.[40]

Twelve

BATTERED VICTOR

*F*amily, friends, and local officials did all in their power to keep the wounded hero at home, to no avail. Not even his newborn daughter or his postpartum wife could persuade Chamberlain that his place was with those who loved him, not with those who followed him into battle. For two months, as the bitter winter worked its will upon the Maine countryside, he kept to his sickbed, by candlelight scouring the newspapers for word of his corps' activities, wishing he were sharing in them.

As his latest recuperation wore on, he found an ever greater incentive to return as swiftly as possible to the seat of war. Even before heading north he had heard rumors that General Bartlett was about to leave the 3rd Brigade on an extended sick leave, raising the probability that Chamberlain, as senior brigade leader in the corps, would succeed him. Early in February, the restless patient (who reported himself as "fast recovering") learned that the rumor had come true: Bartlett had hobbled home to Massachusetts. Upon his return, Chamberlain might find himself transferred back to his old brigade. While he had no reservations about leading his present command into action at Petersburg, the thought of renewing his association with the 20th Maine, after so long an estrangement, captured his imagination. And yet he was in no mood to be picky. "I want to be at any post," he wrote his father. "The campaign will soon open, & it will open strong."[1]

Despite his prospects in the army, Chamberlain must have given some consideration to the opportunities available to him at home. By the second week in February, with his recovery nearly complete, he was mulling over an offer recently tendered him by state officials, that of collector of customs in neighboring Bath. It was, he admitted, a plum position, second in terms of salary and prestige only to the collectorship of Portland, which had been bestowed on former Governor Washburn. Yet in the end—as his father must have anticipated—he rejected the sinecure in favor of retaking the field, "where my services were never more needed, or more valuable than now." When his parents protested his decision, he admonished them that, "I owe the Country three years service. It is a time when every man should stand by his guns. And I am not scared or hurt enough yet to be willing to face to the rear, when other men are marching to the front."[2]

In a second letter to his father, a week after the first, Chamberlain finally addressed the subject of his responsibilities to his family. His view of the matter does not surprise. While the interests of "my young & dependent family" remained uppermost in his mind, he was unwilling to leave to it a divided nation and a land without peace. If Chamberlain ever entertained guilt feelings over his continual leave-taking of Fannie and the children, he could always tell himself, as he did now, that he was responding to a higher calling, a cause that transcended personal hopes and desires, whose success would benefit the Chamberlains and everyone else in the long run. This vision of a greater good would have provided all the balm his conscience required.[3]

For a second job offer—to return to his teaching duties at Bowdoin—he entertained no enthusiasm. As he told his father, should the war drag on beyond summer, he would probably resign his professorship. Even if Grant subdued Lee as soon as the roads dried, he preferred to "throw myself on the current of affairs ... or strike into some other enterprise of a more bold & stirring character than a College chair affords." To one who had spent months engaged in mortal combat, a schoolroom seemed a listless, lifeless workplace.[4]

Chamberlain concluded his letter to his father with an expression of the firmest resolve: "At all events I must return to the army." And return he did, the very next day. On February 21 he kissed the four people dearest to him and went through the door with a heart both heavy and light—saddened by this new, untimely parting, brightened by the prospect of high drama just ahead.[5]

Those he left behind appear to have reacted to the separation less matter-of-factly than he. His departures, especially as they almost always found him restored to something less than full health, seemed to rob his family of vitality and peace of mind. For Fannie Chamberlain, this leave-taking may well have been the hardest of all to bear. This time not only had she lost a loved one—for good, perhaps—but their marriage had lost something integral and unrecoverable. The strain of saying goodbye too many times to a husband driven as much by love of war as by patriotism had taken its toll. Ever after, nothing between them would be the same.

* * *

In Chamberlain's absence, his brigade, deftly managed by Horatio Sickel, had successfully engaged the Rebels. On February 5, during an advance by the Second and Fifth Corps, Sickel's troops clashed with the foe about seven miles southwest of Petersburg, near the point at which the Boydton Plank Road crossed Hatcher's Run, a major route of supply for Lee's army. Following a general engagement, during which the 1st Brigade drove a sizable force from the field at a cost of three dozen casualties, the attackers lay claim to a long stretch of the road.

This accomplishment had enabled Grant and Meade to stretch Lee's line to a distance of 35 miles above and below Petersburg. That line was now held by approximately 35,000 effectives, less than one third as many men as the Army of the Potomac and Army of the James could hurl against them. As Chamberlain had so vividly foreseen, the end was coming fast; he had returned none too soon.[6]

Reporting on February 27 at his brigade's new camp four miles beyond Poplar Spring Church, Chamberlain astonished officers and men who feared they had seen the last of him. Visiting corps headquarters, he learned that General Bartlett was back in command of the 3rd Brigade. Thus Chamberlain relinquished his dream of returning to the 20th Maine's brigade, perhaps adding its regiments to his own.

Almost as soon as he relieved General Sickel, Chamberlain busied himself in studying maps and situation reports, debriefing the leaders of scouting parties, and interrogating prisoners from the front. Before long, signs suggested another offensive. A series of dress parades, often a prelude to a general movement, were held throughout the army as Grant, Meade, and visitors such as President Lincoln and William T. Sherman, the latter just up from his armies' new position in North Carolina, turned out to review the troops. On March 6, in the temporary absence of General Griffin, Chamberlain had the honor of commanding the 1st Division during one of these morale-building exercises. He was proud to observe that the 1,750 men in General Sickel's charge looked as impressive on parade as they had on the drill-plain.[7]

He was likewise gratified by the continuing and noticeable improvement in his health. As the weather warmed, he felt an increase in stamina, a sign that he would be able to endure the campaigning ahead, as brief or as extended as it proved to be. "You cannot imagine how favorable this kind of life is to my health," he wrote on March 9 to Sae. "One would not think me fit to walk a half mile if I was home; but here I ride as fast & far as the best, and ask no favors. I have no doubt that my recovery will be greatly promoted by my return to the field...."[8]

His revived health was fast approaching the critical test—hard and sustained campaigning. A preliminary engagement occurred on March 25, when Robert E. Lee conducted the final offensive of his military career. The Confederate commander had received word that Phil Sheridan, having stamped out organized opposition in the Shenandoah Valley, had begun his return march to Petersburg in company with two cavalry divisions plus the infantry and artillery of the Sixth Corps. Hoping to break Grant's siege before Sheridan could join him, in the pre-dawn hours of the 25th Lee made a surprise assault on Ninth Corps positions along the northeastern environs of Petersburg. Lee's gamble failed. Although the attackers briefly seized a major fort and outlying defenses, they were hurled back by Meade's application of overwhelming force.[9]

The offensive was not limited to Petersburg. Attackers also struck the lines of the Second Corps, now under Major General Andrew A. Humphreys, near Hatcher's Run. Early that morning General Warren moved elements of Griffin's division into supporting distance. From 8:00 A.M. until dark, Chamberlain's brigade trekked to several points under assault, ready to help as needed. Close to sundown, the command was placed in the rear and on the flank of a Second Corps division, which it helped in repulsing an attack that Chamberlain described as made with "great vigor and boldness, though not in heavy force." The brigade hardly worked up a sweat—only two of its men had been wounded, none killed—but the day's action provided a nice tune-up to the larger, more decisive work that lay ahead.[10]

* * *

The day following its support of General Humphreys, Griffin's division was told to prepare to march at a moment's notice. That day Chamberlain's people drew 50 rounds of ammunition per man as well as four days' rations of beef, hard bread, salt, coffee, and sugar. Clerks and other noncombatants were evicted from camp, and surplus baggage was carted off to City Point. It took another three days, however, for marching orders to arrive. Some time after 5:00 A.M. on March 29, the 1st Brigade, 1st Division, Fifth Army Corps turned it back on winter quarters and took to southward-leading roads. No bugles or drums sounded during the movement, which told Chamberlain and anyone else with a logical mind that the objective of their movement lay not far away.

Chamberlain's brigade, which led the advance of its division, made up a minute part of the force in motion this morning. All around it, the rest of the Fifth Corps pressed south on parallel roads. On the right of the corps marched Humphreys's troops, and in front, in rear, and on the flanks, trotted the cavalry divisions of the Army of the Potomac and Sheridan's Army of the Shenandoah, under Major General George Crook and Brevet Major General Wesley Merritt, respectively. Although General Meade accompanied the massive advance in the role of expeditionary leader, Grant had made Sheridan—today strictly in charge of the cavalry—an independent commander and thus removed from Meade's authority. The command arrangements may have seemed unusual, perhaps unwieldy, but Grant felt he owed Sheridan, who had commanded a full-size army in the Shenandoah, autonomy in the present situation. For one thing, the commanding general considered the Irishman a more decisive and combative soldier than the older, more conservative Meade. If given the authority and the resources, Sheridan might bring Lee to bay in a matter of hours; Grant doubted that Meade, if left to his own devices, would accomplish as much in a fortnight.[11]

Whether they knew it or not the advancing troops were heading for the extended right flank of Lee's army, anchored in the countryside southwest of Petersburg. Months given to countering Union probes below the Cockade City had left that flank so fragile that, if pressed, it might shatter. Grant had sent Meade and Sheridan to pass around the end of that flank, a line of entrenchments astride the White Oak Road near Burgess's Mill, about three miles east of a strategic crossroads known as Five Forks. The flank cleared, the Federals could move as far north as the Petersburg & Lynchburg (more familiarly known as the Southside) Railroad. The Weldon line and other rail routes to Petersburg had been cut or otherwise neutralized; the Southside represented Lee's last line of supply as well as the only practical route of withdrawal should he somehow break free of investment. Grant believed that once the Southside Railroad came into his possession, the enemy would resist no further.

To reach their objective, cavalry and infantry crossed Rowanty Creek on a hastily constructed pontoon span before veering westward onto the Vaughan Road and marching in the direction of Dinwiddie Court House. Soon after falling out for a roadside rest, Griffin's division, at Meade's order, retraced its path on the Vaughan Road until it could be guided northward along the Quaker Road in the direction of Burgess's Mill. The brigade advanced as far as Gravelly Run, north of which it spied breastworks occupied by men in gray and butternut. Chamberlain halted his people on the south bank until Griffin arrived with an order that the brigade cross the creek in line of battle. Chamberlain complied by culling out a battalion of the 198th Pennsylvania, placing it under one of his most trusted subordinates, Major Edwin A. Glenn, and throwing it in advance of the main body as skirmishers.[12]

At a prearranged signal, Glenn's troops splashed across the cold, waist-deep water while the 185th New York, in their immediate rear, laid down a covering fire. Weapons and ammunition held above their heads, Glenn's skirmishers made choice targets for Confederate marksmen on the north bank, who laced them with a volley. Several Pennsylvanians sank into the water, never to rise. Once across the stream, the enraged survivors struck the enemy in flank and chased those they did not kill for about a mile to the north. There the fugitives sought refuge among a few dozen comrades ensconced behind earthworks bolstered by fallen trees. Once all were over the stream, Glenn's skirmishers resumed their advance. In their rear Chamberlain formed a line across the Quaker Road with the balance of Glenn's regiment, under General Sickel, to the right of the road, and Colonel Sniper and his 185th New York on the left.[13]

Fulfilling his superior's expectations, Glenn gouged the enemy out of their works with swift precision, then chased them through a woods as far as a landmark known as the Lewis house. When the reinforced enemy—troops of Major General Bushrod Rust Johnson's division, part of a larger force that Lee had hustled down to foil Warren's and Humphreys's advance—made a stand at the edge of the trees, Chamberlain halted the skirmish line until Sickel and Sniper joined it in the woods. Once his force had regained cohesiveness, Chamberlain conferred with Griffin, who told him, quite simply, to attack. To obey meant to leave the shelter of the trees for a perilous stretch of open ground. Johnson's position, hard by a sawmill and a massive pile of sawdust that made a natural earthwork, could be reached only by crossing a clearing perhaps a thousand yards both in length and width. Cannon in front commanded the ground and sharpshooters had been posted in woodlots along either flank.[14]

The task ahead had its hazards, but for mortal risk Chamberlain doubted that it matched Rives's Salient. Even Charlemagne, though badly wounded in that assault, had survived its terrors; Chamberlain was astride him now as he scanned the Rebel works one last time through his fieldglasses. With calm deliberation he reinforced Glenn's battalion with a company of New Yorkers. He conferred briefly with Sickel and Sniper, ensuring each subordinate knew what was expected of him. Then he turned toward the main body, unsheathed his sword, raised it above his head, shouted a command, and started forward. Behind him nearly 2,000 soldiers moved at a rapid walk, then shifted into the double-quick, overflowing the Quaker Road and seeping into the woods beyond.

Determined to keep ahead of them, their leader spurred his charger toward the spitting rifles of the enemy. Just before he reached their line he began to repent of his rashness. Hauling back on the reins, he caused Charlemagne to rear. In that instant Chamberlain was struck in the chest by a sharpshooter's bullet, rendering him briefly unconscious. As he recounted in his memoir of the Appomattox campaign, *The Passing of the Armies*, the missile had passed through the neck muscle of his mount before striking him just below the heart, passing along his bridle arm "and also I may say through a leather case of field orders and a brass-mounted hand-mirror in my breast-pocket," before it "demolished the pistol in the belt of my aide Lieutenant Vogel, and knocked him out of the saddle."[15]

An unconscious Chamberlain could not have witnessed the effects of the rifle shot; therefore he may be forgiven this flight of fancy. No Civil War firearm possessed the muzzle velocity necessary for a minie ball to have passed through so many animate and inanimate objects. Most likely two bullets, fired simultaneously at targets in close proximity to each other, accounted for the damage done to and near Chamberlain. A curious commentary on the incident comes from Ellis Spear, who was serving as a 3rd Brigade staff officer this day. Spear, who was in such close contact with Chamberlain that he gave him a drink from a flask filled with wine, later denied that his old commander had been shot at all. "He was not wounded on the Quaker road," Spear would maintain in a postwar letter to Oliver Norton. "I know that absolutely, as I was with him part of the time and not far off any time." Spear claimed that Chamberlain's only damage was to his coat, which was perforated by a near-miss.[16]

While Spear's claim is difficult to accept, Chamberlain's contention that the bullet was deflected "around two ribs so as to come out at the back seam of my coat" appears to defy the laws of both physics and probability. Then, too, the severity of the wound that Chamberlain describes, especially given its inability to drive him from the field, invites dispute. Writing long after the war, Norton raised a provocative question: "How can any reasonable person suppose that if Chamberlain had been wounded ... as he states in his book, he could have been able to resume his command on the 30th and 31st of March.... A ball striking a rib and going all around his left side, even if the rib was not shattered, would certainly have him out of commission longer than the succeeding two or three days."[17]

Whatever the nature of his injury, Chamberlain regained his senses quickly enough to direct Charlemagne out of the line of fire before either horse or rider went down. When in a position of relative safety, however, he saw that all was not well with his brigade. Despite its speed and enthusiasm, Chamberlain's attack had lost its momentum, and part of his command—the right flank of Sickel's regiment—"was now broken and flying before the enemy like leaves before the wind." When General Griffin rode up to his wounded subordinate with a look of concern and worried aloud that Chamberlain was "gone," the latter agreed, believing his boss was referring to the 1st Brigade.[18]

But the brigade was not gone, not yet. Sickel himself rushed into the breach, steadying the battle line. "The men," wrote one of the Pennsylvanians, "soon responded to these efforts, and, rallying, they drove the rebels entirely back into their works." In the process Sickle took a severe wound in the left arm, "notwithstanding which he fought on like a hero." Sickle's wound troubled Chamberlain, who believed he could not afford to lose such a worthy subordinate. He was saddened, too, by the loss of a young man he had come to know quite well, Major Charles I. Maceuen of Sickel's regiment, "a gallant and noble young officer," who had toppled dead virtually at Chamberlain's feet.[19]

Once Griffin left, Chamberlain rode Charlemagne at an easy gait toward the rear, until it became apparent that the warhorse had gone as far as he could. Dismounting slowly and painfully, the brigadier began to advance on foot toward the center of his still-moving line, hopeful of turning rally into triumph. Wandering too far afield, however, he found himself surrounded by the enemy; for the third time in his military career he had to talk his way out of capture. "Surrender?" he claims to have shouted at the hesitant Confederates. "What's the matter with you? What do you take me for? Don't you see these Yanks right onto us? Come along with me and let us break 'em." According to Chamberlain, his would-be captors followed his waving sword toward the rear of his own brigade, whose members turned about and took them prisoner.[20]

Just as Sickel's men seemed about to carry the works near the sawdust pile, Chamberlain's other regiment wavered and nearly broke under the pressure of opposing reinforcements. Within minutes, Sniper's New Yorkers were forced into a position almost parallel with the Quaker Road, facing primarily westward. They needed a helping hand, and quickly.

Chamberlain sent a courier to seek aid from the force on his far left, the 2nd Brigade of Griffin's division, under Brevet Brigadier General Edgar M. Gregory. It was this command that Griffin had promised to place under Chamberlain's control whenever possible. Gregory was asked to strike the enemy in flank, but passing time brought no perceptible improvement in Colonel Sniper's situation. Minutes seemed to lumber by as the battle hung in the balance, but finally help arrived and in quantity, thanks to General Griffin's solicitude. First, Lieutenant John Mitchell's Battery B, 4th United States Artillery ran into position to sweep the Rebel right, easing the pressure on Sniper. Then one of Gregory's regiments marched up from the west to reinforce the 185th New York. Next, Brevet Brigadier General Alfred L. Pearson led his 155th Pennsylvania Zouaves, part of Bartlett's brigade, into the melee in the direction of Chamberlain's center. Like Colonel Sniper minutes before, Pearson led his troops in a charge while hoisting the regimental colors; his men responded with wild enthusiasm.[21]

The combination of artillery cover and fresh infantry feeding into his line enabled Chamberlain to prod the Confederates, who had withstood two hours of combat, into retreat. Once they made up their mind to leave, they did so in such haste that they left their dead—130 of them— and dozens of their wounded on the field; almost 200 others were cut off in mid-flight and persuaded to surrender. The victory had been gained at a cost of 328 killed and wounded in the 1st Brigade plus unknown losses in the units that had reinforced it. Casualties comprised 16 officers in addition to Sickel and Maceuen, including every member of Chamberlain's staff.[22]

The statistics indicate the gravity of Chamberlain's situation. For much of the fight, he had been outnumbered and, for a part of it, hard-pressed. Yet, he had held the line until supports could fight their way through to him. Fittingly, he won lofty praise for the steadiness and fortitude he and his men had displayed throughout the fight. General Warren announced that his "splendid work" rated a tangible reward—promotion to brevet major general of volunteers "for conspicuous gallantry in action."[23]

* * *

Mounted on a borrowed horse, Chamberlain rode the length of his line in the early, rainy hours of evening, supervising the erecting of strong fieldworks. He also saw to the positioning of troops from those commands on his flanks, while seeking information about the day's outcome in other sectors. He learned that the Second Corps had gone into position near, but not always connecting with, Warren's right. Meanwhile, about two and a half miles to the southwest, Sheridan and his three cavalry divisions had taken position near Dinwiddie Court House, within striking distance of infantry and cavalry guarding Lee's far right. The next day Sheridan would seek a way to break or circumvent that flank, move into the Rebels' rear, and play havoc with their last railroad.[24]

Returning to his field headquarters at the Lewis farmhouse, Chamberlain tried to comfort the sorrowing members of a burial party, then himself grieved over one object of their attention, the body of Major Maceuen. After a few moments given to prayer, he entered the kitchen of the house to compose by candlelight a letter of condolence to the major's father. Later he looked in on the wounded General Sickel, who reportedly paid tribute to his emotionally distressed superior. "General Chamberlain," Sickel is quoted as saying, "you have the soul of a lion and the heart of a woman." This compliment was first recorded (in slightly different words) in a regimental history published in 1884, to which Chamberlain contributed material. It has come to be regarded as perfectly expressive of Chamberlain's salient qualities. It has even provided the title of one of his biographies.[25]

No historian has ever studied the origin or questioned the validity of the quote, which on its face seems rather too good to be true. While it is difficult to imagine Chamberlain inventing it, it is equally difficult to believe such a lyrically effusive compliment could come from the mouth of a hard-bitten combat leader who never gave indication of being poet or toady. Rather than a complete fabrication, the quote may have its origins in a less grandiose tribute, one its recipient embellished. This theory is strengthened by the fact that its theme was quite meaningful to Chamberlain. He reprises it in his magazine article about Fredericksburg when he emphasizes the compassion that "brave men show to comrades when direst need befalls," the "tenderness of the stern and strong [that] recalls the Scripture phrase, 'passing the love of women'."[26]

* * *

Throughout rainy, ice-cold March 30th, Chamberlain convalesced from the accumulated effect of wounds old and recent. His men, and their comrades elsewhere on the Fifth Corps' front and along the still-disconnected line of General Humphreys's corps farther east, strengthened their works while simultaneously confronting rumors that an offensive was imminent.

If it came, the movement would have to be launched in two directions at the same time. North of the Lewis house, Johnson's division and other Confederate infantry huddled inside their breast-works along the White Oak Road. Farther west, at Five Forks, General Lee had created a new anchor for his right flank. Late that afternoon 9,200 troops of all arms, under the tragic hero of Gettysburg, Major General George Edward Pickett, took possession of the crossroads vicinity and fortified it, albeit imperfectly. Pickett's mission was not merely defensive; on March 31 he was to advance against Sheridan in conjunction with an offensive against the Second and Fifth Corps by other Confederate forces. The overall objective was to drive Meade's left flank as far as possible from the Southside Railroad.[27]

The last day of March found General Warren planning an advance of his own. The previous day Grant had suggested to Meade that the left flank of the Fifth Corps be extended as far north as the White Oak Road, within striking distance of the entrenchments near Burgess's Mill. Such a move would enable the Federals not only to attack the trenches but to interpose between them and Pickett's position.[28]

Before sunrise members of the Second Corps relieved Griffin's division, whereupon Griffin joined the rest of Warren's corps, the divisions of Romeyn Ayres and Samuel Crawford, in moving up to the White Oak Road. Chamberlain's role in the movement was to provide a reserve force as well as to guard the left flank of the main lines, a dual mission that created what he called a "ticklish situation." To play that role, he led his troops up the Boydton Plank Road almost as far as the crossing of Gravelly Run. Astride Charlemagne, who had returned to service that morning as if from the dead, he spent much of the morning positioning not only his own troops but also Gregory's, as well as a pair of light batteries that had been assigned him this day.[29]

Fighting began sometime after 10:00 A.M., when a party of Ayres's division, while making a reconnaissance of the White Oak Road, attracted enemy attention and then an attack, two brigades strong. Although Ayres initially offered stout resistance, one of his brigades, under Brevet Brigadier General Frederick Winthrop, a close acquaintance of Chamberlain's, suddenly broke, its men racing to the rear as though the fires of perdition were licking at their heels. Winthrop managed to stem a rout, but the panic communicated itself to the rest of Ayres's division, then to Crawford's, in Ayres's right rear. Although enough men rallied to temporarily halt the onslaught, help was urgently needed.[30]

At the critical moment, Griffin ordered Chamberlain into the breach. His men hustled to the south side of Gravelly Run just as demoralized comrades rushed down the other bank into the water. Before their pursuers could reach the stream, Chamberlain led his men across, on the far side forming them into two lines, the 198th Pennsylvania, commanded this day by Major Glenn, in front and toward the left, and Sniper's New Yorkers in the right rear. Gregory's brigade, also deployed in two lines, battalions in echelon, came up on the right of Chamberlain. Remnants of Ayres's division formed on Chamberlain's left, rallied units of Crawford's command in his rear. The skirmishers of Griffin's division, led by General Pearson, covered the gap between Chamberlain's left and Ayres's right. Finally, the Second Corps division of Brevet Major General Nelson A. Miles moved forward to attack on the far right; it faced half of the Confederate force that had demoralized Ayres and Crawford.[31]

When his line was ready, Chamberlain advanced for more than a mile, Gregory keeping pace on the right, Pearson to the left. The moving troops drove a force of skirmishers across a wide field toward the point at which the fight had begun. Before midway across that field, however, Chamberlain's men began to absorb something more than a skirmish fire. Across the open ground a gray battle line drifted out of a woods, "its force," Chamberlain noted, "at least equal to our own." He was about to advance in turn when an order from General Warren shunted him onto the defensive. His superior later claimed that the tactical situation, rather than any explicit instructions, brought Chamberlain's line to a halt. Whatever the case, the men of the 1st Brigade dropped their weapons and began to dig rifle pits across the field.[32]

Defensive tactics had their limitations, as became clear when the brigade took an enfilading fire from woods on both of its flanks. Chamberlain's right, hit especially hard, began to waver. The precarious position led him to seek out General Griffin with an urgent proposal: "It appeared that the enemy's position might be carried with no greater loss than it would cost us merely to hold our ground, and the men were eager to charge over the field." To Chamberlain's relief, Griffin approved a renewal of the attack. As his superior turned to the rear, he alluded sharply to the panic-stricken flight of the other divisions: "I ['ll] tell Warren you will wipe out this disgrace... !"[33]

With a shout, Chamberlain's men leapt to their feet, abandoned their hastily built works, and surged across the grassy field. As before, Gregory's brigade kept pace, aiming for the woods where the most destructive fire had originated. Despite a barrage from cannon supporting the enemy line, Chamberlain and Gregory struck that line virtually simultaneously. Both brigades surmounted the breastworks in their front and grappled with their defenders. Farther to the right, Miles's division thudded into the extreme left flank of the Rebel line, putting most of its personnel to flight.[34]

The result was, as Chamberlain exulted, "a complete success." After a brief but intense struggle, the Rebel infantry turned and ran back through the woods, their artillery comrades trundling along beside. All headed for the Burgess's Mill defenses. Galvanized by their victory, the troops of Chamberlain and Gregory pursued across the White Oak Road until, as the latter noted proudly, "the ground lost in the morning was handsomely retaken." In restoring the reputation of the Fifth Corps, Chamberlain had lost close to 80 officers and men, but in three hours' fighting he had inflicted more than twice as many casualties. Prisoners alone numbered in the hundreds; they included a Virginia regiment captured whole.[35]

The victory inserted thousands of Federals between Burgess's Mill and Five Forks. Chamberlain's final position of the day, assumed at about 6:00 P.M., placed his left flank 300 yards above the White Oak Road. Farther south, Gregory's brigade, which remained on Chamberlain's right, stretched to a point just below that long-coveted thoroughfare. The members of both brigades faced in a common direction, toward the Rebel defenses near Burgess's.[36]

The aftermath of battle could be summed up briefly. "During the night," Chamberlain reported, "we buried our dead and cared for our wounded, and bivouacked on the line."[37]

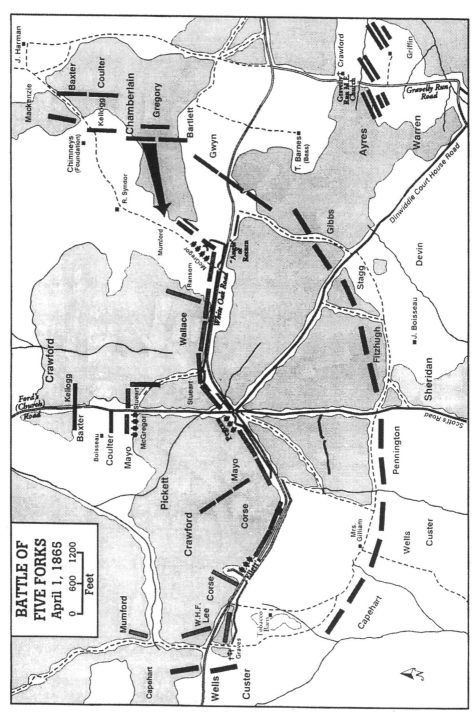

BATTLE OF
FIVE FORKS
April 1, 1865

0   600   1200
Feet

Thirteen

GENEROUS ENEMY

While Meade's infantry had turned a bad day into a memorably good one, Sheridan's cavalry had suffered through a day everyone from "Little Phil" down to the lowliest trooper wished to forget. Expecting to give George Pickett a hard time between Five Forks and Dinwiddie Court House, Sheridan instead found himself forced out of one position after another, hard pressed by both infantry and horsemen on all parts of the field. By evening, he was regrouping inside a defensive line less than a mile above the courthouse.[1]

Sheridan's predicament had cost him neither his combativeness nor his optimism. When he became aware that Chamberlain had cut the White Oak Road, isolating Pickett from comrades closer to Petersburg, the cavalry leader-turned-independent commander realized just how vulnerable his enemy had become. That evening he requested that Grant send him the Sixth Corps, which had fought under him in the Shenandoah. Backed by troops he trusted, Sheridan was confident that he could "turn the enemy's left or break through his lines," before rolling up that line eastward. Grant saw the potential in such strategy but informed Sheridan that the Sixth Corps was too far off to reach Dinwiddie in time for a dawn advance. Instead, Grant had Meade order Warren's troops to Sheridan's assistance. Without consulting

Meade, Grant promised Sheridan that the Fifth Corps would report to him by midnight.[2]

Grant's timetable was unrealistic, for the rains had turned the roads between Warren's and Sheridan's headquarters—nearly four miles of them—into quagmires, brooks into freshets. Warren did not receive the order to aid Sheridan until after 9:00 P.M. on the 31st; even superhuman marching would not get his entire corps to Sheridan in less than three hours.

Warren made what he always considered his best effort to comply, and Chamberlain would back him up on this issue. Dutifully the corps leader sent word for Griffin's division to prepare to head down the Boydton Plank Road to Dinwiddie. In order to comply, Chamberlain regretfully relinquished his hard-won position north of the White Oak Road. Disengaging from close contact with the enemy took time, as did forming a marching column in the inky darkness. Other elements of the division, including Bartlett's brigade, which hours earlier had been moved to within sight of Pickett's defenses, had to be recalled—another time-consuming process.[3]

The delay finally prompted Warren to send Ayres's division along the plank road in advance of the rest of the corps. But Ayres was halted by Gravelly Run, which had overflowed its banks. Lacking pontoons, Warren's engineers dismantled houses to bridge the stream. Some time after 2:00 A.M. on April 1 Ayres finally headed for Dinwiddie Court House. Instead of starting Griffin's division as soon as Ayres moved out, the cautious Warren waited until after 4:30 to order Griffin south. As per the high command's instructions, Griffin did not take the plank road, the most direct route to Sheridan, instead moving to the Crump Road, a more westerly thoroughfare, one roughly parallel to Ayres's route. Chamberlain's brigade did not reach the Crump Road until well after 5:00 A.M.

Ayres's division reached Sheridan about an hour before daybreak. Warned by the proximity of Bartlett's brigade, Pickett's foot and horse soldiers had long since retreated from their exposed position above the courthouse, falling back to the prepared defenses at Five Forks. His plans ruined by the Fifth Corps' failure to reach him hours sooner, Sheridan had been forced to plot anew. His new strategy was aimed at evicting Pickett's men from the crossroads. While his three cavalry divisions struck the enemy's right and center, Sheridan would hurl Warren's infantry at the Rebel left. The combined assault, if properly coordinated, promised to reduce Lee's extended flank to rubble in a matter of hours.[4]

* * *

Griffin's column, Chamberlain at its head, with Crawford's division in its rear, made contact with Sheridan's horsemen at 7:00. The impatient Irishman rode out to greet the new arrivals, but did not extend a warm welcome. He immediately inquired of General Warren's whereabouts; when Chamberlain surmised that he was riding with Crawford in the rear, Sheridan snapped, "that is where I expected to find him!" Then Chamberlain faced a barrage of angry questions, all relating to Warren's inability to adhere to the schedule Grant had established. Chamberlain, who was aware of the animus between his two superiors, feared that the Fifth Corps was in for a hard day. The situation worsened some time before noon, when Sheridan received an oral message from Grant reminding him that as an independent commander he possessed the authority to relieve Warren from command should his dilatory habits continue.[5]

It was 1:00 P.M. before Sheridan could confer with Warren and Warren could get his men into position to follow Sheridan toward Five Forks. The cavalry proceeded up the main road from Dinwiddie Court House, which meandered along a northwestward course toward the center of Pickett's line. Warren's infantry—Crawford's division now in the lead, tailed by Griffin's, then Ayres's—followed for a distance before taking a muddy road that branched off to the right and that met the White Oak Road a mile or more east of Five Forks.

Two hours after leaving Dinwiddie Court House and shortly before reaching the White Oak Road, Warren halted near Gravelly Run Church to form lines of battle. Just to the north lay Warren's objective, the refused left flank of Pickett's position. Near the church Sheridan conferred with Warren one last time. For a while Chamberlain, who was again commanding Gregory's brigade as well as his own, observed the proceedings, committing to memory his role in the day's plan.

Then he broke away from the strategy session to share a midday meal with the visiting General Winthrop, whose brigade had absorbed the initial shock of the previous day's attack. Chamberlain predicted that the pair would have time for "only a hasty bite" before their brigades were ordered up. It would be Winthrop's last meal; within a few hours he would fall mortally wounded.[6]

After Ayres's division came up and deployed for battle on the left side of the road, linking with Crawford's on the right, Sheridan gave the order to attack. It was well past 4:00 P.M. and daylight was beginning to fade. Ayres's and Crawford's men went forward, Griffin's following to the right and rear. Well to the west, Sheridan's three cavalry divisions prepared to attack mounted and afoot against the center and right, forcing Pickett to defend all sectors of his line simultaneously.

As Chamberlain had feared, the day began badly for the men of the Fifth Corps, but the fault was not its alone. Warren's oral orders and a diagram he distributed to his commanders conveyed conflicting information about their route and the points of attack. Warren's orders had all three divisions reaching the White Oak Road before attacking westward, Ayres striking the refused angle of the line, while Crawford and Griffin flanked the works and took them in rear. However, Warren's diagram (which Sheridan had approved) showed all three divisions obliquing to the northwest, Crawford aiming at the angle and Ayres attacking farther to the left; thus, everyone would strike the enemy before they did the road. When Chamberlain asked Griffin about the conflict, he was told not to worry, that if he followed Crawford's right all would be well.[7]

A more troublesome problem this day was that Sheridan's people had inadequately reconnoitered Pickett's line, the flank of which was anchored 1,200 yards to the west of the point that Warren had been directed to strike. The upshot was that Crawford strayed too far north before turning westward. Crossing the White Oak Road, his men passed the refused flank instead of hitting it. Instead of Rebel infantry, they encountered dismounted cavalry that had been trying to close the gap between Pickett and the works closer to Petersburg. Although the horsemen were already opposed by Brigadier General Ranald S. Mackenzie's cavalry division of the Army of the James, which had been instructed to guard the right flank of the Fifth Corps, Crawford pursued the gray troopers as if they were his primary objective.

Meanwhile, moving westward below the White Oak Road, the flank of Ayres's leading brigade found itself raked by an enfilading fire from the enemy defenses. After some confusion, the division leader changed front and attacked head-on with good results, especially after Sheridan's cavalry moved against Pickett's right and center. Eventually Ayres carried the defenses in his front, taking many captives, but for a critical period Crawford's errant advance left him without support.[8]

The quick-thinking General Griffin realized that a mistake had been made. When he heard heavy firing to his left, the division leader quit his assigned position and turned the head of his column sharply to the west, crossing the southeastern corner of a large clearing known as the Syndor Field. Chamberlain also sensed the error. Without orders but suspecting that Crawford had gone too far north—his own brigade was now almost in line with Crawford's left flank instead of its right rear—Chamberlain followed the divisional headquarters flag, his wounds entirely forgotten. As he recalled years later, "I moved south at the *first rip* of Ayres' fight ... and as fast as I could march." His brigade, followed closely by Gregory's, broke out of a woodlot, waded a stream, crossed a ravine, and rushed toward the sound of musketry.[9]

While his men pushed forward, Chamberlain helped turn Bartlett's brigade—three of its regiments, at any rate, including the 20th Maine—in the same direction that he was moving. Griffin's division, now nearly intact, looped around the Rebel flank and attacked its works in the rear. With Colonel Sniper's New Yorkers and a battalion of Pennsylvanians under Major Glenn on the right, Gregory's brigade directly behind it, Chamberlain's command swept across the Rebel rear, spraying it with musketry. Simultaneously, the rest of the 198th Pennsylvania hit the upper edge of the refused flank. Six hundred yards to the south, Ayres's division struck Pickett's left from the opposite side; looking in that direction, Chamberlain observed "a confused whirl of struggling groups, with fitful firing." Under the multi-directional pounding, a rising tide of Confederates threw down their weapons and threw up their hands.[10]

Chamberlain's men did not have everything their own way. When the 20th Maine and the two other outfits of Bartlett's brigade attacked on Chamberlain's left, they encountered a much heavier fire than had the 1st and 2nd Brigades. Its right flank blasted almost to pieces, Bartlett's command threatened to come apart, perhaps taking Chamberlain's column with it. As it was, numerous members of both brigades sought refuge behind the works from which they had driven their enemy. Fortunately, at the height of the threat to Chamberlain's right, he spied in his rear the flag of Brevet Brigadier General James Gwyn's brigade of Ayres's division. He petitioned Gwyn to move up on his left, promising his colleague that he would take the responsibility and give Gwyn credit for any success. Later Chamberlain could report that, "this assistance was most cheerfully and promptly rendered, and contributed in a good degree to our success." He added, however, that the result was not due solely to Gwyn's assistance: "It required the utmost personal efforts of every general and staff officer present to ... repulse the attack."[11]

No sooner was that crisis defused than another loomed. An enemy force, apparently larger than Chamberlain's command, began to threaten his left rear. At his order, the left battalions faced away from the enemy in their front, wheeled to the rear, and met the new threat. To the surprise and relief of everyone in blue, Chamberlain not excepted, the Confederates surrendered en masse. Thankful for large favors, Chamberlain then helped General Bartlett round up 150 to 200 Federal stragglers. Chamberlain coaxed one from behind a stump that would have stopped few bullets. Under his and Bartlett's prodding, most of these demoralized men returned to the firing lines.

When Chamberlain turned back to the offensive, he found it difficult to distinguish his troops from those of Gregory, Bartlett, Gwyn, and elements of Crawford's division that General Warren had finally shuttled into the fight. "Our commands," he wrote, "were queerly mixed; men of every division of the corps came within my jurisdiction; and something like this was probably the case with several other commanders. But that made no difference; men and officers were good friends. There was no jealousy among us subordinate commanders...."[12]

The various units combined to capture hundreds of Rebels as well as artillery pieces both in the works and along a northward-running line that guarded Pickett's principal avenue of retreat. The blue mass pressed on, led by Griffin's three brigades, "driving the enemy," as Chamberlain wrote, "far up the road to the distance, I should judge, of a mile or more." At one point in the kaleidoscope of action he had the pleasure of observing his old 20th Maine "at the post of honor and peril," fighting its way through the disordered ranks of the enemy with a vigor that would have made any commander proud. To the west, meanwhile, Sheridan's horsemen had carried the works in their front through a series of stunning assaults, forcing the occupants to fall or flee, and rendering Picket's entire position untenable.[13]

At Sheridan's direct order, Chamberlain took charge of whatever infantry he found near him and led the commingled mass along the White Oak Road toward Five Forks. En route he swept up demoralized Confederates by the score. However, near Ford's Road, which led north from the crossroads, the left center of his column encountered unexpected opposition from a section of Pickett's works still held in some force. Hesitating only briefly, Chamberlain sent forward the 198th Pennsylvania. Up and over went the Pennsylvanians, carrying the position in minutes and choking off the last resistance Chamberlain would encounter this day.

By now darkness was total, effectively ending the fight and preventing a concerted pursuit. Chamberlain halted, regrouped his scattered ranks, and began counting. The two brigades under his command had accounted for fully a quarter of the 6,000 prisoners captured this day; they had also seized great quantities of weapons as well as five battle flags. "My loss," he reported, "was not heavy in comparison with that of previous days, but cannot be considered otherwise than severe." The 39 casualties included "that thorough soldier" Edwin Glenn, who at Chamberlain's order and promise of promotion, had led the final charge near Ford's Road, capturing a Rebel flag before being struck down. The indirect role he had played in Glenn's mortal wounding prompted Chamberlain to promote the officer, on his deathbed, to brevet colonel. Supposedly, the incident haunted him for the rest of his life.[14]

The loss of good soldiers such as Glenn diminished Chamberlain's pleasure at his command's exemplary performance. So too did rumors, received late in the fighting, of General Warren's relief from command. At first Chamberlain considered the story a poor joke, a fitting end to this All Fools' Day. When it proved true, his mood plummeted. Sheridan, incensed by Warren's slow advance to Dinwiddie Court House, his errant attack across the White Oak Road, and his inaccessibility at a critical point, had used the authority given him to place Charles Griffin in command of the Fifth Corps and order Warren to the rear in disgrace.[15]

The shake-up advanced General Bartlett to the command of the 1st Division. Reportedly, Bartlett gave Chamberlain the opportunity to return to his old brigade and the 20th Maine. Now that a long-cherished goal was in his hands, Chamberlain refused the offer. The historian of the 198th Pennsylvania believed he knew why—Chamberlain had made a more extensive combat record with his current command than he had with the 3rd Brigade after Gettysburg or with the Keystone Brigade at Petersburg. Chamberlain's New Yorkers and Pennsylvanians might be few in comparison to the other brigades in this army, but they had proved themselves worthy of his continuance in command.[16]

The loss of Warren, whom Chamberlain had long admired despite his faults, was a blow that took a long time to absorb. Not only did Sheridan's action rub some of the luster from the victory, it muted Chamberlain's gratification at the praise superiors such as Griffin and Bartlett heaped on him. Several times during the fight Sheridan had also commented favorably on Chamberlain's performance, despite at one point holding him responsible for firing on friendly cavalry. Sheridan's cry at the height of the battle—"By God, that's what I want to see, general officers at the front!"—seemed to augur well for Chamberlain's future in this new order of things.[17]

But Sheridan had said other things, too, in the heat of battle, including a boast that reeked of naked ambition: "We have a record to make before that sun goes down that will make hell tremble...." It appeared that Sheridan had sacrificed Warren to that ambition. Chamberlain must have wondered if he cared to succeed in an army that celebrated those who achieved at any cost and jettisoned others who regarded the lives of their men more highly than the scalps of their enemy.[18]

* * *

What followed Pickett's annihilation at Five Forks smacked of anticlimax, as if the war were over but had to go on due to contractual obligations. When he received news of Sheridan's great victory, Grant put the last touches to a multi-column assault on the Petersburg works, many of which fell to attackers on the morning of Sunday, April 2. Afterward, Lee realized that he could not hope to hold the city for more than a few hours; he was all too aware that with Petersburg gone, Richmond must be evacuated. While attending church in the capital, Jefferson Davis received the news that the end had come. That day the Confederate government fled Richmond, and that night Lee's troops pulled out of both cities, streaming southward and westward. They headed for Amelia Court House on the Richmond & Danville, a few miles above that railroad's junction with the Southside line.[19]

Even before the long-range effects of April 1 became clear, Sheridan put his people—which now included Miles's division of the Second Corps as well as the troops that had carried Five Forks—in motion. The Irishman's objective, as it had been for the past several days, was that last enemy railroad, the Southside, along which many of Pickett's fugitives had rallied. Yet Sheridan did not start until midafternoon, by which time he had learned of gains farther down the line, including General Humphreys's capture of the heavy works near Burgess's Mill.

When the Fifth Corps did move, the two brigades under Chamberlain took the advance up Ford's Road. To reach the Southside the Federals had to cross Hatcher's Run, where they found a Rebel force of indeterminate size holding the north bank. At Chamberlain's word, Colonel Sniper led the 185th New York across the narrow stream and straight at the enemy's ranks, which crumbled at first contact. In their flight the enemy uncovered the road to the Southside, which Chamberlain's main body reached in time to flag down a train carrying Rebel officers.

As 1st Division commander, General Bartlett ordered Chamberlain's men up the tracks toward the Cox Road, an expected route of retreat for the troops evacuating Petersburg. The 1st and 2nd Brigades pushed on, only to be stopped where the Southside crossed the road by perhaps 1,500 dismounted cavalry from the division of Robert E. Lee's nephew, Major General Fitzhugh Lee. The previous day, the troopers had given a strong account of themselves; they seemed determined to repeat the performance. But appearances deceived. As soon as Chamberlain sent forward Sniper's New Yorkers, supported by one of General Gregory's regiments, the horsemen remounted and rode off.

Chamberlain thus held the road open with a strong skirmish line until General Sheridan came up, nodded in approval of his perform-ance, and led the infantry westward toward Amelia Court House. That night Chamberlain's troops, worn out by a combination of hiking and shooting, slept soundly along the Namozine Road, miles to the southwest of now-occupied Petersburg. The march resumed on the morning of the 3rd, the column "shrouded in smoke and dust" as it moved along the south bank of the Appomattox River. In its rear came much of Meade's army as well as a cooperating force largely drawn from the Twenty-fourth Corps, Army of the James, under Major General Edward O. C. Ord, successor to the inept and unlucky Ben Butler. Everyone in the enlarged pursuit column realized that the fugitives from Petersburg were on the roads ahead of them, soon to be joined by the evacuees of Richmond retreating along the Richmond & Danville railroad.[20]

The Fifth Corps failed to reach Amelia Court House before sun-down, being forced to bivouac on the same road it had trodden all day. Soon after breaking camp in the pre-dawn murk of April 4, however, the advance echelon struck the R & D at Jetersville, eight miles west of Amelia. To the north were numerous Rebels, dug in behind works. These, the last vestiges of the Army of Northern Virginia, looked so feisty that Sheridan had the infantry build opposing defenses. The men remained under arms throughout April 5, expecting a major confron-tation, especially after being moved out the direct road to Amelia Court House. To their chagrin, Chamberlain's men merely supported the cavalry in escorting to the rear dozens of prisoners, the awareness of defeat written on every face.[21]

By the morning of April 6 Griffin's corps, in concert with recently arrived elements of the Second and Sixth Corps, moved cross-country toward Amelia. Everyone was halted short of his objective as soon as it was learned that Lee had decided against committing his famished, footsore troops to battle. Instead, he had pushed westward in the direction of Lynchburg. Veering sharply in the same direction, Chamberlain's command, which headed Griffin's column, staged a "rapid and tiresome" march that failed to overtake the enemy but succeeded in enriching the pursuers' vocabularies. Ellis Spear, who three days before had returned to Chamberlain's side as provisional commander of the 198th Pennsylvania, "could hear the men behind me cursing their commanding officers indiscriminately, and hoping that we would come into [contact with] the enemy, since fighting would be a relief to the pain of marching."[22]

This day Chamberlain's skirmishers rounded up about 150 stragglers and took possession of dozens of supply wagons captured by the cavalry or abandoned by their drivers. The wagons Chamberlain's ax-wielding pioneers reduced to kindling. The brigade camped for the night along Sailor's Creek, about 30 miles east of a courthouse village named Appomattox. That day the creek had witnessed a one-sided battle between the Sixth Corps and Lee's rearguard, in which the retreating army lost upwards of 6,000 men, most of them as prisoners.[23]

Early on the 7th, with the inevitable confrontation drawing near, the pursuers curved southwestward, passing High Bridge over the Appomattox River. Although heavy firing could be heard off to the right, Chamberlain's men followed the Second and Sixth Corps to Prince Edward Court House, where they camped for the night, their fast-moving enemy still at arm's length. Up and moving again in the small hours of the 8th, they soon gained the pike that ran to Lynchburg. This day they moved behind a phalanx of infantry from General Ord's command. Chamberlain noted that the column included black soldiers, "pressing forward to save the white man's country."[24]

Now marching in the rear of Griffin's main body, Chamberlain found the going stop-and-start, and progress hard to quantify. He also found his composure difficult to maintain after Charlemagne slipped into the depths of the Buffalo River during a watering stop, throwing his rider. By the time Chamberlain clambered up the slippery bank to

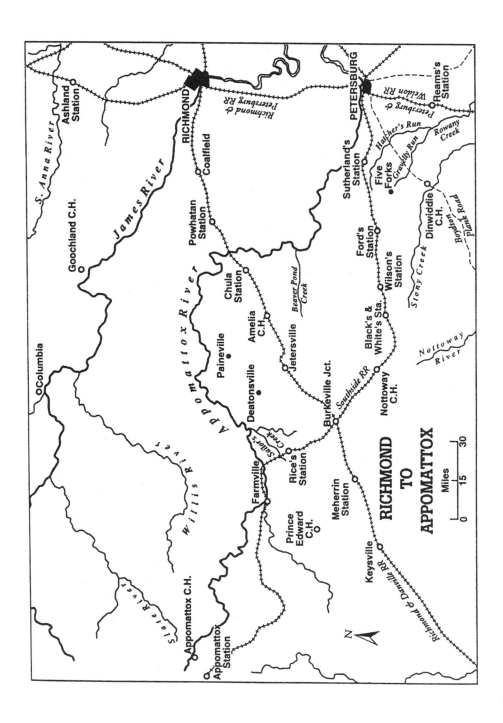

RICHMOND
TO
APPOMATTOX

Miles

0   15   30

N

safety, he was coated with mud from head to toe. Soldiers then worked beside him to save Charlemagne from a watery grave.

Chamberlain's tumble failed to raise his men's spirits. Having been forced on the 8th to travel almost 30 miles under a hot sun, everyone was too tired, too much out of sorts, even to crack a smile. Their mood quickly turned foul. When a few soldiers attempted to clear the road of wagons and other impediments, teamsters took umbrage and a brawl erupted, one that expanded to include several Fifth Corps regiments. Despite the intervention of officers, some antagonists did not stop throwing punches until after dark.[25]

Its near-exhaustion notwithstanding, when Chamberlain's command went into bivouac every man was alert to rumors that Lee's army was now within striking distance. Sheridan had pounded off to the west where, as some had heard, his cavalry had cut across the road in the Rebels' front. Suddenly Ord's white and black soldiers were gone, too, apparently hoping to reinforce the cavalry before Lee hit it. Then Fifth Corps headquarters received a hasty note from Sheridan at Appomattox Station, a "short distance" to the west: "If you can possibly push your infantry up here tonight, we will have great results in the morning." Griffin and Chamberlain understood Sheridan's urgency. The staying-power of horse soldiers, even fighting on foot behind cover, was notoriously low. Unless infantry and artillery arrived to provide some muscle, the potential roadblock would melt away under the weight of Lee's 26,000 still-potent fighters.[26]

* * *

Chamberlain's men were back on the road by 4:00 on Palm Sunday morning, April 9. Again they had the advance, the post of honor in Griffin's column. The way led to and beyond Appomattox Station, then toward the courthouse village of the same name, two and a half miles northeast of the depot. Perhaps halfway to the town, Chamberlain was met by an orderly sent by Sheridan to facilitate his march. Without taking time to seek the approval of a superior, Chamberlain waved his column onto a side road down which the orderly had galloped, and hastened Gregory's brigade, as well as his own, to the north. "In good season," the head of the column emerged into a field, on the far side of which Chamberlain found Sheridan's horsemen "warmly engaged" with enemy troops of all arms.[27]

Chamberlain discovered that his men had gained the Lynchburg Road ahead of Major General John Brown Gordon's corps, Army of Northern Virginia, with Appomattox Court House between them. As he crossed the road he spied Ord's troops in the act of relieving cavalry units that had been trying to bar Gordon's path. Meanwhile, miles to the rear, elements of Humphreys's and Wright's corps were blocking the escape of a second, smaller column under General Longstreet.

Chamberlain vowed to close his part of the trap. As he moved up to the scene of action, he shook out a skirmish line behind which the embattled cavalry could rally. The tired, dusty, ammunition-poor troopers, who had fought a delaying action reminiscent of John Buford's stand on the first day at Gettysburg, took grateful refuge in the skirmishers' rear.

As Chamberlain wheeled his men to face Gordon, Phil Sheridan rode past on his coal-black charger, making a characteristic appeal to violence: "Smash 'em ... smash 'em!" At first, however, it seemed as if the new arrivals would be smashed. When Chamberlain's skirmish line reached the outskirts of the courthouse town, a Rebel battery shelled the main body of the brigade, killing one and wounding another. The fatality, Lieutenant Hiram Scott of the 185th New York, would be the final casualty of the war in Chamberlain's ranks.[28]

Under the continuing barrage, Chamberlain patiently formed a line of battle, then led it forward. It did not get far, but it did not have to. As it joined the skirmishers on the edge of town, a lone Confederate officer rode toward it, waving a white towel in lieu of a flag. Years later, making dramatic use of the present tense as well as of his trademark prose, Chamberlain recalled the workings of his mind at that moment:

> "Now I see the white flag earnestly borne, and its possible purposes sweeps before my inner vision like a wraith of morning mist. He comes steadily on, the mysterious form in gray, my mood so whimsically sensitive that I could even smile at the material of the flag—wondering where in either army was found a towel, and one so white. But it bore a mighty message....

"The messenger draws near, dismounts with graceful salutation and, hardly suppressed emotion, delivers his message: 'Sir, I am from General Gordon. General Lee desires a cessation of hostilities until he can hear from General Grant as to the proposed surrender.'

"What word is this! ... 'Surrender.' It takes a moment to gather one's speech. 'Sir,' I answer, 'that matter exceeds my authority. I will send to my superior. General Lee is right. He can do no more.' All this with a forced calmness, covering a tumult of heart and brain. I bid him wait awhile, and the message goes up to my corps commander, General Griffin, leaving me amazed at the boding change...."[29]

Minutes after Griffin received the rider's news, he ordered all skirmishing to cease. A lull ensued, the firing slowly dying out along the line. Then word came that Grant and Lee were going to meet in the village to arrange the surrender of the Army of Northern Virginia. When more truce flags went up from various Confederate positions, the rumor seemed easier to believe. Still, the quiet that settled over the Appomattox vicinity had a temporary quality. While it lasted, Chamberlain rode down to the courthouse to mingle with high-ranking officers on both sides, including General Gordon. Several in the gathering had been friends in the Old Army; they shared reminiscences along with coffee and hard bread. War had turned to peace, with startling suddenness.

But would peace last? At an agreed-upon time, the truce expired and the old friends parted to return to their original positions. Chamberlain faced the prospect of fighting to the death against some of the officers he had been chatting and joking with minutes before. When he rejoined his command, bugles were blowing and men who had been lounging by the roadside were hustling into line. Mounted on Charlemagne, Chamberlain tensely awaited the word to advance, aware that the renewed fight ahead would be brief but brutal. The enemy that had been brought to bay was capable of taking hundreds of Yankees down with it.

Suddenly, as Chamberlain recorded, he beheld with "awe and

admiration" the unmistakable figure of Robert E. Lee, mounted on his warhorse Traveler, accompanied by a single staff officer, riding slowly toward his enemy's lines. Along those lines, bands began to play and men to rejoice, shouting at the top of their lungs, tossing headgear and accouterments into the air in delirious celebration. These demonstrations had their effect. With a rush of relief and joy, Chamberlain realized that the fight was over and the cause won—fair pay, he thought, for every wound, every hardship, every privation he had suffered during the past two and a half years.[30]

*　*　*

Once Lee's surrender was announced, the Fifth Corps was ordered into camp and division leaders were enjoined to "make their men comfortable." They also made comfortable numerous Confederates who strayed inside their lines in search of food and a hospitable fire. Grant and Meade saw to it that their opponents, who had far outrun their commissary trains, were fed.[31]

After entertaining some of these enemies-turned-countrymen, Chamberlain turned in, expecting to sleep as he "had not slept in four years. There was, of course, a great deal of unrestrained jubilation, but … before long the camp over which peace after strife had settled was sleeping with no fear of a night alarm. We awoke next morning to find the Confederates peering down into our faces, and involuntarily reached for our arms, but once the recollections of the previous day's stirring events came crowding back to mind, all fear fled…."[32]

In fact, he was not permitted the luxury of uninterrupted sleep. Late in the night he was summoned to corps headquarters, where General Griffin gave him an unusual assignment and an unexpected honor. He had been chosen to command the parade that would be held three days hence when Lee's army formally surrendered its weapons and colors. Griffin explained that although the Confederates had begged to be permitted to stack arms in their present position and go home, General Grant "did not think this quite respectful enough to anybody, including the United States of America." While he would respect all private property and would permit officers to retain their side-arms, the commanding general had insisted, "that the surrendering army as such should march out in due order, and lay down all tokens of Confederate authority and organized hostility to the United States, in immediate presence of some representative portion of the Union army." Grant wished the ceremony to be simple but meaningful, with no intent to humiliate the foe.[33]

Such a high-visibility assignment gratified Chamberlain—here was another indication of his superiors' regard. His desire to make a good impression on both comrades and enemies must have filled his mind throughout the intervening days. On April 10 he received permission from General Bartlett to supervise the ceremony at the head of the 20th Maine and the rest of his old 3rd Brigade. In thus parting with the command he had led for the past five months, Chamberlain promulgated an order that lauded the "soldierly behavior and gallant conduct" of its officers and men and that conveyed his pleasure over the fact "that the whole course of this brief campaign found the 1st Brigade in the front line and at its triumphant close they exchanged the last shots with the enemy...."[34]

While his successor, General Pearson, led the 1st Brigade to its new camp half a mile from Appomattox, Chamberlain mingled with the men of the 3rd Brigade for the first time in several months. April 11 was given over to renewing old acquaintances and to discussing with his regimental commanders the details of the surrender ceremony. Also on the 11th, Bartlett's division moved into position near the courthouse to relieve the Twenty-fourth Corps, whose men had been receiving cannon, muskets, and sabers surrendered by Confederate units along General Ord's front.[35]

The 3rd Brigade remained in camp until shortly before 9:00 A.M. on the 12th. At that hour, under a gunmetal sky and against a chill wind, the surrender ceremony began astride the Lynchburg Road. Casualty-depleted units of Gordon's corps began to file past the carefully aligned ranks of the 3rd Brigade, stacking arms and furling shot-torn, blood-stained banners. Many of the passing Confederates appeared overcome by emotion; some were openly downcast, others sullen and defiant, a few teary-eyed. To victor and vanquished alike the ceremony had a funereal quality, signifying as it did the death of an army, a nation, and a dream.

Chamberlain had given much thought to how his men should act on this day, a day for the history books. "The momentous meaning of this occasion impressed me deeply," he would write years later. "I resolved to mark it by some token of recognition, which could be no other than a salute of arms." He foresaw possible consequences—a gesture of respect to the enemy might stir controversy, bring criticism, have political repercussions. And yet "nothing of that kind could move me in the least.... Before us in proud humiliation stood the embodiment of manhood: men whom neither toils and sufferings, nor the fact of death, nor disaster, nor hopelessness could bend from their resolve; standing before us now, thin, worn, and famished, but erect, and with eyes looking level into ours, waking memories that bound us together as no other bond;—was not such manhood to be welcomed back into a Union so tested and assured?"[36]

Welcome them he did. As the head of each Confederate division or remnant thereof came opposite the forward flank of the 3rd Brigade, Chamberlain's bugles sounded and the "whole line, from right to left, regiment by regiment in succession, gives the soldier's salutation, from the 'order arms' to the old 'carry'—the marching salute."[37]

Having expected no such tribute, the startled Confederates did not at once respond. Then General Gordon, "riding with heavy spirit and downcast face," looked up, surveyed the scene, wheeled about on his horse, and "with profound salutation" returned the gesture by lowering his saber to the toe of his boot. The Georgian then ordered each following brigade to carry arms as they passed the 3rd Brigade, "honor answering honor. On our part," Chamberlain continued, "not a sound of trumpet more, nor roll of drum; not a cheer, nor word nor whisper of vain-glorying, nor motion of man standing again at the order; but an awed stillness rather and breath-holding, as if it were the passing of the dead!"[38]

By the turn of the 20th century, after Chamberlain had commemorated the surrender parade in numerous speeches and publications, some of the Union participants would quarrel with his presentation of events. They would charge him with making it appear that his brigade alone took part in the ceremony, ignoring other elements of the Fifth Corps also present for Gordon's surrender as well as to receive the surrender of General Longstreet's corps that same afternoon. These critics would also charge Chamberlain with implying that he had received arms and flags throughout morning and afternoon instead of during only a portion of the day as evidence suggested. Other veterans would claim that General Bartlett, not Chamberlain, had been Grant's choice to preside at the parade and that Chamberlain took over only because his superior was summoned elsewhere at the last minute. Critics of a later day would even deny that Chamberlain and Gordon had exchanged salutes of honor.[39]

These criticisms notwithstanding, it seems clear that some gesture on Chamberlain's part that day made the surrender ceremony something other than the degrading, humiliating experience Lee's army might otherwise have found it. At any rate, the veterans of the Army of Northern Virginia remembered the occasion as the start of a long, difficult, but very necessary healing process. Sixty years later a Virginian who had been present at Appomattox on April 12, 1865, asserted that "reunion began with that order to present arms."[40]

Fourteen

FIGHTING CIVILIAN

The day after the surrender parade, most of the prisoners having been paroled and many already started on the long road home, Chamberlain wrote his sister that, "I am glad I was not tempted to leave the army this Spring. I would not for a fortune have missed the experience of the last two weeks. It seems like two years, so many, & such important events have taken place, within that time. Father said in his last letter to me that 'the glory of battles was over.' But if he had seen some of these we have had of late, in which we captured the enemy by thousands & carried their positions by a dash, and at last at Appomattox Court House received the surrender of Genl Lee & his whole army he would think differently." He added some pardonable bragging, but he stretched the truth by claiming that two of the recent battles had been fought "entirely under my own direction" and that the last shots and casualties of the war had occurred on his front. He closed by recounting the scene of the previous day, when 15,000 arms and 72 flags had been piled at his feet.[1]

He waited almost a week to write Fannie. Perhaps he had learned his wife was visiting relatives or off on another shopping junket and had only just returned. Writing now from Burkeville Junction, to which his troops had moved three days after the surrender, he showered his wife with romantic allusions. After professing his love he repeated many of the same claims he had made to Sae, improving on some—now he had confiscated 26,000 weapons, 73 banners—and not failing to mention that, "I receive many congratulatory letters" from superiors, subordinates, and civilians who had read of his exploits.[2]

In lush prose he also informed Fannie of shocking news received two days before: "In the midst of all this triumph—in this hour of exultation, in this day of power & joy & hope, when our starry flag floats amid the stars of Heaven, suddenly it falls to *half-mast*—'Darkness sweeps athwart the sky,' & the President of the United States, with his heart full of conciliation & forgiveness is struck down by the assassin's hand. Word will not tell the feeling with which this Army receives this news."[3]

Shortly before writing, he had held a memorial service for the slain president in the camp of the 1st Division, Fifth Corps, which he now commanded, General Bartlett having transferred to the Ninth Corps. The solemn occasion had turned into a spectacle when the Irish chaplain conducting it had started shouting for revenge ("you should have been here," he told Fannie, knowing she would have enjoyed the priest's outburst). "These are terrible times," he added, "but I believe in God, & he will bring good at last." Promising to relate every breathless detail of the past fortnight as soon as they were together again, he signed off with imaginary kisses to wife and children.[4]

Two days after he wrote, his newly enlarged command was deployed to cover a 20-mile stretch of the Southside Railroad, from Wilson's Station as far east as Sutherland Station, one of his objectives in the aftermath of Five Forks. The 1st Division remained on occupation duty in that area for the next two weeks, Chamberlain serving as military governor of the surrounding countryside. It was a multi-faceted job. He helped disarm local Confederates who had not surrendered at Appomattox. He protected civilians' homes against depredations by men in blue and gray alike. When he found much of the populace bereft of the necessities of life, he seized local stores and mills, saw to their efficient operation, and distributed their goods among the citizenry. He acted as sheriff and sometimes also as judge when dealing with lawbreakers in and out of the service. Whenever time permitted, he tended to his command's personnel matters, recommending re-assignments, transfers, and promotions.[5]

Somehow he found the time to compose reports covering the operations on the Quaker and White Oak Roads and at Five Forks. Although uncharacteristically brief in their summary of military operations, they paint a clear, concise picture of the service rendered by Chamberlain's command, devoid as they are of the hyperbole, purple rhetoric, and egoism found in his earlier reports.[6]

By the last days of April Chamberlain's domain had expanded to include the territory adjoining Petersburg, itself in the midst of army occupation. His line of camps and picket posts now stretched for 30 miles through farm lands and villages devastated by the fighting of recent weeks. "It was painful," he later recalled, "to be brought into contact with the ruin, waste, and desolation that had been wrought upon proud old Virginia, and her once prosperous homes."[7]

A considerable amount of his time was taken up by dealing with recently liberated slaves. His commentary on the black population in his realm is instructive, for it reveals that the war had not materially altered his view of race relations. He had come to view African-Americans in arms as a valuable military experiment, especially so because it turned the Confederacy's own resources against it. He did not, however, believe that a black man achieved equality with his white comrade simply by donning a uniform.

He had an even dimmer view of black civilians, especially those recently released from bondage, who seemed not to know how to use their freedom productively. He lamented that "all restraints which had hitherto held them in check were set loose by the sudden collapse of the rebel armies. The flood-gates were opened to the rush of animal instinct. The only notion of freedom apparently entertained by these bewildered people was to do as they pleased."[8]

The effects of this tendency to idleness and mischief were aggravated by the sheer size of the mob: "Numbers gave them a kind of frenzy. Without accustomed support, without food, or opportunity to work, they not unnaturally banded together; and without any serious organization and probably without much deliberate planning of evil, they still spread terror across the country." By this last phrase he meant outrage against white citizens, the safeguarding of whom he considered one of his primary duties. "They swarmed through houses and homes demanding food, seizing all goods they could lay their hands on, abusing the weak, terrifying women, and threatening to burn and destroy."[9]

Chamberlain could not abide the thought of ex-slaves running wild through his district: "This was an evil that had to be met properly, and we construed our orders to protect the country literally." While he strove to suppress all forms of lawlessness, his soldiers were sent out "more especially against the depredations of the lawless negro bands." Through what he called "a constant reconnaissance," troops broke up bands of black civilians upon the merest suspicion of trouble. "In cases of personal violence or outrage," his men had the authority to mete out punishment "more summary than that authorized by courts."[10]

Given his social and political influences, it is perhaps not surprising that Chamberlain entertained such a low opinion of the black civilians he encountered after Appomattox. Certainly he had a right to condemn African-Americans guilty of looting, vandalism, and assault. But the general impression one gets from his writings on the subject—that ex-slaves tended to childlike behavior, were driven by base instincts and ungoverned passions, and gravitated between idleness and violence—makes Chamberlain sound more like a member of the planter class than a representative of the armies that put an end to two and a half centuries of chattel slavery in America.

* * *

Despite having strong feelings about the job, Chamberlain never felt entirely comfortable in the role of military governor. Thus he was pleased when on the last day of April he received orders to march, two days hence, to Richmond via Petersburg. Even so, the communiqué left him with some regrets, prompted by "the thought of leaving these stricken and helpless people," especially those of the upper classes, whose courtliness and deferential attitude had surprised and gratified him. He especially regretted leaving such people under siege by their black neighbors. Still, he could dwell on the fact that the move east was a prelude to a longer march north that would carry him and everyone in his command back home.[11]

The latter thought sustained him as he started his division for Petersburg at 5:30 A.M. on May 2. That evening the men went into bivouac near Sutherland Station, which Chamberlain's brigade had first visited exactly a month ago but which other units knew from earlier campaigning. After supper, several officers wandered across local sites that stirred memories. Ellis Spear visited the works near Peebles's Farm, where the Fifth Corps had seen hard fighting last September while Chamberlain recuperated from his Petersburg wound. Chamberlain himself recalled the fighting on the nearby Quaker Road, "where my stubborn little 1st Brigade made the costly overture of the last campaign."[12]

Next day, the 3rd, he entered Petersburg at the head of his division. There he met with General Warren, now commanding the city's occupation troops, a lowly position that only added to the mortification he had felt since April 1. Chamberlain was pleased when General Griffin had the men give their old corps commander a salute of honor as they passed his headquarters.[13]

Two days later, Chamberlain's division took to "a fine, smooth road" that led north past Drewry's Bluff to Manchester, within sight of the former Confederate capital. After a day spent in a rain-drenched bivouac, the troops passed through the streets of Richmond, where Chamberlain took in the sights. They included Libby Prison, his imagined destination on the three occasions when he had barely eluded capture. In Richmond the Fifth Army Corps, along with the recently arrived Second Corps, was saluted by the occupation forces, who paraded in their honor. Onlookers included General Meade and Major General Henry W. Halleck, former chief of staff of the army, now commanding the Military Division of the James.

From Richmond, with unexpected haste, the Fifth Corps pushed on to Hanover Junction on the Virginia Central Railroad, where, 20 miles from their previous camp, they halted on the evening of May 6. Chamberlain not only considered the pace too quick, he thought the route too straight; had it been left to him, his men would have marched along "a line running through soldiers' hearts" across nearby fields on which they had covered themselves with glory if not always with victory.[14]

Those fields lay closer to Chamberlain's route than he imagined. That night Charlemagne uncovered some human bones from a shallow grave near his master's tent. Going forth to investigate, Chamberlain unknowingly trampled "a body half buried by the fallen pine-cones and needles so long undisturbed." Other skeletons protruded from ground all around him; the macabre sight shocked and saddened him. Before he departed next morning, he had his men gather up the remains—enough to account for dozens of Union soldiers—and store them in hardtack boxes for future delivery to next of kin. Personal belongings found among the bones identified several as the lost comrades of soldiers in Chamberlain's division.[15]

On May 7 the Fifth Corps moved on to Concord Church, and the following day to Milford Station. The day after that, the corps crossed the Rappahannock and an old campground of the 20th Maine. Not until May 12, however, did Chamberlain's division halt near another well-remembered campsite, this on Arlington Heights outside Washington City.

For Chamberlain and his men—indeed, for the great majority of the units in the Army of the Potomac—Washington was their next-to-last destination, one stop short of Maine, or Pennsylvania, or Michigan, or wherever home happened to be. "We took, therefore," he wrote, "a certain pride in this last encampment; we looked upon this as the graduation day of our Alma Mater."[16]

Their stay, which for most of them lasted until a muster-out process of massive proportions could be completed, was for the most part uneventful and promotive of boredom and dissatisfaction. The period, however, was less bleak for Chamberlain than for many of his men. He went sightseeing in the capital, alone and in the company of others. He recalled the past and ruminated on the future with old acquaintances such as Ellis Spear and members of his staff, which now included Captain Thomas D. Chamberlain. He orated at the presentation of a gift from the officers of the 1st Division to General Griffin: a diamond pin that Tiffany's had fashioned in the shape of a flag bearing a red Maltese Cross. More than once he met with such celebrities as Grant and Sheridan. He was even able to squire his visiting father-in-law around the neighboring camps. Doctor Adams, who not long ago had doubted that his son-in-law would amount to much, was impressed not only by Chamberlain's rank and authority but by the respect paid him by every officer and enlisted man.[17]

Chamberlain was not the only soldier deserving of respect; the government wished to pay tribute to all who had helped sustain it throughout the crisis just ended. On May 23, after much preparation on the part of Chamberlain and his colleagues, the corps, divisions, brigades, and regiments of the Army of the Potomac paraded through Washington past throngs of well-wishers: the high command, statesmen including President Andrew Johnson, diplomats, foreign dignitaries, the citizenry of Washington, and visitors from all corners of the Union. The following day General Sherman's troops, just up from the Carolinas, were honored on day two of this Grand Review of the Armies of the United States.

Chamberlain would never forget his part in this, the last formal proceeding of his military career. As he rode up Pennsylvania Avenue in the role of honorary commander of the Fifth Corps, he was able to recapture the sense of satisfaction over a difficult job well done that he had last experienced on April 9 at Appomattox Court House. It is also possible, even as he basked in the adulation of the public, that he was looking ahead to an uncertain future, to a life that promised none of the glory, honor, and power that war had lavished on him.[18]

* * *

In the last days of May and the first of June, Chamberlain's regiments were mustered out of service and left Arlington Heights for points north and west. On June 5 he bade farewell to the proud, battle-torn 20th Maine as it took the train north (leaving behind Tom Chamberlain, who had been retained in service as a member of the reconstituted regiment, made up of recruits and the consolidated fragments of other Maine outfits). Soon Tom's brother commanded a division that existed primarily on paper. "You doubtless know very well," he wrote his sister, "that we are reducing the army as fast as possible. What will happen next we do not know."[19]

If the unknown bothered him, he gave no sign, reminding Sae that, as so often before, "Providence will both open & guide my way." One immediate hope was to gain the full major generalship of volunteers that "all my superior officers" had promised him. He doubted, however, that he would capture the promotion. Notwithstanding the close relationships he had maintained with Governor Cony and Adjutant General Hodsdon, and despite the efforts Fannie and he had made in his behalf whenever opportunity had presented itself, he lacked political support back home. He exaggerated his handicaps, insisting to Sae that, "I am far better known in New York or Pennsylvania than in my own State." In fact, he was well known in his native region; but his political affiliation may have hurt his prospects for higher rank. Though he had voted for Lincoln as a candidate on the bipartisan Union ticket, Chamberlain still considered himself a War Democrat. That, however, would soon change.[20]

His lament would appear to have been premature. For one thing, not until July 1, which date found him still on Arlington Heights, did he receive and formally accept the brevet major generalship he had won on the Quaker Road. Mistakenly dated from April 9, the brevet was later backdated to March 29 through the efforts of General Griffin. Curiously, although citing the "especial ability" Chamberlain had displayed on the latter date, the brevet contained no mention of the wounds he had reported receiving—wounds that Ellis Spear swore were fictitious. The corrected brevet did not reach its recipient until the end of July, by which time Chamberlain was back in Maine.[21]

Three weeks after Appomattox, Griffin, himself now a two-star general by actual rank, had recommended Chamberlain for the full major generalship he coveted. The recommendation was duly endorsed by Meade and Grant and sent to the War Department and the White House for action. The upshot remains a mystery. In 1865 Chamberlain informed General Hodsdon that the recommendation was tabled by politicians who chose to ignore his contributions. But almost 30 years later he claimed that an appointment as major general reached his hands but "for reasons then unknown to me, was asked to be returned in a private letter from the Secretary of War. I since learned that there was another major general to be appointed from Maine, and so its 'quota' would be full."[22]

If Chamberlain's second explanation is accurate—it cannot be verified at this late date—the officer who took the commission he considered his may have been Francis Fessenden, who was named a major general in November 1865. If so, Chamberlain might have had grounds for calling foul. Fessenden's war record could not match up to that of the savior of Little Round Top, but the fact that his father had been a United States senator as well as Lincoln's secretary of the treasury might be viewed as giving him an unfair advantage.[23]

Steps were taken to keep Chamberlain in uniform. In late June, when the Army of the Potomac officially ceased to exist, Griffin chose him to command one of three brigades that the single remaining division of the Fifth Corps would contribute to a holding organization for men not eligible for early muster-out. Chamberlain later claimed he also was assigned to head a provisional corps to be sent to the Rio Grande under Sheridan to contain and perhaps overawe the French invaders of Mexico. Then, too, several of Chamberlain's patrons including Generals Warren and Griffin tried to procure for him a commission in the Regular Army.

None of these opportunities panned out. The command composed of long-term recruits existed for only a month before the government decided to discharge virtually everyone remaining in the volunteer service. "Skillful diplomacy," as Chamberlain noted, made a French intervention unnecessary. And despite the fact that when the Regulars were reorganized early in 1866 he was offered a colonelcy "with the privilege of retiring with the rank of brigadier general," he was several months at home by that time, his wounds were giving him increasing trouble, and he was not disposed to return to public life.[24]

And yet his primary reason for rejecting a position in the regulars had nothing to do with a settled home life or poor health. War had enabled him to achieve, to grow as a person, to prove unfounded his worst fears about himself, and to validate the heroic self-image he had nurtured since boyhood. The peacetime army offered only the prospect of hard work, low pay, wretched living conditions, the disinterest of the government, and the back hand of the public. For Chamberlain, to be "a soldier in time of peace" was to live a life replete with all the trials and privations of war, and none of the glory. Trials and privations he could still endure, but the absence of glory was something he would not abide.[25]

* * *

Before July ended, he went home to Fannie, the children including tiny, sickly Gertrude Loraine, and the rest of his extended family. His return followed by days that of brother Tom and the last remnants of the 20th Maine. Chamberlain's wounds bothered him enough that he was content to spend quiet days in Brunswick, but his sabbatical was cut short by Bowdoin's annual commencement and a recently announced reunion of her graduates just returned from the war.

Despite his health problems Chamberlain was prevailed upon to help with the preparations. He proved his value to the organizers by inviting General Grant, who happened to be visiting in Portland, to attend the commencement. To the gratification of all involved, Grant accepted. The Chamberlains received him at their home, where he stayed throughout his time in Brunswick. During the commencement, at which the general-in-chief received an honorary doctorate, Chamberlain offered an appropriate oration. Then he conducted the visitor through an admiring throng to the First Parish Church, which, festooned with patriotic bunting, hosted a reception in Grant's honor.[26]

When the great day ended and the guest of honor returned to Washington, Chamberlain resumed a more mundane and much less attractive existence. He returned to the chair of rhetoric and oratory at his alma mater, something he had vowed, less than six months ago, never to do. In August he shared the family's bereavement at the death of their youngest child. He attempted to write a book-length account of the battles and campaigns of the Fifth Army Corps, but the distractions and tragedies of his home life and the burdens that accompanied the resumption of teaching kept him from making much progress. Ultimately the book would be written by William Henry Powell, although it would not appear in print until 1896.[27]

Through the rest of the summer and into the fall Chamberlain struggled to climb out of what one historian calls "an emotional abyss."

It was not long before he and Fannie were again apart, each traveling alone on personal business to Portland, Boston, and New York. Both began to sense that more than miles were keeping them apart. Worried that their ability to communicate had begun to deteriorate, Fannie wrote him from Manhattan, not knowing if he was at home or himself traveling: "Why don't you let me know more about things, dear? ... where are you and the children? " She closed with a lament for a happier time: "Dear, dear Lawrence write me one of the old letters.... I am as in the old times gone bye [sic] Your Fannie." Replying from Brunswick, her husband addressed the widening gulf between them, one created at least in part by his physical limitations: "There is not much left in me to love. I feel that too well."28

While he could do little to repair his shattered sexuality, he hoped to alleviate his near-constant suffering. In August 1865 he chanced to meet Governor Cony, who, inquiring of Chamberlain's health, was concerned to learn that his wounds would require additional surgery. Doubting that the general could easily afford the cost, Cony immediately contacted Maine's senior senator, Lot Morrill, for help. Morrill alerted the state's congressional delegation, which almost as a group petitioned President Johnson to restore Chamberlain to active service long enough to undergo surgery at the government's expense. Once General Grant added his hearty approval, the plan was quickly implemented. That December Chamberlain returned to the active duty list, had his operation, and was mustered out a second and final time on January 15, 1866.29

The surgery was successful enough to restore Chamberlain at least to his pre-Appomattox condition. Other events at this same time aided him psychologically, including a round of speeches to veterans' organizations. On these occasions he drank in the applause and praise of ex-soldiers not only from Maine but from across the North. In February 1866 he delivered a well-received address in Philadelphia at the founding of the Union officers' association known as the Military Order of the Loyal Legion of the United States (later he would help establish Maine's chapter, or commandery, of the organization). In Philadelphia he declaimed on the subject of loyalty, later recalling that his "analysis of that sentiment, referring to its principles more vital than laws and constitutions, produced a profound effect" on his audience. Three years later he would orate at the founding of another major veterans' organization, the Society of the Army of the Potomac, whose president he would become in 1888. In 1872 he would return to Philadelphia to speak before "one of the most distinguished audiences ever gathered in America" at a memorial service for the recently deceased George Gordon Meade.[30]

By the spring of 1866 Chamberlain was on a multi-city speaking tour, shaking the hands of men he had led into combat as well as those of veterans he had never met but whom he could easily regard as comrades. These engagements buoyed his spirit, helping him submerge the tribulations and uncertainties of the present in a warm sea of shared experience. They also kept his name and face before the public, especially the good folk of Maine, before whom he delivered many of his speeches. Exposure made him something of a celebrity. Early in 1866 state Republican officials, realizing they could do worse than run a wounded war hero, asked him to stand as their party's candidate for governor in the fall election.[31]

The prospect of a political career, especially as a Republican, must have given Chamberlain pause. He knew nothing of politics except the army variety; moreover, as a life-long Democrat he would have regarded with a certain suspicion the objectives and tactics of the opposition party, especially those of its radical wing. On the other hand, he had adopted Union Party principles in the war's last year, having come to detest the peace faction of the Democrats, which by its disloyal utterances and activities had sullied its party's reputation.

With some misgivings, he gave his consent to the Republican managers, and at the party's state convention that June (which he did not attend) he easily won the nomination. The news elicited enough favorable commentary to make him feel somewhat more comfortable about his decision to run. Well-wishers included General Warren, who wrote warmly from New York City, where he remained on duty as an engineer officer despite the blow Sheridan had dealt his career. Warren expressed his pleasure at his old subordinate's nomination, adding that "from what I know of the parties in Maine I presume your election is a certainty."[32]

Such commendation may have helped Chamberlain repress the guilt he felt at having overridden his wife's objections to public service. Fannie, who never wanted to be a soldier's wife, was equally opposed to being the wife of a politician. She resented the disruption of their home life that his candidacy precipitated, and she did not want her husband to sever his connection with Bowdoin, which now included the posts of trustee as well as acting-president in the wake of the resignation of Dr. Leonard Woods. But Chamberlain had been restive at Bowdoin, his increased responsibilities notwithstanding, and he longed to return to the public arena—if not in uniform, then in morning-coat and silk hat. The governorship connoted power and authority, both of which he craved and neither of which he could find in academe.[33]

General Warren's prediction of a preordained victory seemed a safe one, as both houses of the state legislature were firmly in Republican hands and no Regular Democrat had occupied the governor's mansion for a decade. Predictably enough, that September he trounced his Democratic opponent, Eben F. Pillsbury of Augusta, a member of his party's extreme faction. Only the margin of victory was a surprise—almost 28,000 votes, largest in state history.

He may have won the governor's mansion, but Fannie did not join him there. She preferred to live in Brunswick with the children while he served what she expected would be a single one-year term. Only on occasion would she take the train to Augusta to preside over a state reception or a holiday celebration. Better than any words she might have directed at her husband, Fannie's protracted absence from the capital bespoke her attitude toward his political ambitions.

She had to make the best of a situation more disagreeable than she could have imagined, for her husband won reelection three times, defeating the hapless Pillsbury on two of those occasions. In 1869 he exceeded an unwritten rule by running for a fourth term, this time beating both Democrat Franklin Smith and Temperance Party candidate N. G. Hitchborn. Not until the last day of December 1870 did be leave the State House to return to Brunswick and Bowdoin. That period saw her husband ascend to the summit of state power, only to descend into political oblivion. It also saw her marriage to Joshua

Chamberlain begin to crack under the stress of their attempts to balance their public and private lives.[34]

* * *

As governor, Chamberlain advanced—sometimes enthusiastically, sometimes half-heartedly—the Republican agenda. Several issues gained his undivided attention and strong support. Recognizing his party's reliance on the soldier vote, he promoted the welfare of Maine's 50,000 veterans by creating jobs for them, granting pensions and medical care to those "worn away by the hardships and exposures of the campaigns," and seeking to instill in the general populace the patriotic values for which these men had fought and suffered. He energetically promoted state aid to the widows and orphans of the state's many war dead. Hearkening back to his own service, he also called for reorganizing the state militia into 10 companies of volunteers, a move that he believed would "renew the companionships and preserve the proud memories of the old service." He had no way of knowing that within five years he would be the commanding officer of those volunteers.[35]

Unsurprisingly, he promoted education on many levels. He suggested improvements to two recently established institutions, the state agricultural college at Orono (later the University of Maine) and the state normal school at Farrington, while proposing that a second teachers' college be founded at Castine. He called for separating the state's reform school from the penal system and for establishing an "industrial school" for truant girls. He recommended an addition to the state insane asylum, arguing that "a brief treatment of a sane man in these crowded corridors would very soon give him a title to stay there." He also sought to enlarge the state prison and to provide it with a full-time chaplain.[36]

Chamberlain devoted his most strenuous efforts to improving the industrial and agricultural climate throughout Maine and to reverse the general decline of commerce. He repeatedly advised his state to discontinue its policy of refusing aid to public enterprises and growth investment. This repressive policy had its roots in the Panic of 1837, when numerous state-subsidized banks had failed, threatening the state's credit. He also called on Mainers to stop exporting their most abundant raw materials—lumber, seafood, agricultural products—in such quantities as had been the norm over the past several years. He felt that instead of importing grain, the state should grow wheat on a large scale; it should redouble its efforts at manufacturing and infuse new life into the shipbuilding industry, which had been hurt by a new trend toward ironclad vessels; and Maine should also devote more attention to conservation and reforestation, while better harnessing its water power.

Chamberlain championed rail commerce, promoting the Portland & Ogdensburg Railroad, whose terminus was in western New York State, and the newly laid European & North American line, which sought to connect Boston with Halifax, Nova Scotia, from which ships could carry passengers to England and the Continent. He called for commercial improvements to the port of Portland, potentially the most valuable port east of New York City. And he supported a hydrographic survey of Maine's principal waterways.[37]

To enable his state to compete successfully for economic opportunities, he supported efforts to stop the growing exodus of young Mainers lured away to Boston, New York, and other industrialized cities. "It is doubtful," he warned the legislature during one of his annual addresses, "whether the state can longer afford to be a nursery for the missionaries of civilization." To redress the population imbalance—which amounted to a net loss of 5,000 residents each year—he encouraged attempts to attract desirable immigrants, especially hard-working, middle-class, Protestant-affiliated Scandinavians. Their coming would help counter the continuing migration of French Canadians and the recent influx of southern Europeans, both peoples being mainly lower-class Catholics and Jews. His efforts were rewarded when a New Sweden took root in Aroostook County in the summer of 1870. Thanks largely to Chamberlain's solicitude, the colony grew and prospered.[38]

Time and again Chamberlain proved unafraid to tackle controversial issues. On the subject of the state's capital punishment statute, which had been enforced only once in 30 years, he urged that either general practice be made to conform to the law, or vice-versa. He successfully overturned a law that authorized a state constabulary to enforce prohibition, which he considered an example of misguided social engineering. His consistent and vocal opposition to prohibition laws, which he believed trampled citizens' rights and invaded their privacy, earned him the wrath of temperance leagues, religious institutions, and reform movements. These opponents not only attacked his public utterances but distorted their meaning; more than their vilification of him, Chamberlain, who drank in strict moderation, took umbrage at what he called the reformers' "unscrupulous misrepresentation." Because these groups exerted a much greater influence than their numbers appeared to warrant, he managed to mitigate but not overturn a law that mandated prison sentences for liquor dealers—the outgrowth of the lead role Maine had played in the temperance movement since going dry in 1846.[39]

On issues of nationwide significance, Chamberlain urged a quick return of the Southern States to the Union consistent with congressional guidance, and he opposed enfranchising recently liberated slaves. The latter issue, he believed, should be decided by "the best minds of the South, and by no means by hasty and sweeping measures tending to give political preponderance to the most inferior." Here was a clear and concise explication of his attitude toward African-Americans at this point in his life.[40]

* * *

Chamberlain's opposition to black suffrage, especially after Congress' passage, and Maine's ratification, of the 15th Amendment early in his third term, cost him politically. Despite his outspokenness on this policy matter and others, he always retained the loyalty of a large portion of the state's voters. Moreover, influential editors consistently praised his erudition, his managerial ability and, of course, his war record. But Chamberlain was not always popular with the leaders of his party, which included the chairman of the Republican State Committee, James Gillespie Blaine of Augusta. As Chamberlain later admitted, his stands on certain divisive issues "were undoubtedly contrary to the prevailing party sentiment, and hence afforded a happy occasion for those so inclined to foment a feeling of party distrust towards him."[41]

Views, statements, and actions that ran counter to Republican orthodoxy had national as well as local implications. In the spring of 1868 he opposed his party's desire to impeach and convict Andrew Johnson of high crimes and misdemeanors. He did so by praising the decision of a fellow free-thinker from Maine, Senator Fessenden, to vote against conviction, one of only seven Republicans to do so. Chamberlain may have sustained Fessenden, whose action was instrumental in Johnson's acquittal, as a means of repaying political debts. Even so, he sincerely believed that Johnson's only crime was to thwart the machinations of Radical Republicans, a species of politician Chamberlain disliked and distrusted as much as the president.[42]

On other issues, too, Chamberlain violated Republican principles. His consistent opposition to liquor controls led temperance-minded members of the party to desert it in the spring of 1869 and form their own political organization. This was enough to discomfit the party chiefs; they winced again when Chamberlain tactlessly assaulted the motives and ethics of the new party. Republican regulars also disapproved of his seemingly avid promotion of the death penalty. They were especially displeased by his successful efforts to put to death a convicted murderer and rapist, a former slave named Harris, who had turned state's evidence. Harris's execution not only ran counter to the views of the state's attorney general but incensed liberals and opponents of capital punishment throughout New England. It played a role in Maine's 1872 abolition of the death penalty, only the fourth state to do so.[43]

Chamberlain also hurt himself by daring to explore the transactions between the state and the federal government relative to the recruiting and equipping of Maine volunteers during the early months of the war for the Union. The unprecedented pressures that period had placed on both ruling bodies had produced what one historian calls "doubtful actions and questionable dealings." By supporting the work of ex-Governor Cony, whom he appointed to head a commission charged with investigating the state's mobilization claims against the government, Chamberlain made lifelong enemies both within and outside his party.[44]

These and other unpopular acts conspired to erode his base of support. His huge victory margin of 1866 was more than halved the following year. Although it rebounded to more than 19,000 votes in 1868, it dwindled to little more than 12,000 in '69. Neither Chamberlain nor party leaders had expected him to run for that fourth term; he did so upon the urging of influential citizens and because no other viable candidate came forward. At the state party's convention in the summer of 1870 the governor's name was not placed in nomination. The fact did not seem to bother him; by this point he had become weary of partisan squabbles and political deal-making. He did not cherish the thought of participating in another election; for this reason, as well as because of the loyalty he still felt toward his party, he rejected overtures from Democratic leaders to switch sides for the coming race. Even so, it must have been comforting to learn that his status as Maine's most revered warrior continued to attract political offers.[45]

On leaving office, Chamberlain could look back on a record of success and failure, triumph and defeat, one that featured few compromises of position and none of principle. Had he been more tactful, more accommodating—more of a politician—he might have achieved more, but notable accomplishments were not lacking. He had placed the militia on a firm organizational and operational foundation. He had given a needed boost to education. The hydrographic survey proved to be a boon to commerce. His support of railroad development helped further the state's transportation industry. He helped settle the state's early-war accounts with Washington, while also procuring payment of the joint war claims of Massachusetts and Maine for advances made to the government during the War of 1812. He had established strict laws for fish and game protection, had helped pass a general incorporation act, and had seen to the appointment of banking and insurance commissioners. Whatever criticism might be leveled at his administration, the outgoing governor could tell himself that he had left his state in a better industrial, commercial, financial, and cultural condition than he had found it.[46]

* * *

When he left the governor's mansion, Chamberlain may have sensed that the only political aspiration he continued to entertain—to win a seat in the United States Senate—would avail him nothing. Already his hopes had been cruelly dashed. Upon Fessenden's death in 1869, Chamberlain appeared a likely candidate to replace him. However, after Lot Morrill, who had lost his own seat that year, was appointed to fill the vacancy, the legislature elected him to a full term.

Disappointment would dog Chamberlain for years to come. In 1876 political insiders would make him the odds-on choice to succeed Morrill, who had resigned his seat to become secretary of the treasury. This time, Party Chairman Blaine, who had shored up his position as the most powerful Republican in the state, would snatch the prize from him. An opportunity for even higher office would come Chamberlain's way in 1872, but he would decline the second spot on a Liberal Republican ticket headed by *New York Tribune* editor Horace Greeley. As he later explained, bolting to a disaffected faction of his party "would misrepresent [my] position on the main questions then at issue before the country."[47]

Sorrow and regret had many sources. During his governorship, family matters continually vied with policy matters for his attention. Some were happy distractions, such as his children's graduation from school and his sister's marriage to Brewer merchant Charles Farrington in 1867. Tragedies also intervened. In late summer of that same year, following two years of deteriorating health, John Chamberlain died of consumption, the same malady that had claimed the life of his older brother. The family dealt with the loss as best it could, grieving quietly for the deceased and seeking to assist his widow, Delia, in any way it could. In this effort, Brother Tom took the lead; in 1870 he secured Delia's place in the family fold by marrying her.[48]

Soon after losing his brother Chamberlain nearly lost his marriage. In November 1868, after almost three years of living alone and seeing no prospect that her husband would curtail his political career, Fannie threatened him with divorce. By then Chamberlain had learned of her discontent from family friends to whom she had complained, but he had not expected her to take such a drastic step. He was also shocked and saddened by her allegations. According to State House gossips, Fannie had charged him with physical abuse, among other offenses.

At first, he did not know how to react. Unable to go home to her just then, he pleaded with Fannie by letter to stop making false allegations, predicting that if she did not their marriage "will end in *hell*." Knowing no other course, he proposed a trial separation, all the while professing his love and devotion and promising in some way, any way, to make things right.[49]

It is doubtful that Chamberlain had assaulted his wife, although, as one recent biographer points out, his denial of the charge does not acquit him of it. More likely, Fannie's chronic depression, her sense of being neglected if not abandoned, and her status as an unappreciated appendage to her celebrated husband's public career caused her to retaliate in a manner calculated to get Chamberlain's attention while visiting on him some of the misery she had long endured.[50]

Somehow—no one is privy to the mechanics of the process—the couple reconciled. Perhaps now that she had drawn blood, Fannie could forgive even if she could not forget. On his part, Governor Chamberlain may have made peace as a means of saving his political career, or he may have decided that she had just cause to inflict on him such a painful and embarrassing wound. There was yet another reason for his willingness to patch things up. Deep in his heart, as always, he loved his wife very much.

Fifteen

WANING STAR

*B*y the most fortuitous timing, Chamberlain landed a new job— one commensurate with his station in life—a few months after leaving the State House in Augusta. When Bowdoin President Samuel Harris, Leonard Woods's successor, resigned his post to accept a professorship at Yale University, former Governor Chamberlain appeared the perfect replacement. Like the state Republican leadership in 1866, the college's board of overseers and trustees understood that Chamberlain's military stature would help promote their agenda as well as succeed at the all-important art of fundraising, for which President Harris had shown only moderate talent. Whatever political gifts Chamberlain had ac-quired during the past four years would also come in handy as a college executive. Flattered by his alma mater's interest in him, Chamberlain accepted her call in time to assume his duties at the outset of the 1871-72 academic year.

A major reason for his taking the post was his desire to institute a raft of educational reforms. He had accepted on the condition that the school would adopt a policy of expansion and innovation. During his undergraduate days he had been frustrated by what he considered Bowdoin's backward, fusty attitude toward academics as well as by its sometimes suffocating emphasis on religious education. For the college to prosper through the rest of the century, it would have to give priority to preparing young men to enter professions other than the ministry. Chamberlain would concentrate his efforts on improving class offerings in the sciences, constitutional and international law, modern languages, and classical literature, believing that instruction in these subjects would prove more relevant to students' needs than the study of Greek, Latin, and scriptural history. He was convinced that such emphasis would "secure a more active interest in the college on the part of the graduates"—thus leading to an increase in alumni donations.[1]

The overriding problem he faced in advocating such reforms, which only a few decades later became what one editor called "the common-places of professional educational discussion," was the college's lack of funds to implement them completely and make them effective. Building expansion was limited, many facilities continued to be inadequate, and pay was low. Chamberlain himself received an annual salary of $2,600, with a $300 allowance to maintain his home, which in 1871 he moved to a corner lot on Maine Street opposite the campus. On the other hand, tuition remained relatively high, which caused a drain of would-be students who opted instead for the lower cost of attending Massachusetts Institute of Technology, or the agricultural college at Orono where tuition was free and admission standards were not as strict.[2]

Another problem Chamberlain faced was that many of his innovations were ahead of their time. He persuaded the administration to add a separate scientific department, which included a course in civil and mechanical engineering, leading to a bachelor of science degree. While the department was a step in the direction of the future, it drew too few students and too much opposition from faculty and alumni who regarded science as the enemy of religion. They chose to disregard the new president's assurances that religious people had nothing to fear from scientists, "for after all they are following in God's ways, and whether they see him now or not, these lines will surely lead to him at the end."[3]

Mainly because the scientific department could not pay its own way, in 1880 the administration closed it down. The following year, a newly separate engineering department was eliminated as well. By then, the programs had turned out numerous civil engineers as well as a future dean of M.I.T. and Arctic explorer Robert Peary, discoverer of the North Pole.[4]

* * *

Most of President Chamberlain's setbacks and frustrations were private affairs, known to few beyond the college's extended family, and lacking major repercussions. One such defeat, however—a source of lingering embarrassment if not humiliation to Chamberlain—had long-range effects and received widespread publicity. It is the one episode in Chamberlain's life in which even his most sympathetic biographers find fault with him.

One of the many curriculum reforms he sought to institute was based on his desire to give Bowdoin's student body instruction in the rudiments of military science. He believed that if enough college-age males learned the basics of soldiering, future wars would not find the country hamstrung, as it was in 1861, by an almost total ignorance of army life. By March 1872, Chamberlain had appointed a drill instructor, had obtained training aids including four light 12-pounder cannon, and had procured West Point-style uniforms for every Bowdoin student.[5]

Infantry and artillery drill began happily enough; the glamour of soldiering lasted through the semester as well as throughout the following academic year. Then, in September 1873, the administration made the mistake of voting to charge the students $6.00 apiece for their military attire, including blouse, cap, belt, and gloves. Almost everyone fought the regulation. The student newspaper called the action "the last, worst, and most unpopular act of ... a military despotism...." As a result, few students showed up for daily instruction, and the "Drill Rebellion" was on.[6]

Instead of investigating the basis of the dissatisfaction, Chamberlain acted to fend off what he saw as a threat to his authority. He counterattacked by announcing that each student who refused to pay for his uniform would be promptly expelled. Later he would proclaim that he had secured a promise from an institution supposedly sympathetic to the dissenters, Dartmouth College, that no student dismissed by Bowdoin would find refuge in New Hampshire. Incensed by this punitive measure, a delegation of complainants went to the board of overseers, whom they presented with a petition signed by 126 students (representing all but seven students in the upper three classes) demanding, for numerous reasons of which cost of clothing was only one, the abolition of drill. They got nowhere. The board members, who believed the grievances should have been presented first to Bowdoin's faculty board, took no action.

Frustrated and angry, the students plotted their future course. In the meantime, news of the crisis had spread from campus to countryside, from Brunswick throughout New England and the East. Newspapers began to editorialize on the matter. Most took the side of Chamberlain and the administration, attacking the recalcitrant students as "Miss Nancies"—effeminate, degenerate youth.[7]

The drill opponents lay low until the spring semester, when their discontent took the form of profane outbursts on the school's makeshift parade ground. When their instructor called for silence, a student shouted him down to the cheers of dozens of his mates. Calling the faculty into session, Chamberlain prevailed on it to approve the expulsion of the outspoken student and the suspension of five other junior classmen, all instigators of rebellion. Word of Chamberlain's action merely stoked the resentment of other students, most of whom formally declared they would never soldier again. When they failed to appear for the next day's drill, all were sent home.

If the crisis reminded Chamberlain of his own schoolboy determination to suffer expulsion rather than compromise his principles, he gave no indication of it. Instead, he sent letters to the students' parents, seeking their help in persuading their sons to return to campus within 10 days. The president enjoyed a temporary triumph when all but three holdouts returned within the appointed time. Soon, however, the editors of a few major newspapers began to attack Chamberlain's "craze for epaulets and gold" and his "sickly longing for the exercise of autocratic power."[8]

He fought off these assaults, but a few months after the students returned he took a blow from the blind side. In June the overseers, whom Chamberlain had considered a source of firm support, voted to make drill an option rather than a requirement. Some years later the faculty administered further injury by recommending the practice be entirely abolished, which it was.

Chamberlain felt betrayed by the opposition of those he had labored so hard to serve. He never appreciated that he had stooped to harsh inflexibility when patience and understanding would have served him infinitely better. In a sense, he never recovered from this defeat. In its own way, the outcome of the Drill Rebellion rivaled the pain, sorrow, and frustration he had experienced at Fredericksburg, Chancellorsville, and Rives's Salient.[9]

* * *

Along with dramatic setbacks, President Chamberlain could claim notable accomplishments. He made a success of fundraising, traveling far and wide (all the way to Chicago, in one instance) to solicit donations, encourage endowments, and fund academic chairs costing $3,000 annually. By leaving no potential source untapped, his efforts easily eclipsed those of his predecessor. At times, however, he may have gone too far, as when he sought a donation from ex-General Adelbert Ames. The victim of unwise investments during his term as "carpet-bagger governor" of Mississippi, an embarrassed Ames had to turn down his old subordinate, pleading financial distress.[10]

Other achievements on Chamberlain's record include the completion during his tenure of Memorial Hall, the reconstruction of Massachusetts Hall, the thorough renovation of campus dormitories, and the funding of a gymnasium as well as 10 new professorships by 1874. He increased the budget of the college library, whose staff had once been forced to reach into their own pockets to buy books and subscribe to magazines. He took steps to loosen the college's puritanically strict disciplinary code and to lessen the effect of demerits on academic rankings—thus treating students more like adults than truants. He tried hard to police the fraternity system and to abolish hazing. He discontinued some of the school's religious practices such as evening prayers (except on Sundays). And he materially altered the academic year calendar, abolishing the long winter vacation, lengthening the summer recess, and rescheduling commencement to June.[11]

Chamberlain instituted the school's first graduate courses, part of a two-year program leading to a master of arts degree in science, letters, and philosophy. He instituted a policy to open the college's "advantages in all possible ways to the community instead of shutting it in for a few students." By this he appeared to mean making higher education available to more than the traditional student of the day. For one thing, he advocated a college career for women—if not today, then definitely tomorrow. Although he felt constrained to deny the application of one young woman to Bowdoin's medical school, he believed that all females who could meet admission standards should be permitted to "rise to these high harmonies of spiritual science in which ... true life lies."[12]

Evidently, none of these accomplishments gave Chamberlain a lasting sense of satisfaction. In later years he brooded over the demise of his scientific and engineering programs. He also looked back upon the criticism of college officials and alumni who believed his policies had betrayed Bowdoin's Congregationalist traditions in order to give the school a gloss of modernity and to fill its classrooms with warm bodies. Had these critics been more honest, they would have admitted that the severing of religious ties was an idea whose time had come; under Chamberlain's successor, Bowdoin would become strictly non-denominational.

Recalling such criticism years later, Chamberlain termed his years as president "thankless and wasteful." In a sense, he was right. He had given Bowdoin an impetus to expand, innovate, and look ahead, an impetus that would serve it well through the years. But of the many specific reforms he sought to institute, only one—his relaxing of the disciplinary code—achieved any sort of permanence.[13]

The strident opposition his policies encountered led Chamberlain to tender his resignation in 1873. The trustees and overseers managed to dissuade him from his course, and he stayed on for another decade. By 1883, however, his continuing bouts with students, faculty, and alumni, plus the nagging effects of his war wounds, had worn him out and he was permitted to resign. Supposedly three other institutions of higher learning immediately tried to make him their president, but he declined each offer. He agreed to remain at Bowdoin as a lecturer, but the classroom experience yielded diminishing returns and in 1885 he severed all professional ties with his alma mater. By then, his attention had been drawn to other enterprises, other areas of endeavor, and other fields of conflict.[14]

* * *

Diversions provided needed relief from Chamberlain's sometimes-tumultuous reign as Bowdoin's president. In May of 1871 he realized a lifelong dream of yachting by purchasing *Wildflower,* a six-ton sloop which he sailed around Casco Bay and down the coast to Portland. Four years later he acquired a 10-ton schooner he christened *Pinafore.* Small as his president's salary was— supplemented only by a $30-per-month pension courtesy of his war wounds—in the autumn of 1871 he was able to transform his half-story Cape Cod home into a small mansion. Workers elevated the original structure 11 feet and built a new first floor beneath it. The ground floor encompassed rooms in which Chamberlain entertained faculty and pupils as well as a never-ending flow of guests including presidents, secretaries of state, generals in both of the Civil War armies, and poets such as Longfellow, who slept in his old bedroom upstairs when brought to Bowdoin in June 1875 upon the 50th anniversary of his graduation.[15]

In the 1880s Chamberlain purchased and renovated buildings from an abandoned shipyard along Middle Bay near Mere Point; the result was a summer home that he named "Domhegan." The promontory on which the five-acre site squatted had been, two centuries ago, a launching point for Indians' canoes—the home's name was that of a chief of their tribe. From the promontory Chamberlain himself launched *Pinafore* out into the bay, sometimes with Fannie as his passenger, more often with Daisy and Wyllys as his crew. At other times he trotted along a shoreline "squirrel-path" aboard the warhorse he had brought back from Virginia. According to local legend, following his death Charlemagne was buried at Domhegan.[16]

Because they always seemed in short supply, Chamberlain cherished the days he spent at home, be it in his new manse or on Middle Bay. While at Bowdoin his fund-raising duties frequently called him away, and in June 1878 his family accompanied him on a several-month excursion to Europe. He went in the prestigious capacity of United

States commissioner of education to the Universal Exposition in Paris, where the French government honored his services with a decoration.[17]

Other responsibilities, perhaps not as enjoyable as an European tour, also kept him on the road. More than ever, he was in demand as a speaker on various topics: war and patriotism, as before—now also education and government, including one of his newly acquired causes, civil service reform. When speaking outside her borders, he was also a spokesman for his state. He gave one of his most memorable orations in Philadelphia during America's 100th year. On November 4, 1876, as part of "Maine Day" at the Centennial Exposition, he offered an address—so lengthy it was later published in book form—on the history of the state he loved.

He waxed especially poetic when recounting her natural beauties: "Maine has many things yet to take hold of human interests, and to stir life and love. Her thousand lakes embosomed in deep forests,—her Mount Katahdin, sombre and solitary, more wonderful in some ways even than the White Hills, with its strange craters and battlemented peaks, its wider vision of far-stretching woods in a net-work of countless silver-threaded streams and blue waters,—and this great and wide sea—this wonderful shore—these beaches and bays and harbors, and bold headlands sun-steeped in loveliness or storm-swept in grandeur,—these things invite the brave, the noble, the cultured; those who love nature's simplicity, and are partakers of her sacraments...."[18]

While most of his speeches met unalloyed acclaim, at least a few drew the wrath of influential men, imperiling any political ambitions he might have retained. When a fellow Civil War general, Rutherford B. Hayes of Ohio, won the Republican presidential nomination in 1876, Chamberlain worked diligently for his election in any capacity he could. He stood by Hayes through a contentious post-election dispute involving an apparently fraudulent vote count in three southern states. When Hayes's backers struck a deal that permitted their man to occupy the White House in exchange for an early withdrawal of occupation forces from the former Confederate states, Chamberlain publicly endorsed the bargain despite taking criticism in many quarters. Yet Chamberlain never doubted he was in tune with the national sentiment; in their centennial year, Americans everywhere desired to banish those ill feelings stemming from the war and achieve true nationhood.[19]

Chamberlain placed himself in the forefront of the let-bygones-be-bygones movement and promoted it to all who would listen. In November 1877 he urged an audience at Boston's Faneuil Hall to "be considerate in our treatment of those who … fought for … the doctrine of states' rights." He had come to sympathize more with white Southerners oppressed by Reconstruction than with the black citizens whose rights had been cruelly trampled. When Adelbert Ames wrote from Mississippi suggesting that Chamberlain did not understand the situation in the South and hoped that "the north will stand true to the rights of the colored men," his correspondent shrugged. Joshua Lawrence Chamberlain had gone to war to save his country from sectionalism, not to promote minority rights. Now that reunion had been achieved, now that the political problems that had divided white men were settled, he believed social difficulties would work themselves out.[20]

In promoting his views on Reconstruction, he sometimes appeared to invite opposition. At a Memorial Day speech in Lewiston, Maine, in 1879, he went so far as to suggest that his region had overreacted by going to war in 1861 ("I am not aware that the material interests of the North were seriously threatened by the secession of the Southern States"), and he wondered if by enlisting he had joined a misguided crusade. The speech received a torrent of criticism across the Northeast. A typical response was the supposition of the editor of the *Oxford Democrat* (Paris, Maine), that Chamberlain "had changed his residence from Maine to South Carolina and that the orator of the day was a Confederate Brigadier."[21]

A quick end to Reconstruction—which was duly achieved in mid-1877 with the removal of federal troops from the last occupied city, New Orleans—was not the only issue emanating from the recent presidential campaign with which Chamberlain was in agreement. He applauded Hayes's stand on the so-called "Catholic Question," which Chamberlain formally supported in a resolution put forth at a Maine Republican rally in August 1877.

Chamberlain's standard-bearer had raised the issue as a means of defending the public educational system and to rebuke his Democratic opponents for their "subserviency to Roman Catholic demands." In recent months Catholics in some cities had successfully protested the singing of Protestant hymns and the reading of the King James Bible in public schools. Hayes and many of his supporters, seemingly including Chamberlain, viewed these actions as well as the agitation of some Catholic groups to seek federal funding for parochial schools as undemocratic, perhaps even un-American. Although the president did not share some of his Protestant followers' disdain for Catholicism, he opposed Catholic power in American politics and was not averse to stirring up prejudice against the church. Chamberlain's support of the president on this issue appears to signal his approval of anti-Catholic tactics.[22]

Although his stand on religious issues probably failed to harm his chances for regaining public office, Chamberlain's views on the evils of Reconstruction and his overtures to white Southerners may have. When criticizing his Memorial Day address, the Paris newspaper had called him "A Dead Senator."[23]

A dead senator he might have been, but in the 1870s Chamberlain began to entertain hopes of landing a diplomatic post if not a political office. Late in the administration of Hayes's predecessor, Ulysses Grant, he had been touted as a candidate for minister to the Court of St. James. When that opportunity fell through, he hoped that Hayes would prove more receptive to his candidacy for a ministerial appointment. He must have believed that his vocal support of the new president's policies would stand him in good stead. Whether or not he was correct, he failed to gain the ambassadorship to Paris that he coveted. Some years later he expressed interest in an ambassadorship to Russia or Turkey, but those posts eluded him as well. One can only assume, as Chamberlain himself never did, that while the leaders of his party believed he possessed many gifts, diplomacy was not one of them.[24]

* * *

As a way of maintaining his interest in things military, in June 1872 Chamberlain accepted command of Maine's volunteer militia with the rank of major general. The position was an honor, recognizing his status as Maine's most revered living soldier; its duties were heavily administrative and largely ceremonial. Seven years later, however, Chamberlain suddenly realized how responsible the position could become under the right circumstances.[25]

The event that made this point was Maine's gubernatorial election of September 1879, which had attracted no fewer than four candidates. The field included Joseph L. Smith, nominee of the newly formed Greenback Party; Republican Daniel F. Davis; a "maverick Democrat," Bion Bradbury; and the Democratic incumbent, Dr. Alonzo Garcelon. By splitting the popular vote so many ways the candidates ensured that no one would win a majority. Because the Republican Davis came within 600 votes of outright victory it was assumed that he would prevail when, as provided by law, the recently elected members of the state legislature—most of whom were Republican—chose the governor. Yet when rumors began to circulate, mainly in Democratic circles, that some of the legislators had been elected through fraud, all bets were off.

Another statute called for the lists of votes cast statewide to be sent to the governor who, working with his state council, would affirm or reject the results. In December, when Garcelon and the Democrat-controlled council sorted through the lists, they found, or professed to find, enough irregularities to void the election of a dozen Republican legislators. Before the "count-out," Republicans had a majority in both houses; when governor and council were through, Greenbackers controlled the senate and Democrats the house of representatives. Under these conditions, there was no doubt that the next governor would be something other than a Republican.[26]

Naturally, Republican leaders called foul. They were especially incensed when Garcelon refused to submit the results of the count-out to the state's supreme court for final adjudication. In January 1880, the Democrats and Greenbackers, who had united on a fusion ticket to deny the governorship to Davis, took control of the State House, and the governor placed 100 armed men around the building to prevent trouble. Of course, that only served to broaden and deepen the crisis.[27]

With storms of protest rolling across the state, James G. Blaine left Washington, where he had been trying to launch a presidential bid, and returned home to direct the Republican opposition to the count-out. From his Augusta home he discussed with his subordinates plans to lead a Republican mob to the State House, there to overawe and eject the opposition and rule the state by force of arms. Blaine also orchestrated a series of "indignation meetings" across the state, calculated to whip the Republican faithful into fighting spirit. Blaine even requested his old rival, Chamberlain, as Brunswick's leading political figure, to chair a local meeting. He was upset when the general refused, declaring his unwillingness to engage in rabble-rousing.[28]

Already Chamberlain had been prevailed upon to ask Garcelon—unsuccessfully, as it turned out—to moderate his course. The militia commander hoped this would be the extent of his involvement in the ugly affair. But on January 5, fearful at last of the storm he had helped create, the governor ordered Chamberlain to call out the militia to keep peace until the controversy could be defused. Thus began what was later called "The Twelve Days that Shook Maine."

Garcelon believed his call would bring a division of militiamen to Augusta. It brought only Chamberlain, early on the 6th. The general had come alone for fear that armed troops in the capital's streets might touch off the volatile situation.[29]

Despite the vilification both sides would heap on him, Chamberlain showed himself to be the only cool head, and the only effective peacemaker, in Augusta. First, he persuaded Garcelon to remove his guards from the capital grounds and to return two cartloads of guns and ammunition the governor had called up from the arsenal at Bangor. He forced Garcelon to admit that only Maine's supreme court could resolve disputes over the legislative election; eventually the issue was submitted to Chief Justice John Appleton. Then Chamberlain huddled with the sympathetic mayor of Augusta, Charles E. Nash, whose policemen soon replaced the civilian guards around the State House, while patrolling parts of the city where violence by one side or another seemed most likely to occur.[30]

Ultimately, Chamberlain's tactics served to end the crisis without bloodshed. For a week and more, however, he fought a battle almost as fierce as he had at Gettysburg or Petersburg, at one point writing Fannie that "today was another Round Top." When the warring factions failed to win him over to their viewpoint, both threatened his life. The Republicans, who considered him both apostate and traitor, were probably more incensed than the fusionists by Chamberlain's even-handedness. Their ire peaked after he turned away one of their emissaries to his State House office, a Bowdoin graduate and old acquaintance of Chamberlain's, with the words: "I am going to preserve the peace. I want you and Mr. Blaine and the others to keep away from this building."[31]

Chamberlain's place in the center of the controversy led some agitators to plot his murder. Others planned to kidnap and remove him from Augusta long enough for the antagonists to fight it out. Some of these plots were foiled by the bodyguard Mayor Nash had assigned to Chamberlain; others were thwarted by Chamberlain's nightly change of sleeping quarters.

He could not avoid every attempt on his life. On one occasion, an angry mob burst into his office and threatened to lay hands on him. An unfazed Chamberlain is supposed to have met his visitors at the top of a stairway where he glared down at them and declared that if they had come to kill him they should know that "killing is no new thing to me." He referred to the scars he had received on many battlefields—on some of which, he believed, at least a couple members of the mob had accompanied him. Then he announced his duty to "see that the laws of this state are put into effect, without fraud, without force, but with calm thought and purpose." Finally, with the courage of a soldier and the flair of a showman, he unbuttoned his coat and invited a shot through the heart.[32]

His words, it is said, had such an effect that a member of the mob, a veteran of the same fields on which Chamberlain had bled, loudly threatened to shoot "the first man that dares to lay a hand on you." Moments later, the speaker's embarrassed cohorts slunk away. No further threats were made on the general's life.[33]

Chamberlain emerged from the "Twelve Days" with his reputation for impartiality and fair play intact. After January 16, when the state supreme court reinstated the counted-out legislators and named David Davis governor, the crisis cooled and the general returned home to bask in the praise of admirers from across the state and around the country. Few knew at the time that in his zeal to end the crisis Chamberlain had flagrantly overstepped his authority.

Of the many men who had come to him during the crisis claiming the right to occupy the governor's chair, only one had impressed Chamberlain—James B. Lamson of Freedom, a Democrat whom the rump legislature had elected president of the senate. Affable and principled, Lamson had treated Chamberlain with deference while his opponents resorted to threats and intimidation. After a state supreme court justice told Chamberlain in confidence that he regarded Lamson as *de facto* governor, Chamberlain wrote to Chief Justice Appleton suggesting that the man be recognized. When the story became public a year later, the general claimed he had suggested only "partial recognition," whatever that meant. Few believed him. In any event, by trying surreptitiously to influence the outcome of the controversy Chamberlain not only violated his neutrality but compromised his integrity.[34]

* * *

The march of time began to echo more and more in Chamberlain's ear. In August 1880 the father who had taught him the value of hard work and the power of the Scriptures, died. The following spring 22-year-old Wyllys was graduated from Bowdoin. The young man prepared to take his master's degree at the college prior to entering Boston University's law school. At about the same time Chamberlain gave his beloved Daisy (whom he once described as "a splendid soul" who "belong[ed] to eternity") in marriage to Boston attorney Horace G. Allen; her wedding was held, as her parents' had been, in Brunswick's First Parish Church. Meanwhile, Chamberlain's marriage seemed to be back on course; everyday contact with Fannie helped keep it there.[35]

In May 1880 he traveled to New York to testify in behalf of his former corps commander at the army's long-delayed inquiry into Gouverner Warren's relief from command at Five Forks. Outside the hearing rooms Chamberlain was greeted by colleagues he had not laid eyes on for years, including Phil Sheridan. The witness provided testimony he considered both accurate and favorable to the applicant, who in November 1882 was exonerated of most of the charges Sheridan had lodged against him in the long-ago heat of battle. For Warren, however, vindication came too late—he had died the previous August of what his supporters called a broken heart.[36]

Foreseeing the end of his professional connection with his alma mater, Chamberlain began to examine other business ventures. Beginning in 1881, he purchased real estate in Florida where, as he wrote his sister, "there are great opportunities to get health and wealth." Visiting the object of his growing attention early the following year, he soon decided to join the legions of investors who had descended on that sparsely settled but land-rich state. That year he became an executive of the Florida West Coast Improvement Company, which bought up Gulf Coast property in the hopes of attracting settlers, tourists, and those seeking relief from health problems. The venture made Chamberlain see himself as both pioneer and missionary: "I always wanted," he told Sae, "to be at the head of some enterprise to transform the wilderness into a garden both materially and spiritually...."[37]

To make his dream a reality, he had to move. Early in 1884 he and Wyllys went to live in Ocala, Florida, where Chamberlain joined what became known as the Homosassa Company. The concern planned to construct a local hotel that would develop into a tourist mecca, as well as permanent dwellings for year-round residents. But that stretch of the coast in which the firm invested proved so overgrown with vegetation and so susceptible to harsh weather that landholdings deteriorated and the grand hotel never materialized. While his father labored to commercialize the area despite declining health, his son tried to practice law in Ocala. Neither turned a profit.

The Homosassa Company began to fear that its enterprise would waste away unless a railroad linked the Gulf with transportation lines farther north. In May 1888 an association of developers reincorporated the Silver Springs, Ocala & Gulf Railroad Company, which had languished since its founding nine years before. The developers made Chamberlain vice-president of both the railroad and the improvement company that would build the proposed line from Silver Springs to the Gulf via Levy County. The venture was well capitalized and its holdings were properly extensive; company offices stretched as far north as Boston and as far west as St. Louis.[38]

Chamberlain found that running his Florida ventures meant living hundreds of miles away. Through the latter 1880s he divided his time between Ocala and New York City, where from corporate offices on Wall Street he raised funds for his railroad and improvement companies. For a time he lodged at the Alpine Hotel in downtown Manhattan; later he leased an apartment on West Fifty-seventh Street. Occasionally—sometimes for long periods, and in 1887-88 for the entire winter—Fannie lived with him in the city. It appears that, like many another Civil War general with a high-profile involvement in railway enterprises, Chamberlain's primary job was to line up investors. Many of his days were spent wining and dining potential subscribers who must have been pleased and flattered by the attention shown them by one of the nation's best-known soldiers.[39]

On his part, Chamberlain was not pleased by the remuneration he received for his efforts to bankroll his railroad. Eventually the construction firm succeeded in building a spur to the coast. In 1901 the short line merged with the Savannah, Florida & Western Railway Company and the following year became a part of the Atlantic Coast Line system. On its own, however, the spur attracted minimal traffic, and profits fell far short of expectations. Highly disappointed, Chamberlain gradually sold most of his Florida holdings for what he could get and headed north for good, his well-meaning but ineffectual son in tow. His effort at "making history" in the Sunshine State was over.[40]

After the railroad venture failed, he made his name and influence available to investors in other enterprises. He was not averse to driving what other parties considered a hard bargain. He engineered one such deal in February 1892, when the man he had saluted at Appomattox, John Brown Gordon, now a United States senator from Georgia, asked him to enlist capitalists in a business he was trying to launch in his state. The fee that Chamberlain quoted for his services and the percentage of future profits he demanded for his investors shocked and dismayed Gordon. It would be, the senator declared, "a great sacrifice" to accept Chamberlain's terms. He implied, however, that his old enemy had him at a disadvantage and left him no choice but to submit.[41]

While in New York Chamberlain became involved, either actively or as a silent partner, in various corporations and business enterprises. He was president of the New Jersey Construction Company, another venture in railroad building; Manhattan's Mutual Town and Bond Company; and the Kinetic Power Company, which developed motors for streetcars and elevated trains. He was also involved in an executive capacity in textile companies, real estate firms, and a tourist promotion business. In 1893 he began a several-year stint as president of New York's Institute for Artists-Artisans, which provided a moderate-priced education not only in the fine arts but in domestic arts such as metal work and ceramics. While holding these several and demanding positions, he maintained a full slate of speaking engagements before veteran, civic, and educational associations not only in New York but in Philadelphia, Washington, D. C., and throughout New England.[42]

Juggling so many responsibilities sapped his already fragile health. In April 1883 he was forced to have extensive surgery on his war wounds, and through the rest of the decade and well into the next he was severely ill on several occasions and close to death on at least one. Each time he recovered, as though he could not afford to leave the scene just yet. Too much remained to be done: attending Grant's burial, sharing the dignitaries' platform at the unveiling of the Statue of Liberty, speaking at Gettysburg on the 25th anniversary of his day of glory, attending Republican state and national conventions, spending time with the grandchildren Daisy gave him, navigating the choppy waters of Middle Bay.[43]

* * *

In the last quarter-century of his life, Chamberlain divested himself of most of his professional interests. The free time he acquired enabled him to maintain an active membership in dozens of clubs, associations, and learned societies. A partial list of his affiliations shows how diverse were the interests he kept up in his later years: the Chamberlain Association of America, the Alpha Delta Phi Fraternity, the Maine Historical Society, the American Huguenot Society, the American

National Institute in Paris, the Philosophical Society of Great Britain, the Egyptian Exploration Society, the American Bible Society, the Military Historical Society of Massachusetts, the Board of Commissioners for Foreign Missions, the Humane Education Society, the Colonial Society of Massachusetts, the American Historical Association, the National Geographic Society, and the American Red Cross.[44]

More and more he cherished his association with military organizations: the Grand Army of the Republic, the Loyal Legion, and especially the Society of the Army of the Potomac. He was always available to speak at veterans' gatherings such as the Grand Reunion of Maine Soldiers and Sailors, held at Portland in August 1881, which doubled as the second reunion of the 20th Maine Regimental Association. He also enjoyed taking part in veterans' activities. In October 1882 he supervised a committee of 20th Maine survivors in plotting the July 2, 1863, position of the regiment and in determining a site for a monument on Little Round Top, erected four years later. Historians would criticize the boundaries laid out for the regiment, which Chamberlain had approved, as being inconsistent with contemporary accounts of the outfit's service at Gettysburg.[45]

In October 1889, the 61-year-old Chamberlain was on hand to help dedicate the regiment's monument as well as a marker commemorating the service at Gettysburg of the 20th Maine's Company B. Physical contact with once-bloody fields never failed to move him to eloquence. In his evening address on October 3, he declared that "no chemistry of frost or rain, no overlaying mould of the season's recurrent life and death, can ever separate from the soil of these consecrated fields the life-blood so deeply commingled and incorporated here…. In great deeds something abides. On great fields something stays. Forms change and pass; bodies disappear; but spirits linger, to consecrate ground for the vision-place of souls…." He believed in a spiritual continuity of the human race; he knew that generations to come would symbolically share the sacrifice of those who went, and fought, before them: "This is the great reward of service, to live, far out and on, in the life of others; this is the mystery of the Christ,—to give life's best for such high sake that it shall be found again unto life eternal."[46]

Memories of his service on Little Round Top may have inspired him to noble thoughts and poetic expressions, but the memories of his former enemies did not. Twenty years after Chamberlain's moving address at Gettysburg, the commander of the 15th Alabama on that field, ex-Congressman William C. Oates, began an effort to place atop Vincent's Spur a monument to his old regiment. The modest memorial would also honor the service of Oates's younger brother and lieutenant, who had fallen mortally wounded on the ground. The Gettysburg Battlefield Commission, which Union veterans dominated, did not think much of the idea and enlisted Chamberlain's help in rejecting it.

At first Chamberlain frustrated the commissioners, but then he learned that Oates wished to place his monument around the east side of the spur by the great boulder in rear of the 20th Maine's original line. To agree to the placement would force Chamberlain to admit that during the height of the battle Oates had turned his left flank and that of Vincent's brigade as well—something the hero of Little Round Top was not about to do. The actual disparity in the men's recollections of the 15th Alabama's farthest position was small enough to have fore-stalled the nasty dispute that ensued. Oates never got his monument, and Chamberlain came away from the controversy looking petty and retaliatory.[47]

* * *

If the details of Chamberlain's service on July 2, 1863, were open to dispute, that service was deemed worthy of government recognition, in a major way. In May 1893 Thomas M. Hubbard, Bowdoin '57, a brevet brigadier general at the close of the Civil War and now a partner in a Wall Street law firm, applied to the Chief of the U. S. Army's Record and Pension Office for a Congressional Medal of Honor for Chamberlain. Soon other endorsements of Chamberlain's fitness for the award, sent in by luminaries including Fitz John Porter and General Alexander S. Webb as well as by military and political movers in Maine, began to reach the War Department. In time Chamberlain lobbied the army in his own behalf.

After reviewing the pertinent documentation, on August 11 of that year Secretary of War Daniel S. Lamont directed that a Medal of Honor be issued to the hero of Gettysburg. Chamberlain acknowledged its receipt on September 16; 14 years later he accepted a redesigned medal as a replacement for the old. Although privately gratified and honored by the award, its recipient publicly regarded it as debased, calling it "no sure token of distinguished service or merit."[48]

Properly honored or not, his service to his country was a continuing thing; he stood ready to serve whenever crisis or war loomed. In April 1898, with conflict between the United States and the Spanish Empire only days away, Chamberlain, then 70 years old and handicapped by increasing infirmities, offered his services in a military capacity to Governor Llewellyn Powers of Maine. Two weeks later, with hostilities begun, he made the same offer to Secretary of War Russell A. Alger. Although Civil War colleagues including Adelbert Ames had gained star rank at the outset of the hostilities with Spain, the officials merely thanked Chamberlain for his interest and permanently filed his application.[49]

Not to be outdone, Chamberlain offered to reorganize the Maine militia for war service, with himself commanding an expanded division for field service. Resolutely he told Senator William P. Frye of Maine that, "I think my day is not yet over for the service of my Country." Four months later, when the war ended with the overthrow of Spain's forces in Cuba, Chamberlain tried equally hard and just as unsuccessfully for a seat on the peace commission that settled the terms of the enemy's defeat.[50]

His letters to Powers, Alger, and Frye give a sad indication of how badly Chamberlain missed a position of prominence in military affairs. Though aged and debilitated, he longed for a return to uniform, that he might savor one last time the gifts of wartime service: honor, valor, sacrifice, corporate endeavor, dedication to cause. War imposed order on a man's life and made him care about things he ought to care about—proving his masculinity, preserving his honor, subordinating his individuality to the good of his unit (read his family), and killing or being killed in the moment of truth.

Chamberlain's desire to serve in a war knew few bounds—the conflict need not even involve his country. Although none of his friends—perhaps not even his family—knew of his action, in July 1870, when in his fourth term as governor of his state, he had tendered an offer of his military services to the King of Prussia "in the war now opening in Europe." Evidently King William gave him no encouragement, and Chamberlain never served against the French Empire. But the incident illustrates that for Chamberlain a war, *any* war, was preferable to the stasis and barrenness of peace.[51]

* * *

Chamberlain's mother died in Brewer, in her 85th year, in November 1888; eight years later his brother Tom, who had contracted heart and lung disease, a condition aggravated by his descent into alcoholism, died at 55. By the turn of the century Fannie had gone blind, thus realizing her lifelong fear, and Chamberlain, who himself passed from one health crisis to another as the new century began, took care of her as best he could with the assistance of her housekeepers. He was now employed as customs surveyor of the port of Portland, a patronage job tendered him by Republican President William McKinley. Chamberlain and his many friends and supporters had hoped he would become collector of the port, but his political stock had dropped too low to grant him that more prestigious and higher-paying position.[52]

The sinecure forced him to live apart from Fannie, who remained in Brunswick. For a time he commuted daily between Portland and home before taking hotel rooms, and then a house, near his job. The post also provided benefits he would not otherwise have enjoyed. Thanks to its steady income (something he had lacked for some years since severing his professional ties in New York and Florida), in the fall of 1900 he traveled to Egypt, Italy, and other foreign shores. In later years he made final tours of his Civil War sites including his Pennsylvania shrine, where "Chamberlain Avenue" was laid out below Little Round Top in 1902. When health permitted, he delivered speeches and gave papers, mostly on military topics, before invariably appreciative audiences.[53]

In October 1905 Fannie Chamberlain, who had been a semi-invalid since breaking her hip in June, died in the family home in Brunswick. Chamberlain grieved over her passing for the rest of his life. One suspects that grief was tinged with remorse and perhaps also with guilt.[54]

He spent his last decade much as he had the preceding half-century and more, working, reading, writing, speaking, traveling, and dictating to his personal secretary the memoir of the Appomattox campaign that would be published a year after his death. He advocated penal and civil service reform, supported the erecting of monuments to his Civil War superiors, hosted old comrades and former enemies in his home including the widow of General Pickett, and served as trustee for several estates.[55]

Chamberlain's patronage job in Portland never seemed secure; he fought off several attempts to abolish it. From 1906 to 1909, although pushing 80 and in precarious health, he worked long and hard to secure congressional action on a bill that would place him on the army's retired list as a brigadier general, thus granting him an annual pension in excess of $4,000. Despite his many contributions to the army, however, the bill received little serious consideration.[56]

In 1913 Chamberlain was able to supplement his income by publishing articles about his service at Fredericksburg and Gettysburg in two popular magazines, *Cosmopolitan* and *Hearst's,* both of which were commemorating the 50th anniversary of his war. Both pieces were edited heavily, but although Chamberlain deplored the overly dramatic "connective tissue" added to them he never denied that he was responsible for the bulk of their content. The articles contained statements that exaggerated the importance of his contributions to both battles and also, it would appear, some outright fabrications. In combination with papers and publications in which he had made questionable assertions, the pair of articles disappointed and upset surviving members of the 20th Maine including Ellis Spear, who felt impelled to refute some of Chamberlain's claims.[57]

Chamberlain lived out his years in his little house at 499 Ocean Avenue, Portland. There in late 1913 he suffered a flare-up of his old ailment, for which little could be done medically and which sometimes left him, as he informed his sister, in "unspeakable agony." On the frigid morning of February 24, 1914, death released him from his suffering—50 years after receiving that grievous wound at Petersburg, it killed him. His funeral, held in Augusta three days later, drew 2,000 mourners and tributes from across the country. He was buried beside his wife in Pine Grove Cemetery, just behind the campus where he had learned, taught, and presided. The headstone is modest; it carries only his name and his life dates. Perhaps he had come at last to see that he need add nothing to his record, that his position in the history of his state and his nation was secure. "That is the way he wanted it," his secretary recalled 60 years later, "to be beside his wife and members of his family with the Bowdoin pines towering nearby."[58]

* * *

Joshua Lawrence Chamberlain is as clearly defined through his contradictions as through any behavior that might be regarded as in keeping with his nature. From boyhood he was a dutiful and obedient son, adhering closely to the social, political, and religious values of his family and his region. Yet even in his youth he displayed a streak of independence and an iconoclastic spirit while developing an appreciation for music, literature, and heroic endeavor that few of his neighbors would have shared.

Usually personable and outgoing, he could also be aloof and moody. In young adulthood he was beset—as was his future wife—by fits of deep depression. Though devoutly religious and once a candidate for the ministry, he was overtly sexual in his approach to pre-marital and marital relations. By turns a loving and a harassing suitor, he showered affection on the woman whom at times he appeared to browbeat into adopting his vision of their future together.

A devotee of the success ethic, Chamberlain managed to excel in many fields including those for which he appeared to have little aptitude. A brilliant but restless scholar, he traded the peaceful, predictable existence of a professor for the danger and uncertainty of a soldier's life. Despite his inexperience, he rose to the upper levels of his adopted profession. Blessed with courage bordering on foolhardiness, a born leader, with a good eye for terrain and a firm grasp of tactics, he refused to let disabling wounds prevent him from helping reunite his divided nation. While his actions may not have saved the day on any particular field, he rendered conspicuous service at Gettysburg, Petersburg, on the Quaker and White Oak Roads, at Five Forks, and in other engagements. And as soon as the guns fell silent, he took the lead in helping heal the wounds of war.

In the postwar civilian world, he was a progressive and principled politician whose clashes with party leaders limited his effectiveness as governor of his native state. Later, as president of his alma mater, he helped modernize and secularize Bowdoin College but found that not all students appreciate being treated like soldiers. During "The Twelve Days That Shook Maine" he filled well the roles of soldier and peacemaker, but by seeking to impose an end to the crisis he exceeded his authority and violated his impartiality. As a businessman he worked hard to develop the economy of the capital-depleted South. Yet he appears to have been too willing to use his name and reputation to lure investors into business ventures in which he himself did not invest.

A committed husband and father, at times he forfeited his wife's love and respect. His emotional clashes with Fannie Chamberlain stemmed as much from his neglect of her and his occasional willingness to treat her as a child as from her own fragile psyche. Although it is unlikely that Chamberlain physically abused his spouse, his willingness to subordinate his family to his personal and professional ambition hurt Fannie as much as any body-blow.

Chamberlain overcame a speech impediment to become an accomplished orator as well as a sometimes-eloquent, sometimes-grandiloquent writer on subjects including his war experiences and the overriding importance of duty, honor, and service to one's country. But as an historian he cannot always be trusted; he seems to have been more interested in the thematic significance of events than in recording them accurately. His writings lose some of their power to uplift because they glorify the admirable byproducts of war as often as they condemn war's pervasive evil. And despite his piety and progressive outlook, through words and deeds he sometimes appeared negrophobic and anti-Catholic.

Chamberlain was much more complex and complicated than historians would have us believe. He could be different things to different people, as though unwilling to lend himself to easy definitions of character and personality. Among other qualities, he was abstruse and direct, caring and insensitive, modest and pretentious, selfless and self-consumed, tolerant and narrow-minded.

He was, in other words, a human being.

General Joshua L. Chamberlain, 1905.
(Courtesy Library of Congress)

Afterword

JOSHUA CHAMBERLAIN

A Psychological Portrait

by

Gary K. Leak

Department of Psychology, Creighton University

We know many of the details of Joshua Lawrence Chamberlain's life, but who was Chamberlain, the person? While much is already known about the significant events in Chamberlain's life and his personal characteristics, much remains unexamined beneath the surface actions of his life and the simple sketches of the man that have been presented to date. Modern personality theory and assessment offers keys to understanding Chamberlain by answering certain critical questions: What dominant motives and goals energized and directed his life, providing him with such a strong sense of duty, determination, and will to succeed? What were Chamberlain's most salient personality traits, and how did they relate to other aspects of his life? Given his extraordinary accomplishments as a soldier in the Civil War, with enough glory to last a lifetime, why was he so despondent after returning to the warmth of home and family? And how can we come to understand the *unifying themes* behind his lifelong physical and psychological journeys that touched on such apparently diverse domains as student and scholar, lover and husband, military leader and hero, politician, administrator, trustee, and entrepreneur?[1]

Before proceeding with the task of constructing a psychological profile and analysis that may aid in answering those questions, a basic issue must first be addressed: What does it mean to "know" a person from a psychological point of view?[2]

Given the richness and complexity of human personality, it is essential to examine lives from multiple, complementary perspectives. This study will explore the psychological make-up of Joshua Lawrence Chamberlain from two complementary perspectives that hold the keys to understanding any individual.[3]

Level I: Traits

The first perspective or level of analysis has long been the bedrock of personality assessment. It describes one's personality in terms of enduring traits and basic dispositions. Level I traits have been used for decades by psychologists, as well as for centuries by lay people, as a way to account for a person's consistency of behavior across diverse situations and over time. Recent work has shown convincingly that traits are indeed important; because they are consistent during adulthood, they can be useful in predicting behavior.

Perhaps the greatest boon to personality psychology during the past 15 years is the emerging consensus on the so-called "Big Five" traits of personality, often referred to as the Five Factor Model of personality description. This model claims that five fundamental traits are necessary for understanding a person. These five domains of personality are: Extraversion (quantity and intensity of interpersonal interaction, activity level, need for stimulation), Agreeableness (quality of interpersonal interaction, ranging from compassion to antagonism), Conscientiousness (degree of organization, persistence, and achievement orientation), Neuroticism (emotional instability), and Openness or Intellect (openness to experiences). The importance of these five dimensions of personality is that they have been found to relate to physical and mental health and interpersonal adjustment.

Constructing a personality profile of Joshua Lawrence Chamberlain requires use of the Five Factor Model because those traits are the building blocks of personality. However, Level I description does not, by itself, provide a complete description of a person; a person is more than his or her pattern of traits.

Level II: Psychological Needs and Goals

Level II description is concerned with attributes that depend, relative to Level I, on one's situation for their expression. In other words, personal characteristics may interact with specific environments to determine what someone will do. Level II description concerns such things as one's strivings, aspirations, and goals, social and impersonal motives, attitudes, the nature of attachment to loved ones, and so on. These things concern what people want and how they go about getting it. A great deal of attention will be devoted to an assessment of Chamberlain in terms of two key Level II characteristics and to documenting their relevance for understanding his most noteworthy accomplishments.

Description of Chamberlain in Terms of Level I Traits.

The method used to obtain data on Chamberlain's Big Five traits:

Three professional Civil War historians who have demonstrated a knowledge of Chamberlain through their writings were contacted by the author. In addition, two other individuals who have a background in psychology and have extensively studied Chamberlain through his writings (correspondence, speeches, autobiography, etc.) and earlier biographies participated in this study. These individuals—considered highly knowledgeable about Chamberlain—were asked to provide a description of him using Saucier's 40 trait adjectives.[4] In addition, they rated Chamberlain on 30 sets of adjectives, taken from the Adjective Checklist. Each of these sets has been found to capture one of the six facets that make up each of the five main dimensions of personality (e.g., the adjective set of "friendly, warm, sociable, and cheerful" assesses the facet of Warmth, and Warmth is one of the six facets that comprise the Big Five dimension of Extraversion).[5] These two instruments were designed to provide information about and insights into Chamberlain's location on the Big Five personality traits. The scores in each domain were averaged across raters to enhance reliability and provide one score per domain for Chamberlain.[6]

A description of Chamberlain using the Big Five.

Based on the information from the ratings provided by experts, Chamberlain seems to have been extremely high on Agreeableness, Conscientiousness, and Openness to Experience (average rating near 8.0 on a 9-point rating scale, a score corresponding to "very accurate" as a description of Chamberlain). His domain score on Extraversion was 6.9 (i.e., the traits that comprise Extraversion were seen as "moderately accurate" as descriptions of Chamberlain), and 3.6 on Neuroticism (he was seen as emotionally calm and well-adjusted).

Using Costa and McCrae's descriptions of these domains as well as their underlying facets, and based upon rating information provided by experts, one can offer the following profile of Chamberlain from the perspective of the Five Factor Model. His low score on Neuroticism indicates that Chamberlain was likely to have been very effective in coping with stress and in control of his impulses, rather than over-reacting to problems or being vulnerable to life's downdrafts. People low in Neuroticism are seen by others as emotionally stable, calm, hardy, secure, and unself-conscious.

His very high rating on Conscientiousness was expected because there is abundant evidence in the historical record for the existence of this trait throughout his life. In fact, he was rated very high on all six facets of the global dimension of Conscientiousness: Competence (capable, sensible, and effective); Order (being well-organized); Dutifulness (having a strong conscience and tending to adhere strictly to ethical values and to scrupulous fulfillment of moral obligations); Achievement Striving (having high aspirations and working hard to achieve long-term goals); Self-Discipline (self-motivated, persistent at tasks and unlikely to be discouraged when working toward goals even if bored or fatigued); and Deliberation (thinking carefully before acting).

Chamberlain was also seen by the experts as very high in Openness to experience. Combining his overall level of Openness with his high scores or ratings on four of the six facets leads to the conclusion that he had a vivid imagination; a deep appreciation for the arts, natural beauty, sensuous experiences; a preference for variety over familiar and routine activities; openness to change; and a tendency to intellectual curiosity and open-mindedness.

Chamberlain appears to have been very high in Agreeableness, which is somewhat surprising. The results paint the picture of someone cooperative, trusting, soft-hearted, good-natured, straightforward, and guileless. His facet scale ratings indicate a person who believes others to be honest and well-intentioned, is concerned with others' welfare, and is humble and self-effacing without compromising his self-esteem.

His score on Extraversion is also high. He is highest on the three facets scales of Warmth, Assertiveness, and Activity. The results suggest that Chamberlain was capable of intimacy, a trait reflected in genuine liking for people, friendliness, and even affection. At the same time, he did not necessarily prefer frequent company (i.e., he preferred quality over quantity of companionship). His assertiveness rating was high, indicating that he had some of the traits of a leader: dominance and forcefulness, persuasiveness in social situations, and social poise. Finally, high Activity suggests that Chamberlain was a vigorous individual who had a high energy level, liked to keep busy, and preferred a fast-paced life.

An Analysis of Chamberlain Using the Adjective Check List Inventory

A subsequent step in understanding Chamberlain involves examining biographies and his correspondence for statements made by others concerning his personality traits. For example, in one letter Fannie called him "fastidious," "open," and "guileless," while Trulock refers to him in various places as "serious," "earnest," "honest," "quiet," "wise," "mystical," and "having a keen mind." From these various sources—contemporaries of Chamberlain and his most recent biographers—two psychologists developed a comprehensive list of Chamberlain's traits. Based on the twin assumptions that he was (a) known best by close relatives and friends and (b) described accurately by his most recent biographers, those traits attributed to Chamberlain became the basis for endorsing or checking adjective traits on the Adjective Check List Inventory (ACL).[7] From these endorsed or selected adjectives, an Adjective Check List profile was developed for Chamberlain.

Chamberlain's ACL profile, based on traits attributed to him by others who knew him well, indicates that he was unusually high (above the 90th percentile) on the psychological needs for Achievement (to strive to be outstanding in pursuit of socially recognized significance), Endurance (to persist in any task undertaken), and Order (to place special emphasis on neatness, organization, and planning in one's activities). He was also very high on the scales of Ideal Self (strong sense of personal worth, harmony between what one is and what one wants to be) and Military Leadership (steadiness, self-discipline, and good judgment of the kind required of a ranking officer). The results of the ACL also show that he was definitely above average (approximately the 85th percentile) on scales measuring Self-control, Self-confidence, and Personal Adjustment. He appears to be extremely high on a scale measuring attitudes of independence, objectivity, and industriousness, ideal traits for a professor. Finally, he appears to be high on a scale to measure rationality over emotion (high scores suggest logicality, industriousness, and cognitive clarity).[8]

Chamberlain's high score on the Military Leadership scale suggests that his success as an army officer was a product of his basic personality structure and enduring motivations. In other words, his personality traits proved an excellent fit with the requirements of military service. This conclusion stands in contrast to those of other historians who have attributed his success as a leader to far more specific causes, such as duty to his country or, as Desjardin believes, a compensatory need to overcome earlier life failures.

Several key themes emerge again and again from the analysis using the ACL: Chamberlain appears to have been socially poised, conscientious, hard-working, goal-directed, ambitious, energetic, emotionally stable, conservative, rational, of high aspirations, with a strong sense of duty, and in control of his impulses. It will be documented later that these traits provide an almost perfect description of someone very high in achievement motivation. The description of Chamberlain from the ACL overlapped a great deal with the description provided by the

Five Factor Model. The convergence was especially striking with respect to the traits of extraversion, conscientiousness, and emotional stability. Because the sources of information about Chamberlain, as well as the raters themselves, differed across the two projects, it becomes unlikely that the results were a product of one person's idiosyncratic impression of Chamberlain. The important conclusion is that the results may reflect things about Chamberlain, rather than things about a rater.[9]

One final trait that seems to characterize Chamberlain and may help us to understand him more fully is Zuckerman's concept of "sensation seeking."[10] People high on this trait are continually seeking out "... new, complex, varied, exciting, and often arousing experiences."[11] We do not have any *direct* evidence that Chamberlain could be labeled a sensation-seeker, only an inference that can reasonably be made from events in his life (e.g., his vigorous nature, love of the outdoors, willingness to change careers—all consistent with the need to seek new experiences). Nevertheless, if he had been high on the trait of sensation seeking, it would make understandable such dramatic traits as his need to repeatedly leave the security (read "boredom" to a sensation-seeker) of his profession and home for the hardships of military life during time of war (he "chafed under the inaction" at times, and he stated, "... no danger & no hardship ever makes me wish to get back to that college life again.... Why I would spend my whole life campaigning rather than endure that again.") Yet he imagined the life of a career military officer in peacetime to be unsatisfying for him. His early preference for a career as a minister, *if* it could be practiced through missionary work in foreign lands, makes sense from the point of view of Chamberlain as a sensation-seeker, as do the more prosaic aspects of his life, such as his love of travel, public speaking, and military reunions.

Description of Chamberlain in Terms of Level II Needs and Motives

Even without the Civil War, Joshua Lawrence Chamberlain was a remarkable man who led a remarkable life: diligent scholar, innovative administrator, successful politician, energetic entrepreneur, and re-spected member of his community. But the Civil War is the key to comprehending him as well as our fascination with him. The war transformed Chamberlain's life from the realm of the remarkable to the realm of the extraordinary.

Motives explain one's choice of goals, persistence toward those goals, and the manner in which the goals are pursued. Two crucial Level II motives go a long way in helping us understand his "fire in the belly": what directed his life—before, during, and after the war—and caused him to pursue various avenues of personal accomplishment and influence over others with such single-mindedness. The most critical events of his life become understandable when examined in the context of his pattern of motives.

The diversity of specific human motives can be seen as derivatives of two basic forces of human existence: themes of *agency* and *communion*.[12] These two great forces have been common themes in writings from antiquity to 20th-century theorizing on the nature of human existence.

Agency is manifested in the desire to separate from others and the urge to master the environment; it occurs when people assert, expand, and project themselves as independent actors on the world stage. It encompasses more specific psychological concepts such as needs for achievement, power, and control. *Communion,* on the other hand, involves themes of union with others and the surrender of individuality to a larger whole. It is manifested in love, intimacy, merger, reconciliation, care, cooperation, and openness to and with others. As one can see, agency and communion are extremely broad tendencies that encompass motivation, values, and traits.

The motives or needs that best reflect agency in human activities are the needs for power and achievement, and the motive that best reflects communion is the need for intimacy. While these three are not the only human motives that matter, they are among the most important for understanding individuals and their behavior. Power and intimacy emerge as the two fundamental, universal dimensions of social behavior and underly numerous interpersonal traits.[13]

More specifically, the need for achievement involves a concern for excellence, ambition, and a high energy level. The emphasis is on the person's desire for significant or unique accomplishments, success in competition, mastery of complex skills or ideas, and striving to attain a high standard. Research has revealed several things about people high in achievement motivation that will prove important in our understanding of Chamberlain. They excel in tasks where evaluation is available and when they have high but realistic aspirations. They work with a restless vigor and persistence, especially when the tasks are difficult. They exercise self-control and delay rewards in order to gain greater awards in the future.

People high in the need for power are concerned with enhancing their reputation; they wish to convey to others an impression of someone who is authoritative and influential. These people are attracted to power-related careers such as teacher, politician, and clergyman. They tend to be excellent leaders in organizations and they produce high subordinate morale. They become highly visible (e.g., through the acquisition of prestige possessions) and they arouse strong emotions in others.

Measurement of achievement, power, affiliation. The assessment of these needs typically comes from scoring respondents' construction of stories on the Thematic Assessment Test (TAT). Other techniques based on the TAT scoring scheme have been developed and refined. They are highly flexible and can be used to assess motives in almost any verbal material, such as historical speeches, diaries, and letters, and this makes them valuable for use in historical interpretation where they can be "used with psychometric confidence."[14] Given the validity of these methods for assessing needs, and thus the validity of the motive scores obtained from them, researchers can use those scores to construct motive profiles of historical figures.

An Analysis of Chamberlain's Motives

Rationale. As mentioned earlier, motives can be assessed "at a distance" through a systematic content analysis of almost any verbal material such as autobiographies or speeches. Motive scores derived from text can then be used to develop a personality profile (description) and explain the reasons underlying an historical figure's key attributes and accomplishments (understanding). For example, one noted psychologist found that the motive pattern of U.S. presidents as assessed through an analysis of inaugural addresses related to presidential behaviors in expected ways. Power-oriented presidents, rated as "great" by historians, are seen as charismatic, while affiliative presidents seek internal harmony and peaceful relations with other nations.[15] This indirect method of assessment has the advantage of bypassing conscious distortions contained in direct reports of motives provided by the subject. Thus an intensive study of an historical figure using these systematic and objective techniques can advance our understanding of the person over the use of ad hoc explanations favored by many historians and especially by psychobiographers.

Procedure and results. Following established procedures for the assessment of motives "at a distance" from text, an expert scorer trained in Winter's system[16] evaluated Chamberlain's first and last gubernatorial addresses. The expert also scored Chamberlain's autobiographical sketch for the three motives to provide an assessment from a different perspective.

Chamberlain's "raw motive scores" were calculated in the traditional manner, with motive images per 1,000 words of text serving as the unit of statistical analysis. The analysis revealed that Chamberlain was high on two motives: power and achievement, and very low on affiliation.[17] Specifically, his power, achievement, and affiliation images per 1,000 words were 7.64, 6.29, and 0.92, respectively, for his first address (1867), and 6.25, 6.70, and 0.29 for his final address (1870). His autobiography also yielded information on his motive profile: it was similar to the impression from his inaugural addresses. His motive scores for power, achievement, and affiliation were 6.1, 6.6, and 2.8, respectively. If one can form an overall conclusion, Chamberlain was high (and approximately equally so) on power and achievement, and quite low on affiliation. Statements about "high" and "low" on motives are made relative to the established motives scores of U.S. presidents of his era, a group likely to be quite high in power and achievement needs relative to the general population. Now, let us see how Chamberlain's motive profile of high power and achievement and low affiliation can shed light on the major landmarks in his career.

Using Power, Achievement, and Affiliation Motives to Explain Significant and Perplexing Events in Chamberlain's Life

Perhaps the most psychologically interesting aspect of Joshua Lawrence Chamberlain's life is the apparent "contradiction" between his simple, prosaic life as a scholar coupled with a tranquil home life, and his extraordinary war record and unsurpassed devotion to duty and willingness for personal sacrifice. At first glance, one might require postulating two fundamentally different personalities and motive patterns that could generate two quite different "persons" within one man (the scholar and the war hero). However, a great deal of Chamberlain's life "makes sense" from his pattern of motives and traits; any apparent contradiction can be resolved and shown to make sense psychologically.

Before he established a career, Chamberlain seemed to be adrift—being open to career suggestions from his parents and attracted to the military as well as to church service (two seemingly very different occupations).[18] Finally, he settled on the life of a scholar, teaching at Bowdoin. Note, however, that all three options—military, clergy, and teaching—were avenues for the expression of needs for power. All three are "power-related careers" that provide an opportunity for holding formal, institutionally sanctioned power[19] (e.g., being able to direct and control others within a legitimate institutional structure). The careers are also highly visible to others, and they are connotive of prestige, status, and the accumulation of prestige possessions. People who pursue such careers tend to arouse strong emotions in others. (In Chamberlain's case, some examples are his wartime associates, his political supporters and enemies when governor, opponents of his drill policy while college administrator, and Ellis Spear's antagonism toward him in later life). It does not require much imagination to see Chamberlain during any phase of his life as someone who fits into this need-for-power framework. His high need for power may also serve to explain his cordial relationships with subordinates and the lofty morale among his men (recall that such individuals can be excellent leaders who instill loyalty in their subordinates).

In addition to power, Chamberlain was high in the need for achievement. A high need for achievement is reflected in such things as a concern with overcoming obstacles, with outperforming others, with meeting internal standards of excellence, with doing something unique, and with being involved in long-term achievement projects. Chamberlain's accomplishments as a student, scholar, and officer are certainly consistent with this motive and likely were manifestations of it. For example, his need for achievement motivated him to overcome obstacles as a student (e.g., stuttering, a weakness in mathematics) and as an officer (learning tactics by candlelight, longing to return to duty after being wounded, achieving distinction within institutional structures) that allowed for moderate, reasonable risk taking (note his hesitation when given the *un*reasonable, *high*-risk order for a suicide charge at Petersburg), and where feedback of results was available. His remarkable achievements, especially as a student, reflect classic achievement concerns: outperforming others, displaying unique accomplishments, meeting high personal standards of excellence, and being successful in long-term, achievement-related projects. His high levels of achievement motivation, coupled with his personality traits of conscientiousness, emotional stability, and openness or "intellectance," made his academic success a *fait accompli*. His high levels of power and achievement motivation, combined with the traits of emotional stability and conscientiousness, also made military success likely.

Chamberlain was very low in affiliation motivation. This suggests that he was able to concentrate his efforts on the tasks at hand and not be burdened by an oversensitivity to others, their criticisms, and their demands. This may account for such diverse characteristics as his independence from peers in school and his insensitivity to his wife and her needs.[20] If he liked being liked, he nevertheless had the courage to resist acquiescence to the whims of his peers if doing so would violate his personal standards. His rectitude and commitment to responsibility may have come from multiple sources (e.g., the personality trait of conscientiousness nurtured in him by both parents, the "superego" in Freudian terminology), but it also may be based in part on his freedom to choose among options, a freedom that comes from being relatively independent of the "tyranny of the herd." In other words, his ability to "do the right thing"—to do his duty as he saw it and to be faithful to internal standards of conduct—may have come from being low in the need for approval and affiliation. Thus his traits and motives provided him with the resources to make choices based on internal rather than external considerations.

To put the point directly: any seeming "contradiction" between the quiet scholar (with the "heart of a woman") who succeeds within the world of academia versus the heroic warrior (with the "soul of a lion") who thrives within a military structure, is illusory. Bowdoin College as well as the Army of the Potomac offered him an opportunity for the manifestation of needs for both achievement and power, while his low levels of affiliation freed him from external social constraints and thus enabled him to act in accordance with internal standards of excellence. His pattern of needs may also explain why he may have performed his duty to his country with greater enthusiasm than his duty to his spouse.

Why His Extreme Devotion to Military Service?

The role of achievement and power motivation. Despite the analysis above, a very significant question lingers: Why did he seem to *thrive*, to be so much "at home" and personally fulfilled, within the military but not at home in Brunswick? That may be the most provocative of all questions about Chamberlain. My answer is that service in the American Civil War offered him the most suitable or fitting opportunity to express his twin motives for success and influence. During the war, everything was magnified: one's life-as-drama could be played out on a much grander, significant, and heroic scale. A war, especially one fought for such noble causes as Chamberlain's, can be a haven for someone high in power and achievement motivations. In terms of those two motivations alone war offers an extreme challenge with numerous and important avenues for obtaining success, the need to work with vigor and persistence toward goals, the opportunity to obtain status and prestige, and the ability to exert influence over others within an institutional structure.

After the war Chamberlain gravitated to careers, such as politics and college administration, in which he could act upon his fundamental motivations to achieve success and to influence others as well as the course of events. But only the Civil War could offer Brevet Major General Chamberlain the opportunity to satisfy deeply ingrained needs for influence and accomplishment; no later life experience could provide the same scope for the gratification of these twin needs. From this empirically based perspective, one does not have to invent pathological origins for his heroism, such as Desjardin's thesis that Chamberlain's success is traceable to an overcompensation for childhood failures, stuttering in particular. Instead, Chamberlain's choices and outcomes in life stem from high levels of two *normal* human motivations.[21]

Satisfaction of needs for autonomy and competence. Another perspective may shed light on Chamberlain's being so "at home" in the army or "alive" during the war. Recent work in personality psychology has emphasized the role of three key factors deemed necessary for healthy and optimal psychological functioning: a sense of mastery or competence, a feeling of being autonomous and the belief that one's actions are determined by the self, and relatedness to others. Research has shown that feelings of competence and autonomy in particular have salutary psychological consequences.[22] A sense of competence and autonomy are associated with greater physical and psychological well-being, happiness and satisfaction with life, more positive emotions, and a sense of vitality characterized by positive energy, liveliness, zeal, and a sense of purpose.[23]

The Civil War offered Chamberlain the greatest opportunity of his life to experience feelings of competence (mastery) and autonomy (doing what he loved and was most psychologically suited for). He was an able officer, demonstrating skill and serving with gallantry and distinction in numerous battles. In addition, his sense of autonomy—doing what seemed most right, natural, and authentic for him—was at its peak. While on active duty he lamented returning to college life, reported being in the saddle for 15 hours a day and relishing the experience, and was despondent and anxious when prevented from serving in the field. What he was asked to do as an officer, the goals he had to pursue, meshed well with what he found of value and importance.

Well-being and happiness depend on frequent opportunities for the satisfaction of basic needs for autonomy and competence; these the Civil War provided him. The conflict offered him the most personally authentic and meaningful time of his life because it provided an ideal fit between who he was as a person and what circumstances and duty required of him. Combining modern views on the importance of self-determination and authenticity for psychological adjustment and felt vitality, along with the importance of power and achievement motivation as a means of understanding a person, it is no wonder that

Chamberlain was so despondent immediately after the war. Nor is it any wonder he thought so frequently and wrote so poetically about his experiences.

Personality trait of sensation-seeking. Remember that Chamberlain can be classified as possessing high levels of extraversion, conscientiousness, and emotional stability. It is apparent that individuals who possess the traits of conscientiousness and stability do well within a military system with its emphasis on attainment of objectives, fulfillment of obligations, invulnerability to fear, and so on. However, the trait of extraversion provides an interesting clue to understanding Chamberlain's love of the extremes of military life, because it embraces the concept of sensation-seeking.

It seems likely that Chamberlain possessed at least some of the characteristics of the sensation-seeker. His strong need to leave his family and career against the wishes of everyone important to him cries out for an explanation. In addition to the role of motives and the need for self-determination, his sensation-seeking may provide a complementary perspective on the profound question of why Chamberlain so loved that part of his life. It is possible that he was never happier or more fulfilled at any time in his life than during his years in the military. Recall that he was concerned that a career in the ministry or military in times of peace would be too confining and inflexible, a sentiment expected of someone high in openness to experience and sensation-seeking. But the military in time of war and the ministry in a missionary capacity provided an opportunity for experiencing change and stimulating events. So what might seem to some as a pathological need for combat may in fact be a result of the multiple influences of normal psychological needs and traits possessed to a high degree. Chamberlain's war experiences enabled him to act on his motivations and express his personality traits on a grand scale and within a context sanctioned by society.

The need to achieve identity. Erik Erikson posits that one's sense of identity can be determined when one can feel himself "most deeply and intensely active and alive. At such moments there is a voice inside which speaks and says: '*This* is the real me'."[24] Chamberlain was most alive, vital, and fulfilled during the Civil War, perhaps because his identity formation prior to that time was incomplete—that is, he saw his sense of self, of what he should do with his life, as incomplete. This need for Chamberlain to find his real self at Camp Mason, on the heights south of Gettysburg, or at Rives's Salient may have been the product of an incomplete identity formation based on strong family identifications (see footnote 18). If his prewar life was only partially fulfilling, the war may have offered a new avenue for identity and purpose.

Joshua Lawrence Chamberlain and the "Psychology of History"

The psychology of history attempts to understand historical phenomena through the study of eminent individuals using principles of psychology.[25] Simonton asks such questions as: What personalities are likely to "move and shake" the world? He replies that motives provide a partial answer to why people achieve greatness. Specifically, high levels of power and achievement combined with low levels of affiliation are associated with political greatness.[26] In terms of developmental influences, great leaders tend to be first-borns like Chamberlain: conservative, status-quo oriented people rather than boat-rockers or rebels.[27] Greatness is also associated with overcoming early adversity (ill health, for instance) as well as with stimulation in the home. Successful leaders also tend to come from the homes of business and professional people. In addition to motivational and developmental factors, intelligence is a strong predictor of greatness. Intelligence predicts fame, job prestige, and political leadership.[28] Intelligence, however, is not everything: persistence also matters. Fame and achievement are the products of intelligence acting in tandem with persistence, two qualities Chamberlain had in abundance. In fact, Chamberlain's greatness was certainly the product of several converging influences.

A Postscript: Our Fascination with Chamberlain

Why do so many find Chamberlain so fascinating? To be sure, he was physically and morally courageous, but such traits fail to separate him from many others of his era who do not hold our fascination. He was devoted to a cause, but so were thousands of his contemporaries. Perhaps it is his apparent complexity: the scholar-turned-warrior-turned-distinguished-citizen who left us a generous legacy.[29]

It is not too simplistic to say that his life is interesting for the same reason that a good story is interesting. In a good story the characters' actions "make sense," as Chamberlain's appear to. In addition, Chamberlain's life-as-story suggests a "romance" tale characterized by trial, testing, and adventure. McAdams describes such a story as "a series of heroic exploits as the protagonist oftentimes proceeds on a perilous journey, encounters fierce rivals, and emerges triumphant and exalted in the end."[39] Elsbree's classification of story plots also describes universal action sequences. These plots (adapted from McAdams) can be applied to Chamberlain's life: (a) establishing a home or family, (b) engaging in a contest or fighting a battle, (c) taking a journey, (d) enduring inordinate suffering, and (e) pursuing a consummation in which the hero finds self-fulfillment or liberation in a single-minded devotion to a cause.[31]

When we consider why we find Chamberlain so interesting, we happen on a specific and relevant theme: his life is a story of repeated redemption (i.e., something bad becoming good). This stands in marked contrast to Desjardin's thesis that Chamberlain was deeply unhappy during the last quarter-century of his life (a "contamination" theme: something good becomes bad). A more balanced view is that Chamberlain, by dint of effort, overcame his rural background and lack of educational opportunities to become a successful student at Bowdoin. He mastered his weakest subjects. He overcame an illness that almost killed him while he was a student. Nearly expelled, he became well-liked and respected by fellow students and faculty. He overcame a speech impediment to become an accomplished, prize-winning orator. He had a long and difficult courtship during which he was subject to periods of depression and loneliness, but eventually he married and raised a family. His marriage survived serious threats to its existence, but Lawrence and his wife grew closer in her later years.

The Civil War is a prototype illustration of the theme of redemption in Chamberlain's life. But while the conflict affirmed many of Chamberlain's key traits, it was only one of many experiences in his life, the interplay of which defines the man as well as the soldier. Under this many-faceted redemption theme, failures become successes, weaknesses become strengths, shame and humiliation become triumphs, ignorance is replaced by knowledge, wounds respond to healing, conflicts are eventually resolved, separation yields to union, and the physical and psychological hardships and privations of army life are made meaningful—redeemed—through Union victory and his cathartic comments on the conflict. In one of the best-known of these observations, Chamberlain noted that "in great deeds something abides. On great fields something stays ... and generations that know us not and that we know not of, heart-drawn to see where and by whom great things were suffered and done for them, shall come to this deathless field, to ponder and dream; and lo! The shadow of a mighty presence shall wrap them in its bosom, and the power of the vision pass into their souls."[32]

NOTES

Abbreviations Used in Notes:

BC	Hawthorne-Longfellow Library, Bowdoin College
CBF	Commission Branch File
FAC	Frances Adams Chamberlain
GNMPL	Gettysburg National Military Park Library
JLC	Joshua Lawrence Chamberlain
LC	Library of Congress
MHS	Maine Historical Society
M-, R-	Microcopy, Reel
MOLLUS	Military Order of the Loyal Legion of the United States
MSA	Maine State Archives
MSS	Correspondence/Papers
NA	National Archives
OR	*War of the Rebellion: A Compilation of the Official Records of the Union and Confederate Armies*
PHS	Pejepscot Historical Society
RC	Schlesinger Library, Radcliffe College
RG-, E-	Record Group, Entry
SSMH	Soldiers and Sailors Memorial Hall
TS	Typescript
UM	Raymond H. Fogler Library, University of Maine
USAMHI	U.S. Army Military History Institute

ONE:

1. JLC, *Joshua Lawrence Chamberlain: A Sketch* (n.p., ca. 1906), 3-5.

2. JLC to FAC, May 30, 1854, RC.

3. JLC, *Joshua Lawrence Chamberlain*, 3; "Chamberlain Family [Genealogy]," n.p., TS in JLC MSS, UM; George T. Little, ed., *Genealogical and Family History of the State of Maine* (4 vols. New York, 1909), 1: 132-38; Howard Kenney, "The Chamberlain Family," n.p., TS in JLC MSS, PHS.

4. JLC, "Do It! That's How," *Bowdoin Magazine* 64 (Spring-Summer 1991): 3-4; Alice Rains Trulock, *In the Hands of Providence: Joshua L. Chamberlain and the American Civil War* (Chapel Hill, N. C., 1992), 25-26, 33-34; JLC to Sarah B. Chamberlain, Feb. 8, 1860, LC.

5. JLC, *Joshua Lawrence Chamberlain*, 4-6; JLC, "Do It! That's How," 3; Trulock, *In the Hands of Providence*, 27-35.

6. JLC, *Joshua Lawrence Chamberlain*, 3; "History of the First Parish Church as Part of the Life and Times of Joshua L. Chamberlain," [3], TS in PHS.

7. JLC, *Joshua Lawrence Chamberlain*, 4; Willard M. Wallace, *Soul of the Lion: A Biography of General Joshua L. Chamberlain* (New York, 1960), 21; Robert M. Cross, "Joshua Lawrence Chamberlain," 3-4, TS in BC.

8. JLC, *Joshua Lawrence Chamberlain*, 7; Trulock, *In the Hands of Providence*, 34-35; Mark Perry, *Conceived in Liberty: Joshua Chamberlain, William Oates, and the American Civil War* (New York, 1997), 42-46; Michael Golay, *To Gettysburg and Beyond: The Parallel Lives of Joshua Lawrence Chamberlain and Edward Porter Alexander* (New York, 1994), 12.

9. JLC, "Early Memoirs, J. L. Chamberlain," 51, BC; JLC, "Do It! That's How," 3; JLC, *Joshua Lawrence Chamberlain*, 7.

10. JLC, "Do It! That's How," 8; Trulock, *In the Hands of Providence*, 41, 47.

11. Thomas A. Desjardin, *Stand Firm Ye Boys from Maine: The 20th Maine and the Gettysburg Campaign* (Gettysburg, Pa., 1995), 144-47.

12. JLC, *Joshua Lawrence Chamberlain*, 7-9; JLC to "My Dear Pastor," May 5, 1848, BC; Cross, "Joshua Lawrence Chamberlain," 5.

13. JLC, *Joshua Lawrence Chamberlain*, 6-7; Trulock, *In the Hands of Providence*, 35-36.

14. JLC, *Joshua Lawrence Chamberlain*, 7; JLC to Sarah B. Shepard, Feb. 8, 1847, UM.

15. JLC, "Do It! That's How," 5.

16. JLC to "My Dear Pastor," May 5, 1848, BC.

17. JLC, "Do It! That's How," 6-8.

18. JLC to "My Dear Pastor," May 5, 1848, BC; Trulock, *In the Hands of Providence*, 42-43; Thompson Eldridge Ashby, *A History of the First Parish Church in Brunswick, Maine*, ed. by Louise R. Helmreich (Brunswick, Me., 1969), 156-57.

19. JLC, "Do It! That's How," 9; Golay, *To Gettysburg and Beyond*, 32.

20. JLC, "Do It! That's How," 9-10; JLC to FAC, Aug. 22, 1851, PHS; JLC to FAC, n.d. [1851], RC; Cross, "Joshua Lawrence Chamberlain," 6-9.

21. JLC, "Early Memoirs, J. L. Chamberlain," 69, BC; JLC, "Do It! That's How," 10; Trulock, *In the Hands of Providence*, 42-43.

22. James M. McPherson, introduction to JLC, *The Passing of the Armies: An Account of the Final Campaign of the Army of the Potomac* ... (New York, 1993), xiv; JLC, Postwar speech on "Loyalty," BC; JLC to Sarah D. B. Chamberlain, n.d. [Sept. 1864], ibid.

23. Trulock, *In the Hands of Providence*, 26-27, 43-44; Little, *Genealogical and Family History* 1: 138; Jennifer Lund Smith, "Strains of Post-Military Matrimony: The Estrangement of Fannie and Lawrence Chamberlain," 1-2, TS in PHS.

24. JLC, *Joshua Lawrence Chamberlain*, 26-27.

25. FAC to JLC, Apr. 1, 1853, RC; JLC to FAC, June 7, 1852, MHS.

26. Trulock, *In the Hands of Providence*, 44-45.

27. Ibid., 45; JLC to FAC, June 7, 1852, MHS.

28. JLC to FAC, Aug. 22, 1851, RC.

29. Benjamin Browne Foster, *Down East Diary*, ed. by Charles H. Foster (Orono, Me., 1975), 333, 337; JLC to FAC, May 16, 17, 1852, n.d. [1854], RC.

30. Stephen M. Allen to FAC, Jan. 9, 1852, ibid.; Stephen M. Allen to FAC, Feb. 8, 1852, MHS; JLC to FAC, May 21, 1852, RC; JLC to FAC, May 28, June 7, 1852, MHS.

TWO:

1. JLC, "Do It! That's How," 10; JLC to U. S. State Dept. ["Notes of Description, Joshua L. Chamberlain, Brunswick, Maine"], Oct. 25, 1900, PHS.

2. JLC, "Early Memoirs, J. L. Chamberlain," 70-71, BC; JLC to Sarah B. Chamberlain, Aug. 6, 1852, UM.

3. JLC, "Do It! That's How," 10; JLC, Journal, July 4, 1853, BC; Golay, *To Gettysburg and Beyond*, 36.

4. JLC, *Joshua Lawrence Chamberlain*, 8; JLC to FAC, n.d. [ca. Aug. 1852], Frost Family MSS, Yale Univ. Lib., New Haven, Conn.; *Catalogue of the Theological Seminary, Bangor, 1853* (Bangor, Me., 1853), 1-12.

5. JLC to FAC, June 7, 1852, MHS; FAC to "My Dear Charlotte," Jan. 10, 1853, ibid.; Deborah Folsom to FAC, Jan. 12, 1854, ibid.; FAC to JLC, June 23, 1853, RC; Smith, "Strains of Post-Military Matrimony," 2-3.

6. JLC, "Do It! That's How," 10-11; JLC, *Joshua Lawrence Chamberlain*, 8; Richard L. Sherman, *Joshua Lawrence Chamberlain, 1828-1914: A Sesquicentennial Tribute* (Brunswick, Me., 1978), 7; JLC to FAC, Sept. 28, 1854, RC.

7. JLC to FAC, n.d. [ca. Jan. 1853, MS 1], ibid.

8. FAC to JLC, Feb. 22, 1854, ibid.; Karen Lystra, *Searching the Heart: Women, Men, and Romantic Love in Nineteenth-Century America,* (New York, 1989), 56-87; Trulock, *In the Hands of Providence*, 49; Ellen K. Rothman, *Hands and Hearts: A History of Courtship in America* (New York, 1984), 132-33; Perry, *Conceived in Liberty*, 93; JLC to FAC, Feb. 1, 1856, RC; FAC to JLC, Feb. 8, 1857, ibid; FAC to JLC, Jan. 1, Sept. 22, 1852, "Love Letters from Joshua Chamberlain to Fanny Chamberlain" Internet Site.

9. JLC to FAC, n.d. [ca. Jan. 1853, MS 2], RC.

10. Rothman, *Hands and Hearts*, 132-34.

11. JLC to FAC, Apr. 20, June 3, 1853, RC; JLC to FAC, n.d. [ca. Jan. 1853, MS 2], ibid.

12. JLC to FAC, n.d. [ca. Aug. 1852], Frost Family MSS, Yale Univ. Lib.; JLC to FAC, n.d. [ca. Jan. 1853, MS 2], Mar. 6, 1853, Apr. 6, 1855, RC.

13. JLC to FAC, Oct. 31, 1852, n.d. [ca. Jan. 1853, MS 2], ibid.

14. JLC to FAC, n.d. [ca. Jan. 1853, MS 2], June 3, 1853, Apr. 11, 1854, ibid.; JLC to FAC, May 28 [1852], MHS; Trulock, *In the Hands of Providence*, 51; Perry, *Conceived in Liberty*, 91-99; JLC, Warrantee Deed, Bangor, Me., Nov. 3, 1854, LC.

15. Cross, "Joshua Lawrence Chamberlain," 9; JLC to FAC, n.d. [ca. Jan. 1853, MS 1], RC.

16. JLC to FAC, June 3, 1853, Apr. 6, 1855, ibid.; "To Former Students of Bangor Theological Seminary [with JLC's responses]," n.d., PHS;

Moulton Library, Bangor Theological Seminary, Bangor, Me., to Alice Rains Trulock, 25 Mar. 1988, ibid.

17. FAC to JLC, Feb. 22, 1854, RC; JLC to FAC, Mar. 27, 1855, ibid.

18. FAC to JLC, June 23, 1853, Feb. 22, 1854, n.d. [ca. Oct. 1854], ibid.; JLC to FAC, Apr. 22, May 30, July 1, 4, 30, Nov. 6, 1854, Sept. 21 [1855], ibid.

19. JLC to FAC, n.d. [1854], Mar. 10, 14, Apr. 22, Nov. 6, 1854, Mar. 27, 1855, ibid.; FAC to JLC, Aug. 12, Sept. 20, 1855, ibid.

20. Rothman, *Hands and Hearts*, 157-58; FAC to JLC, Feb. 22, 1854, Aug. 12, Sept. 20, 1855, RC.

21. FAC to JLC, Aug. 12, Sept. 20, Oct. 2, 1855, ibid.

22. JLC to FAC, Mar. 10, 14, Nov. 6, 1854, ibid.; JLC to "Dear Annie," Nov. 10, 1854, ibid.

23. JLC, *Joshua Lawrence Chamberlain*, 9; JLC, "Do It! That's How," 11.

24. Ibid.; Wallace, *Soul of the Lion*, 28-29.

25. Cross, "Joshua Lawrence Chamberlain," 11; JLC to Sarah D. B. Chamberlain, n.d. [Sept. 1864], BC.

26. JLC to FAC, Sept. 21 [1855], Oct. 2, 1855, RC.

27. "Your Affectionate Pupils" to JLC, Nov. 19, 1855, BC.

28. Trulock, *In the Hands of Providence*, 53-54; Ashby, *First Parish Church*, 367; "History of the First Parish Church," [4], TS in PHS.

THREE:

1. George E. Adams Diary, Dec. 7, 1855, First Parish Church, Brunswick, Me.

2. FAC to JLC, Feb. 8, 1857, RC; JLC to FAC, Feb. 1, 1856 [1857], ibid.

3. JLC, *Joshua Lawrence Chamberlain*, 9; JLC, "Do It! That's How," 11; FAC to JLC, Mar. 6, May 17, 1857, RC.

4. JLC to FAC, May 20, 1857, MHS; FAC to JLC, Mar. 6, May 17, 1857, RC; Trulock, *In the Hands of Providence*, 53, 55-56; Little, *Genealogical and Family History of the State of Maine* 1: 133.

5. FAC to JLC, Feb. 5, 1857, n.d. [Jan. 31, 1857], RC; JLC to FAC, n.d. [ca. Oct. 1856], MHS; JLC to FAC, Feb. 25, 1857, RC; JLC to Sarah B. Chamberlain, Feb. 19, 1860, LC; JLC, "Early Memoirs, J. L. Chamberlain," 74, BC; JLC, "Do It! That's How," 11; Trulock, *In the Hands of Providence*, 54-56; Wallace, *Soul of the Lion*, 31-32.

6. Cross, "Joshua Lawrence Chamberlain," 82-83; Jason Stone, "Joshua Chamberlain," *Down East* 34 (Mar. 1987): 46, 48.

7. FAC to JLC, n.d. [ca. Jan. 1857], RC; JLC to FAC, Jan. 26, Feb. 8, 25, Dec. 30, 1857, ibid.; JLC to FAC, May 20, 1857, MHS.

8. FAC to JLC, n.d. [Feb. 1857], RC; JLC to FAC, Feb. 25, 1867, ibid.

9. JLC to Sarah D. B. Chamberlain, Jan. 31, 1860, BC; JLC to Sarah D. B. Chamberlain, Feb. 8, 1860, LC.

10. JLC to Sarah D. B. Chamberlain, Jan. 31, 1860, BC; JLC, *Joshua Lawrence Chamberlain*, 9; JLC, "Do It! That's How," 11.

11. Cross, "Joshua Lawrence Chamberlain," 11-12; Golay, *To Gettysburg and Beyond*, 55-56; *Portland Evening Express & Daily Advertiser*, Feb. 27, 1914.

12. JLC to Sarah B. Chamberlain, Feb. 19, 1860, LC; JLC, "Do It! That's How," 12.

13. Ibid.; FAC to JLC, Dec. 2, 8, 1861, RC; JLC to Sarah B. Chamberlain, Feb. 4, 1862, BC; JLC to "Dear Sir," Apr. 10, 1862, ibid.

14. Ashby, *First Parish Church*, 252; Golay, *To Gettysburg and Beyond*, 57-58.

15. JLC to FAC, Apr. 22, 1861, RC; Ashby, *First Parish Church*, 248; Americus Fuller to Oliver O. Howard, June 15, 1861, Howard MSS, BC.

16. JLC, Postwar speech on "Loyalty," BC; JLC, "Do It! That's How," 12.

17. *OR*, III, 3: 180-81, 187, 200-01, 266.

18. Golay, *To Gettysburg and Beyond*, 59; JLC to anon., Sept. 24, 1861, 20th Maine Records, MSA; JLC to "whom it may concern," July 23, 1862, ibid.

19. Walter Poor to JLC, Oct. 13, 1861, LC.

20. JLC, "Do It! That's How," 12.

21. Ibid.; JLC to anon., Apr. 10, 1862, BC; JLC [memorandum on European sabbatical], Aug. 25, 1862, LC; JLC to John L. Hodsdon [summary of military service], n.d., PHS; Americus Fuller to Oliver O. Howard, June 15, 1861, Howard MSS.

22. JLC, "Do It! That's How," 12; JLC to Israel Washburn, July 17, 1862, 20th Maine Records, MSA; Golay, *To Gettysburg and Beyond*, 63; Wallace, *Soul of the Lion*, 35.

23. JLC to Israel Washburn, July 14, 1862, 20th Maine Records, MSA.

24. Ibid.

25. JLC to Israel Washburn, July 17, 1862, ibid.

26. JLC, "Do It! That's How," 12; Trulock, *In the Hands of Providence*, 10.

27. JLC, "Do It! That's How," 12; Trulock, *In the Hands of Providence*, 10-11; JLC, "Early Memoirs," 76-77, BC; Josiah Drummond to Israel Washburn, July 21, 1862, 20th Maine Records, MSA.

28. JLC to Israel Washburn, July 22, Aug. 8, 1862, ibid.

29. John D. Lincoln to Israel Washburn, July 17, 1862, ibid.

30. General Order 20, HQ Adj. Gen.'s Office, State of Maine, Aug. 7, 1862, ibid.; JLC to Israel Washburn, Aug. 8, 1862, ibid.; Israel Washburn to JLC, Aug. 8, 1862, LC.

31. Generals' Reports of Service, War of the Rebellion, 4: 1-2, RG-94, E-160, NA; Ezra J. Warner, *Generals in Blue: Lives of the Union Commanders* (Baton Rouge, La., 1964), 5-6.

32. John J. Pullen, *The 20th Maine: A Volunteer Regiment in the Civil War* (Philadelphia, 1957), 1-2; Blanche A. Ames, *Adelbert Ames, 1835-1933: General, Senator, Governor* (New York, 1964), 93-95; Stuart B. Lord, "Adelbert Ames, Soldier & Politician: A Reevaluation," *Maine Historical Society Quarterly* 13 (1973): 81-84; Maine Congressional Delegation to Israel Washburn, July 16, 1862, 20th Maine Records, MSA; Charles Shiels Wainwright, *A Diary of Battle: The Personal Journals of Colonel Charles S. Wainwright, 1861-1865*, ed. by Allan Nevins (New York, 1962), 242.

33. Trulock, *In the Hands of Providence*, 23, 25; Joshua Chamberlain, Jr., to JLC, n.d. [Sept., 1862], RC.

FOUR:

1. JLC to Eugene Hale, Aug. 15, 1862, 20th Maine Records, MSA; Pullen, *20th Maine*, 4; Ellis Spear, *The Story of the Raising and Organization of a Regiment of Volunteers in 1862: MOLLUS, Commandery of the District of Columbia*, War Paper 46 (Washington, D.C., n.d.), 7; Petition [in behalf of Maj. Charles D. Gilmore], July 3, 1862, 20th Maine Records, MSA; "In Re[gard to] Charles D. Gilmore," 1-2, TS in GNMPL.

2. Wallace, *Soul of the Lion*, 38; Pullen, *20th Maine*, 2; William P. Lamson, Jr., *Maine to the Wilderness: The Civil War Letters of Pvt. William Lamson, 20th Maine Infantry*, ed. by Roderick M. Engert (Orange, Va., 1993), 16.

3. Officers of 20th Maine to anon., Feb. 5, 1863, 20th Maine Records, MSA; Gary Kross, "The Alanamians' Attack on Little Round Top," *Blue & Gray* 13 (Feb. 1996): 59; JLC to FAC, Oct. 26, 1862, LC.

4. Grady McWhiney and Perry D. Jamieson, *Attack and Die: Civil War Military Tactics and the Southern Heritage* (University, Ala., 1982), 48-58.

5. Spear, *Story of a Regiment*, 8-9.

6. Trulock, *In the Hands of Providence*, 12, 16, 64, 83, 177; Pullen, *20th Maine*, 2-5; Desjardin, *Stand Firm Ye Boys from Maine*, 9, 148-50; Erastus Foote to anon., July 10, 1862, 20th Maine Records, MSA; W. Hubbard to Israel Washburn, Aug. 8, 1862, ibid.

7. JLC to Eugene Hale, Aug. 15, 1862, ibid.; Desjardin, *Stand Firm Ye Boys from Maine*, 1-2, 9, 24, 37; Wallace, *Soul of the Lion*, 39.

8. Holman S. Melcher, *With a Flash of His Sword: The Writings of Major Holman S. Melcher, 20th Maine Infantry*, ed. by William B. Syple (Kearny, N.J., 1994), 2.

9. Ibid., 252; Nathan S. Clark memoirs, 4, MSA; Spear, *Story of a Regiment*, 13; JLC, [memorandum on European sabbatical], Aug. 25, 1862, LC.

10. Spear, *Story of a Regiment*, 5-6; Ellis Spear, *The Hoe Cake of Appomattox: MOLLUS, Commandery of the District of Columbia, War Paper 93* (Washington, D.C., 1913), 5.

11. Stephen W. Sears, *Landscape Turned Red: The Battle of Antietam* (New York, 1983), 74-79.

12. Spear, *Story of a Regiment*, 10.

13. Nathan S. Clark memoirs, 4, MSA; Trulock, *In the Hands of Providence*, 3-5, 20.

14. George E. Adams diary, Sept. 1, 1862, First Parish Church, Brunswick Me.; JLC, "Early Memoirs, J. L. Chamberlain," 62-63, BC; Nathan S. Clark memoirs, 5, MSA.

15. Ibid.; Melcher, *With a Flash of His Sword*, 3; Alva B. Small to his brother, Sept. 10, 1862, "20th Maine Casualties at Little Round Top" Internet Site; Elliott S. Fogg to his mother, Oct. 5, 1862, ibid.; Theodore Gerrish, *Army Life: A Private's Reminiscences of the Civil War* (Portland, Me., 1882), 13-15.

16. Ibid., 15.

17. Alva B. Small to his brother, Sept. 10, 1862, "20th Maine Casualties at Little Round Top" Internet Site; Nathan S. Clark memoirs, 6, MSA.

18. Ordnance return, 20th Maine Vol. Inf., Sept. 8, 1862, JLC MSS, LC; Gerrish, *Army Life*, 18-19; JLC to FAC, Sept. 29, 1862, in possession of Mr. Tony Lemut, Parma, Ohio.

19. Spear, *Story of the Regiment*, 14; Melcher, *With a Flash of His Sword*, 3-4, 252; William E. S. Whitman and Charles H. True, *Maine In the War for the Union: A History of the Part Borne by Maine Troops in the Suppression of the American Rebellion* (Lewiston, Me., 1865), 491; E. B.

Long, *The Civil War Day by Day: An Alamnac, 1861-1865* (Garden City, N.Y., 1971), 263.

20. JLC to John L. Hodsdon [summary of military service], n.d., PHS; Melcher, *With a Flash of His Sword*, 4, 252; Pullen, *20th Maine*, 20-24.

21. Mark Mayo Boatner III, *The Civil War Dictionary* (New York, 1959), 110-11, 190, 661-63; Warner, *Generals in Blue*, 62, 378-79.

22. Melcher, *With a Flash of His Sword*, 4, 252-53; John Marshall Brown to John L. Hodsdon, Sept. 23, 1862, 20th Maine Records, MSA; Eugene A. Nash, *A History of the Forty-fourth Regiment New York Volunteer Infantry in the Civil War, 1861-1865* (Chicago, 1911), 103.

23. Melcher, *With a Flash of His Sword*, 252; *OR*, I, 19, pt. 1: 175.

24. Special Order 3, HQ 20th Maine Vol. Inf., Sept. 10, 1862, 20th Maine MSS, NA.

25. Melcher, *With a Flash of His Sword*, 4, 252; John Marshall Brown to John L. Hodsdon, Sept. 23, 1862, 20th Maine Records, MSA.

26. Melcher, *With a Flash of His Sword*, 4, 253; William L. Davis to his parents, Sept. 23, 1862, "20th Maine Company E Soldier Research Data Section" Internet Site; Elliott S. Fogg to his mother, Oct. 5, 1862, "20th Maine Casualties at Little Round Top" Internet Site.

27. Melcher, *With a Flash of His Sword*, 5; John Marshall Brown to John L. Hodsdon, Sept. 23, 1862, 20th Maine Records, MSA.

28. Melcher, *With a Flash of His Sword*, 5, 253; Pullen, *20th Maine*, 24-25; JLC to FAC, Sept. 17, 1862, "Love Letters from Joshua Chamberlain to Fanny Chamberlain" Internet Site; Trulock, *In the Hands of Providence*, 68-69.

29. Gerrish, *Army Life*, 28; Pullen, *20th Maine*, 24-25; JLC to FAC, Sept. 26, 29, 1862, in possession of Mr. Tony Lemut, Parma, Ohio.

30. JLC to FAC, Sept. 17, 1862, "Love Letters from Joshua Chamberlain to Fanny Chamberlain" Internet Site.

31. JLC to FAC, Nov. 4, 1862, LC; Ellis Spear, Postwar speech on war memories, 10, TS in Spear MSS, MSA.

32. Sears, *Landscape Turned Red*, 296; JLC to FAC, Sept. 17, 1862, "Love Letters from Joshua Chamberlain to Fanny Chamberlain" Internet Site.

FIVE:

1. John Marshall Brown to John L. Hodsdon, Sept. 23, 1862, 20th Maine Records, MSA; Melcher, *With a Flash of His Sword*, 253; Pullen, *20th Maine*, 25-27; A. M. Judson, *History of the Eighty-third Regiment Pennsylvania Volunteers* (Erie, Pa., 1865), 53-54; *OR*, I, 19, pt. 1: 421.

2. Sears, *Landscape Turned Red*, 44-45, 48, 303-07, 317-18, 334; Long, *Civil War Day by Day*, 268; JLC, Postwar speech on "Loyalty," BC.

3. *OR*, I, 19, pt. 1: 349-50; Warner, *Generals in Blue*, 190-91; Melcher, *With a Flash of His Sword*, 253; Avery Harris memoirs, 200, USAMHI.

4. *OR*, I, 19, pt. 1: 67-68.

5. Pullen, *20th Maine*, 28; John Marshall Brown to John L. Hodsdon, Sept. 23, 1862, 20th Maine Records, MSA; William H. Powell, *The Fifth Army Corps (Army of the Potomac): A Record of Operations during the Civil War* (New York, 1896), 300-01; Judson, *Eighty-third Pennsylvania*, 54; Daniel B. Foote to "My Kind Friend," Sept. 29, 1862, Foote MSS, USAMHI; William L. Davis to his parents, Sept. 23, 1862, "20th Maine Company E Soldier Research Data Section" Internet Site; Alva B. Small to his parents, Sept. 23, 1862, "20th Maine Casualties at Little Round Top" Internet Site.

6. *OR*, I, 19, pt. 1: 204; JLC to John L. Hodsdon [summary of military service], n.d., PHS; Powell, *Fifth Army Corps*, 301; Hezekiah Long to his wife, Sept. 23, 1862, TS in PHS.

7. Pullen, *20th Maine*, 27-30; John Marshall Brown to John L. Hodsdon, Sept. 23, 1862, 20th Maine Records, MSA; Hezekiah Long to his wife, Sept. 23, 1862, TS in PHS.

8. Melcher, *With a Flash of His Sword*, 5; JLC to FAC, Sept. 26, 1862, in possession of Mr. Tony Lemut, Parma, Ohio.

9. JLC to FAC, Oct. 26, 1862, LC.

10. General Order 6, HQ 20th Me. Vol. Inf., Sept. 24, 1862, 20th Maine Records, NA; Russell Booth, "Butterfield and 'Taps'," *Civil War Times Illustrated* 16 (Dec. 1977): 35-39.

11. General Order 7, HQ 20th Me. Vol. Inf., Oct. 1, 1862, 20th Maine Records, NA.

12. JLC to FAC, Oct. 26, 1862, LC; JLC to FAC, Dec. 4, 1862, "Love Letters from Joshua Chamberlain to Fanny Chamberlain" Internet Site.

13. JLC to FAC, Oct. 26, 1862, LC; George W. Carleton to A. B. Farwell, Jan. 8, 1866, Frost Family MSS, Yale Univ. Lib.

14. Long, *Civil War Day by Day*, 274; General Order 8, HQ 20th Me. Vol. Inf., Oct. 2, 1862, 20th Maine Records, NA.

15. Pullen, *20th Maine*, 30-31; JLC, "My Story of Fredericksburg," *Cosmopolitan Magazine* 54 (Dec. 1912): 148-49.

16. Ellis Spear, "'My Story of Fredericksburg,' by Lt. Col. Joshua L. Chamberlain (later Brig. General) and Comments Thereon By One who was There, Capt. Ellis Spear (later Brig. General)," 4-5, TS in

Ames Family MSS, Sophia Smith Coll., Smith College, Northampton, Mass.

17. JLC, *"Bayonet! Forward": My Civil War Reminiscences* (Gettysburg, Pa., 1994), 257-58.

18. Melcher, *With a Flash of His Sword*, 254; JLC to John L. Hodsdon [summary of military service], n.d., PHS.

19. Melcher, *With a Flash of His Sword*, 254; Ames, *Adelbert Ames*, 97.

20. Ellis Spear, Postwar speech on war memories, 13, TS in Spear MSS, MSA; Melcher, *With a Flash of His Sword*, 254.

21. Ibid., 8, 254; *OR*, I, 19, pt. 1: 87; Judson, *Eighty-third Pennsylvania*, 55.

22. JLC to FAC, Nov. 3, 4, 1862, LC.

23. Melcher, *With a Flash of His Sword*, 255; Judson, *Eighty-third Pennsylvania*, 55; *OR*, I, 19, pt. 2: 555; Pullen, *20th Maine*, 41-42; Sears, *Landscape Turned Red*, 340-45.

24. *OR*, I, 19, pt. 1: 88; Warner, *Generals in Blue*, 57, 62, 234, 331, 379.

25. JLC, "My Story of Fredericksburg," 149; Spear, "'My Story of Fredericksburg' and Comments Thereon," 6.

26. Wallace, *Soul of the Lion*, 50-51; *OR*, I, 19, pt. 2: 552-54; 21: 83-84; Melcher, *With a Flash of His Sword*, 255.

27. *OR*, I, 21: 84-86, 103-04, 550-51.

28. Pullen, *20th Maine*, 43; Edward Simonton, "Recollections of the Battle of Fredericksburg," *Glimpses of the Nation's Struggle: Papers Read Before the Minnesota Commandery, MOLLUS* 2: 248.

29. FAC to JLC, Nov. 27, 1862, RC.

30. JLC to FAC, Dec. 2, 1862, "Love Letters from Joshua Chamberlain to Fanny Chamberlain" Internet Site.

31. JLC to FAC, Dec. 3, 1862, ibid.

32. Melcher, *With a Flash of His Sword*, 10; Simonton, "Recollections of the Battle of Fredericksburg," 250.

33. JLC, *Through Blood & Fire: Selected Civil War Papers of Major General Joshua Chamberlain*, ed. by Mark Nesbitt (Mechanicsburg, Pa., 1996), 37-45; JLC, "My Story of Fredericksburg," 148-59; Spear, "'My Story of Fredericksburg' and Comments Thereon," 1-37; Abbott Spear, "The 20th Maine at Fredericksburg: The 1913 Accounts of Generals Chamberlain and Spear," 1-10, MSA.

34. JLC, *Through Blood & Fire*, 38; *OR*, I, 21: 88-89.

35. JLC, "My Story of Fredericksburg," 150; Spear, "'My Story of Fredericksburg' and Comments Thereon," 6-7; "Women Rallied to

Preserve Mary Washington Gravesite," *The Free Lance-Star* (Fredericksburg, Va.), Apr. 29, 1994; Edward Alvey, Jr., "The Mary Washington Monument Centennial," *Fredericksburg Times Magazine 10* (May 1994): 13-23.

36. JLC, *Through Blood & Fire*, 38.

37. Ibid., 39; Trulock, *In the Hands of Providence*, 92-96; OR, I, 21: 53-55.

38. JLC, "My Story of Fredericksburg," 152; Spear, "'My Story of Fredericksburg' and Comments Thereon," 7-8.

39. JLC, "My Story of Fredericksburg," 152; Spear, "'My Story of Fredericksburg' and Comments Thereon," 8.

40. JLC, "My Story of Fredericksburg," 152; Spear, "'My Story of Fredericksburg' and Comments Thereon," 9.

41. JLC, "My Story of Fredericksburg," 152; Spear, "'My Story of Fredericksburg' and Comments Thereon," 9-10.

42. JLC, "My Story of Fredericksburg," 152-53; Spear, "'My Story of Fredericksburg' and Comments Thereon," 10-11.

43. JLC, "My Story of Fredericksburg," 153; Spear, "'My Story of Fredericksburg' and Comments Thereon," 11-12.

44. JLC, "My Story of Fredericksburg," 153; Spear, "'My Story of Fredericksburg' and Comments Thereon," 13-14.

45. JLC, "My Story of Fredericksburg," 153-54.

46. Spear, "'My Story of Fredericksburg' and Comments Thereon," 13-17; Trulock, *In the Hands of Providence*, 97; OR, I, 21: 136, 411.

47. Spear, "'My Story of Fredericksburg' and Comments Thereon," 17-18.

48. Ibid., 16.

49. Desjardin, *Stand Firm Ye Boys from Maine*, 151.

SIX:

1. JLC, "My Story of Fredericksburg," 154; Spear, "'My Story of Fredericksburg' and Comments Thereon," 19-21.

2. JLC, "My Story of Fredericksburg," 155-56.

3. JLC, *Through Blood & Fire*, 43.

4. JLC, "My Story of Fredericksburg," 156; Spear, "'My Story of Fredericksburg' and Comments Thereon," 24.

5. JLC, "My Story of Fredericksburg," 156; Spear, "'My Story of Fredericksburg' and Comments Thereon," 26-27.

6. JLC, "My Story of Fredericksburg," 156-58.

7. Spear, "'My Story of Fredericksburg' and Comments Thereon," 34.

8. *OR*, I, 21: 136-37, 142; Pullen, *20th Maine*, 62; JLC to Abner Coburn, Feb. 25, 1863, 20th Maine Records, MSA; Ames, *Adelbert Ames*, 109.

9. Desjardin, *Stand Firm Ye Boys from Maine*, 146.

10. Glenn LaFantasie, "Joshua Chamberlain and the American Dream," in *The Gettysburg Nobody Knows*, ed. by Gabor S. Boritt (New York, 1997), 38-40. When the collection of 100-some Chamberlain letters currently owned by the City of Harrisburg, Pennsylvania, is made available to researchers, Chamberlain's driving ambition and his eager quest to gain promotion will become public knowledge.

11. Melcher, *With a Flash of His Sword*, 20-21; Pullen, *20th Maine*, 62-63; Trulock, *In the Hands of Providence*, 106.

12. Special Order 30, HQ 20th Me. Vol. Inf., Jan. 6, 1863, 20th Maine Records, NA.

13 Pullen, *20th Maine*, 65-66; *OR*, I, 21: 900-01.

14. Pullen, *20th Maine*, 68-69; Melcher, *With a Flash of His Sword*, 17-18; Ellis Spear, *The Civil War Recollections of General Ellis Spear*, ed. by Abbott Spear et al. (Orono, Me., 1997), 197-98; Whitman and True, *Maine in the War for the Union*, 492.

15. Nash, *Forty-fourth New York*, 123; Powell, *Fifth Army Corps*, 409; Spear, *Civil War Recollections*, 198.

16. LaFantasie, "Joshua Chamberlain and the American Dream," 33-34; JLC to FAC, Sept. 29, 1862, in possession of Mr. Tony Lemut, Parma, Ohio; JLC to John Marshall Brown, Jan. 28, 1863, PHS.

17. Warner, *Generals in Blue*, 58, 234; *OR*, I, 21: 96, 1004-05.

18. Thomas D. Chamberlain to Sarah B. Chamberlain, Feb. 2, 1863, UM; Trulock, *In the Hands of Providence*, 53, 57, 117-18, 339-40. Details of the lives and careers of JLC's siblings can be found in Diana H. Loski, *The Chamberlains of Brewer* (Gettysburg, Pa., 1998).

19. JLC to Abner Coburn, Feb. 26, 1863, 20th Maine Records, MSA; Special Order 16, HQ 20th Me. Vol. Inf., Apr. 5, 1863, 20th Maine Records, NA.

20. Alva B. Small to his parents, Feb. 26 [1863], "20th Maine Casualties at Little Round Top" Internet Site; Willard W. Buxton to his father, Feb. 24, 1863, ibid.

21. A. W. Clark et al. to "whom it may concern," Feb. 5, 1863, 20th Maine Records, MSA.

22. Alva B. Small to his parents, Feb. 26 [1863], "20th Maine Casualties at Little Round Top" Internet Site; Bruce Catton, *Glory Road: The Bloody Route from Fredericksburg to Gettysburg* (Garden City, N. Y., 1952), 140-47.

23. Lamson, *Maine to the Wilderness*, 61.

24. Pullen, *20th Maine*, 72; JLC, "Oration on Lincoln," 257-58, BC.

25. E. B. French to "Lieut. Col. Conrad," Apr. 9, 1863, PHS; JLC to FAC, Apr. 24, 1863, LC; Field and Staff Muster Roll, Mar. and Apr., 1863, JLC's Compiled Military Service Record, RG-94, E-519, NA.

26. Pullen, *20th Maine*, 73-75; Melcher, *With a Flash of His Sword*, 23.

27. Wallace, *Soul of the Lion*, 66; William F. Breakey, "Recollections and Incidents of Medical Military Service," *War Papers: Read Before the Commandery of Michigan, MOLLUS* 2: 137-38; Gerrish, *Army Life*, 86.

28. JLC to Daniel Butterfield, Apr. 20, 1863, LC.

29. JLC to FAC, Apr. 24, 1863, ibid.

30. Ames, *Adelbert Ames*, 109.

31. Generals' Reports of Service, War of the Rebellion, 4: 1, RG-94, E-160, NA; John Lenfest to his wife, May 1, 1863, TS in Trulock Coll., PHS; Elliott Fogg to his mother, May 23, 1863, "20th Maine Casualties at Little Round Top" Internet Site; Pullen, *20th Maine*, 131-32; Nathan S. Clark memoirs, 19, MSA; *OR*, I, 25, pt. 1: 519; "In Re Charles D. Gilmore," [1], TS in "20th Maine Inf. Reg." File, GNMPL.

32. JLC to John L. Hodsdon [summary of military service], n.d., PHS.

33. Spear, *Civil War Recollections*, 207; Circular, HQ 20th Me. Vol. Inf., May 2, 1863, 20th Maine Records, NA; Gerrish, *Army Life*, 86; John Lenfest to his wife, May 1, 1863, TS in Trulock Coll., PHS; Hezekiah Long to "Dear Sarah," May 1 [1863], TS in ibid.; JLC to Abner Coburn, May 25, 1863, 20th Maine Records, MSA.

34. Trulock, *In the Hands of Providence*, 111; Catton, *Glory Road*, 171-88.

35. JLC to John L. Hodsdon [summary of military service], n.d., PHS; Wallace, *Soul of the Lion*, 67.

SEVEN:

1. JLC to "My dear little Daisy," May —, 1863, BC.

2. HQ 3rd Brig. [1st Div., 5th A. C.] to JLC, May 13, 1863, LC; Spear, *Civil War Recollections*, 209; Melcher, *With a Flash of His Sword*, 27-28; Albert E. Fernald diary, May 17, 1863, TS in Trulock Coll., PHS; Special Order 255, Adj. Gen.'s Office, June 8, 1863, 20th Maine Records, MSA.

3. JLC and Charles D. Gilmore to Israel Washburn, Nov. 16, 1862, ibid.; Charles D. Gilmore to John L. Hodsdon, May 26, 1863, ibid.

4. Melcher, *With a Flash of His Sword*, 25-27; Willard W. Buxton to his

father, May 24, 1863, "20th Maine Casualties at Little Round Top" Internet Site.

5. Ibid.; Warner, *Generals in Blue*, 527-28; Desjardin, *Stand Firm Ye Boys from Maine*, 15-16; Spear, *Civil War Recollections*, 209; Judson, *Eighty-third Pennsylvania*, 63; Daniel B. Foote to "My Dear Friend," May 25 [1863], USAMHI.

6. JLC, Muster-in Roll, May 20, 1863, LC; copy in JLC, Compiled Military Service Record, RG-94, E-519, NA; JLC to Abner Coburn, May 25, 1863, 20th Maine Records, MSA; Charles D. Gilmore to John L. Hodsdon, Sept. 2, 1863, ibid.; Spear, *Civil War Recollections*, 307-08; Thomas D. Chamberlain et al. to Abner Coburn, May 22, 1863, ibid.

7. Trulock, *In the Hands of Providence*, 114.

8. Judson, *Eighty-third Pennsylvania*, 63; *OR*, I, 25, pt. 2: 579 and n.; Oliver W. Norton to Boyd Vincent, Aug. 3, 1914, Norton MSS, Clarke Hist. Lib., Central Mich. Univ., Mt. Pleasant, Mich.; Albert E. Fernald diary, May 20, 1863, TS in Trulock Coll., PHS; Charles W. Billings to his father, May 19, 31, 1863, "20th Maine Casualties at Little Round Top" Internet Site.

9. John Lenfest to his wife, May 24, 1863, TS in Trulock Coll., PHS; Albert E. Fernald diary, May 23, 1863, TS in ibid.; Pullen, *20th Maine*, 77-79; JLC to John L. Hodsdon [summary of military service] n.d., PHS.

10. Ibid.; JLC to Abner Coburn, May 25, 27, 1863, 20th Maine Records, MSA; Pullen, *20th Maine*, 80-81.

11. John O'Connell memoirs, 40-41, Civil War Misc. Coll., USAMHI; JLC, "Through Blood and Fire at Gettysburg," *Hearst's Magazine* 23 (1913): 899-900.

12. Ibid.; JLC to John L. Hodsdon [summary of military service] n.d., PHS.

13. *OR*, I, 25, pt. 2: 534-38; Albert E. Fernald diary, May 28, 1863, TS in Trulock Coll., PHS; Charles W. Billings to his father, May 31, 1863, "20th Maine Casualties at Little Round Top" Internet Site.

14. Ibid.; JLC to "Lieut.," June 3, 1863, LC; Albert E. Fernald diary, May 28-29, 1863, TS in Trulock Coll., PHS.

15. Charles W. Billings to his father, May 31, 1863, "20th Maine Casualties at Little Round Top" Internet Site.

16. Albert E. Fernald diary, June 4, 1863, TS in Trulock Coll., PHS; Melcher, *With a Flash of His Sword*, 29-30.

17. Ibid., 32; Albert E. Fernald diary, June 10, 1863, TS in Trulock Coll., PHS.

18. Melcher, *With a Flash of His Sword*, 257; Nathan S. Clark memoirs, 24, MSA; Albert E. Fernald diary, June 14, 15, 1863, TS in Trulock Coll., PHS; Spear, *Civil War Recollections*, 212-14; Judson, *Eighty-third Pennsylvania*, 63.

19. *OR*, I, 27, pt. 3: 70-75, 80-93, 95-97, 99-115; Pullen, *20th Maine*, 83-84.

20. Albert E. Fernald diary, June 15, 1864, TS in Trulock Coll., PHS; JLC to "Dear Aunty," June 15, 1863, LC.

21. Ibid.; Trulock, *In the Hands of Providence*, 120, 161; Desjardin, *Stand Firm Ye Boys from Maine*, 146.

22. Sarah B. Chamberlain to Thomas D. Chamberlain, May 26, 1863, RC; Trulock, *In the Hands of Providence*, 120.

23. Ibid., 43-45, 86, 119-20, 161, 410n., 420n.; Perry, *Concieved in Liberty*, 100, 177-79. The tensions caused by the wartime estrangement of JLC and FAC can be traced in Smith, "Strains of Post-Military Matrimony." The avoidant attachment style is summarized in Cindy Hazan and Philip R. Shaver, "Attachment as an Organizational Framework for Research on Close Relationships," *Psychology Inquiry* 5 (1994): 1-22.

24. Nathan S. Clark memoirs, 24, MSA.

25. Albert E. Fernald diary, June 17, 18, 1863, TS in Trulock Coll., PHS.; Pullen, *20th Maine*, 84; Spear, *Civil War Recollections*, 213; Nathan S. Clark memoirs, 24, MSA.

26. Ibid., 25; *OR*, I, 27, pt. 1: 598, 613-14.

27. *OR*, I, 27, pt. 1: 598-99, 613-15; Pullen, *20th Maine*, 85-87; Henry Lytle to "Dear Brother," June 28, 1863, TS in Lewis Leigh Coll., USAMHI; John O'Connell memoirs, 45, Civil War Misc. Coll., ibid.; Albert E. Fernald diary, June 21, 1863, TS in Trulock Coll., PHS; Spear, *Civil War Recollections*, 214; Judson, *Eighty-third Pennsylvania*, 63-64; Melcher, *With a Flash of His Sword*, 33-34, 257.

28. John C. Chamberlain diary, [1]-[9], TS in PHS; Spear, *Civil War Recollections*, 213-14.

29. John C. Chamberlain diary, [9], TS in PHS.

30. Melcher, *With a Flash of His Sword*, 35; Trulock, *In the Hands of Providence*, 121.

31. John C. Chamberlain diary, [9]-[10], TS in PHS; John O'Connell memoirs, 46-47, Civil War Misc. Coll., USAMHI; Albert E. Fernald diary, June 26, 1863, TS in Trulock Coll., PHS.

32. Spear, *Civil War Recollections*, 30, 214; "In Re Charles D. Gilmore," TS in "20th Maine Inf. Reg." File, GNMPL.

33. Spear, *Civil War Recollections*, 214.

34. Albert E. Fernald diary, June 28, 1863, TS in Trulock Coll., PHS; Judson, *Eighty-third Pennsylvania*, 65; Breakey, "Recollections and Incidents of Medical Military Service," 139.

35. Spear, *Civil War Recollections*, 214-15; Desjardin, *Stand Firm Ye Boys from Maine*, 23-24; John O'Connell memoirs, 48-49, Civil War Misc. Coll., USAMHI.

36. Pullen, *20th Maine*, 94-96; Melcher, *With a Flash of His Sword*, 76-77; Nathan S. Clark memoirs, 27, MSA; John O'Connell memoirs, 50, Civil War Misc. Coll., USAMHI; Gerrish, *Army Life*, 100; Lamson, *Maine to the Wilderness*, 70; Judson, *Eighty-third Pennsylvania*, 66; JLC, "Through Blood and Fire at Gettysburg," 895-96; *OR*, I, 27, pt. 1: 621-22. Although JLC's *OR* report was written from memory twenty years after the events depicted, a few statements, including this one, may be accepted at face value with some confidence.

37. Ibid., 622.

38. Ibid., 592, 600; JLC, "Through Blood and Fire at Gettysburg," 896-98; Oliver Willcox Norton, *The Attack and Defense of Little Round Top, Gettysburg, July 2, 1863* (New York, 1913), 262; Oliver W. Norton to Frank Huntington, Sept. 28, 1888, "July 2nd: Little Round Top (Vincent & Weed vs. Law & Robertson)" File, GNMPL; Melcher, *With a Flash of His Sword*, 96; John O'Connell memoirs, 50, Civil War Misc. Coll., USAMHI; William T. Livermore diary, July 2, 1863, TS in Ellis Spear MSS, MSA.

39. *OR*, I, 27, pt. 1: 622; Spear, *Civil War Recollections*, 215; Catton, *Glory Road*, 266-67.

40. *OR*, I, 27, pt. 1: 622; Thomas L. Livermore diary, July 2, 1863, TS in Ellis Spear MSS, MSA; Samuel L. Miller to JLC, May 15, 1895, JLC MSS, LC; Norton, *Attack and Defense of Little Round Top*, 238, 294; Trulock, *In the Hands of Providence*, 128.

41. Edwin B. Coddington, *The Gettysburg Campaign: A Study in Command* (New York, 1968), 385-99.

42. Norton, *Attack and Defense of Little Round Top*, 240, 263-64, 292-93, 307-32; Oliver Willcox Norton, *Strong Vincent and His Brigade at Gettysburg, July 2, 1863* (Chicago, 1909), 10-13; Powell, *Fifth Army Corps*, 521-22; Coddington, *Gettysburg Campaign*, 387-88, 740n.-41n.; Emerson Gifford Taylor, *Gouverneur Kemble Warren: The Life and Letters of an American Soldier, 1830-1882* (Boston, 1932), 126-30;

Harry W. Pfanz, *Gettysburg, the Second Day* (Chapel Hill, N. C., 1987), 205-06.

43. *OR*, I, 27, pt. 1: 592-93, 598, 616-17; Norton, *Attack and Defense of Little Round Top*, 264, 293; Norton, *Strong Vincent and His Brigade at Gettysburg*, 5-7; Oliver W. Norton to Frank Huntington, Sept. 28, 1888, "July 2nd: Little Round Top (Vincent & Weed vs. Law & Robertson)" File, GNMPL; Oliver W. Norton to JLC, May 8, 1901, JLC MSS, MHS; Coddington, *Gettysburg Campaign*, 388-89; Pfanz, *Gettysburg, the Second Day*, 208-09.

44. *OR*, I, 27, pt. 1: 616-17, 622-23; Norton, *Attack and Defense of Little Round Top*, 264-67; Morris M. Penny and J. Gary Laine, *Struggle for the Round Tops: Law's Alabama Brigade at the Battle of Gettysburg* (Shippensburg, Pa., 1999), 72-74; JLC, "Through Blood and Fire at Gettysburg," 899.

45. Ibid.; JLC to George B. Herendeen, July 6, 1863, MSA. The latter is JLC's original Gettysburg report.

46. Ibid.

EIGHT:

1. Norton, *Attack and Defense of Little Round Top*, 167, 189-92, 238, 264, 295-96; Melcher, *With a Flash of His Sword*, 99-100; Pullen, *20th Maine*, 109-10; Oliver W. Norton to Frank Huntington, Sept. 28, 1888, "July 2nd: Little Round Top (Vincent & Weed vs. Law & Robertson)" File, GNMPL; Oliver W. Norton to JLC, May 8, 1901, JLC MSS, MHS; Norton, *Strong Vincent and His Brigade at Gettysburg*, 6-7; Pfanz, *Gettysburg, the Second Day*, 209-13; Gary Kross, "The Confederate Approach to Little Round Top: A March of Attrition," *Blue & Gray* 13 (Feb. 1996): 23; Coddington, *Gettysburg Campaign*, 389-90, 741n.; *OR*, I, 27, pt. 1: 616-17.

2. JLC to George B. Herendeen, July 6, 1863, MSA; Nathan S. Clark memoirs, 27-29, ibid.; William T. Livermore diary, July 2, 1863, TS in Spear MSS, ibid.; Albert E. Fernald diary, July 2, 1863, TS in Trulock Coll., PHS; Pullen, *20th Maine*, 111.

3. David L. Ladd and Audrey J. Ladd, eds., *The Bachelder Papers: Gettysburg in Their Own Words...* (Dayton, Ohio, 1994), 1029-30; Spear, *Civil War Recollections*, 313; Melcher, *With a Flash of His Sword*, 48-49, 61, 66, 258; Walter G. Morrill to JLC, July 8, 1863, TS in JLC MSS, PHS; Ellis Spear, Postwar paper on Civil War tactics, 14-15, Spear MSS, MSA.

4. *OR*, I, 27, pt. 2: 391-96, 404-14; Norton, *Attack and Defense of Little Round Top*, 141-44, 146-66, 172-81, 253-59; Melcher, *With a Flash of*

His Sword, 102-03; Elisha Coan, "Round Top: A Shot from the 20th Maine...," *National Tribune*, June 4, 1885; Kross, "Confederate Approach to Little Round Top," 7-8, 10; Richard Pindell, "The True High-Water Mark of the Confederacy," *Blue & Gray* 1 (Dec. 1983-Jan. 1984), 8.

5. *OR*, I, 27, pt. 2: 392, 395; William C. Oates, *The War Between the Union and the Confederacy and Its Lost Opportunities ...* (New York, 1905), 206-08; Norton, *Attack and Defense of Little Round Top*, 144, 148, 176-77, 258; Holman S. Melcher, "The 20th Maine at Little Round Top," *Battles and Leaders of the Civil War* 3 (1887-88): 314-15; Pullen, *20th Maine*, 114; Pfanz, *Gettysburg, the Second Day*, 217-19. For a biography of Oates, see Perry, *Conceived in Liberty*, especially pp. 17-23, 27-37, 75-83, 113-15, and Glenn LaFantasie, "The Other Man," *MHQ: The Quarterly Journal of Military History* 5 (Summer 1993): 69-75.

6. *OR*, I, 27, pt. 2: 392, 395; Oates, *War Between the Union and the Confederacy*, 210-11; Norton, *Attack and Defense of Little Round Top*, 144-45, 176; Melcher, *With a Flash of His Sword*, 103; Pullen, *20th Maine*, 113; Trulock, *In the Hands of Providence*, 139; Kross, "Confederate Approach to Little Round Top," 10-12, 14, 17, 19-20, 22.

7. Oates, *War Between the Union and the Confederacy*, 210-13; William C. Oates to William M. Robbins, Feb. 14, 1903, "July 2nd: Little Round Top (20th Maine Inf. vs. 15th Alabama Inf.)" File, GNMPL; William C. Oates to Elihu Root, n.d. [ca. June 1903], ibid.; Norton, *Attack and Defense of Little Round Top*, 144-46.

8. Oates, *War Between the Union and the Confederacy*, 212, 214; Desjardin, *Stand Firm Ye Boys from Maine*, 42; Kross, "Confederate Approach to Little Round Top," 12, 24.

9. JLC to George B. Herendeen, July 6, 1863, MSA; Norton, *Attack and Defense of Little Round Top*, 172-75, 258-60; Desjardin, *Stand Firm Ye Boys from Maine*, 48.

10. *OR*, I, 27, pt. 2: 392-93; Kross, "Alabamians' Attack on Little Round Top," 54.

11. JLC to John B. Bachelder, n.d. [c. 1884], Bachelder MSS, New Hampshire Hist. Soc., Concord; JLC, "Through Blood and Fire at Gettysburg," 902; JLC to George B. Herendeen, July 6, 1863, MSA.

12. JLC to John B. Bachelder, n.d. [c. 1884], Bachelder MSS; JLC to George B. Herendeen, July 6, 1863, MSA; *OR*, I, 27, pt. 1: 617; Melcher, *With a Flash of His Sword*, 59-60, 258; Ellis Spear to John B. Bachelder, Nov. 15, 1892, "20th Maine Inf. Reg." File, GNMPL; Ellis

Spear to JLC, May 22, 1895, JLC MSS, LC; Ellis Spear, Postwar speech on Gettysburg, July 2, 1863, 1-3, TS in Trulock Coll., PHS; Pullen, *20th Maine*, 117-18; Janet B. Hewett et al., comps., *Supplement to the Official Records of the Union and Confederate Armies* (80 vols. to date. Wilmington, N. C., 1994-), 5: 196-97.

13. Oates, *War Between the Union and the Confederacy*, 214.

14. Oliver W. Norton to Boyd Vincent, Aug. 3, 1914, Norton MSS, Clarke Hist. Lib.; JLC to FAC, July 4, 1863, LC; JLC to John B. Bachelder, n.d. [ca. 1884], Bachelder MSS; Oliver W. Norton to JLC, May 8, 1901, JLC MSS, MHS; Oliver W. Norton to Frank Huntington, Sept. 28, 1888, "July 2nd: Little Round Top (Vincent & Weed vs. Law & Robertson)" File, GNMPL; Washington A. Roebling to James E. Smith, July 5, 1913, Roebling MSS, Alexander Lib., Rutgers Univ., New Brunswick, N. J.; *OR*, I, 27, pt. 1: 617, 620, 628; Norton, *Attack and Defense of Little Round Top*, 220-21, 242-45, 260, 267-69, 271, 298-99; Norton, *Strong Vincent and His Brigade at Gettysburg*, 8-18; Judson, *Eighty-third Pennsylvania*, 67; Powell, *Fifth Army Corps*, 523-25; Coddington, *Gettysburg Campaign*, 394-96; Pfanz, *Gettysburg, the Second Day*, 224-31, 510n.

15. *OR*, I, 27, pt. 1: 624.

16. JLC, *"Bayonet! Forward"*, 186; Melcher, *With a Flash of His Sword*, 121-22; JLC to George B. Herendeen, July 6, 1863, MSA; Spear, *Civil War Recollections*, 34; Desjardin, *Stand Firm Ye Boys from Maine*, 51, 54, 57, 63.

17. JLC to George B. Herendeen, July 6, 1863, MSA; Judson, *Eighty-third Pennsylvania*, 68; Trulock, *In the Hands of Providence*, 145-46.

18. JLC, "Through Blood and Fire at Gettysburg," 904-05; Gerrish, *Army Life*, 69-70; Trulock, *In the Hands of Providence*, 146, 442n.; Desjardin, *Stand Firm Ye Boys from Maine*, 60, 131-32.

19. *OR*, I, 27, pt. 2: 393; Oates, *War Between the Union and the Confederacy*, 218-19.

20. William C. Oates, "Gettysburg, the Battle on the Right," *Southern Historical Society Papers* 6 (1878): 172-82; Kross, "Alabamians' Attack on Little Round Top," 54, 57, 60-61.

21. JLC to George B. Herendeen, July 6, 1863, MSA; Trulock, *In the Hands of Providence*, 147; Pullen, *20th Maine*, 123; Pfanz, *Gettysburg, the Second Day*, 233.

22. Robert D. Heinl, Jr., comp., *Dictionary of Military and Naval Quotations* (Annapolis, Md., 1966), 20-21.

23. Kross, "Alabamians' Attack on Little Round Top," 57-59.

24. JLC to George B. Herendeen, July 6, 1863, MSA; JLC to John L. Hodsdon [summary of military service], n.d., PHS; JLC, *"Bayonet! Forward"*, 186; Nathan S. Clark memoirs, 28-29, MSA; Spear, *Civil War Recollections*, 34-35; Melcher, *With a Flash of His Sword*, 68, 115; John O'Connell memoirs, 54, Civil War Misc. Coll., USAMHI; Gerrish, *Army Life*, 110; Theodore Gerrish and John S. Hutchinson, *The Blue and the Gray: A Graphic History of the Army of the Potomac...* (Bangor, Me., 1884), 359; JLC, "Through Blood and Fire at Gettysburg," 905-06; Hewett et al., comps., *Supplement to the Official Records*, 5: 197.

25. Ellis Spear to JLC, May 22, 1895, JLC MSS, LC; Spear, *Civil War Recollections*, 35-36, 315-16; Ellis Spear, "Recollections," 45, unedited copy in "20th Maine Inf. Reg." File, GNMPL; Ellis Spear, Postwar speech on war memories, 25, TS in Spear MSS, MSA; Ellis Spear, Postwar paper on Civil War tactics, 15-16, ibid.; Melcher, *With a Flash of His Sword*, 133, 143; James Morgan, "Who Saved Little Round Top?" (Internet copy), 1-2.

26. Melcher, *With a Flash of His Sword*, 143; LaFantasie, "Joshua Chamberlain and the American Dream," 227n.

27. JLC to George B. Herendeen, July 6, 1863, MSA; JLC to Ellis Spear, Nov. 27, 1896, Spear MSS, MSA; JLC to John B. Bachelder, n.d. [ca. 1884], "20th Maine Inf. Reg." File, GNMPL; Ellis Spear to John B. Bachelder, Nov. 15, 1892, ibid.; JLC, *"Bayonet! Forward"*, 186; Joseph B. Mitchell, *The Badge of Gallantry: Recollections of Civil War Congressional Medal of Honor Winners ...* (New York, 1968), 130; Melcher, *With a Flash of His Sword*, 296.

28. Oates, *War Between the Union and the Confederacy*, 220; William C. Oates to William M. Robbins, Feb. 14, 1903, "July 2nd: Little Round Top (20th Maine Inf. vs. 15th Alabama Inf.)" File, GNMPL; William C. Jordan, *Some Events and Incidents during the Civil War* (Montgomery, Ala., 1909), 43-44; JLC, *"Bayonet! Forward"*, 186; JLC, "Through Blood and Fire at Gettysburg," 906-08; Melcher, *With a Flash of His Sword*, 296; Powell, *Fifth Army Corps*, 530; Trulock, *In the Hands of Providence*, 147.

29. Spear, *Civil War Recollections*, 314; Spear, "Recollections," 45-46, unedited copy in "20th Maine Inf. Reg." File, GNMPL; Pullen, *20th Maine*, 124; Morgan, "Who Saved Little Round Top?", 2-3; Nathan S. Clark memoirs, 28-29, MSA.

30. Ladd and Ladd, eds., *Bachelder Papers*, 1029-30; Gerrish, *Army Life*, 107, 111; John O'Connell memoirs, 55, Civil War Misc. Coll., USAMHI.

31. Oates, *War Between the Union and the Confederacy*, 220-21; Spear, *Civil War Recollections*, 314-15; Spear, "Recollections," 46, unedited copy in "20th Maine Inf. Reg." File, GNMPL; Melcher, *With a Flash of His Sword*, 57; Ladd and Ladd, eds., *Bachelder Papers*, 1029-30; Kross, "Alabamians' Attack on Little Round Top," 58.

32. JLC, "Through Blood and Fire at Gettysburg," 907; Mitchell, *Badge of Gallantry*, 131.

33. JLC to George B. Herendeen, July 6, 1863, MSA; *OR*, I, 27, pt. 1: 179; Hewett et al., comps., *Supplement to the Official Records*, 5: 197; JLC to FAC, July 17, 1863, LC.

34. Elisha Coan to "My Dear Brother," Aug. 5, 1863, Coan MSS, BC; William T. Livermore to JLC, May 22, 1877, JLC MSS, MHS; copy in "20th Maine Inf. Reg." File, GNMPL.

35. Kross, "Confederate Approach to Little Round Top," 24; Kross, "Alabamians' Attack on Little Round Top," 59; Desjardin, *Stand Firm Ye Boys from Maine*, 157-58.

36. Ibid., 158.

37. Coddington, *Gettysburg Campaign*, 395-96; Pfanz, *Gettysburg, the Second Day*, 223-40; JLC to George B. Herendeen, July 6, 1863, MSA.

38. Ibid.; Melcher, *With a Flash of His Sword*, 127-28; JLC to "My Dear Colonel," Jan. 25, 1884, "20th Maine Inf. Reg." File, GNMPL; copy in PHS; Nash, *Forty-fourth New York*, 148; *OR*, I, 27, pt. 1: 618; Hewett et al., comps., *Supplement to the Official Records*, 5: 198; Norton, *Attack and Defense of Little Round Top*, 269-70.

39. JLC to George B. Herendeen, July 6, 1863, MSA; JLC to "My Dear Colonel," Jan. 25, 1864, "20th Maine Inf. Reg." File, GNMPL; copy in PHS; *OR*, I, 27, pt. 1: 604; William T. Livermore diary, July 2, 1863, TS in Spear MSS, MSA; Pfanz, *Gettysburg, the Second Day*, 402-03.

40. JLC to George B. Herendeen, July 6, 1863, MSA; Hewett et al., comps., *Supplement to the Official Records*, 5: 198-99; JLC to "My Dear Colonel," Jan. 25, 1884, "20th Maine Inf. Reg." File, GNMPL; copy in PHS; Spear, "Recollections," 49-50, unedited copy in "20th Maine Inf. Reg." File, GNMPL; Norton, *Attack and Defense of Little Round Top*, 270.

41. JLC to George B. Herendeen, July 6, 1863, MSA; JLC to FAC, July 17, 1863, LC; JLC to "My Dear Colonel," Jan. 25, 1884, "20th Maine Inf. Reg." File, GNMPL; copy in PHS; *OR*, I, 27, pt. 1: 654, 658; Nash, *Forty-fourth New York*, 148; Judson, *Eighty-third Pennsylvania*, 68-69; Norton, *Attack and Defense of Little Round Top*, 270-71.

NINE:

1. JLC to FAC, July 17, 1863, LC; William T. Livermore diary, July 3, 1863, TS in Spear MSS, MSA.

2. Ibid.; Melcher, *With a Flash of His Sword*, 130; Adelbert Ames to JLC, July 3, 1863, JLC's CBF, M-1064, R-248, NA.

3. John O'Connell memoirs, 56-57, Civil War Misc. Coll., USAMHI; Lamson, *Maine to the Wilderness*, 73.

4. JLC to George B. Herendeen, July 6, 1863, MSA; JLC, "Through Blood and Fire at Gettysburg," 909.

5. N. P. Monroe to Israel Washburn, Mar. 25, 1863, 20th Maine Records, MSA; Adelbert Ames to John L. Hodsdon, Mar. 29, 1863, ibid.; Special Order 204, Adj. Gen.'s Office, May 6, 1863, ibid.; Adelbert Ames to Abner Coburn, May 16, 1863, ibid.; Special Order 221, Adj. Gen.'s Office, May 18, 1863, ibid.; JLC to Abner Coburn, May 25, 27, 1863, ibid.; Ellis Spear to JLC, May 22, 1895, JLC MSS, LC; JLC to Abner Coburn, July 21, 1863, 20th Maine Records, MSA.

6. JLC to FAC, July 4, 1863, LC.

7. Trulock, *In the Hands of Providence*, 156; Desjardin, *Stand Firm Ye Boys from Maine*, 99-103; Lamson, *Maine to the Wilderness*, 73.

8. William T. Livermore diary, July 3, 1863, TS in Spear MSS, MSA; William T. Livermore to Charles Livermore, July 6, 1863, TS in Trulock Coll., PHS.

9. Ibid.

10. Trulock, *In the Hands of Providence*, 157; Desjardin, *Stand Firm Ye Boys from Maine*, 99-101.

11. Oliver W. Norton to JLC, May 8, 1901, JLC MSS, MHS; *OR*, I, 27, pt. 1: 627; Trulock, *In the Hands of Providence*, 159-60.

12. JLC to George B. Herendeen, July 6, 1863, MSA.

13. *OR*, I, 27, pt. 1: 621, 627; Pullen, *20th Maine*, 146; Albert E. Fernald diary, July 7, 8, 1863, TS in Trulock Coll., PHS; Surgeon's Certificate, July 27, 1863, JLC's Medical File, RG-94, E-534, NA; Orsell Cook Brown to "Dear Sister," July 8, 1863, Brown MSS, New York State Lib., Albany; Trulock, *In the Hands of Providence*, 160.

14. *OR*, I, 27, pt. 1: 627; JLC to John L. Hodsdon, July 11, 1863, 20th Maine Records, MSA; John O'Connell memoirs, 58-59, Civil War Misc. Coll., USAMHI; Judson, *Eighty-third Pennsylvania*, 74.

15. General Order 5, HQ 3rd Brig., 1st Div., 5th A. C., July 12, 1863, copy in Orsell Cook Brown MSS, New York State Lib.; JLC to FAC, July 17, 1863, LC; Judson, *Eighty-third Pennsylvania*, 71-73; Trulock, *In the Hands of Providence*, 160.

16. *OR*, I, 27, pt. 1: 621, 627; Coddington, *Gettysburg Campaign*, 566-74.

17. *OR*, I, 27, pt. 1: 627; Judson, *Eighty-third Pennsylvania*, 75; Gerrish, *Army Life*, 121.

18. Special Order 34, HQ 20th Maine Vol. Inf., July 21, 1863, 20th Maine Records, NA; Melcher, *With a Flash of His Sword*, 144-45; Israel Thickston to "Brother Comp," July 17, 1863, Thickston Family MSS, USAMHI.

19. JLC to FAC, July 17, 1863, LC.

20. Ibid.

21. JLC to Abner Coburn, July 21, 1863, 20th Maine Records, MSA.

22. Trulock, *In the Hands of Providence*, 161; Nash, *Forty-fourth New York*, 161-62.

23. Edward G. Longacre, *General John Buford: A Military Biography* (Conshohocken, Pa., 1995), 223-25; *OR*, I, 27, pt. 1: 627; Melcher, *With a Flash of His Sword*, 149; Gerrish, *Army Life*, 121.

24. Melcher, *With a Flash of His Sword*, 149, 260.

25. JLC to FAC, July 24, 1863, "Love Letters from Joshua Chamberlain to Fanny Chamberlain" Internet site.

26. *OR*, I, 27, pt. 1: 99.

27. JLC to FAC, July 24, 1863, "Love Letters from Joshua Chamberlain to Fanny Chamberlain" Internet site.

28. Ibid.

29. *OR*, I, 27, pt. 1: 627; John O'Connell memoirs, 59, Civil War Misc. Coll., USAMHI; Spear, *Civil War Recollections*, 220-21; Surgeon's Certificate, July 27, 1863, JLC's Medical File, RG-94, E-534, NA; JLC to F. T. Locke, July 27, 1863, ibid.

30. Surgeon's Certificates, July 27, Aug. 3, 1863, ibid.; Hospital admittance form, n.d. [July 31, 1863], ibid.

31. JLC to FAC, Aug. 31, 1863, LC; Golay, *To Gettysburg and Beyond*, 198; James C. Rice to JLC, Aug. 16, 1863, JLC MSS, LC; Surgeon's Certificate, Aug. 17, 1863, JLC's Medical File, RG-94, E-534, NA.

32. Spear, *Civil War Recollections*, 189, 222-23; Charles D. Gilmore to HQ 5th A. C., Sept. 12, 1863, Gilmore's CBF, NA; Special Order 252, HQ Army of the Potomac, Sept. 18, 1863, ibid.

33. JLC to Abner Coburn, Aug. 25, 1863, 20th Maine Records, NA.

34. Monthly Return, Aug. 1863, JLC's Compiled Military Service Record, RG-94, E-519, NA; Trulock, *In the Hands of Providence*, 163.

35. Nash, *Forty-fourth New York*, 164; Oliver Willcox Norton, *Army*

Letters, 1861-1865: Being Extracts from Private Letters... (Chicago, 1903), 176, 178.

36. Spear, *Civil War Recollections*, 223; Gerrish, *Army Life*, 123-28; Pullen, *20th Maine*, 153-57.

37. Ibid., 157; John O'Connell memoirs, 59-60, Civil War Misc. Coll., USAMHI; JLC to FAC, Aug. 31, Sept. 12, 1863, LC.

38. James C. Rice to William P. Fessenden, Sept. 8, 1863, JLC MSS, LC; James Barnes to JLC, Sept. 14, 1863, JLC's CBF, M-1064, R-248, NA.

39. Adelbert Ames to Edwin M. Stanton, Sept. 21, 1863, ibid.; Abner Coburn to Edwin M. Stanton, Sept. 27, 1863, ibid.; Charles Griffin to Seth Williams, Oct. 7, 1863, ibid.; Hannibal Hamlin to Abraham Lincoln, Oct. 16, 1863, JLC MSS, PHS.

40. Melcher, *With a Flash of His Sword*, 261; Judson, *Eighty-third Pennsylvania*, 77; John O'Connell memoirs, 61, Civil War Misc. Coll., USAMHI.

41. JLC to Abner Coburn, Sept. 19, 1863, 20th Maine Records, MSA; Charles D. Gilmore to HQ 5th A. C., Sept. 12, 1863, Gilmore's CBF, NA; Spear, *Civil War Recollections*, 227-28.

42. Circulars, HQ 3rd Brig., 1st Div., 5th A. C., Sept. 28, 29, 1863, RG-393, pt. 2, E-4314, NA.

43. Norton, *Army Letters*, 183.

44. *OR*, I, 29, pt. 1: 148-95; pt. 2: 754, 756-59, 766, 769, 780.

45. Judson, *Eighty-third Pennsylvania*, 77; John O'Connell memoirs, 62-63, Civil War Misc. Coll., USAMHI; Trulock, *In the Hands of Providence*, 170.

46. Ibid.; John O'Connell memoirs, 63-64, Civil War Misc. Coll., USAMHI.

47. Judson, *Eighty-third Pennsylvania*, 77; Orsell Cook Brown to "Dear Sister," Oct. 16, 1863, Brown MSS, New York State Lib.

48. John O'Connell memoirs, 64-65, Civil War Misc. Coll., USAMHI; Nash, *Forty-fourth New York*, 168.

49. Ibid., 168-69.

50. John O'Connell memoirs, 66, Civil War Misc. Coll., USAMHI; Spear, *Civil War Recollections*, 229; Orsell Cook Brown to "Dearly Loved Sister," Oct. 25, 1863, Brown MSS, New York State Lib.

51. Spear, *Civil War Recollections*, 229; Orsell Cook Brown to "My Own Loved Sister," Nov. 4, 1863, Brown MSS, New York State Lib.; Charles P. Mattocks, *"Unspoiled Heart": The Journal of Charles Mattocks*

of the 17th Maine, ed. by Philip N. Racine (Knoxville, Tenn., 1994), 76.

52. Orsell Cook Brown to "My Own Darling Ollie," Nov. 12, 1863, Brown MSS, New York State Lib.; Melcher, *With a Flash of His Sword*, 55-56, 262; Pullen, *20th Maine*, 161-65; John O'Connell memoirs, 66-67, Civil War Misc. Coll., USAMHI; Hezekiah Long to his wife, Nov. 12, 1863, TS in Trulock Coll., PHS; Judson, *Eighty-third Pennsylvania*, 78-79; Whitman and True, *Maine in the War for the Union*, 494-95; Trulock, *In the Hands of Providence*, 171-73.

53. Ibid., 173; Pullen, *20th Maine*, 166.

54. JLC to John L. Hodsdon [summary of military service], n.d., PHS; Wallace, *Soul of the Lion*, 119-20.

55. JLC to HQ 1st Div., 5th A. C., Nov. 15, 1863, RG-393, pt. 2, E-4305, NA; Surgeon's Certificate, Nov. 15, 1863, JLC's Medical File, RG-94, E-534, ibid.; Hospital admittance form, n.d. [Feb. 1864], ibid.; William E. Dowell to FAC, Nov. 16, 1863, JLC MSS, LC.

56. JLC to John L. Hodsdon [summary of military service], n.d., PHS.

TEN:

1. Hospital admittance form, n.d. [Feb. 1864], JLC's Medical File, RG-94, E-534, NA; Surgeon's Certificate, Nov. 28, 1863, ibid.; Wallace, *Soul of the Lion*, 120.

2. Ibid., 120-21.

3, Medical furlough form, n.d. [Jan. 1864], JLC's Medical File, RG-94, E-534, NA; Trulock, *In the Hands of Providence*, 174; Pullen, *20th Maine*, 166-68; *OR*, I, 29, pt. 1: 578-79.

4. Medical furlough form, n.d. [Jan. 1864], JLC's Medical File, RG-94, E-534, NA; Special Order 141, Adj. Gen.'s Office, Jan. 27, 1864, JLC's CBF, M-1064, R-248, ibid.; JLC to E. D. Townsend, May 9, 1864, ibid.

5. JLC to anon., Mar. 10, 1864, 20th Maine Records, MSA; JLC to Samuel Cony, Mar. 15, Apr. 25, 1864, ibid.; JLC to anon., Jan. 24, 1864, LC.

6. G. F. Balch to JLC, Feb. 8, 1864, ibid.

7. FAC to "Auntie," Apr. 14, 1864, MHS.

8. Bruce Catton, *A Stillness at Appomattox* (Garden City, N. Y., 1953), 36-39; *OR*, I, 36, pt. 1: 573; JLC to E. D. Townsend, May 9, 1864, JLC's CBF, M-1064, R-248, NA.

9. Special Order 173, Adj. Gen.'s Office, May 10, 1864, 20th Maine Records, MSA; FAC to "My Dear Aunty," n.d. [May 1864], MHS.

10. JLC to John L. Hodsdon [summary of military service] n.d., PHS; Spear, *Civil War Recollections*, 242; Catton, *A Stillness at Appomattox*, 55-128.

11. Ibid., 49-50; *OR*, I, 36, pt. 1: 611, 625, 905.

12. Ibid., 109; Warner, *Generals in Blue*, 23-24.

13. Ibid., 541-42; Edward G. Longacre, "Gouverneur K. Warren," *Civil War Times Illustrated* 10 (Jan. 1972): 11-20; Wainwright, *Diary of Battle*, 396, 509.

14. Catton, *A Stillness at Appomattox*, 91-92.

15. Spear, *Civil War Recollections*, 240-43; *OR*, I, 36, pt. 1: 123.

16. Ibid., 109; Spear, *Civil War Recollections*, 242.

17. *OR*, I, 36, pt. 1: 541-42, 547, 659-60.

18. Trulock, *In the Hands of Providence*, 177; Sherman, *Joshua Lawrence Chamberlain*, 13; JLC to Samuel Cony, May 18, 1864, 20th Maine Records, MSA; JLC to John L. Hodsdon [summary of military service], n.d., PHS.

19. *OR*, I, 36, pt. 2: 12, 37-40, 116-17, 196-204.

20. JLC to Samuel Cony, May 18, 1864, 20th Maine Records, MSA.

21. Spear, *Civil War Recollections*, 243-44; Trulock, *In the Hands of Providence*, 181.

22. Ibid.; Spear, *Civil War Recollections*, 244; J. Michael Miller, *The North Anna Campaign: "Even to Hell Itself," May 21-26, 1864* (Lynchburg, Va., 1989), 44.

23. Trulock, *In the Hands of Providence*, 182; Pullen, *20th Maine*, 203-04; Spear, *Civil War Recollections*, 244; George W. Carleton to A. B. Farwell, Jan. 8, 1866, Frost Family MSS, Yale Univ. Lib.

24. Ibid.

25. Trulock, *In the Hands of Providence*, 182; Pullen, *20th Maine*, 205; Spear, *Civil War Recollections*, 244.

26. Joseph P. Cullen, "When Grant Faced Lee Across the North Anna," *Civil War Times Illustrated* 3 (Feb. 1965): 16-23; *OR*, I, 36, pt. 1: 543, 550, 553; Pullen, *20th Maine*, 205; Spear, *Civil War Recollections*, 244.

27. Trulock, *In the Hands of Providence*, 182-83; Miller, *North Anna Campaign*, 94.

28. *OR*, I, 36, pt. 1: 193, 543; Trulock, *In the Hands of Providence*, 183-84.

29. Ibid., 184; *OR*, I, 36, pt. 1: 543.

30. Ibid., 543, 553; Pullen, *20th Maine*, 205; Spear, *Civil War Recollections*, 246.

31. Ibid.; Trulock, *In the Hands of Providence*, 185; *OR*, I, 36, pt. 3: 336, 339-41, 346, 351, 361; "Gen. Chamberlain's Narrative of the [Army of the] Potomac," *Nation*, Dec. 30, 1915.

32. Spear, *Civil War Recollections*, 246; George W. Carleton to A. B. Farwell, Jan. 8, 1866, Frost Family MSS, Yale Univ. Lib.

33. Spear, *Civil War Recollections*, 247; *OR*, I, 36, pt. 1: 543, 574; Catton, *A Stillness at Appomattox*, 149-53; George W. Carleton to A. B. Farwell, Jan. 8, 1866, Frost Family MSS, Yale Univ. Lib.

34. *OR*, I, 36, pt. 1: 170, 180; Geoffrey Perret, *Ulysses S. Grant, Soldier & President* (New York, 1997), 331-32.

35. Special Order 154, HQ 5th A. C., June 6, 1864, JLC's CBF, M-1064, R-248, NA; *OR*, I, 36, pt. 1: 111, 125, 169 & n., 610-11, 614-15; pt. 3: 613; 40, pt. 3: 520; Wallace, *Soul of the Lion*, 125-26; Trulock, *In the Hands of Providence*, 188-89, 192-93; Lysander Cutler to Charles Griffin, June 6, 1864, JLC MSS, LC; John Irvin diary, June 4, 6, 1864, Hist. Soc. of Penna., Philadelphia; Samuel T. Keene to his wife, n.d. [ca. June 6, 1864], Spear MSS, MSA; Spear, *Civil War Recollections*, 248; Thomas Chamberlin, *History of the One Hundred and Fiftieth Regiment Pennsylvania Volunteers ...* (Philadelphia, 1905), 258, 263; James M. Gibbs, comp., *History of the ... 187th Regiment Pennsylvania Volunteer Infantry: Six Months and Three Years Service, Civil War, 1863-1865* (Harrisburg, Pa., 1905), 85; Avery Harris memoirs, 200-01, USAMHI.

36. *OR*, I, 36, pt. 3: 652, 709-10; Joseph J. Bartlett to Seth Williams, June 6, 1864 [with endorsements by Gouverneur K. Warren and Charles Griffin], JLC's CBF, M-1064, R-248, NA.

37. Trulock, *In the Hands of Providence*, 188; Avery Harris memoirs, 207, USAMHI.

38. JLC to John L. Hodsdon [summary of military service], n.d., PHS.

39. Horatio N. Warren to JLC, July 7, 1888, JLC MSS, LC; Abraham Harshberger memoirs, 19, *Civil War Times Illustrated* Coll., USAMHI.

40. Ibid., 17; John Irvin diary, June 7, 1864, Hist. Soc. of Penna.; Avery Harris memoirs, 201, USAMHI.

41. JLC, *Joshua Lawrence Chamberlain*, 38-39.

42. Powell, *Fifth Army Corps*, 677; John W. Nesbit, comp., *... General History of Company D, 149th Pennsylvania Volunteers and Personal Sketches of the Members* (Oakdale, Pa., 1908), 33; Chamberlin, *One Hundred and Fiftieth Pennsylvania*, 259; Gibbs, comp., *187th*

Pennsylvania, 89; Samuel T. Keene to "My Dear Brothers & Sister," June 19, 1864, Spear MSS, MSA; Avery Harris memoirs, 201, USAMHI.

43. Ibid., 203; John Irvin diary, June 16, 17, 1864, Hist. Soc. of Penna.; Abraham Harshberger memoirs, 18, *Civil Wars Times Illustrated* Coll., USAMHI; Spear, *Civil War Recollections*, 250; Powell, *Fifth Army Corps*, 699; Chamberlin, *One Hundred and Fifteith Pennsylvania*, 259; Nesbit, comp., *Company D, 149th Pennsylvania*, 33-34; Horatio N. Warren, *Two Reunions of the 142d Regiment, Pa. Vols...* (Buffalo, N. Y., 1890), 33-34; Harry M. Kieffer, *The Recollections of a Drummer-Boy* (Boston, 1889), 200.

44. Avery Harris memoirs, 205, USAMHI.; Trulock, *In the Hands of Providence*, 198.

45. Ibid., 198-99; JLC, *"Bayonet! Forward"*, 46-47.

46. *OR*, I, 40, pt. 1: 455-57; Trulock, *In the Hands of Providence*, 200-01; Warren, *Two Reunions of 142d Pennsylvania*, 34-35; Gibbs, comp., *187th Pennsylvania*, 94.

47. *OR*, I, 40, pt. 1: 482; Trulock, *In the Hands of Providence*, 201-02; JLC, *Joshua Lawrence Chamberlain*, 32; JLC to John L. Hodsdon [summary of military service], n.d., PHS.

48. JLC to Gouverneur K. Warren, June 18, 1864, TS in MHS; JLC, *"Bayonet! Forward"*, 47-48; Patrick DeLacy to JLC, Jan. 15, 1904, JLC MSS, LC; Pullen, *20th Maine*, 210-11; Chamberlin, *One Hundred and Fiftieth Pennsylvania*, 263-64.

49. JLC to anon., n.d. [June 18, 1864], MHS; Trulock, *In the Hands of Providence*, 204-05.

50. Golay, *To Gettysburg and Beyond*, 229; Patrick DeLacy to JLC, Jan. 15, 1904, JLC MSS, LC; Warren, *Two Reunions of 142d Pennsylvania*, 35.

51. JLC, *Joshua Lawrence Chamberlain*, 32; Patrick DeLacy to JLC, Jan. 15, 1904, JLC MSS, LC; Chamberlin, *One Hundred and Fiftieth Pennsylvania*, 261-62; Gibbs, comp., *187th Pennsylvania*, 94-98; Nesbit, comp., *Company D, 149th Pennsylvania*, 34; *History of the 121st Regiment Pennsylvania Volunteers ... "An Account from the Ranks"* (Philadelphia, 1893), 79-80; Warren, *Two Reunions of 142d Pennsylvania*, 35-36.

52. Avery Harris memoirs, 206-07, USAMHI; JLC, *Joshua Lawrence Chamberlain*, 32-33; Patrick DeLacy to JLC, Oct. 27, 1885, JLC MSS, LC; JLC to John L. Hodsdon [summary of military service], n.d., PHS; JLC, *"Bayonet! Forward"*, 48; Thomas J. Howe, *The Petersburg Campaign: Wasted Valor, June 15-18, 1864* (Lynchburg, Va., 1988), 129.

JOSHUA CHAMBERLAIN

ELEVEN:

1. Trulock, *In the Hands of Providence*, 209; JLC, *"Bayonet! Forward"*, 48.

2. *OR*, I, 40, pt. 2: 182; Warren, *Two Reunions of 142d Pennsylvania*, 36-37; Avery Harris memoirs, 207-08, USAMHI; Gibbs, comp., *187th Pennsylvania*, 95; Howe, *Petersburg Campaign*, 129.

3. Trulock, *In the Hands of Providence*, 212; JLC, *"Bayonet! Forward"*, 48.

4. Trulock, *In the Hands of Providence*, 213-14; Wallace, *Soul of the Lion*, 133-34.

5. Trulock, *In the Hands of Providence*, 214; Golay, *To Gettysburg and Beyond*, 234.

6. Ibid., 214, 466n.; *The Medical and Surgical History of the War of the Rebellion* (3 vols. in 6. Washington, D. C., 1870-88), 2, pt. 2: 363; Hospital records, June 19, 1864, JLC's CBF, M-1064, R-248, NA; Hospital admittance records, June 19, 20, 1864, JLC's Medical File, RG-94, E-534, ibid.

7. Ellis Spear to Oliver W. Norton, Jan. 18, 1916, Norton MSS, Clarke Hist. Lib.; Edwin J. March to JLC, June 8, 1895, JLC MSS, MHS; *OR*, I, 40, pt. 2: 216-17.

8. Gouverneur K. Warren to George G. Meade, June 19, 1864, JLC MSS, LC; Ulysses S. Grant to Edwin M. Stanton, June 20, 1864, ibid.; Ulysses S. Grant, *Personal Memoirs of U. S. Grant* (2 vols. New York, 1885-86), 2: 297; Special Order 39, HQ Armies of the U. S., June 20, 1864, JLC's CBF, M-1064, R-248, NA.

9. Hospital admittance records, June 19, 20, 1864, JLC's Medical File, RG-94, E-534, NA.

10. Charles D. Gilmore to John L. Hodsdon, July 5, 1864, 20th Maine Records, MSA.

11. Oliver W. Norton to Boyd Vincent, Jan. 5, Feb. 18, 1916, Norton MSS, Clarke Hist. Lib.; Ellis Spear to Oliver W. Norton, Jan. 18, 1916, ibid.

12. JLC to FAC, June 19, 1864, BC.

13. *New York Herald*, June 21, 1864; *Boston Evening Transcript*, June 21, 1864; Sarah B. Chamberlain to JLC, June 23, 1864, RC.

14. Ibid.; *New York Herald*, June 22, 1864; Trulock, *In the Hands of Providence*, 215-16.

15. JLC to Lorenzo Thomas, July 4, 1864, JLC's CBF, M-1064, R-248, NA; Charles D. Gilmore to John L. Hodsdon, July 5, 1864, 20th Maine Records, MSA; Spear, *Civil War Recollections*, 153.

342

16. John C. Chamberlain to John L. Hodsdon, July 22, 1864, 20th Maine Records, MSA.

17. Smith, "Strains of Post-Military Matrimony," 9.

18. Trulock, *In the Hands of Providence*, 224, 331; Golay, *To Gettysburg and Beyond*, 282.

19. Norval Welch to JLC, July 28, 1864, JLC MSS, LC; Holman Melcher to anon., n.d. [ca. Aug. 15, 1864], JLC MSS, PHS.

20. JLC to Samuel Cony, Aug. 31, 1864, 20th Maine Records, MSA; JLC to Sarah D. B. Chamberlain, n.d. [Sept. 1864], BC.

21. Catton, *A Stillness at Appomattox*, 294-317.

22. Special Order 313, HQ 5th A. C., Sept. 21, 1864, JLC's General's Papers, R-94, E-159, NA; JLC to Lorenzo Thomas, Sept. 30, 1864, ibid.; Trulock, *In the Hands of Providence*, 219.

23. Adelbert Ames to JLC, Oct. 18, 1864, JLC MSS, LC.

24. Smith, "Strains of Post-Military Matrimony," 9.

25. Special Order 395, HQ Army of the Potomac, Nov. 12, 1864, JLC's General's Papers, RG-94, E-159, NA; JLC to Lorenzo Thomas, Jan. 1, 1865, RG-393, pt. 2, E-259, NA; *OR*, I, 42, pt. 3: 661-63.

26. Ibid., 663; Special Order 166, HQ 1st Div., 5th A. C., Nov. 19, 1864, JLC's CBF, M-1064, R-248, NA.

27. *OR*, I, 42, pt. 3: 63, 74, 460; 46, pt. 1: 267, 569.

28. Ibid., 42, pt. 3: 1117; Nelson Wilbur to his wife, Feb. 17, 1865, Wilbur MSS, SSMH; Mark M. Boatner III, *The Civil War Dictionary* (New York, 1959), 760, 777.

29. Nelson Wilbur to his wife, Nov. 26, 1864, Wilbur MSS, SSMH.

30. Harold B. Raymond, "Joshua Chamberlain's Retirement Bill," *Colby Library Quarterly* 7 (1966): 348; JLC, *The Passing of the Armies: An Account of the Final Campaign of the Army of the Potomac ...* (New York, 1915), 256-57; JLC, "The Last Review of the Army of the Potomac, May 23, 1865," *War Papers: Read Before the Maine Commandery, MOLLUS* 3: 319; Thomas D. Chamberlain to John C. Chamberlain, Dec. 18, 1864, JLC MSS, BC.

31. Josiah Shuman diary, Nov. 24, 29, Dec. 3, 4, 1864, TS in Civil War Misc. Coll., USAMHI.

32. Ibid., Dec. 6-7, 1864; JLC to Sarah B. Chamberlain, n.d. [Dec. 1864], BC.

33. Circular, HQ 1st Brig., 1st Div., 5th A. C., Dec. 8, 1864, JLC MSS, LC; JLC to Sarah B. Chamberlain, n.d. [Dec. 1864], BC; Pullen, *20th Maine*, 232-33.

34. JLC to John L. Hodsdon [summary of military service], n.d., PHS; JLC to Sarah B. Chamberlain, n.d. [Dec. 1864], BC; JLC to John C. Chamberlain, Dec. 19, 1864, ibid.; Josiah Shuman diary, Dec. 8-12, 1864, TS in Civil War Misc. Coll., USAMHI.

35. JLC to Sarah B. Chamberlain, n.d. [Dec. 1864], BC; JLC to John C. Chamberlain, Dec. 19, 1864, ibid.

36. Josiah Shuman diary, Dec. 12, 22-26, 1864, TS in Civil War Misc. Coll., USAMHI; Thomas D. Chamberlain to Sarah B. Chamberlain, Dec. 13, 1864, JLC MSS, BC; JLC to John C. Chamberlain, Dec. 19, 1864, ibid.

37. Sarah D. B. Chamberlain to JLC, Jan. 1, 1865, PHS; JLC to John L. Hodsdon [summary of military service], n.d., ibid.; JLC to F. T. Locke, Jan. 9, 1865, JLC's General's Papers, RG-94, E-159, NA; Surgeon's Certificate, Jan. 9, 1865, ibid.

38. *OR*, I, 46, pt. 2: 193; Spear, *Civil War Recollections*, 267; Melcher, *With a Flash of His Sword*, 190; JLC to Sarah B. Chamberlain, Mar. 9, 1865, BC.

39. Ibid.

40. JLC to Joshua Chamberlain Jr., Feb. 12, 1865, PHS.

TWELVE:

1. Trulock, *In the Hands of Providence*, 223-24; JLC to Joshua Chamberlain Jr., Feb. 12, 1865, PHS.

2. Ibid.

3. JLC to Joshua Chamberlain Jr., Feb. 20, 1865, BC; Smith, "Strains of Post-Military Matrimony," 10.

4. JLC to Joshua Chamberlain Jr., Feb. 12, 1865, PHS.

5. JLC to Joshua Chamberlain Jr., Feb. 20, 1865, BC; JLC to John L. Hodsdon [summary of military service], n.d., PHS.

6. *OR*, I, 46, pt. 1: 253-57, 265-67; Josiah Shuman diary, Feb. 5, 1865, TS in Civil War Misc. Coll., USAMHI; Evan M. Woodward, *History of the One Hundred and Ninety-eighth Pennsylvania Volunteers ...* (Trenton, N. J., 1884), 29-32.

7. JLC's Staff Officers' File for Mar. 1865, RG-94, NA; Trulock, *In the Hands of Providence*, 225; Circular, HQ 1st Div., 5th A. C., Mar. 26, 1865, RG-393, pt. 2, E-259, NA; JLC to HQ 1st Div., 5th A. C., Mar. 2, 1865, ibid.

8. JLC to Sarah B. Chamberlain, Mar. 9, 1865, BC.

9. *OR*, I, 46, pt. 1: 316-19; Catton, *A Stillness at Appomattox*, 335-38.

10. *OR*, I, 46, pt. 1: 267-73; Josiah Shuman diary, Mar. 25, 1865, TS in Civil War Misc. Coll., USAMHI; Nelson Wilbur to his wife, Mar. 26, 1865, Wilbur MSS, SSMH.

11. JLC to HQ, 1st Div., 5th A. C., Mar. 26, 1865, RG-393, pt. 2, E-259, NA; Circular, HQ 1st Brig., 1st Div., 5th A. C., Mar. 28, 1865, ibid., E-263; Catton, *A Stillness at Appomattox*, 343-44.

12. JLC, *Military Operations on the White Oak Road, Virginia, March 31, 1865* (Portland, Me., 1897), 7-9; Pullen, *20th Maine*, 241.

13. *OR*, I, 46, pt. 1: 847; Philip Van Doren Stern, *An End to Valor: The Last Days of the Civil War* (Boston, 1958), 113.

14. *OR*, I, 46, pt. 1: 847; Pullen, *20th Maine*, 243-44; Woodward, *One Hundred ad Ninety-eighth Pennsylvania*, 36-37.

15. JLC, *Passing of the Armies*, 45-46; *OR*, I, 46, pt. 1: 800, 847; pt. 3: 731; JLC to John L. Hodsdon [summary of military service], n.d., PHS; Melcher, *With a Flash of His Sword*, 210.

16. Ellis Spear to Oliver W. Norton, Jan. 18, 1916, Norton MSS, Clarke Hist. Lib.; Pullen, *20th Maine*, 245.

17. JLC, *Passing of the Armies*, 46; Oliver W. Norton to Boyd Vincent, Feb. 10, 1916, Norton MSS, Clarke Hist. Lib.

18. JLC, *Passing of the Armies*, 46; *OR*, I, 46, pt. 1: 848; Pullen, *20th Maine*, 244.

19. *OR*, I, 46, pt. 1: 848; Woodward, *One Hundred and Ninety-eighth Pennsylvania*, 37.

20. JLC, *Passing of the Armies*, 48.

21. *OR*, I, 46, pt. 1: 848, 853, 856, 858; John Mitchell to JLC, Jan. 26, 1868, JLC MSS, LC; Woodward, *One Hundred and Ninety-eighth Pennsylvania*, 37-38; Edmund N. Hatcher, *The Last Four Weeks of the War* (Columbus, Ohio, 1892), 65-66.

22. *OR*, I, 46, pt. 1: 301, 848; JLC, *Operations on the White Oak Road*, 9; JLC to John L. Hodsdon [summary of military service], n.d., PHS.

23. Ibid.; JLC, *Passing of the Armies*, 56; *OR*, I, 46, pt. 1: 800; pt. 3: 308, 731.

24. JLC, *Operations on the White Oak Road*, 11-12; *OR*, I, 46, pt. 1: 676, 1101-02.

25. Trulock, *In the Hands of Providence*, 241; JLC, *Passing of the Armies*, 57; Woodward, *One Hundred and Ninety-eighth Pennsylvania*, 38.

26. JLC, "My Story of Fredericksburg," 154.

27. JLC, *Passing of the Armies*, 60-65; Edward G. Longacre, *Pickett, Leader*

of the Charge: A Biography of General George E. Pickett, C. S. A. (Shippensburg, Pa., 1995), 163-64.

28. *OR,* I, 46, pt. 3: 282, 298, 361.

29. Ibid., pt. 1: 849; JLC, *Passing of the Armies,* 65-67; Woodward, *One Hundred and Ninety-eighth Pennsylvania,* 39.

30. *OR,* I, 46, pt. 1: 815, 868, 882, 896; JLC, *Passing of the Armies,* 70-72.

31. *OR,* I, 46, pt. 1: 710-11, 849, 853; JLC, *Passing of the Armies,* 72-74; Woodward, *One Hundred and Ninety-eighth Pennsylvania,* 39-41.

32. *OR,* I, 46, pt. 1: 849; Gouverneur K. Warren to JLC, Dec. 22, 1865, JLC MSS, LC; JLC, *Passing of the Armies,* 72-73; JLC to John L. Hodsdon [summary of military service], n.d., PHS.

33. JLC, *Passing of the Armies,* 72-74.

34. *OR,* I, 46, pt. 1: 849; JLC, *Passing of the Armies,* 74; Woodward, *One Hundred and Ninety-eighth Pennsylvania,* 41-42; Josiah Shuman diary, Mar. 31, 1865, TS in Civil War Misc. Coll., USAMHI.

35. *OR,* I, 46, pt. 1: 849, 853; JLC to John L. Hodsdon [summary of military service], n.d., PHS; Trulock, *In the Hands of Providence,* 250-51.

36. *OR,* I, 46, pt. 1: 849, 853.

37. Ibid., 849.

THIRTEEN:

1. Philip H. Sheridan, *Personal Memoirs of P. H. Sheridan, General United States Army* (2 vols. New York, 1888), 2: 149-54; *OR,* I, 46, pt. 3: 381.

2. Ibid.; Sheridan, *Personal Memoirs,* 2: 154-55.

3. JLC, *Passing of the Armies,* 89-107; *OR,* I, 46, pt. 1: 819-26; pt. 3: 365-68; Taylor, *Gouverneur Kemble Warren,* 213-17.

4. JLC, *Passing of the Armies,* 92-93, 103-04; *OR,* I, 46, pt. 3: 366-70, 417-18; Sheridan, *Personal Memoirs,* 2: 155-60; Longacre, *Pickett, Leader of the Charge,* 164; Trulock, *In the Hands of Providence,* 256-57.

5. Ibid., 259-60; JLC, *Passing of the Armies,* 104, 119; *OR,* I, 46, pt. 3: 418.

6. Sheridan, *Personal Memoirs,* 2: 160-61; *OR,* I, 46, pt. 1: 850; JLC, *Passing of the Armies,* 120-24; JLC, "Chamberlain's answer[s] to questions of Genl Warren," n.d. [ca. 1880], LC.

7. JLC, *Passing of the Armies,* 122-26.

8. *OR,* I, 46, pt. 1: 869-70, 879-80; JLC, *Passing of the Armies,* 126-28; Noah Andre Trudeau, *Out of the Storm: The End of the Civil War, April-June 1865* (Boston, 1994), 33-36.

9. *OR*, I, 46, pt. 1: 838-39, 850; JLC to Aurestus S. Perham, Jan. 21, 1902, Perham MSS, MHS; JLC, *Passing of the Armies*, 128-29; Pullen, *20th Maine*, 253-54.

10. *OR*, I, 46, pt. 1: 850; JLC, *Passing of the Armies*, 128-29.

11. *OR*, I, 46, pt. 1: 850; JLC, *Passing of the Armies*, 131-32.

12. *OR*, I, 46, pt. 1: 850-51; JLC to John L. Hodsdon [summary of military service], n.d., PHS; JLC, *Passing of the Armies*, 130-37.

13. *OR*, I, 46, pt. 1: 851; JLC to John L. Hodsdon [summary of military service], n.d., PHS.

14. *OR*, I, 46, pt. 1: 839-40, 851; pt. 3: 924; JLC, *Passing of the Armies*, 138-40; Woodward, *One Hundred and Ninety-eighth Pennsylvania*, 45; Trulock, *In the Hands of Providence*, 278-79.

15. *OR*, I, 46, pt. 1: 828, 839; pt. 3: 420; Taylor, *Gouverneur Kemble Warren*, 221-23, 228-29.

16. Woodward, *One Hundred and Ninety-eighth Pennsylvania*, 46.

17. *OR*, I, 46, pt. 1: 839, 846; JLC, *Passing of the Armies*, 130, 132-33.

18. Ibid., 142-44.

19. *OR*, I, 46, pt. 1: 902-04, 1016-19, 1160-61; Catton, *A Stillness at Appomattox*, 360-63.

20. *OR*, I, 46, pt. 1: 851; JLC, *Passing of the Armies*, 184-94.

21. *OR*, I, 46, pt. 1: 851; JLC, *Passing of the Armies*, 194-206; JLC, "The Last Salute of the Army of Northern Virginia," *Southern Historical Society Papers* 32 (1904): 357.

22. *OR*, I, 46, pt. 1: 852; JLC, *Passing of the Armies*, 206-11; Woodward, *One Hundred and Ninety-eighth Pennsylvania*, 52-53; Special Order 31, HQ 1st Brig., 1st Div., 5th A. C., Apr. 3, 1865, RG-393, pt. 2, E-262, NA; Spear, *Civil War Recollections*, 179-80, 271.

23. *OR*, I, 46, pt. 1: 682, 852, 905-07; JLC, *Passing of the Armies*, 212-19.

24. *OR*, I, 46, pt. 1: 852; JLC, *Passing of the Armies*, 220-23, 232; Josiah Shuman diary, Apr. 7, 1865, TS in Civil War Misc. Coll., USAMHI.

25. *OR*, I, 46, pt. 1: 852; JLC, *Passing of the Armies*, 223-24; Trulock, *In the Hands of Providence*, 289-90.

26. *OR*, I, 46, pt. 1: 852; JLC, *Passing of the Armies*, 225-30.

27. *OR*, I, 46, pt. 1: 852; JLC, *Passing of the Armies*, 231-32; Pullen, *20th Maine*, 263-64; Ellis Spear, Postwar speech on war memories, 32-33, TS in Spear MSS, MSA; Spear, *Civil War Recollections*, 180, 272.

28. *OR*, I, 46, pt. 1: 852; JLC, *Passing of the Armies*, 233-42; Spear, *Civil*

War Recollections, 180-81; Ellis Spear, Postwar speech on war memories, 33, TS in Spear MSS, MSA.

29. *OR*, I, 46, pt. 1: 852; JLC, *Passing of the Armies*, 239-40; JLC to anon., Jan. 2, 1906 [1907], LC; Edward W. Whitaker to JLC, Jan. 7, 1907, ibid.; JLC, "Last Salute of the Army of Northern Virginia," 358-59; Walter Jones, "The Flag of Truce at Appomattox," *Confederate Veteran* 39 (1931): 302.

30. JLC, *Passing of the Armies*, 240-47.

31. Circular, HQ 5th A. C., Apr. 9, 1865, JLC MSS, LC.

32. JLC, "Last Salute of the Army of Northern Virginia," 359.

33. JLC, *Passing of the Armies*, 248-49.

34. *OR*, I, 46, pt. 3: 691, 707.

35. Josiah Shuman diary, Apr. 11, 1865, TS in Civil War Misc. Coll., USAMHI; JLC, *Passing of the Armies*, 254-57.

36. Ibid., 260; *OR*, I, 46, pt. 3: 706, 731; Spear, *Civil War Recollections*, 272; Gerrish, *Army Life*, 260-61.

37. JLC, *Passing of the Armies*, 261.

38. Ibid.; JLC to Sarah B. Chamberlain, Apr. 13, 1865, BC; JLC, "Last Salute of the Army of Northern Virginia," 361-62; JLC, "The Third Brigade at Appomattox," in *Proceedings of the Third Brigade Association, First Division, Fifth Army Corps, Army of the Potomac ...* (New York, 1894), 341; John B. Gordon, *Reminiscences of the Civil War* (New York, 1904), 444; Richard B. Harwell, ed., *Honor Answering Honor* (Brunswick, Me., 1965), [1]-[2]; Douglas Southall Freeman, *Lee's Lieutenants: A Study in Command* (3 vols. New York, 1942-44), 3: 744-47.

39. Oliver W. Norton to Mrs. General Vincent, Aug. 22, 1913, Norton MSS, Clarke Hist. Lib.; Oliver W. Norton to Boyd Vincent, Jan. 5, Feb. 8, 10, 1916, ibid.; Ellis Spear to Oliver W. Norton, Jan. 8, Feb. 1, 1916, ibid; William G. Marvel, "A Question of Rhetoric," *North & South* 2 (June 1999): 80-85.

40. "Coming Home Again," *Confederate Veteran* 36 (1928): 50.

FOURTEEN:

1. JLC to Sarah B. Chamberlain, Apr. 13, 1865, BC.

2. JLC to FAC, Apr. 19, 1865, PHS.

3. Ibid.; JLC, *Passing of the Armies*, 277-86.

4. JLC to FAC, Apr. 19, 1865, PHS; JLC, *"Bayonet! Forward"*, 259-60; Trulock, *In the Hands of Providence*, 315, 505n.

5. *OR*, I, 46, pt. 3: 863, 995; Woodward, *One Hundred and Ninety-eighth Pennsylvania*, 62; JLC, *Passing of the Armies*, 287-96; JLC, *Joshua Lawrence Chamberlain*, 14.

6. *OR*, I, 46, pt. 1: 847-52.

7. JLC to John L. Hodsdon [summary of military service], n.d., PHS; JLC, *Joshua Lawrence Chamberlain*, 14; *OR*, I, 46, pt. 3: 922, 924; JLC, *Passing of the Armies*, 288.

8. Ibid., 289.

9. Ibid.

10. Ibid., 289-96.

11. Ibid., 297.

12. Ibid., 297-301; Spear, *Civil War Recollections*, 275.

13. Ibid.; JLC, *Passing of the Armies*, 302; Josiah Shuman diary, May 3, 1865, TS in Civil War Misc. Coll., USAMHI; Pullen, *20th Maine*, 280.

14. JLC, *Passing of the Armies*, 303-08; Warner, *Generals in Blue*, 196.

15. JLC, *Passing of the Armies*, 308-10.

16. Ibid., 311-18; Josiah Shuman diary, May 12, 1865, TS in Civil War Misc. Coll., USAMHI; *OR*, I, 46, pt. 3: 1107, 1115, 1119-20, 1128, 1135.

17. Trulock, *In the Hands of Providence*, 318-25; George E. Adams diary, May 14-29, 1865, First Parish Church.

18. Ibid., May 23, 1865; JLC, *Passing of the Armies*, 326-63; *OR*, I, 46, pt. 3: 1186-88.

19. Josiah Shuman diary, May 31, 1865, TS in Civil War Misc. Coll., USAMHI; Woodward, *One Hundred and Ninety-eighth Pennsylvania*, 63; JLC to Sarah B. Chamberlain, June 6, 1865, BC.

20. Ibid.

21. JLC to Lorenzo Thomas, July 1, 31, 1865, JLC's CBF, M-1064, R-248, NA; Charles Griffin to Adj. Gen., USA, Apr. 13, July 19, 1865, ibid.

22. *OR*, I, 46, pt. 3: 1011; JLC to John L. Hodsdon, Dec. 6, 1865, 20th Maine Records, MSA; JLC to Alexander S. Webb, May 18, 1893, Webb MSS, Yale Univ. Lib.

23. Warner, *Generals in Blue*, 152-53.

24. JLC to Charlton T. Lewis, June 26, 1865, Lewis MSS, Yale Univ. Lib.; *OR*, I, 46, pt. 3: 1292, 1302; Trulock, *In the Hands of Providence*, 329-30, 335; JLC, *Joshua Lawrence Chamberlain*, 15.

25. Ibid.

26. JLC to Ulysses S. Grant, July 31, 1865, PHS.

27. Ibid.; Golay, *To Gettysburg and Beyond*, 282; Philip S. Wilder, "Chamberlain: Student, Scholar and Educator," 3, BC; JLC to John L. Hodsdon, Nov. 11, 1865, 20th Maine Records, MSA; JLC to Morris Schaff, n.d., Frost Family MSS, Yale Univ. Lib.; FAC to JLC, May 1, 1866, RC; William S. Tilton to JLC, Oct. 6, 1865, JLC MSS, LC; John Robertson to JLC, Oct. 25, 1865, ibid.; William H. Powell to JLC, Apr. 20, 1894, JLC MSS, MHS.

28. Smith, "Strains of Post-Military Matrimony," 10-12; FAC to JLC, Mar. 8, 19, 1866, RC; JLC to FAC, Mar. 20, 1866, ibid.

29. Samuel Cony to Lot M. Morrill, Sept. 5, 1865, JLC's CBF, M-1064, R-248, NA; Lot M. Morrill et al. to Andrew Johnson, Dec. 20, 1865, JLC MSS, LC; Ulysses S. Grant to Edwin M. Stanton, Jan. 16, 1866 [and Stanton's endorsement], ibid.; Wallace, *Soul of the Lion*, 203.

30. JLC, *Joshua Lawrence Chamberlain*, 23; *MOLLUS, Commandery of the State of Maine: In Memoriam, Joshua Lawrence Chamberlain, Late Major General U. S. V.* (Portland, Me., 1914), 11; Cross, "Joshua Lawrence Chamberlain," 81; JLC to Grace D. C. Allen, July 13, 1888, BC.

31. JLC to FAC, Mar. 21, Apr. 7, 1866, RC; FAC to JLC, May 1, 1866, ibid.; Trulock, *In the Hands of Providence*, 334-35.

32. Wallace, *Soul of the Lion*, 205; Gouverneur K. Warren to JLC, June 24, 1866, JLC MSS, LC.

33. Trulock, *In the Hands of Providence*, 335; JLC to Board of Overseers and Trustees, Bowdoin Coll., Nov. 13, 1866, BC; Perry, *Conceived in Liberty*, 315-16, 331-32.

34. Ibid., 338-40; Cross, "Joshua Lawrence Chamberlain," 33-34, 38-39, 43, 46-47; Eugene A. Mawhinney, "Joshua L. Chamberlain, Governor of Maine, 1867, 1868, 1869, 1870," 1-2, PHS.

35. Cross, "Joshua Lawrence Chamberlain," 34-35, 39; Mawhinney, "Joshua L. Chamberlain, Governor," 3-4.

36. JLC, *Joshua Lawrence Chamberlain*, 18; Mawhinney, "Joshua L. Chamberlain, Governor," 4; Cross, "Joshua Lawrence Chamberlain," 35, 39, 47-48.

37. Ibid., 212-13; JLC, *Joshua Lawrence Chamberlain*, 18; Mawhinney, "Joshua L. Chamberlain, Governor," 5-8; Cross, "Joshua Lawrence Chamberlain," 36, 39-40, 43-44, 47-48, 52-53.

38. Ibid., 39, 53-54; JLC, *Joshua Lawrence Chamberlain*, 18; Mawhinney, "Joshua L. Chamberlain, Governor," 5, 14-15.

39. JLC, *Joshua Lawrence Chamberlain*, 17-18; Mawhinney, "Joshua L.

Chamberlain, Governor," 11-14; Cross, "Joshua Lawrence
Chamberlain," 35, 42, 45, 49; Wallace, *Soul of the Lion*, 210-11, 214,
216-19, 221.

40. Ibid., 218-19; JLC, *Joshua Lawrence Chamberlain*, 18-19; Cross,
"Joshua Lawrence Chamberlain," 50.

41. JLC, *Joshua Lawrence Chamberlain*, 19; Cross, "Joshua Lawrence
Chamberlain," 42-43, 46, 50.

42. JLC, *Joshua Lawrence Chamberlain*, 19; JLC to William P. Fessenden,
Jan. 17, 1868, UM; Cross, "Joshua Lawrence Chamberlain," 42.

43. Cross, "Joshua Lawrence Chamberlain," 43, 45, 49; Mawhinney,
"Joshua L. Chamberlain, Governor," 11.

44. JLC, *Joshua Lawrence Chamberlain*, 16-17; Cross, "Joshua Lawrence
Chamberlain," 53.

45. Ibid., 46, 50; Wallace, *Soul of the Lion*, 219-22.

46. Cross, "Joshua Lawrence Chamberlain," 50-51.

47. JLC, *Joshua Lawrence Chamberlain*, 19-21; Daniel Wright to Charles
D. Gilmore, Jan. 12, 1869, Frost Family MSS, Yale Univ. Lib.; Charles
D. Gilmore to JLC, Jan. 14, 1868 [1869], ibid.; Cross, "Joshua
Lawrence Chamberlain," 50-54.

48. Trulock, *In the Hands of Providence*, 340, 360, 368, 524n.; Thomas D.
Chamberlain to JLC, Jan. 14, 1867, RC; Sarah B. Chamberlain and
Thomas D. Chamberlain to JLC, Jan. 16, 1867, MHS.

49. JLC to FAC, Nov. 20, 1868, Frost Family MSS, Yale Univ. Lib.;
Smith, "Strains of Post-Military Matrimony," 12; Trulock, *In the
Hands of Providence*, 341.

50. Perry, *Conceived in Liberty*, 338-40, 356-57, 460n.

FIFTEEN:

1. JLC, *Joshua Lawrence Chamberlain*, 19; *General Catalogue of Bowdoin
College, and the Medical School of Maine, 1794-1894* (Brunswick, Me.,
1894), xc; Louis C. Hatch, *The History of Bowdoin College* (Portland,
Me., 1927), 129-30; Perry, *Conceived in Liberty*, 372-73; Cross,
"Joshua Lawrence Chamberlain," 55-57.

2. *Portland Evening Express & Daily Advertiser*, Feb. 27, 1914; Trulock, *In
the Hands of Providence*, 343, 347-48; "President Chamberlain,
Bowdoin College, 1871-1883," 2, PHS.

3. *Portland Evening Express & Daily Advertiser*, Feb. 27, 1914; Hatch,
History of Bowdoin College, 155-62; Wallace, *Soul of the Lion*, 230-33,
244; Cross, "Joshua Lawrence Chamberlain," 58.

4. Hatch, *History of Bowdoin College*, 162; Wallace, *Soul of the Lion*, 231, 243-44.

5. Ibid., 234; Hatch, *History of Bowdoin College*, 133; Trulock, *In the Hands of Providence*, 345-46.

6. Ibid., 346; Petition, Students of Bowdoin College, Nov. 12, 1873, JLC MSS, BC.

7. Wallace, *Soul of the Lion*, 238-39; Trulock, *In the Hands of Providence*, 346-47; "President Chamberlain, Bowdoin College, 1871-1883," 1-2, PHS.

8. Hatch, *History of Bowdoin College*, 140-41; Wallace, *Soul of the Lion*, 237-39.

9. Ibid., 240; Hatch, *History of Bowdoin College*, 142-48.

10. JLC to FAC, May 2, 1875, RC; JLC to S. T. Hersey, Jan. 20, 1873, PHS; JLC to J. W. Bradbury, Jan. 20, 1873, ibid.; JLC to "My Dear Mr. Blake," May 22, 1873, ibid.; JLC to William H. Willcox, Oct. 5, 1876, ibid.; JLC to Abner Coburn, Jan. 7, 1878, ibid.; Adelbert Ames to JLC, Jan. 22, 1875, JLC MSS, LC.

11. JLC, *Joshua Lawrence Chamberlain*, 19; *General Catalogue of Bowdoin College*, xc-xci; Richard L. Sherman, "An Innovative College President," *Brunswick Times-Record*, Aug. 3, 1978; Cross, "Joshua Lawrence Chamberlain," 55-62.

12. JLC, *Joshua Lawrence Chamberlain*, 19-20; JLC to "Miss Low," Oct. 9, 1872, BC; Trulock, *In the Hands of Providence*, 344.

13. Wallace, *Soul of the Lion*, 235-36, 240-41; JLC to C. H. Wheeler, Sept. 19, 1876, PHS; Hatch, *History of Bowdoin College*, 179; R. Lewis McHenry, "Dawning of a New Elizabethan Age: The [Bowdoin College] Presidency of Joshua Lawrence Chamberlain," 16, BC; Cross, "Joshua Lawrence Chamberlain," 67-68.

14. JLC to Board of Overseers and Trustees, Bowdoin Coll., July 8, 1873, June 26, 1876, MHS; JLC to "Rev. Dr. Mason," Sept. 19, 1876, PHS; Sherman, *Joshua Lawrence Chamberlain*, 21.

15. JLC to FAC, Apr. 7, 1866, RC; FAC to JLC, Apr. 15, 1866, ibid.; JLC to Henry W. Longfellow, Mar. 22, June 19, 22, 1875, Feb. 27, 1877, Feb. 27, 1882, Houghton Lib., Harvard Univ., Cambridge, Mass.; Stone, "Joshua Chamberlain," 58; Cross, "Joshua Lawrence Chamberlain," 83-84; Catherine T. Smith interview, [2]-[3], [5], "Interview with JLC's Personal Secretary" Internet site.

16. Ibid., [5], [10]; JLC to Henry W. Longfellow, Mar. 22, June 19, 1875, Harvard Univ. Lib.; Trulock, *In the Hands of Providence*, 347, 350.

17. JLC, *Joshua Lawrence Chamberlain*, 20; William M. Evarts to JLC,

Mar. 19, 1878, JLC MSS, LC; JLC to Peleg W. Chandler, Mar. 7, 1878, Rutherford B. Hayes Pres. Cntr., Fremont, O.; JLC to FAC, Mar. —, 1878, RC; JLC to his parents, June 14, 1878, BC; Wallace, *Soul of the Lion*, 250-53.

18. Selden Connor to JLC, Feb. 28, 1876, JLC MSS, LC; JLC, *Joshua Lawrence Chamberlain*, 23; Cross, "Joshua Lawrence Chamberlain," 97-98; JLC, *Maine: Her Place in History* (Augusta, Me., 1877).

19. JLC to Drake DeKay, Sept. 19, 1876, PHS; JLC to Rutherford B. Hayes, Mar. 8, 1877, ibid.; JLC to Carl Schurz, Apr. 5, 1877, ibid.

20. *Boston Journal*, Jan. 4, 1878; Adelbert Ames to JLC, Jan. 22, 1875, JLC MSS, LC.

21. *Oxford Democrat* (Paris, Me.), June 10, 1879.

22. E. H. Ferrell to JLC, Aug. 10, 1877, JLC MSS, BC; Ari Hoogenboom, *Rutherford B. Hayes, Warrior and President* (Lawrence, Kan., 1995), 257-58, 268-69, 575n.; Harry Barnard, *Rutherford B. Hayes and His America* (Indianapolis, 1954), 195-96, 412.

23. *Oxford Democrat*, June 10, 1879.

24. Nathaniel P. Banks to JLC, May 8, 1876, JLC MSS, LC; Presidential staff to JLC, Mar. 7, 1884, ibid.; William P. Frye to JLC, Apr. 5, 1897, ibid.; JLC to Chester A. Arthur, Mar. 1, 1884, Frost Family MSS, Yale Univ. Lib.

25. General Order 4, Adj. Gen., State of Maine, June 25, 1872, PHS.

26. JLC, *Joshua Lawrence Chamberlain, Supplement: The Twelve Days at Augusta, 1880* (Portland, Me., 1906), 3-4; William McDonald, *The Government of Maine: Its History and Administration* (New York, 1902), 18-19; Whitmore Barron Garland, "Pine Tree Politics: Maine Political Party Battles, 1820-1972" (Ph.D. diss., Univ. of Massachusetts, 1979), 51-53; Eugene A. Mawhinney, "Joshua Chamberlain and the Twelve Days Which Shook Maine, January 6-17, 1880," 1-2, PHS.

27. Ibid., 3; JLC to Alonzo Garcelon, Jan. 6, 1880, JLC MSS, MHS; JLC, *Joshua Lawrence Chamberlain, Supplement*, 4-5.

28. JLC to James G. Blaine, Jan. 16, 1880, PHS; James G. Blaine to JLC, Jan. 14 [two letters], 16, 1880, ibid.; JLC, *Joshua Lawrence Chamberlain, Supplement*, 5; Mawhinney, "Joshua Chamberlain and the Twelve Days," 3.

29. General Order 12, Adj. Gen., State of Maine, Jan. 5, 1880, JLC MSS, MHS; General Order 1, HQ 1st Div. Maine Militia, Jan. 6, 1880, Election Crisis of 1880 File, Maine State Lib., Augusta; Stone, "Joshua Chamberlain," 49.

30. Special Orders 3, 4, HQ 1st Div., Maine Militia, Jan. 9, 1880,

Election Crisis of 1880 File, Maine State Lib.; JLC to Alonzo Garcelon, Jan. 7, 1880, MHS; JLC to anon., n.d. [ca. Jan. 7, 1880], PHS; JLC to FAC, Jan. 7, 1880, ibid.; W. H. Brown to JLC, Jan. 10, 1880 [telegram], BC; JLC, *Joshua Lawrence Chamberlain, Supplement,* 6, 14-15.

31. JLC to FAC, Jan. 15, 1880, BC; JLC, *Joshua Lawrence Chamberlain, Supplement,* 13-15, 19-20; Mawhinney, "Joshua Chamberlain and the Twelve Days," 4.

32. Ibid., 4-5; Cross, "Joshua Lawrence Chamberlain," 73; JLC, *Joshua Lawrence Chamberlain, Supplement,* 24-25.

33. Ibid., 25.

34. Daniel F. Davis to JLC, Jan. 17, 1880 [circular], JLC MSS, MHS; JLC to "Judge Appleton," Jan. 12, 1880, ibid.; James E. McMullan to JLC, Jan. 13, 1880, Election Crisis of 1880 File, Maine State Lib.; J. W. Spaulding to John Marshall Brown, Jan. 19, 1880, ibid.; James D. Lamson to JLC, Jan. 13, 1880 [and JLC's endorsement], JLC MSS, LC; J. W. Spaulding to anon., Dec. 31, 1880, JLC MSS, PHS; JLC, *Joshua Lawrence Chamberlain, Supplement,* 10-11, 14, 20-21, 25; Cross, "Joshua Lawrence Chamberlain," 74-75.

35. Trulock, *In the Hands of Providence,* 360-62; Wallace, *Soul of the Lion,* 244-45.

36. JLC to FAC, May 11, 1880, RC; Gouverneur K. Warren to JLC, Oct. 20, 1880, BC; Hewett et al., comps., *Supplement to the Official Records,* 8: 228-37, 271-89, 1081-86; Trudeau, *Out of the Storm,* 407-18.

37. JLC to Sarah B. C. Farrington, Jan. 29, 1882, UM; Wallace, *Soul of the Lion,* 274-75.

38. JLC to FAC, —- 20, 1883, BC; H. Wyllys Chamberlain to Grace D. C. Allen, Aug. 9, 1886, ibid.; JLC to C. O. Langham, Aug. 24, 1887, ibid.; JLC, *Joshua Lawrence Chamberlain,* 22; Wallace, *Soul of the Lion,* 275-77; Cross, "Joshua Lawrence Chamberlain," 76-79; Dudley S. Johnson, "The Railroads of Florida, 1865-1900" (Ph.D. diss., Florida State Univ., 1965), A-21; Silver Springs, Ocala & Gulf Railroad Company Articles of Association, Land Grant and Mortgage, and List of Deeds, Fla. State Archives, Tallahassee.

39. JLC to Grace D. C. Allen, Feb. 15, Oct. 20, 1887, n.d. [1887], Feb. 12, Apr. 9, 1888, BC; Henry C. Dean to JLC, July 10, 1890, ibid.; JLC, *Joshua Lawrence Chamberlain,* 22; Cross, "Joshua Lawrence Chamberlain," 77-80.

40. Johnson, "Railroads of Florida," A-21; JLC to FAC, —- 20, 1883, BC; Wallace, *Soul of the Lion,* 277-78.

41. John B. Gordon to JLC, Feb. 26, 1892, Rutherford B. Hayes Pres. Cntr.

42. JLC to Sarah B. C. Farrington, Nov. 15, 1891, UM; Wallace, *Soul of the Lion*, 278-81; JLC to Andrew Carnegie, Mar. 23, 1893, Frost Family MSS, Yale Univ. Lib.; JLC to "Dear Mr. Searles," Nov. 13, 1893, MHS.

43. J. H. Warner to JLC, Mar. 2, 1883, PHS; H. Wyllys Chamberlain to Grace D. C. Allen, Aug. 9, 1886, BC; JLC to Grace D. C. Allen, Dec. 13, 1886, Feb. 15, 1887, July 13, 1888, ibid.; JLC to FAC, Jan. 23, 1894, Apr. 21, 1903, ibid.; JLC to "Dr. Little," Nov. 28, 1911, ibid.; Robert V. Sewell to JLC, Aug. 10, 1913, ibid.; JLC to FAC, Aug. 8, 1885, John Marshall Brown MSS, Maine State Lib.; Pass for JLC, "Inauguration of the Statue of 'Liberty Enlightening the World'," Oct. 27, 1886, JLC MSS, LC.

44. JLC, *Joshua Lawrence Chamberlain*, 25-26.

45. Desjardin, *Stand Firm Ye Boys from Maine*, 136-38.

46. Ibid., 138-39; JLC, *Address of Gen. Joshua L. Chamberlain at the Dedication of the Maine Monuments on the Battlefield of Gettysburg, October 3, 1893* (Augusta, Me., 1895); *Dedication of the 20th Maine Monuments at Gettysburg, October 3, 1889 ...* (Waldoboro, Me., 1891); JLC, *"Bayonet! Forward"*, 184-202.

47. JLC to Ellis Spear, Nov. 27, 1896, Spear MSS, MSA; William C. Oates to Elihu Root, June 2, 1903, JLC MSS, LC; Elihu Root to Gettysburg Natl. Park Comm., Jan. 22, 1904, "July 2nd: Little Round Top (20th Maine Inf. vs. 15th Alabama Inf.)" File, GNMPL; William C. Oates to William M. Robbins, Feb. 14, 1903, ibid.; William C. Oates to Elihu Root, n.d. [ca. June 1903], ibid.; William C. Oates to John P. Nicholson, Dec. 29, 1904, Mar. 1, 1905, ibid.; JLC to John P. Nicholson, Mar. 16, 1906, Aug. 14, 1908, ibid.; JLC to William C. Oates, May 18, 1908, "July 2nd: Little Round Top (Vincent & Weed vs. Law & Robertson)" File, ibid.; Desjardin, *Stand Firm Ye Boys from Maine*, 133-34, 139, 142-43; LaFantasie, "The Other Man," 74-75; Kross, "Alabamians' Attack on Little Round Top," 60-61.

48. F. C. Ainsworth to "Major General Commanding," Mar. 1, 1893, JLC's CBF, M-1064, R-248, NA; F. C. Ainsworth to Thomas M. Hubbard, Aug. 11, 1893, ibid.; Record and Pension Office Memo, Aug. 11, 1893, ibid.; JLC to F. C. Ainsworth, Sept. 16, 1893, Oct. 21, 1907, ibid.; JLC to Alexander S. Webb, May 18, 1893, Oct. 11, 1906, Webb MSS, Yale Univ. Lib.

49. Llewellyn Powers to JLC, Apr. 5, 1898, JLC MSS, LC; Russell A. Alger to JLC, Apr. 30, 1898, JLC's CBF, M-1064, R-248, NA.

50. JLC to William P. Frye, Apr. 22, 1898, ibid.; William P. Frye to JLC, Aug. 20, 1898, JLC MSS, LC.

51. JLC to "His Majesty, William, King of Prussia," July 20, 1870, PHS.

52. JLC, *Joshua Lawrence Chamberlain*, 22; JLC to FAC, June 30, 1896, BC; JLC to Grace D. C. Allen, Dec. 4, 1898, MHS; JLC to Grace D. C. Allen, Jan. 29, 1899, RC; JLC to Eugene Hale, Nov. 27, 1899, MHS; JLC to John T. Richards, Dec. 28, 1899, ibid.; Ellis Spear to Amos L. Allen, Dec. 4, 1899, BC; Amos L. Allen to G. M. Elliott, Dec. 12, 1899, Rutherford B. Hayes Pres. Cntr.; Amos L. Allen to JLC, Feb. 12, 1900, ibid.; Div. of Appts., U. S. Treasury Dept. to JLC, Mar. 27, 1900, PHS.

53. JLC, *Joshua Lawrence Chamberlain*, 22; Catherine T. Smith interview, [1], [6], "Interview with JLC's Personal Secretary" Internet site; JLC to U.S. State Dept., Oct. 25, 1900, PHS; JLC to FAC, Nov. 6, 1900, BC; JLC to John P. Nicholson, Oct. 19, 1910, Gratz Coll.—Union Gens., Hist. Soc. of Penna.; JLC to Perriton Maxwell, May 22, 1913, MHS; JLC to William D. Hyde, May 27, 1913, BC; Desjardin, *Stand Firm Ye Boys from Maine*, 148, 163-66.

54. JLC to Aurestus S. Perham, Sept. 6, 1905, Perham MSS; JLC to Thomas T. Munford, Oct. 25, 1905, Munford-Ellis MSS., William R. Perkins Lib., Duke Univ., Durham, N. C.

55. JLC to John P. Nicholson, June 12, 1899, Simon Gratz Collection—Union Gens., Hist. Soc. of Penna.; Henry S. Burrage to JLC, Dec. 9, 1910, JLC MSS, LC; Catherine T. Smith interview, [2], [5], "Interview with JLC's Personal Secretary" Internet site; Trulock, *In the Hands of Providence*, 374.

56. Raymond, "Joshua Chamberlain's Retirement Bill," 341-54; JLC to Alexander S. Webb, Oct. 11, 1905, Feb. 27, 1906, Webb MSS, Yale Univ. Lib.; JLC to Eugene Hale, June 26, 1906, MHS; William P. Frye to JLC, Dec. 13, 1909, JLC MSS, MHS; Eugene Hale to JLC, Feb. 4, 1910, Rutherford B. Hayes Pres. Cntr.; JLC to C. C. Andrews, Dec. 4, 1909, ibid.

57. Roland Phillips to JLC, Nov. 1, 2, 12, 14, 1912, Feb. 15, 27, 1913, JLC MSS, MHS; Perriton Maxwell to JLC, May 12, Apr. 10, May 22, 1913, ibid.; JLC to Perriton Maxwell, May 22, 1913, ibid.; Ferris Greenslet to JLC, Dec. 23, 1912, ibid.; JLC to Grace D. C. Allen, Feb. 28, 1913, PHS; Desjardin, *Stand Firm Ye Boys from Maine*, 151.

58. JLC to Sidney D. Waldron, June 11, 1912, MHS; Robert V. Sewell to JLC, Aug. 10, 1913, BC; JLC to Sarah B. C. Farrington, Jan. 20, 1914, UM; *Portland Evening Express & Daily Advertiser*, Feb. 24, 1914; *Lewiston Journal*, Feb. 28, 1914; *MOLLUS, Commandery of the State of*

Maine: In Memoriam, 12-14; Cross, "Joshua Lawrence Chamberlain," 86-88; Trulock, *In the Hands of Providence,* 374-79; Wallace, *Soul of the Lion,* 309-12; Golay, *To Gettysburg and Beyond,* 342-43; Catherine T. Smith memoirs, 3, TS in PHS; Catherine T. Smith interview, [6], "Interview with JLC's Personal Secretary" Internet site.

AFTERWORD:

1. Chamberlain appears to have been a perplexing man, and some of the major events in his life may leave one scratching one's head in confusion. For example, he professed a profoundly deep love for wife and children, as well as for members of his first family, but never hesitated to rejoin the army whenever his health permitted. His almost monomaniacal desire to return to duty did not abate even after garnering enough fame and glory to satisfy anyone who might question his patriotism or courage. How can this make sense, and how can psychology shed light on this aspect of his life? His record of fervent service cannot be understood *solely* by recourse to an abstract sense of duty or as some psychologically vague overcompensation for past personal inadequacies, as suggested by Desjardin, although those two factors may have played some role. Another example concerns his diverse occupational pursuits, from teacher to soldier to politician. Do they share a common or unifying theme, one that allows his career changes to make sense and be seen as a reasonable by-product of his psychological make-up?

2. This question is the title of a recent and already influential article by Dan P. McAdams, "What Do We Know When We Know a Person," *Journal of Personality* 63 (1995): 365-96.

3. Understanding personality on various levels is described in R. A. Emmons, "Levels and Domains in Personality: An Introduction," *Journal of Personality* 63 (1995): 341-64.

4. One of the two major approaches to the measurement of the five domains of personality involves asking people to rate themselves using adjectives such as "extroverted" and "kind." Saucier found that 40 specific adjectives provide an excellent assessment of the five major dimensions of personality (e.g., "extroverted" and "energetic" for the domain of Extraversion, "sympathetic" and "kind" for Agreeableness). See Gerard Saucier, "Mini-Markers: A Brief Version of Goldberg's Unipolar Big-Five Markers," *Journal of Personality Assessment* 63 (1994): 506-16.

5. Paul T. Costa and Robert R. McCrae, *Revised NEO Personality Inventory (NEO PI-R) Professional Manual* (Odessa, Fla., 1992), 49.

6. This project was based on a common assessment technique known as "peer ratings" where individuals who know a "target" person well provide information about that person. Using valid tests, convergence between self-ratings and peer-ratings is impressively high (Costa and McCrae, *Revised NEO Personality Inventory* ch. 7). In other words, we can learn something about a person by "listening" to what other individuals, such as peers, say about that person, assuming they know the individual and can be somewhat objective. Of course peer-ratings or evaluations, like self-ratings, cannot be totally objective, but given the distance in time between the raters in this project and their subject, there may actually be less bias than if one could somehow solicit some of Chamberlain's own contemporaries (many of whom would have had a positive or negative bias toward him) to participate in such a project. The experts rated Chamberlain on 40 traits linked to the Big Five. The ratings were on a scale from 1 to 9, with verbal anchors provided. A rating from 1 through 4 reflected gradations in one's perception of the particular trait as being an inaccurate description of Chamberlain, from 1 = extremely inaccurate, to 9 = extremely accurate.

7. Harrison G. Gough and Alfred B. Heilbrun, Jr., *The Adjective Check List manual* (Palo Alto, Calif., 1980)

8. All quotes are from the ACL scale descriptions that accompany the computerized profile report. Extensive research has documented associations between extreme scores (high or low) on particular scales of the ACL and other personality traits, as well as descriptions of those individuals provided by trained psychologists. The following supplemental material comes from the ACL professional manual and provides details on those scales Chamberlain scored especially high on or which seemed especially interesting. They shed light on the personality make-up of someone who answered the ACL with the type of traits attributed to Chamberlain, and thus may increase our understanding of the historical Chamberlain in particular. The reader should try to keep these traits and attributes in mind when reading about the key events in his life highlighted later in this chapter. *Achievement*—high scorers are seen by others as: talkative, fastidious, productive—gets things done, behaves in an assertive fashion, has high aspirations for the self, tends to offer advice, and is power-oriented. Adjectives for those high on achievement are: assertive, bossy, confident, energetic, ambitious, and enterprising. *The Adjective Check List Manual*, 8, provides this overall description for someone high on Achievement: "... is a hard-working, goal-directed individual, who is determined to do well and usually does. The motivation to succeed seems to lie less in competitive drives than in an insistent need to live

up to high and socially commendable criteria of performance. Others acknowledge the energy and enterprise ... but also see elements of coercion, impatience, and self-aggrandizement."

Endurance—seen by others as: fastidious, favors conservative values, is productive, gets things done, is moralistic, has high aspirations, and tends to offer advice (as against engages in fantasy, is unpredictable, needs expressed without control). Adjective descriptions of those who score high on Endurance are: conservative, painstaking, conscientious, and ambitious. "High scorers ... have a strong sense of duty, work conscientiously, and eschew frivolity ...." (*Ibid.*, 9).

Order—seen by others as: fastidious, favors conservative values, prides self on being rational and objective, tends toward over-control of needs, delays gratification unnecessarily, is moralistic, and tends to offer advice. Adjective descriptors are: conservative, painstaking, conventional, and dignified. "The high scorer ... seeks objectivity and rationality, is firm in controlling impulses, and unswerving in the pursuit of goals. Setbacks and distractions are not easily endured, nor are change and variety welcomed". "The high scorer prefers tasks demanding self-discipline and diligent effort ..." (*Ibid.*, 9).

Ideal Self—seen by others as: having a wide range of interests, is productive, gets things done, shows condescending behavior in relations with others, has high aspirations for self, has social poise, appears socially at ease, and tends to offer advice (as opposed to genuinely submissive, accepts domination comfortably, feels a lack of personal meaning in life, gives up easily, is reluctant to commit self to any definite course of action, has a brittle ego, is self-pitying). "High scorers appear to be characterized by interpersonal effectiveness and goal-attaining abilities ... there seem to be elements of narcissistic ego-inflation ... rated well-adjusted by others ..." (*Ibid.*, 18).

Military Leadership Scale— This scale was developed using military personnel from various countries and branches of service. It has been extensively validated in several samples using judgments of performance provided by superiors and promotion boards. Others see people who score high on this scale as: fastidious, favors conservative values, is productive, gets things done, is moralistic, has high aspirations for self, appears straightforward and candid in dealing with others, is subjectively unaware of self-concern, feels satisfied with self, has social poise, tends to offer advice. Applicable adjectives include: ambitious, conscientious, industrious, organized, and conservative. "High scorers ... oriented toward duties and obligations, holds fast to an agreed-upon line of action, and works hard to see that consensual goals are attained ... exerts a steadying influence on others, values good organization and careful planning, and is not temperamental or high-strung (*Ibid.*).

Low Origence, High Intellectence—"The high scorer ... is analytical, logical, astute, intellectually capable and self-disciplined, and fully prepared to undertake the planning and hard work necessary for the attainment of rationally established goals ... and finds it hard to unbend and give in to whim and impulse ..." (*Ibid.*, 26).

Naturally, conclusions from this ACL profile with its associated traits and personal attributes are limited by the validity of the ACL itself and the validity of the information about Chamberlain entered on the checklist of adjectives. The ACL has excellent validity that has been documented in various sources. The usefulness of the information about Chamberlain's likely attributes depends on the accuracy of the information provided about him in the historical record. If one grants that those who knew him well described him accurately, then the results of this exercise will have value.

9. It could be argued that even if many people agreed about someone else's traits, it may reflect a shared but inaccurate bias in judgment about the subject of analysis. It is impossible to empirically or logically disprove that challenge. However, I counter that challenge by reasoning as follows: Something can indeed be learned about a historical person provided knowledgeable people see that person in a consistent way, and if their conclusions are either well-intentioned or well-reasoned (e.g., a biographer) or based on data from the historical record (e.g., contemporaries who knew him well). This method is open to error, of course, but historical analysis cannot proceed if a guarantee of accuracy is required. In other words, potential errors always lurk in any endeavor that requires human judgment, but our confidence in conclusions reached is increased if those conclusions are based on agreement rather than disagreement.

10. M. Zuckerman, *Sensation Seeking: Beyond the Optimal Level of Arousal* (Hillsdale, N.J., 1979).

11. Charles S. Carver and Michael F. Scheier, *Perspective on Personality* (Boston, 1992), 179.

12. David Bakan, *The Duality of Human Existence: Isolation and Communion in Western Man* (Boston, 1966).

13. David G. Winter, *Personality: Analysis and Interpretation of Lives* (New York, 1996), ch. 5.

14. David G. Winter, "Measuring Personality at a Distance: Development of an Integrated System for Scoring Motives in Running Text," in Abigail J. Stewart, J. M. Healy, Jr., and Daniel Ozer, eds., *Perspectives in Personality: Approaches to Understanding Lives* (London, 1991), 62. For a presentation of these methods of personality assessment in

greater detail, see Dan P. McAdams, *Power, Intimacy, and the Life Story* (New York, 1985), ch. 3; Charles P. Smith, ed., *Motivation and Personality: Handbook of Thematic Content Analysis* (New York, 1992); and Winter, *Personality.* A great deal of compelling evidence exists to support the reliability and validity of the TAT and its derivatives as measures of the latent needs for power, affiliation/intimacy, and achievement. See McAdams, *Power, Intimacy and the Life Story;* David C. McClelland, *Human Motivation* (Glenview, Ill., 1985); Smith, *Motivation and Personality;* David G. Winter and Leslie A. Carlson, "Using Motive Scores in the Psychobiographical Study of an Individual: The Case of Richard Nixon," *Journal of Personality* 56 (1988): 75-103; and Winter *Personality.* Validity has a specific meaning and there are established methods for its assessment. If a test or technique is valid, then individuals who score high on the test, designed to measure a certain need, actually possess high levels of that particular need. By way of a medical analogy, a valid measure of blood pressure or temperature is directly related to a person's actual but unobservable blood pressure or temperature. How one goes about establishing the validity of a test or scoring scheme is beyond the scope of this chapter, but the interested reader can consult the references immediately above for more information.

15. David G. Winter, "Leader Appeal, Leader Performance, and the Motive Profiles of Leaders and Followers: A Study of American Presidents and Elections," *Journal of Personality and Social Psychology* 52 (1987): 196-202.

16. The scorer, Marie Naumann, used Winter's *Integrated System for Scoring Motives in Running Text* (1994) and documented her expertise with the scoring system (her overall agreement with calibration materials averaged across the three motives was .94).

17. These comparisons are made with respect to American presidents of the last third of the 19th century, and their previously calculated motive scores (Winter, *Personality,* 161-64).

18. Psychologists interested in the development of personality throughout the lifespan have been most influenced by Erik Erikson (*Identity: Youth and Crisis,* [New York, 1968]). From an Eriksonian point of view, Chamberlain was probably at this time in a stage of identity formation called "moratorium," wherein one has not yet developed a firm sense of identity that results from a conflict or crisis; and the moratorium period provides an opportunity to explore options before a life-long commitment is made. During a moratorium (a crisis preceding commitment), the person is unsure of his or her role in society, and that dilemma is manifested in uncertainty about key aspects of

identity, such as choice of occupation. Yet in other ways Chamberlain seems to have experienced identity "foreclosure," wherein one accepts too readily the identity presented by others. He seems to have experienced little anxiety or crisis about other critical aspects of his identity while growing up, such as a value system, religious beliefs, and political orientation. Unfortunately, there is no precise way to assess identity formation in an historical figure.

19. Winter, *Personality*, ch. 5.

20. Mark Perry, *Conceived in Liberty: Joshua Chamberlain, William Oates, and the American Civil War* (New York, 1997), 333-34, 338-39, makes the case for Fannie as against Chamberlain. Perry's position is that some of Fannie's unpleasant traits, such as her "bitterness" and "resentment" were the products of Chamberlain's indifference to her needs and his treatment of her as if she were a child (pp. 333-34, 338-39).

Recent work on chronic stress during wartime (Elder & Clipp, 1988) sheds light on Chamberlain's relationship with his troops and, indirectly, with Fannie. Soldiers who experience extreme combat often forge extremely close friendships that remain intact for life (Milgram, 1986). Couple this with the finding that individuals who experience periods of hardship or trauma in their youth (i.e., Chamberlain's 'serious illness) become resilient and stronger as a result of the experience provided they have supportive and nurturing caregivers. These caregivers become highly stable "attachment figures" that provide a secure base of support throughout an individual's life and especially during times of stress. Bonds formed by resilient individuals with caregivers during childhood and also by combat veterans (both describe Chamberlain) remain extremely strong throughout their lifetimes (Simpson & Rhodes, 1994).

Perhaps Lawrence's and Fannie's relationship deteriorated after the war because they did not turn to each other during times of stress, which would have functioned to strengthen the relationship bond *(Ibid)*. Instead, Chamberlain may have experienced the strongest attachments of his life during the war and to his original family based on periods of intense stress during his youth. During the war Chamberlain may have felt that Fannie was "not there for him" when she was away from home, and she may have felt the same about him when he chose to join the army.

Given the above background, and given that people like Fannie have had an "avoidant attachment style" (i.e., they emphasize independence in relationships and tend to have less satisfying relationships), it may not be surprising that Chamberlain and his wife had periods of difficulty in their relationship. It is my thesis that these problems are traceable to her attachment style and his intense bonding to key caregivers early in life and to his comrades during the war. If Chamberlain had an extreme attachment to his comrades and his original family, it may not be surprising that his relationship with his wife suffered by comparison. Such a perception on her part could have exacerbated future conflicts they had.

21. This view of Chamberlain in terms of needs for achievement and power is strikingly similar to McAdams, Hoffman, Mansfield, and Day's system for the classification of human agency, found in "Themes of Agency and Communion in Significant Autobiographical Scenes," *Journal of Personality* 64 (1996): 339-77. I will paraphrase their system's key themes for agency, which almost seem to have been written with Chamberlain as the prototype. The point is that people high in achievement and power, such as Chamberlain, can also be described with reference to that fundamental dimension of existence known as "agency." Elements of agency include:
Self-mastery—where one strives to master, control, enlarge or perfect a self through strong, vigorous, forceful, effective actions, thus strengthening the self to become a wiser or more powerful agent.
Status—reflects ambition and dominance whereby one strives for social or institutional position, prestige, and recognition from others, especially in competitive situations; expressions of this aspect of agency include winning competitions and becoming the best in any field of endeavor.
Achievement/Responsibility—relates to persistence, productivity and hard work, represented psychologically in the achievement motive of being successful, attaining goals, and doing things that allow one to feel proud and confident in "meeting significant challenges or overcoming important obstacles concerning instrumental achievement in life or … taking on major responsibilities for other people and assuming roles that require the person to be in charge of things or people."
Empowerment—r eflects feeling powerful through association with powerful agents (those who are stronger and wiser) such as God, nature, or political or military authorities. As a consequence of being empowered through these associations, one feels stronger and gains the courage or inspiration to do one's duty.
An alternative way to understand the elements of the need for power can be seen in McAdams' system. His four main power themes are:
strength (gaining physical, mental, spiritual, or psychological strength from increased knowledge, spiritual inspiration or moral power); *impact* (a person exerts influence over others through persuasion or direct control); *action* (a preference for vigorous action and perhaps even a testing of integrity through pain); and *status* (gaining fame,

prestige, or a sense of pride through accomplishment). Again, Chamberlain is clearly described by these characteristics, and they serve to reinforce the idea that he was high on need for power.

22. Autonomy is distinct from independence, and involves a feeling that one's actions are "self-determined" and stem directly from the self (a feeling that one "owns" one's actions) as against a feeling that one's actions are the product of coercion or imposed standards of conduct (a sense of being controlled from the outside or by internal compunction).

    Much of the research conducted over the past decade within the framework of "self-determination theory" is presented in several sources. Perhaps the most useful are Richard M. Ryan, "Psychological Needs and the Facilitation of Integrative Processes," *Journal of Personality* 63 (1995): 397-427; and Richard M. Ryan, "Agency and Organization: Intrinsic Motivation, Autonomy and the Self in Psychological Development," in Janet Jacobs, ed., *Nebraska Symposium on Motivation* 40: 1-56.

23. Richard M. Ryan and C. Frederick, "On Energy, Personality and Health: Subjective Vitality as a Dynamic Reflection of Well-Being," *Journal of Personality* 65 (1997): 529-65.

24. Erikson, *Identity*, 19.

25. Dean Keith Simonton, *Greatness: Who Makes History and Why* (New York, 1994), 6-8. The psychology of history uses more respected methods than the maligned field of psychohistory, and it attempts to understand greatness in fields such as science, literature, and politics, using psychological principles.

26. Simonton, *Greatness*, ch. 4. Other work by Simonton, such as "Presidential Style: Personality, Biography, and Performance," *Journal of Personality and Social Psychology* 55 (1988): 928-36, can be used to classify Chamberlain in terms of a leadership style. He seems closest to the "creative" presidential leadership style (high on power and achievement motivation combined with openness and conscientiousness). This leadership style is associated with being reelected to political office, provoking assassination attempts (powerful and forceful individuals create extreme antagonisms among enemies), and is the most reliable predictor of presidential greatness, measured subjectively and objectively. It is interesting to note that among American presidents only six "histroiometric" variables predicted greatness; several are relevant to Chamberlain: years in office (as governor), number of years in war, war hero status, and especially intellectual brilliance. Also interesting is that former professors who

became presidents are characterized as dogmatic and inflexible, which could certainly describe Chamberlain at times.

27. Simonton, *Greatness* (1994), ch. 2; Sulloway, *Orthodoxy* (1990).

28. Simonton, *Greatness*, ch. 8.

29. Erikson has stressed that the maturing personality progresses through eight stages of "psychosocial" development. The seventh stage is generativity vs. stagnation. Generativity is concerned with generating useful "products" as gifts to individuals and society as a whole, including succeeding generations, and these gifts imbue one's life with meaning. Generative people contribute to the successful development of others through personal productivity (e.g., transferring skills through teaching at Bowdoin) and to the development and preservation of society through a broad societal concern (e.g., teaching, service to the country during the Civil War, and other leadership positions during his life). "In its most noble manifestations, maturity through generativity involves more than immediate care for one's family and creating a product, but "sacrifice made in the service of unknown others" designed to benefit future generations (Bill E. Peterson and Abigail J. Stewart, "Generativity and Social Motives in Young Adults," *Journal of Personality and Social Psychology* 65 [1993], 187). It could be argued that our concern with and for Chamberlain is based on our respect for his generativity and his legacy of care for his students, his children, the citizens of his state and country, and even future "generations that know us not."

30. McAdams, *Power, Intimacy and the Life Story*, 54.

31. L. Elsbree, *The Rituals of Life: Patterns in Narratives* (Port Washington, N.Y.,1982).

32. I wish to thank the following psychologists and historians who helped in different phases of this project: Drs. Tom Desjardin, Lou Gardner, Bryan LeBeau, Edward G. Longacre, Julia Oehmig, and Mark Ware. I also wish to thank Dr. David Winter for his advice in the assessment of Chamberlain from personal and public documents. Any omissions are the responsibility of the author. Finally, special thanks to Marie Naumann for her Herculean efforts in mastering Winter's coding scheme and also in statistically evaluating Chamberlain's writings for the assessment of his motives for achievement, power, and affiliation.

BIBLIOGRAPHY

I. Unpublished Materials:

Adams, George E. Diaries, 1855-65. First Parish Church, Brunswick, Me.

Ames, Adelbert. Correspondence. Ames Family Papers, Sophia Smith Collection, Smith College Archives, Northampton, Mass.

_____. Generals' Reports of Service, War of the Rebellion. National Archives, Washington, D. C.

_____. Letter of February 18, 1895. Miller Library, Colby College, Waterville, Me.

Barnes, James. Papers. New-York Historical Society, New York, N. Y.

Billings, Charles W. Correspondence (Internet copy). "20th Maine Casualties at Little Round Top" at http://www.metraplex.com/glenn/cw/roundtop.html.

Brown, Orsell Cook. Correspondence. New York State Library, Albany.

Burrage, Henry S. Papers. Maine Historical Society, Portland.

Buxton, Willard W. Correspondence (Internet copy). "20th Maine Casualties at Little Round Top" at http://www.metraplex.com/glenn/cw/roundtop.html.

Carleton, George W. Letter of January 8, 1866. Frost Family Papers, Yale University Library, New Haven, Conn.

Chamberlain, John C. Diary, 1863 (typescript copy). Pejepscot Historical Society.

Chamberlain, Joshua L. Commission Branch File, National Archives.

_____. Compiled Military Service Record. National Archives.

_____. Correspondence. Alexander S. Webb Papers, Yale University Library.

_____. Correspondence. Charlton T. Lewis Papers, Yale University Library.

_____. Correspondence. Election Crisis of 1880 File. Maine State Library.

_____. Correspondence. Ferdinand Dreer Collection, Historical Society of Pennsylvania, Philadelphia.

_____. Correspondence. In possession of Mr. Tony Lemut, Parma, Ohio.

_____. Correspondence. John Bachelder Papers, New Hampshire Historical Society, Concord.

_____. Correspondence. John Marshall Brown Papers, Maine State Library, Augusta.

_____. Correspondence (Internet copy). "Joshua and Fannie" at http://www.arthes.com/gdg/dtluv.html.

_____. Correspondence (Internet copy). "Love Letters from Joshua Chamberlain to Fanny Chamberlain" at http://www. arthes.com/gdg/luvltrs.html.

_____. Correspondence. Rutherford B. Hayes Presidential Center, Fremont, Ohio.

_____. Correspondence. Simon Gratz Collection—Governors of States, Historical Society of Pennsylvania.

_____. Correspondence. Simon Gratz Collection—Union Generals, Historical Society of Pennsylvania.

_____. Correspondence. Special Collections, Raymond H. Fogler Library, University of Maine, Orono.

_____. General's Papers. National Archives.

_____. Letter of April 16, 1909. Anthony Collection, New York Public Library, New York, N. Y.

_____. Letter of February 17, 1883. Civil War Papers, Yale University Library.

_____. Letter of June 16, 1913. Miller Library, Colby College.

_____. Letter of May 10, 1871. Gardiner Collection, Historical Society of Pennsylvania.

_____. Letter of October 25, 1905. Munford-Ellis Collection, William R. Perkins Library, Duke University, Durham, N. C.

_____. Medical File. National Archives.

_____. Papers. Chamberlain-Adams Family Collection, Schlesinger Library, Radcliffe College, Cambridge, Mass.

_____. Papers. Frost Family Collection, Yale University Library.

_____. Papers. Houghton Library, Harvard University, Cambridge, Mass.

_____. Papers. Library of Congress, Washington, D. C.

_____. Papers. Maine Historical Society.

_____. Papers. New-York Historical Society, New York, N. Y.

_____. Papers. Pejepscot Historical Society.

_____. Papers. Special Collections, Hawthorne-Longfellow Library, Bowdoin College, Brunswick, Me.

_____. Papers. Trulock Collection, Pejepscot Historical Society.

_____. Pension File. National Archives.

_____. Staff Officer's File. National Archives.

Clark, Nathan S. Memoirs. Maine State Archives, Augusta.

Coan, Elisha. Papers. Special Collections, Hawthorne-Longfellow Library, Bowdoin College.

Cross, Robert M. "Joshua Lawrence Chamberlain." Special Collections, Hawthorne-Longfellow Library, Bowdoin College.

Curtis, Stephen P. Correspondence. Pejepscot Historical Society.

Cutler, Alvin. Correspondence (Internet copy). "20th Maine Company E Soldier Research Data Section" at http://www.metraplex.com/glenn/cw/res20me. html.

Davis, William L. Correspondence (Internet copy). "20th Maine Company E Soldier Research Data Section" at http://www.metraplex.com/glenn/cw/res20me.html.

Fernald, Albert E. Diary, 1863 (typescript copy). Trulock Collection, Pejepscot Historical Society.

"15th Alabama Inf. Reg." File. Gettysburg National Military Park Library, Gettysburg, Pa.

First Brigade, First Division, Fifth Army Corps Records. National Archives.

Flanders, Lewis G. Correspondence (Internet copy). "20th Maine Company E Soldier Research Data Section" at http://www.metraplex.com/glenn/cw/res20me.html.

Fogg, Elliott S. Correspondence (Internet copy). "20th Maine Casualties at Little Round Top" at http://www.metraplex.com/glenn/cw/roundtop.html.

Foote, Daniel B. Correspondence. U.S. Army Military History Institute, Carlisle Barracks, Pa.

Garland, Whitmore Barron. "Pine Tree Politics: Maine Political Party Battles, 1820-1972." Ph.D. dissertation, University of Massachusetts, 1979.

Gilmore, Charles D. Commission Branch File, National Archives.

Harris, Avery. Memoirs. U.S. Army Military History Institute.

Harshberger, Abraham. Memoirs. *Civil War Times Illustrated* Collection, U.S. Army Military History Institute.

"History of the First Parish Church as Part of the Life and Times of Joshua L. Chamberlain." Pejepscot Historical Society.

Howard, Oliver Otis. Papers. Hawthorne-Longfellow Library, Bowdoin College.

Irvin, John. Diary, 1864. Historical Society of Pennsylvania.

James, David. Diary, 1864. Britta Stamy Collection, American Heritage Center, University of Wyoming, Laramie.

Johnson, Dudley S. "The Railroads of Florida, 1865-1900." Ph.D. dissertation, Florida State University, 1965.

"July 2nd: Little Round Top (20th Maine Inf. vs. 15th Alabama Inf.)" File. Gettysburg National Military Park Library.

"July 2nd: Little Round Top (Vincent & Weed vs. Law & Robertson)" File. Gettysburg National Military Park Library.

Keene, Samuel T. Correspondence. Ellis Spear Papers, Maine State Archives.

Kenney, Howard J. "The Chamberlain Family." Trulock Collection, Pejepscot Historical Society.

Lenfest, John. Correspondence (typescript copies). Trulock Collection, Pejepscot Historical Society.

Livermore, William T. Correspondence (typescript copies). Trulock Collection, Pejepscot Historical Society.

_____. Diary, 1863 (typescript copy). Ellis Spear Papers, Maine State Archives.

Long, Hezekiah. Correspondence (typescript copies). Trulock Collection, Pejepscot Historical Society.

Lunt, Josiah, Jr. Correspondence. Pejepscot Historical Society.

Lytle, Henry. Letter of June 28, 1863 (typescript copy). Lewis Leigh Collection, U.S. Army Military History Institute.

Mawhinney, Eugene A. "Joshua Chamberlain and the Twelve Days Which Shook Maine, January 6-17, 1880." Pejepscot Historical Society.

_____. "Joshua L. Chamberlain, Governor of Maine, 1867, 1868, 1869, 1870." Pejepscot Historical Society.

McHenry, R. Lewis. "Dawning of a New Elizabethan Age: The [Bowdoin College] Presidency of Joshua Lawrence Chamberlain." Hawthorne-Longfellow Library, Bowdoin College.

Melcher, Holman S. Letter of August —, 1864. Pejepscot Historical Society.

_____. "Military and Civil History." Maine Historical Society.

Morrill, Lot M. Papers. Maine Historical Society.

Norton, Oliver W. Papers. Clarke Historical Library, Central Michigan University, Mount Pleasant.

Oates, William C. Account of Battle of Gettysburg. Elisha Coan Papers, Hawthorne-Longfellow Library, Bowdoin College.

_____. Letter of March 8, 1897. Schoff Civil War Collection, William L. Clements Library, University of Michigan, Ann Arbor.

_____. Papers. Alabama Historical Society, Montgomery.

O'Connell, John. Memoirs. Civil War Miscellaney Collection, U.S. Army Military History Institute.

"Participants: Joshua L. Chamberlain" File. Gettysburg National Military Park Library.

Perham, Aurestus S. Papers. Maine Historical Society.

"President Chamberlain, Bowdoin College." Pejepscot Historical Society.

Roebling, Washington A. Papers. Alexander Library, Rutgers University, New Brunswick, N. J.

Sherman, Sylvia J. "'The Shadow of a Mighty Presence': Varney Lecture Presented ... July 12, 1978." Pejepscot Historical Society.

Shuman, Josiah. Diaries, 1864-65 (typescript copy). Civil War Miscellaney Collection, U.S. Army Military History Institute.

Silver Springs, Ocala & Gulf Railroad Company Articles of Association, Land Grant and Mortgage, and List of Deeds. Florida State Archives, Tallahassee.

Small, Alva B. Correspondence (Internet copy). "20th Maine Casualties at Little Round Top" at http://www.metraplex.com/glenn/cw/roundtop.html.

Smith, Catherine T. Interview, ca. 1970 (Internet copy). "Interview with JLC's Personal Secretary" at http://www.curtis-library.com/pejep-scot/csmith.html.

_____. Memoirs (typescript copy). Pejepscot Historical Society.

Smith, Jennifer Lund. "The Strains of Post-Military Matrimony: The Estrangement of Fannie and Lawrence Chamberlain." Pejepscot Historical Society.

Spear, Abbott. "Another Look at Gettysburg: An Address to the Warren County Historical Society, 1966." Pejepscot Historical Society.

_____, ed. "The 20th Maine at Fredericksburg: The 1913 Accounts of Generals Chamberlain and Spear." Maine State Archives.

Spear, Ellis. Diaries, 1863-65 (typescript copies). Maine State Archives.

_____. "'My Story of Fredericksburg,' by Lt. Col. Joshua L. Chamberlain (later Brig. General) and Comments Thereon By One who was There, Capt. Ellis Spear (later Brig. General)" (typescript copy). Ames Family Papers, Sophia Smith Collection, Smith College.

_____. Papers. Maine State Archives.

_____. "Recollections" (typescript copy). "20th Maine Inf. Reg." File, Gettysburg National Military Park Library.

Thickstun, Israel. Correspondence. Thickstun Family Papers, U.S. Army Military History Institute.

"20th Maine Inf. Reg." File. Gettysburg National Military Park Library.

_____. Records, 1862-65. National Archives.

20th Maine Volunteers. Records, 1862-65. National Archives.

Wilbur, Nelson. Correspondence. Soldiers and Sailors Memorial Hall, Pittsburgh, Pa.

Wilder, Philip S. "Chamberlain: Student, Scholar and Educator." Special Collections, Hawthorne-Longfellow Library, Bowdoin College.

II. Newspapers:

Boston Evening Transcript

Boston Journal

Brunswick Telegraph

Brunswick Times-Record

Daily Richmond Enquirer

Free Lance-Star (Fredericksburg, Va.)

Lewiston Journal

Lincoln County News (Waldoboro, Me.)

Nation (New York, N. Y.)

National Tribune (Washington, D. C.)

New York Herald

New York Times

New York Tribune

Oxford Democrat (Paris, Me.)

Petersburg Express

Petersburg Register

Portland Evening Express & Daily Advertiser

Richmond Examiner

III. Articles and Essays:

"Address Delivered at Brunswick by William DeWitt Hyde, President of Bowdoin College." *The Colonial* 2 (March 1914): 13-15.

Allen, Rosamond. "A Personal Memoir of Rosamond Allen, Granddaughter of Union General Joshua Lawrence Chamberlain." *Blue & Gray* 1 (December 1983-January 1984): 16.

Alvey, Edward Jr. "The Mary Washington Monument Centennial." *Fredericksburg Times Magazine* 10 (May 1994): 13-23.

Beauregard, P. G. T. "Four Days of Battle at Petersburg." *Battles and Leaders of the Civil War ...* 4: 540-44.

Booth, Russell. "Butterfield and 'Taps'." *Civil War Times Illustrated* 16 (December 1977): 35-39.

Breakey, William F. "Recollections and Incidents of Medical Military Service." *War Papers: Read Before the Commandery of Michigan, Military Order of the Loyal Legion of the United States* 2: 120-52.

Cameron, Bill. "The Saviors of Little Round Top" (Internet copy) at http://www. arthes.com/gdg/saviorl.html.

Chamberlain, Joshua L. "Do It! That's How," *Bowdoin Magazine* 64 (Spring-Summer 1991): 2-12.

_____. "Five Forks." *War Papers: Read Before the Maine Commandery, Military Order of the Loyal Legion of the United States* 2: 220-67.

_____. "The Last Review of the Army of the Potomac, May 23, 1865," *War Papers: Read Before the Maine Commandery, Military Order of the Loyal Legion of the United States* 3: 306-33.

_____. "The Last Salute of the Army of Northern Virginia." *Southern Historical Society Papers* 32 (1904): 355-63.

_____. "My Story of Fredericksburg." *Cosmopolitan Magazine* 54 (1912): 148-59.

_____. "The Third Brigade at Appomattox." In *Proceedings of the Third Brigade Association, First Division, Fifth Army Corps, Army of the Potomac* ... New York: privately issued, 1894.

_____. "Through Blood and Fire at Gettysburg." *Hearst's Magazine* 23 (1913): 894-909.

Clark, Tim. "A Hard Day for Mother." *Yankee* 43 (July 1979): 126-31.

"Coming Home Again." *Confederate Veteran* 36 (1928): 50-51.

Cox, Jacob D. "The Battle of Antietam." *Battles and Leaders of the Civil War* ... 2: 630-60.

Cullen, Joseph P. "When Grant Faced Lee Across the North Anna." *Civil War Times Illustrated* 3 (February 1965): 16-23.

Fisher, Donald M. "Born in Ireland, Killed at Gettysburg: The Life, Death, and Legacy of Patrick Henry O'Rorke." *Civil War History* 39 (1993): 225-39.

"General Warren at Five Forks, and the Court of Inquiry." *Battles and Leaders of the Civil War* ... 4: 723-24.

Hazan, Cindy, and Philip R. Shaver. "Attachment as an Organizational Framework for Research in Close Relationships," *Psychology Inquiry* 5 (1994): 1-22.

Hunt, Henry J. "The Second Day at Gettysburg." *Battles and Leaders of the Civil War* ... 3: 290-313.

Jacklin, Rufus W. "The Famous Old Third Brigade." *War Papers: Read Before the Michigan Commandery, Military Order of the Loyal Legion of the United States* 2: 39-50.

Jones, Walter. "The Flag of Truce at Appomattox." *Confederate Veteran* 39 (1931): 300-03.

Kross, Gary. "The Alabamians' Attack on Little Round Top." *Blue & Gray* 13 (February 1996): 54-61.

_____. "The Confederate Approach to Little Round Top: A March of Attrition." *Blue & Gray* 13 (February 1996): 7-15, 17-20, 22-24.

LaFantasie, Glenn. "Joshua Chamberlain and the American Dream." In Gabor S. Boritt, ed., *The Gettysburg Nobody Knows.* New York: Oxford University Press, 1997, pp. 31-55.

_____. "The Other Man." *MHQ: The Quarterly Journal of Military History* 5 (Summer 1993): 69-75.

Longacre, Edward G. "Gouverneur K. Warren." *Civil War Times Illustrated* 10 (January 1972): 11-20.

Longstreet, James. "The Battle of Fredericksburg." *Battles and Leaders of the Civil War ...* 3: 70-85.

Lord, Stuart B. "Adelbert Ames, Soldier & Politician: A Reevaluation." *Maine Historical Society Quarterly* 13 (1973): 81-97.

Marvel, William G. "A Question of Rhetoric." *North & South* 2 (June 1999): 80-85.

McClintock, Charles A., ed. "Memories of Appomattox by George McCully Laughlin." *Western Pennsylvania Historical Magazine* 47 (1959): 259-63.

Melcher, Holman S. "An Experience in the Battle of the Wilderness." *War Papers: Read Before the Commandery of Maine, Military Order of the Loyal Legion of the United States* 1: 73-84.

_____. "The 20th Maine at Little Round Top." *Battles and Leaders of the Civil War ...* 3: 314-15.

Morgan, James. "Who Saved Little Round Top?" (Internet copy) at http://www. arthes.com/gdg/flash.html.

Oates, William C. "Gettysburg, the Battle on the Right." *Southern Historical Society Papers* 6 (1878): 172-82.

Perry, Mark. "An Amateur Among Professionals: Joshua Chamberlain at Gettysburg." *The Kepi* 3 (April-May 1985): 18-25.

Pindell, Richard. "Fighting for Little Round Top: The 20th Maine." *Civil War Times Illustrated* 21 (February 1983): 12-20.

_____. "The True High-Water Mark of the Confederacy." *Blue & Gray* 1 (December 1983-January 1984): 6-14.

Porter, Horace. "Five Forks and the Pursuit of Lee." *Battles and Leaders of the Civil War ...* 4: 708-22.

Raymond, Harold B. "Joshua Chamberlain's Retirement Bill." *Colby Library Quarterly* 7 (1966): 341-54.

Simonton, Edward. "Recollections of the Battle of Fredericksburg." *Glimpses of the Nation's Struggle: Papers Read Before the Minnesota Commandery, Military Order of the Loyal Legion of the United States* 2: 245-66.

Smith, Joseph R. "Brunswick, Maine's Unique House on a House." *Blue & Gray* 1 (June-July 1984): 6-8.

Sprague, Charles E. "In the Company Street." *Military Essays and Recollec-*

tions: Papers Read Before the Illinois Commandery, Military Order of the Loyal Legion of the United States 2: 126-39.

Stone, Jason. "Joshua Chamberlain." *Down East* 34 (March 1987): 46-49, 57-59.

Ward, Geoffrey. "Hero of the 20th." *American Heritage* 43 (November 1992): 14-16.

Wittenberg, Eric J. "The Fighting Professor: Joshua Lawrence Chamberlain." *Civil War* 10 (July-August 1992): 8-14.

IV. Books and Pamphlets:

Address of Governor Chamberlain to the Legislature of the State of Maine, January, 1867. Augusta, Me.: Stevens & Sayward, 1867.

Address of Governor Chamberlain to the Legislature of the State of Maine, January, 1869. Augusta, Me.: Owen & Nash, 1869.

Address of Governor Chamberlain to the Legislature of the State of Maine, January, 1870. Augusta, Me.: Sprague, Owen & Nash, 1870.

Ames, Blanche A. *Adelbert Ames, 1835-1933: General, Senator, Governor.* New York: Argosy-Antiquarian Ltd., 1964.

Ashby, Thompson Eldridge. *A History of the First Parish Church in Brunswick, Maine.* Edited by Louise R. Helmreich. Brunswick, Me.: J. H. French & Son, 1969.

Barnard, Harry. *Rutherford B. Hayes and His America.* Indianapolis: Bobbs-Merrill Co., Inc., 1954.

Boatner, Mark M., III. *The Civil War Dictionary.* New York: David McKay Co., Inc., 1959.

Busey, John W. *These Honored Dead: The Union Casualties at Gettysburg.* Hightstown, N.J.: Longstreet House, 1988.

Calkins, Chris M. *The Appomattox Campaign.* Conshohocken, Pa.: Combined Publishing, 1997.

_____. *The Battles of Appomattox Station and Appomattox Court House, April 8-9, 1865.* Lynchburg, Va.: H. E. Howard, Inc., 1987.

Catalogue of the Theological Seminary, Bangor, 1853. Bangor, Me.: Samuel S. Smith, 1853.

Catton, Bruce. *Glory Road: The Bloody Route from Fredericksburg to Gettysburg.* Garden City, N. Y.: Doubleday & Co., Inc., 1952.

_____. *A Stillness at Appomattox.* Garden City, N. Y.: Doubleday & Co., Inc., 1953.

Chamberlain, Joshua L. *Address of Gen. Joshua L. Chamberlain at the Dedi-*

cation of the Maine Monuments, Battlefield of Gettysburg, October 3, 1889: Second Edition. Portland, Me.: Lakeside Press, 1898.

_____. *Address of Gen. Joshua L. Chamberlain at the Dedication of the Maine Monuments on the Battlefield of Gettysburg, October 3, 1893.* Augusta, Me.: Maine Farmers' Almanac Press, 1895.

_____. *Appomattox: Paper Read Before the New York Commandery, [Military Order of the] Loyal Legion of the United States, October Seventh, 1903.* N.p.: privately issued, ca. 1904.

_____. *"Bayonet! Forward": My Civil War Reminiscences.* Gettysburg, Pa.: Stan Clark Military Books, 1994.

_____. *Joshua Lawrence Chamberlain: A Sketch.* N.p.: privately issued, 1906.

_____. *Joshua Lawrence Chamberlain, Supplement: The Twelve Days at Augusta, 1880.* Portland, Me.: Smith & Sale, 1906.

_____. *Maine: Her Place in History.* Augusta, Me.: Sprague, Owen & Nash, 1877.

_____. *Military Operations on the White Oak Road, Virginia, March 31, 1865 ...* Portland, Me.: Thurston Print., 1897.

_____. *The Passing of the Armies: An Account of the Final Campaign of the Army of the Potomac ...* New York: G. P. Putnam's Sons, 1915.

_____. *The Passing of the Armies: An Account of the Final Campaign of the Army of the Potomac ...* Introduction by James M. McPherson. New York: Bantam Books, 1993.

_____. *Through Blood & Fire: Selected Civil War Papers of Major General Joshua Chamberlain.* Edited by Mark Nesbitt. Mechanicsburg, Pa.: Stackpole Books, 1996.

Chamberlin, Thomas. *History of the One Hundred and Fiftieth Regiment Pennsylvania Volunteers ...* Philadelphia: F. McManus, Jr. & Co., 1905.

Clark, Charles E. *Maine: A Bicentennial History.* New York: W. W. Norton & Co., Inc., 1977.

Coddington, Edwin B. *The Gettysburg Campaign: A Study in Command.* New York: Charles Scribner's Sons, 1968.

Cresap, Bernarr. *Appomattox Commander: The Story of General E.O.C. Ord.* San Diego: A. S. Barnes & Co., Inc., 1981.

Davis, Burke. *To Appomattox: Nine April Days, 1865.* New York: Rinehart & Co., Inc., 1959.

Dedication of the 20th Maine Monument at Gettysburg, Oct. 3, 1889, with

Report of Annual Reunion, Oct. 2d, 1889. Waldoboro, Me.: *News* Print., 1891.

Desjardin, Thomas A. *Stand Firm Ye Boys From Maine: The 20th Maine and the Gettysburg Campaign*. Gettysburg, Pa.: Thomas Publications, 1995.

Dunning, Albert E. *Congregationalists in America: A Popular History of Their Origin, Belief, Polity, Growth and Work*. New York: J. A. Hill & Co., 1894.

Foster, Benjamin Browne. *Down East Diary*. Edited by Charles H. Foster. Orono, Me.: University of Maine at Orono Press, 1975.

Freeman, Douglas Southall. *Lee's Lieutenants: A Study in Command*. 3 vols. New York: Charles Scribner's Sons, 1942-44.

General Catalogue of Bowdoin College, and the Medical School of Maine, 1794-1894. Brunswick, Me.: Published by the College, 1894.

Gerrish, Theodore. *Army Life: A Private's Reminiscences of the Civil War*. Portland, Me.: Hoyt, Fogg & Donham, 1882.

_____, and John S. Hutchinson. *The Blue and the Gray: A Graphic History of the Army of the Potomac ...* Bangor, Me.: Brady, Mace & Co., 1884.

Gibbs, James M., comp. *History of the ... 187th Regiment Pennsylvania Volunteer Infantry: Six Months and Three Years Service, Civil War, 1863-1865*. Harrisburg, Pa.: Central Printing & Publishing House, 1905.

Golay, Michael. *To Gettysburg and Beyond: The Parallel Lives of Joshua Lawrence Chamberlain and Edward Porter Alexander*. New York: Crown Publishers, Inc., 1994.

Gordon, John B. *Reminiscences of the Civil War*. New York: Charles Scribner's Sons, 1904.

Graham, Ziba B. *On to Gettysburg: Ten Days from My Diary of 1863*. Detroit: Winn & Hammond, 1893.

Grant, Ulysses S. *Personal Memoirs of U. S. Grant*. 2 vols. New York: Charles L. Webster & Co., 1885-86.

Harwell, Richard B., ed. *Honor Answering Honor*. Brunswick, Me.: Bowdoin College, 1965.

Haskell, Robert L. *Yankee Warrior: The Story of a Civil War Hero from Maine*. Bangor, Me.: Bangor Publishing Co., 1993.

Hatch, Louis C. *The History of Bowdoin College*. Portland, Me.: Loring, Short & Harmon, 1927.

Hatcher, Edmund N. *The Last Four Weeks of the War*. Columbus, Ohio: Co-operative Publishing Co., 1892.

Heinl. Robert D., Jr., comp. *Dictionary of Military and Naval Quotations.* Annapolis, Md.: U. S. Naval Institute Press, 1966.

Hewett, Janet, et al., comps. *Supplement to the Official Records of the Union and Confederate Armies.* 80 vols. to date. Wilmington, N. C.: Broadfoot Publishing Co., 1994- .

Hill, Ralph G., and James H. Pledger. *The Railroads of Florida.* Talahassee: Florida Railroad Commission, 1939.

History of the Corn Exchange Regiment, 118th Pennsylvania Volunteers ... Philadelphia: J. L. Smith, 1888.

History of the 121st Regiment Pennsylvania Volunteers ... "An Account from the Ranks". Philadelphia: Burk & McFetridge Co., 1893.

Hoogenboom, Ari. *Rutherford B. Hayes, Warrior and President.* Lawrence: University Press of Kansas, 1995.

Howe, Thomas J. *The Petersburg Campaign: Wasted Valor, June 15-18, 1864.* Lynchburg, Va.: H. E. Howard, Inc., 1988.

Jordan, William C. *Some Events and Incidents During the Civil War.* Montgomery, Ala.: Paragon Press, 1909.

Judson, A. M. *History of the Eighty-third Regiment Pennsylvania Volunteers.* Erie, Pa.: B. F. H. Lynn, 1865.

Kieffer, Harry M. *The Recollections of a Drummer-Boy.* Boston: Ticknor & Co., 1889.

Kohl, Manfred W. *Congregationalism in America.* Oak Creek, Wis.: Congregational Press, 1977.

Ladd, David L., and Audrey J. Ladd, eds. *The Bachelder Papers: Gettysburg in Their Own Words ...* Dayton, Ohio: Morningside, 1994.

Lamson, William P., Jr. *Maine to the Wilderness: The Civil War Letters of Pvt. William Lamson, 20th Maine Infantry.* Edited by Roderick M. Engert. Orange, Va.: Publisher's Press, Inc., 1993.

Land Grant and Mortgage of the Silver Springs, Ocala and Gulf Railroad Company. New York: Theo. E. Dollard, 1885.

Lemke, William. *A Pride of Lions: Joshua Chamberlain & Other Maine Civil War Heroes.* North Attleborough, Mass.: Covered Bridge Press, 1997.

Linderman, Gerald F. *Embattled Courage: The Experience of Combat in the American Civil War.* New York: Free Press, 1987.

Little, George T., ed. *Genealogical and Family History of the State of Maine.* 4 vols. New York: Lewis Historical Publishing Co., 1909.

Long, E. B., and Barbara Long. *The Civil War Day by Day: An Almnanac, 1861-1865.* Garden City, N. Y.: Doubleday & Co., Inc., 1971.

Longacre, Edward G. *General John Buford: A Military Biography.* Conshohocken, Pa.: Combined Books, 1995.

_____. *Pickett, Leader of the Charge: A Biography of General George E. Pickett, C. S. A.* Shippensburg, Pa.: White Mane Publishing Co., Inc., 1995.

Loski, Diana H. *The Chamberlains of Brewer.* Gettysburg, Pa.: Thomas Publications, 1998.

Lystra, Karen. *Searching the Heart: Women, Men, and Romantic Love in Nineteenth-Century America.* New York: Oxford University Press, 1989.

MacDonald, William. *The Government of Maine: Its History and Administration.* New York: Macmillan Co., 1902.

Maine at Gettysburg: Report of Maine Commissioners, Prepared by the Executive Committee. Portland, Me.: Lakeside Press, 1898.

Mattocks, Charles P. *"Unspoiled Heart": The Journal of Charles Mattocks of the 17th Maine.* Edited by Philip N. Racine. Knoxville: University of Tennessee Press, 1994.

McWhiney, Grady, and Perry D. Jamieson. *Attack and Die: Civil War Military Tactics and the Southern Heritage.* University, Ala.: University of Alabama Press, 1982.

Medical and Surgical History of the War of the Rebellion. 6 vols. in 3. Washington. D. C.: Government Printing Office, 1870-88.

Melcher, Holman S. *With a Flash of His Sword: The Writings of Major Holman S. Melcher, 20th Maine Infantry.* Edited by William B. Styple. Kearny, N.J.: Belle Grove Publishing Co., 1994.

Military Order of the Loyal Legion of the United States, Commandery of the State of Maine: In Memoriam, Joshua Lawrence Chamberlain, Late Major-General U.S.V. Portland, Me.: privately issued, 1914.

Miller, J. Michael. *The North Anna Campaign: "Even to Hell Itself," May 21-26, 1864.* Lynchburg, Va.: H. E. Howard, Inc., 1989.

Mitchell, Joseph B. *The Badge of Gallantry: Recollections of Civil War Congressional Medal of Honor Winners ...* New York: Macmillan Co., 1968.

Morris, Roy, Jr. *Sheridan: The Life and Wars of General Phil Sheridan.* New York: Crown Publishers, Inc., 1992.

Nash, Eugene Arus. *A History of the Forty-fourth Regiment New York Volunteer Infantry in the Civil War, 1861-1865.* Chicago: R. R. Donnelley & Sons Co., 1911.

Nesbit, John W., comp. . . . .General History of Company D, 149th Pennsylvania Volunteers and Personal Sketches of the Members. Oakdale, Pa.: Oakdale Printing and Publishing Co., 1908.

Norton, Oliver Willcox. *Army Letters, 1861-1865: Being Extracts from Private Letters* ... Chicago: O. L. Deming, 1903.

_____. *The Attack and Defense of Little Round Top, Gettysburg, July 2, 1863.* New York: Neale Publishing Co., 1913.

_____. *Strong Vincent and His Brigade at Gettysburg, July 2, 1863.* Chicago: privately issued, 1909.

Nyham, Thomas, comp. *Joshua Lawrence Chamberlain: Day by Day in the Civil War, Brunswick to Appomattox.* Burlingame, Calif.: privately issued, 1993.

Oates, William C. *The War Between the Union and the Confederacy and Its Lost Opportunities* ... New York: Neale Publishing Co., 1905.

Paris, Comte de. *History of the Civil War in America.* 4 vols. Philadelphia: Porter & Coates, 1883.

Penny, Morris M., and J. Gary Laine. *Struggle for the Round Tops: Law's Alabama Brigade at the Battle of Gettysburg.* Shippensburg, Pa.: Burd Street Press, 1999.

Perret, Geoffrey. *Ulysses S. Grant, Soldier & President.* New York: Random House, 1997.

Perry, Mark. *Conceived in Liberty: Joshua Chamberlain, William Oates, and the American Civil War.* New York: Viking, 1997.

Pfanz, Harry W. *Gettysburg, the Second Day.* Chapel Hill: University of North Carolina Press, 1987.

Powell, William H. *The Fifth Army Corps (Army of the Potomac): A Record of Operations during the Civil War* ... New York: G. P. Putnam's Sons, 1896.

Pullen, John J. *Joshua Chamberlain: The Hero's Life and Legacy.* Mechanicsburg, Pa.: Stackpole Books, 1999.

_____. *The 20th Maine: A Volunteer Regiment in the Civil War.* Philadelphia: J. B. Lippincott Co., 1957.

Reunions of the 20th Maine Regiment Association, at Portland. Waldoboro, Me.: Samuel L. Miller, 1881.

Rothman, Ellen K. *Hands and Hearts: A History of Courtship in America.* New York: Basic Books, Inc., 1984.

Royster, Charles. *The Destructive War: William Tecumseh Sherman, Stonewall Jackson, and the Americans.* New York: Alfred A. Knopf, 1991.

Sears, Stephen W. *Landscape Turned Red: The Battle of Antietam.* New York: Ticknor & Fields, 1983.

Sheridan, Philip H. *Personal Memoirs of P. H. Sheridan, General United States Army.* 2 vols. New York: Charles L. Webster & Co., 1888.

Sherman, Richard L. *Joshua Lawrence Chamberlain, 1828-1914: A Sesquicentennial Tribute.* Brunswick, Me.: Brunswick Publishing Co., 1978.

Spear, Ellis. *The Civil War Recollections of General Ellis Spear.* Edited by Abbott Spear, et al. Orono: University of Maine Press, 1997.

_____. *The Hoe Cake of Appomattox: Military Order of the Loyal Legion of the United States, Commandery of the District of Columbia, War Paper 93.* Washington, D.C.: privately issued, 1913.

_____. *The Story of the Raising and Organization of a Regiment of Volunteers in 1862: Military Order of the Loyal Legion of the United States, Commandery of the District of Columbia, War Paper 46.* Washington, D.C.: privately issued, n.d.

Stern, Philip Van Doren. *An End to Valor: The Last Days of the Civil War.* Boston: Houghton, Mifflin Co., 1958.

Stetson, W. W. *History and Civil Government of Maine.* Chicago: Werner School Book Co., 1898.

Tankersley, Allen P. *John B. Gordon: A Study in Gallantry.* Atlanta: Whitehall Press, 1955.

Taylor, Emerson Gifford. *Gouverneur Kemble Warren: The Life and Letters of an American Soldier, 1830-1882.* Boston: Houghton Mifflin Co., 1932.

Trudeau, Noah Andre. *Out of the Storm: The End of the Civil War, April-June 1865.* Boston: Little, Brown & Co., 1994.

Trulock, Alice Rains. *In the Hands of Providence: Joshua L. Chamberlain and the American Civil War.* Chapel Hill: University of North Carolina Press, 1992.

Tucker, Glenn. *High Tide at Gettysburg: The Campaign in Pennsylvania.* Indianapolis: Bobbs-Merrill Co., Inc., 1958.

Wainwright, Charles Shiels. *A Diary of Battle: The Personal Journals of Colonel Charles S. Wainwright, 1861-1865.* Edited by Allan Nevins. New York: Harcourt, Brace & World, 1962.

Wallace, Willard M. *Soul of the Lion: A Biography of General Joshua L. Chamberlain.* New York: Thomas Nelson & Sons, 1960.

Warner, Ezra J. *Generals in Blue: Lives of the Union Commanders.* Baton Rouge: Louisiana State University Press, 1964.

War of the Rebellion: A Compilation of the Official Records of the Union and Confederate Armies. 4 series, 70 vols. in 128. Washington, D.C.: Government Printing Office, 1880-1901.

Warren, Horatio N. *Two Reunions of the 142d Regiment, Pa. Vols....* Buffalo, N.Y.: Courier Co., 1890.

Wescott, Richard R. *New Men, New Issues: The Formation of the Republican Party in Maine.* Portland, Me.: Maine Historical Society, 1986.

Wheeler, Richard. *Witness to Appomattox.* New York: Harper & Row, 1989.

Whitman, William E. S., and Charles H. True. *Maine in the War for the Union: A History of the Part Borne by Maine Troops in the Suppression of the American Rebellion.* Lewiston, Me.: Nelson Dingley, Jr. & Co., 1865.

Woodward, Evan M. *History of the One Hundred and Ninety-eighth Pennsylvania Volunteers ...* Trenton, N.J.: MacCrellish & Quigley, 1884.

Index

120, 127, 128, 137, 154, 156, 164, 177, 197, 205, 207, 209, 254, 255, 258, 267, 289

Clark, Atherton W., 63, 102, 106, 134, 136, 138, 139, 142, 143

Clark, Nathan S., 121

Coan, Elisha S., 137, 144

Coburn, Abner, 105, 111, 115, 156, 163, 164

Conner, Freeman, 112

Cony, Samuel, 179, 203, 256, 259, 265

Crawford, Samuel W., 145, 181, 210, 225, 226, 231, 232, 233, 234

Crook, George, 217

Cutler, Lysander, 181, 182, 185, 186, 192

Davis, David, 281

Davis, Jefferson F., 49, 163, 237

Dowell, William E., 169

Everett, Robert A., 197

Fernald, Albert E., 119

Fessenden, Francis, 257

Fessenden, William, 162, 265, 267

Fisher, Joseph W., 145, 146, 147

Five Forks, VA, 224, 229, 230, 237

Folsom, Deborah, 119, 174, 204

Franklin, William B., 74, 91, 104, 105

Frederick, MD, 72, 123, 153

Fredericksburg, VA, 85-86, 94, 98, 99

French, William H., 158

Frye, William P., 288

Garcelon, Alonzo, 279, 280

Gerrish, Theodore, 66, 67

Gettysburg, PA, 124

Gettysburg Battlefield
-Cemetery Ridge, 125, 126, 144
-Culp's Hill, 126
-Devil's Den, 129, 132
-Emmitsburg Road, 151, 153
-Little Round Top, 126, 127, 128, 129, 131, 132, 134, 135, 136, 141, 142, 143, 144, 145, 149, 156, 163, 176, 286-287
-Plum Run, 129, 133, 134
-Round Top, 126, 131, 133, 134, 142, 146, 147, 148
-Seminary Ridge, 125
-Taneytown Road, 126
-Weikert Farm, 142
-Wheatfield, 127
-Willoughby Run, 151

Gilmore, Charles D., 59, 61, 64, 74, 102, 111, 114, 115, 122, 123, 160, 164, 199, 201

Glenn, Edwin A., 219, 220, 225, 233, 235

Gordon, John B., 242, 243, 245, 246, 247, 284-285

Grant, Ulysses S., 113, 154, 167-168, 174, 175, 176, 177, 179, 180, 183, 184, 185, 188, 196, 199, 200, 204, 208, 215, 216, 218, 225, 229, 230, 231, 237,